Monty Python
FAQ

Monty Python FAQ

All That's Left to Know About Spam, Grails, Spam, Nudging, Bruces, and Spam

Chris Barsanti, Brian Cogan, and Jeff Massey

APPLAUSE
THEATRE & CINEMA BOOKS
An Imprint of Hal Leonard LLC

Published in 2017 by Applause Theatre & Cinema books
An Imprint of Hal Leonard LLC
7777 West Bluemound Road
Milwaukee, WI 53213
Trade Book Division Editorial Offices
33 Plymouth St., Montclair, NJ 07042

All images are from the author's collection unless otherwise noted.

The FAQ series was conceived by Robert Rodriguez and developed with Stuart Shea.
Printed in the United States of America

Book design by Snow Creative

Library of Congress Cataloging-in-Publication Data

Names: Barsanti, Chris author. | Cogan, Brian, 1967– author. | Massey, Jeff author.
Title: Monty Python FAQ : all that's left to know about spam, grails, spam, nudging, bruces, and spam / Chris Barsanti, Brian Cogan, and Jeff Massey.
Description: Milwaukee, WI : Applause Theatre & Cinema Books, 2017. | Includes bibliographical references and index.
Identifiers: LCCN 2016054178 | ISBN 9781495049439 (pbk.)
Subjects: LCSH: Monty Python's flying circus (Television program) | Monty Python (Comedy troupe)
Classification: LCC PN1992.77.M583 B37 2017 | DDC 791.45/72—dc23
LC record available at https://lccn.loc.gov/2016054178

www.applausebooks.com

We would like to apologize for this book.

We are truly, truly sorry for what you are about to read.

Really.

Contents

Acknowledgments ix

Introduction: The Lasting Importance of Monty Python xi

1 Every Sperm Is Sacred: In Which the Pythons Are Born 1
2 The Origins of British Silliness: *The Goon Show* 14
3 Frost/Python: In Which David Frost Gives Comedy a Go 21
4 And Now, for Something Oddly Familiar: *At Last the 1948 Show* 27
5 The Real Pre-Python: *Do Not Adjust Your Set* 40
6 Whither the BBC?: *Monty Python's Flying Circus* and How It Began at the Beginning 46
7 Under the Big Top: *Monty Python's Flying Circus*: Season One 59
8 Spam, Spam, Spam, Spam, Wonderful Spam! *Monty Python's Flying Circus*: Season Two 81
9 The First Rip-Offs: *And Now for Something Completely Different* and *Fliegender Zirkus* 102
10 Blood, Devastation, Death, War, and Horror: *Monty Python's Flying Circus, Season Three* 113
11 All That's Left: *Monty Python* (sans *Flying Circus*): The Final Season 130
12 What Hath We Wrought? The Pythons Storm America 146
13 Of Course It's a Good Idea! *Monty Python and the Holy Grail* 156
14 Moving On: John Cleese Checks into *Fawlty Towers* 179
15 "I'm Not the Messiah!": The Very Naughty *Life of Brian* 194
16 A Fish Film: *The Meaning of Life* 207
17 Post-Python: "Jolly, Jolly Good!": John Cleese—The Most Prolific Python 223
18 Post-Python: "I'm . . . Dead Yet!": Graham Chapman—The Least Alive Python 234
19 Post-Python: "There's Nothing Quite as Wonderful as Money": Eric Idle—The Showman 248
20 Post-Python: "It's Only a Model": Terry Gilliam—The Director-y Python 263
21 Post-Python: "I'm Bounder of Adventure": Michael Palin—The Nicest Python 283

22 Post-Python: "He's a Very Naughty Boy!": Terry Jones:
    The Medieval-est Python   295
23 Seven for Seventh: The Semi-Pythons   309
24 After Python: The Influencers and Referencers   324
25 *Spamalot!* The Pythons Go to Broadway . . . and a Long Line for
    the Restroom Ensues!   332
26 We're Not Dead Yet! The Recurring Resurrections, Reunion
    Tours, and Ex-Chapmans   345

Selected Bibliography   355
Index   363
Index of Bits, Episodes, Sketches, and Songs   371

Acknowledgments

Together, we authors three want to thank all of our friends, family, and everybody else who has had to put up with our relentless Python-quoting lo these many years.

Chris: To my father, who planted the Python seed early and nurtured its silly flowering.

Brian: To Chris and Jeff for putting me as a coauthor despite the fact that all I did during the writing of the book was smoke a pipe, drink gin, and suggest, "The Norwegian blue?" To Lisa for putting up with all of this (again), and all of my many Python friends and reenactors, you know who you are. But especially to my parents, for encouraging forty or so years of Python obsession, making me a very, very silly person.

Jeff: To my cousin Paul, who took an impressionable young man aside one day, held up a bootleg copy of *Brazil*, and asked: "You seen this? You need to see this." Then he locked me in a dark room with a VCR and went back to the party. The world was never quite the same again.

Introduction

The Lasting Importance of Monty Python

From the opening peal of Sousa's "The Liberty Bell (March)" to a closing tally of squealing pigs, viewers who tuned in to the BBC on October 5, 1969, were assaulted (peanut!) by an intellectually surreal television show the likes of which few had ever dreamed. For four seasons (three . . . and a half, m'lord), the Pythons brought inspired lunacy to television. This was comedy that took no prisoners, asked no quarter, and explained no joke; the first episode practically dared viewers to keep up or get out of the way.

Indeed, a ragged castaway (Michael Palin) has scarce surfaced upon the English shore before viewers are bombarded with: a bizarre pastiche of cut-and-paste animation (Terry Gilliam); a gray-suited announcer (Graham Chapman) unexpectedly sitting on a squealing pig; a robed polytechnic professor (Terry Jones) tabulating pig squeals and teaching Italians Italian; Mozart (John Cleese)—as a TV host—introducing the sudden and overdramatic death of Genghis Khan; and Eddie, a cockney sports announcer (Eric Idle), who offers Mozart a chipper postmortem commentary . . . all within the first THREE minutes! The episode bounds from skit to skit—loosely connected by running gags and interstitial cartoons—before "ending" with a sketch hubristically titled "The Funniest Joke in the World," as if to hurl the gauntlet of comedy against the very history of television expectations. When the credits roll and Palin wades back to sea, a final tally is read: "Pigs 9–British Bipeds 4."

In short, Monty Python seemed to burst onto the BBC fully formed, like a demented Venus rising from the surf, knee-slapping its way into the annals of comedy superstardom as the severed genitals of the ruling class washed out to sea.

It's exhausting, confounding, and relentless: as close to synchronized anarchy as anyone had ever seen on television, certainly. Despite an increasingly avant-garde comic counterculture in England at the time (largely thanks to the awe-inspiring radio antics of the Goons and the behind-the-scenes machinations of David Frost), it's safe to say that Britain wasn't entirely prepared for the Pythons. And when a PBS affiliate in Dallas started showing episodes of something called *Monty Python's Flying Circus* to its unsuspecting Texas audience in the summer of 1974, America sure as hell didn't know what it was in for. But boy howdy, did they embrace the comic British Invasion with a verve previously reserved for, well, the previous musical British Invasion.

The Pythons' brand of comedy burned bright and fast, with a résumé that included a BBC TV show that lasted just four seasons, a brief German spin-off, three proper feature films, various concerts (some filmed, many not), and a dozen or so albums that primarily mined older material. It was a relatively short run, really, but their influence endures. Hell, the *Oxford English Dictionary* felt it necessary to include the word *Pythonesque* in their 1989 edition: "Of, pertaining to, or characteristic of *Monty Python's Flying Circus*, a popular British television comedy series of the 1970s, noted esp.

Monty Python (*left to right*): John Cleese, Terry Gilliam, Terry Jones, Graham Chapman, Michael Palin, and Eric Idle.   *BBC/Photofest*

for its absurdist or surreal humour." And if the *OED*—stodgy old bastion of linguistic authority that it is—recognizes your influence, you know you've gone from fringe cult figure to pop culture touchstone. In other words, Python may have begun as an avant-garde counterculture phenomenon with a cultish following, but it is now—like superhero comics and rap music—part of mainstream culture.

Monty Python™ has generated countless T-shirts, dolls (action figures, m'lord!), bloody rabbit slippers, plush grenades, key fobs, giant parrot statues, phone apps, canned meat, and beer. Let's think about that for a moment, shall we? They have their own beer. THEIR OWN BEER. They have inspired nearly every comedy group that came after them (from *Saturday Night Live* and *The Kids in the Hall*, to *South Park*, *Mr. Show*, and *Key and Peele*), but their comedy has never been duplicated. Despite a clear and abiding interest, there is very little in the way of truly Pythonesque comedy today; while many might imitate their style or co-opt their anarchic format, none could truly create, and destroy, comedy as Python did.

But without any direct comedy descendants, what is it about Monty Python that inspired—and continues to inspire—legions of fanatical devotees, quote-spouting acolytes, and falsetto-croaking lumberjacks? It's tricky, analyzing comedy. It's oft been said that dissecting comedy is like nailing down Jell-O: it's terribly messy, rather futile, and inevitably ruins the Jell-O. But in a broad sense, Monty Python was a Trojan horse of comedy, crammed with antiauthoritarianism, designed with Oxbridge erudition, and painted by Salvador Dali. Their work was stuffed with allusions to canonical literature and philosophy and often satirized the establishment, yet it never forgot that sometimes it's just as funny to see somebody getting slapped in the face with a fish.

So, without killing the joke, we'll try to poke around under the hood a bit (beautiful plumage, the Norwegian Blue) and see what makes Monty Python Monty Python. We'll start with a brief history of the Pythons before they were Pythons—back in the incestuous Crock-Pot that was 1960s BBC light entertainment, most of the lads had joined forces in smaller groups before the first peal of "The Liberty Bell (March)" sounded—and talk a bit about the culture that helped spawned them. Your three authors dote on *Flying Circus* (yes, even Season Four), so we will walk through many of those episodes, as well as all of Python's "canonical" films—sometimes with an eye toward their comedy, sometimes toward their historicity, or cinematic prowess, or media criticism, or erudition or . . . well . . . there's a lot to unpack, really.

The Pythons have gone on to have lives after Monty Python, of course, although some were far too brief. We will check in on what the lads have been doing of late, whether in solo endeavors, partial-Python projects, or even—will wonders never cease?!—reunions like the O2 shows in 2014. And, of course, no discussion of Monty Python would be complete without a long and earnest love letter to the woman who propelled many a lad (and no few lasses) into puberty back in the 1970s, a comedienne who needs no introduction, the world's greatest glamour stooge: Carol Cleveland. Er, uhm, we mean, we will present an entirely nonpartisan discussion of who on this great green Earth deserves to be called "The Seventh Python." Ahem.

Along the way, we'll drop various factoids in helpfully marked inserts proclaiming "What's All This, Then?" in honor of the policemen who were forever bounding into *Flying Circus* episodes and demanding to know just what the hell they were up to. These will parse sundry mundane topics, from the Montgolfier Brothers and the Spanish Inquisition to Galactic Cartography and Coconut Orchestras.

It's all here in *Monty Python FAQ*: every silly, weird, bizarre bit of comedy Python ever produced. Your writers (the bickering Three-Headed Knight of media-film-literature) have—at great expense and no small personal peril—burrowed our way into the pulsing heart of the Python corpus and emerged, bloody but unbowed, with a book that tells you everything you positively, absolutely need to know about this fascinating, maddening, overeducated, and relentlessly silly comedic troupe. We hope you'll find something informative in here about Monty Python—and the world that they inhabit—before this is all over. And if not, well, please direct your complaints to Mr. Barnard over in room 12B.

But enough! It's time we all left our parents' basements, anyway. Grab your pith helmet and your butterfly net: it's Python time.

Monty Python
FAQ

Every Sperm Is Sacred

In Which the Pythons Are Born

Post–World War II Britain was a land of contradictions. On the one hand, the British had single-handedly beaten back the "Jerries" (or at least that's what they told themselves after a few G&Ts). But on the other hand, postwar Britain was a metaphorical and literal shambles. Luftwaffe bombing had decimated many British cities, which remained largely unrepaired thanks to the anemic postwar economy. Food staples such as sugar were tight and rationing was the norm. Keith Richards once remarked that the Rolling Stones were so skinny because there was no candy to be had in those days. And as an immortal, what Keith Richards says is worth listening to.

Like the Stones' waistlines, the empire contracted dramatically in the postwar years. India and Burma declared independence in the 1940s, with numerous African colonies like Uganda and Kenya, and Caribbean territories like Jamaica and Barbados, following suit in the 1960s. No longer could anybody say that the sun never set on the British Empire. Traditions and practices that had defined Britain for generations were swept way postwar, leaving an uncertain future for the next generation.

Growing up in the early 1940s and '50s in Britain was not the same predictable existence as it had been for generations. Sure, the class system was still in place and boarding school remained a special hell endured by many middle- and upper-class children, but something was amiss. The glorious empire was gone, and despite the need to keep up appearances, everyone *knew* that their status in the world had drastically changed. While the British Pythons were mostly raised in traditional households, the time was ripe for questioning authority in a way that had not been possible for earlier generations.

In this chapter, we examine how the unique conditions of postwar Britain influenced the Pythons in their rejection of British norms. Being raised in a society where conformity was the mandated norm and allegiance to inherently silly authority figures was expected, the British Pythons grew up to become extremely intelligent, terribly clever, and completely rebellious. Gilliam, the original American Python, grew up in a similarly conservative atmosphere, but also felt outside of mainstream culture. The Pythons were not just born in the right place and time, but with the keen awareness that they were just the ones to give comedy in particular and culture in general a good hard kick in the arse.

Graham Chapman

Chapman was born on January 8, 1941, in Leicester. A genius of comic timing from the start, he made sure to enter the world smack-dab in the middle of a German air raid. His parents sent him to Melton Mowbray Grammar school, where he appeared in plays and showed an aptitude toward general silliness. Like the other British Pythons, Chapman was obsessed with *The Goon Show*, which would later greatly influence his absurdist approach to sketch comedy (and in many ways, his personal life as well).

The academically adept Chapman entered Cambridge to study medicine at Emmanuel College with plans to become a doctor. But he also had another, equally pressing goal: to join the school's prestigious Footlights Club, the center of avant-garde British comedy at the time. Ironically, Chapman's first attempt to join the Footlights was denied by his future employer, David Frost, who informed him that one does not simply "join" the Footlights: one is *asked* to audition. Nevertheless, Chapman impressed Footlights members with appearances in "smokers": informal cabaret sessions where the bar liberally dispensed drinks and the senior Footlights members stopped in to see if any of the new boys were worthy of membership. These were often tactical affairs; Chapman recalled in *The Pythons: Autobiography* organizing a smoker where they gave the audience "gallons of claret and didn't start until they'd drank at least a gallon each." Thus, at an early age, Chapman showed an understanding of comedy's fifth (third, m'lord!) rule: drunk audiences laugh more.

Finally, Chapman won his way into the Footlights, along with his friend and writing partner, Cleese. The lanky duo made a good team, even though Cleese wasn't enamored of Chapman's creative method, which involved drinking, showing up late, fussing with his signature pipe, lazing about quietly, and not doing much actual writing. However, Cleese recalled that those long periods of silence were often worth it: Chapman was very quiet while writing the "Dead Parrot sketch," for example, but he finally blurted out "Norwegian Blue" (they stun easily) while Cleese was struggling for a line.

In 1962, Chapman's comedic destiny took a potential detour when he left Cambridge for an appointment at St. Bartholomew's Hospital to complete his medical training. He seemed prepared to leave the life of comedy behind until an opportunity came along to join Cambridge Circus on their New Zealand tour. Chapman told a story in which he asked the Queen Mother herself for career advice when she was visiting St. Bart's: Should he pursue comedy or medicine? According to Roger Wilmut's *From Fringe to Flying Circus*, she told Chapman that New Zealand "was a beautiful place and [he] must go." This royal command provided cover with his parents. At this point, Chapman put off becoming a full-fledged doctor, although he did practice self-medication for most of his life.

Chapman continued to write after Cambridge Circus. When Cleese was offered a job at *The Frost Report*, Chapman went along. Chapman wrote, frequently with Cleese, and performed on *At Last the 1948 Show*, *Marty*, *Doctor in the House*, and—as was practically a prerequisite in British comedy at the time—various jobs for "the two Ronnies" (Ronnie Barker and Ronnie Corbett). In 1969, Cleese recruited him for *Monty Python's Flying Circus*.

Two things that defined Chapman's life were his drinking and his sexuality. Both were hidden in plain sight for years. Chapman's staggering dedication to drinking was the stuff of legend among his friends and coworkers, who became as accustomed as they could be to its ever-more-obvious negative side effects as the years went on.

Chapman was twenty-five when he consciously embraced his homosexuality. A year earlier, he had a steady girlfriend and was considering marriage. But then in 1966, on a writing trip that he and Cleese took to Ibiza, Chapman met David Sherlock, and the two remained in a long-term relationship for the rest of Graham's life. By the end of 1967 he and Sherlock were living together and keeping up the "just chums" charade was wearing on Chapman. Within the year ("nineteen sixty-thing" as he notes in *A Liar's Autobiography*), Chapman gathered his friends for a coming-out party. While a few were surprised—Cleese had been told a few days earlier but still seemed a bit shocked—almost everyone in his circle was supportive . . . save Chapman's ex-girlfriend who, perhaps understandably, ran out in tears. It was another two years before he broke the news to his parents (needlessly fearing his father's reaction, as it turned out), but Chapman had a supportive set of peers in the BBC light entertainment division.

John Cleese

Cleese, the oldest Python, was also a person very much of his time. He was born on October 27, 1939, in Uphill, a small village near Weston-super-Mare on the Bristol Channel. In a foreshadowing of a certain shop's lack of its namesake product, his family name had originally been "cheese," but his father had changed it to avoid embarrassment for his potential children. It didn't work.

Cleese's family situation was arguably grimmer than the other Pythons, save Idle. In his autobiography, *So, Anyway . . .* , he describes how his mother, who suffered from severe depression, at one point physically attacked his father in front of the younger Cleese. For her entire life, she could never understand what her son was doing with this writing and acting thing, or why it was important or useful. Cleese got along better with his *slightly* more attentive father, who was nonetheless not a man given to praising his offspring. The *How to Irritate People* sketch with the son returning home to his cloying and needy parents is likely based on Cleese's fraught family dynamic, which itself likely helps explain his lifelong immersion in therapy.

Cleese went to St. Peter's Preparatory School at eight years old. He was tall and gangly at a young age, leaving him a ripe target for the bullying that had been turned into an art form by British boarding schools. Despite his father's efforts, the bullies ended up calling him "Cheese" anyway. A lonely and isolated child, Cleese retreated into the world of comedy. Inspired by the Marx Brothers and George Burns, he made some fledgling attempts at acting, appeared in a few school plays, and started writing amusing sketches.

Cleese found a better outlet for his creativity when he attended Clifton College. There, his growing interest in comedy overlapped with the golden years of *The Goon Show*: 1953–1958. While at Clifton, Cleese appeared in Molière's *Tartuffe*, receiving positive reviews from friends and relatives. In normal circumstances, Cleese would have gone straight from there to Downing College at Cambridge to study law, but there was a glut of applications following the end of National Service in 1957 and Cleese was forced to wait. Cleese was surprised to get an invitation from St. Peter's Preparatory school, where he became a teacher for two years while waiting for a spot to open at Cambridge. It was at St. Peter's where Cleese also finally realized the silliness of the British class system. (One memorable memory about trying to get a hapless boy to learn his Latin later became the Roman Centurion Latin teacher scene from *Life of Brian*.) Cleese enjoyed teaching, but thought that law would be a better (and more lucrative) profession when he went to Cambridge.

Once at Cambridge, Cleese immediately tried to join the Footlights. There was only one problem: Cleese could neither sing nor dance. He only mumbled at the audition that he "supposed" he could try to make people laugh. Nevertheless, Cleese was allowed to join and soon started writing for the Footlights; in 1961, he met and struck up a friendship with a young David Frost, a few years Cleese's senior at Cambridge, who would later be key in Cleese's pre-Python career. Despite Cleese's repressed nature and Chapman's repressed sexuality, the two had great success writing for the Footlights and performing the shows on the road. In 1963, Cleese moved on to that year's touring Cambridge Circus revue (known for a time as *A Clump of Plinths*), and gained more exposure at the Edinburgh Festival Fringe.

Cleese was increasingly questioning his imminent law career, then took an offer from the BBC to become a radio writer and soon was working on the Dick Emery show and with future *Frost Report* costar Ronnie Barker on *Not to Worry*. However, Cambridge Circus invited Cleese back for a major tour and much to his parents' chagrin, he ran off to rejoin the circus. The Cambridge Circus tour was a major success and Cleese—along with Chapman and comics like Tim Brooke-Taylor, Bill Oddie, and Jo Kendall, among others—was soon touring New Zealand, which they found quite mysterious, particularly the time a shopkeeper, asked by Oddie for a banana split, cut a banana in half and handed it to him. Fortunately for the very repressed Cleese, New Zealand was also where he started feeling comfortable enough around women: he finally lost his virginity in Auckland just before the end of the tour.

After the rave reviews of their New Zealand adventure, the show transferred to New York for three weeks on Broadway and (after a merciless *New York Times* review) several months off Broadway. When a last-minute producer request for fresh revue material still left them short, they asked Palin and Jones to use their "History of Slapstick" sketch . . . a tiny step toward the formation of Python. The tone-deaf Cleese then had a short-lived Broadway career in *Half a Sixpence*, miming his singing parts. Cleese also met his future wife and writing partner, Connie Booth, whom he eventually married in 1968.

Wanting to stay in the United States to be close to Booth, Cleese worked briefly at *Newsweek* magazine writing obituaries. He also connected with a talented young American illustrator and budding animator, Gilliam, who cast Cleese in a *fumetti* feature (an Italian-style comic strip that told a story by superimposing word balloons on photographs) for *Help!* magazine in which Cleese played a father sexually obsessed with his daughter's Barbie doll. When Gilliam decamped for England, Cleese was the first person whom Gilliam contacted.

New York City connected Cleese with his future wife and a future Python. But it was only after Frost brought him back to England to work on *The Frost Report* in 1966 that his comedy career took off. Cleese never did practice law, much to his parents' regret. Just three years after being plucked from American semi-obscurity, though, he was costarring in and cowriting for *Monty Python's Flying Circus.* Whether this was a series of happy accidents, or canny calculation, or both, Cleese enjoyed the swiftest and most steadily upward journey of any Python.

Terry Gilliam

Gilliam was born on November 22, 1940, in Medicine Lake, Minnesota, in the United States of America, of all places. Ever the subversive one, Gilliam just had to be different and get himself born in the United States instead of in England like the rest of Python. Oh well . . . not really his fault when you think about it. Personally, I blame his parents but . . . [No psychology!—Eds.].

Gilliam's father was a traveling coffee salesman who later stayed at home to work as a carpenter, and his mother a housewife. Gilliam showed promise as an illustrator early, drawing "strange alien creatures" to amuse his parents and siblings. Unlike the wordy British Pythons, Gilliam's work was always more visually oriented. He was drawn early on to the work of American comic artist and visionary Harvey Kurtzman and in particular his *Mad* magazine, which was as subversive as a comic magazine in America in the 1950s could be. At the time, American radio was nowhere near as subversive as it was in England, leaving the likes of Gilliam looking to comics and magazines for their mind-altering substances.

Gilliam, who did not hear *The Goon Show* until the 1960s, later compared the influence of *Mad* magazine on him to that of *The Goon Show* on the British Pythons. Its mad, satirical, and subversive parodies of movies and television shows were enough to make the originally religious and socially conservative Gilliam realize that the norms of the 1950s and '60s were not to his taste.

While the rest of the Pythons moved fairly easily into the top English colleges with clear career paths in front of them, Gilliam's future was less clear. Gilliam attended Occidental College in southern California and changed his major several times. He eventually graduated with a degree in political science and a dislike of the art teachers who had told the young Gilliam that his ideas about art were too far out of the mainstream. This only hardened Gilliam's desire to be an artist himself. While Gilliam was frustrated in college, he nevertheless started working more in the visual arts; Gilliam and some like-minded fiends reinvented *Fang*, the college poetry magazine (Cardinal Fang, anyone?), and turned it into an irreverent, humorous cartoon magazine along the lines of Harvey Kurtzman's *Help!* magazine. Gilliam, eager to impress his idol, sent several issues to Kurtzman, who wrote back several letters of encouragement. After graduation, Gilliam decided to move to New York, leaving behind a budding career in architecture to enter the luxurious world of professional cartooning.

Based on the encouraging letters from Kurtzman, Gilliam showed up at the *Help* offices and was rewarded for his gumption with a job as an editorial assistant. It was during what he termed in his as "*fumetti* press-ganging missions into Greenwich Village" that Gilliam recruited a particularly limber and physically fearless member of the British comic revue Cambridge Circus named John Cleese. (Gilliam also included an up-and-coming Village comic named Woody Allen in one of the *fumetti*, but since the Bard of Manhattan never needed animated interstitials for his later films . . .)

Gilliam bounced around various jobs, working at a low-budget ad agency and eventually a French publication. His then-girlfriend, a French woman, along with some helpful hints from Uncle Sam about his potential future employment in southeast Asia, soon compelled Gilliam to move to England.

Gilliam arrived in England in 1967 with a fairly good portfolio, but few friends. He contributed cartoons to the *Sunday Times* and the *Londoner*, and worked as the art director on *London Life*. But these were tedious, poorly paid jobs and hardly provided the creative outlet that Gilliam was seeking. He soldiered on for as long as he could, before breaking down and calling Cleese, who was by then a fixture of the BBC light entertainment empire. Cleese introduced Gilliam to *Do Not Adjust Your Set* producer Humphrey Barclay, who liked Gilliam's animation of cutout elephants and hired him to provide both animated and written material. The show's writers and stars, future Monty Python members Palin, Idle, and Jones, were initially upset that this cocky Yank was coming in to work on *their* show, but soon grew impressed with his sense of humor.

Now that Gilliam had a full-time gig, he could relax and spend his time at the National Gallery. There, he could buy illustrated books filled with paintings by the greats, which he could then desecrate by cutting and pasting and otherwise doing what the kids today would refer to as "remix culture." One of the paintings he appropriated, Bronzino's *Venus and Cupid*, provided the iconic foot that crushed the logo in the opening credits animation for *Monty Python's Flying Circus*. As Gilliam pointed out to *Film Comment*, cutout animation like this wasn't some daring creative choice: "It was just a pragmatic decision . . . Cutouts are a very cheap and fast way of working." They also allowed him to directly import images from the many books that he collected over the years, mash them up, and toss them around into a kind of crude mélange of Victoriana scored to Sousa, with a side of splatting and grunting noises added for good measure. Gilliam's unique animation style and anarchic, violent sense of humor became crucial ingredients for the tasty stew that would become Monty Python.

Eric Idle

Idle was born on March 29, 1943, in South Shields in County Durham in England, and, like Cleese, also suffered a somewhat bleak childhood. Idle was born while his father was serving in the RAF as a rear gunner on a Wellington bomber. After the war was over, on December 21, 1945, Ernest Idle was hitchhiking home to be reunited with his family. He caught a lift in the back of a truck carrying a load of sheet metal. During the ride home, the truck swerved to avoid an oncoming car, shifting its load, which crushed its passenger in the back.

Idle's mother never recovered from the loss of her husband. Thinking herself unable to raise a child, when he turned seven she sent him off to a Wolverhampton boarding school designated for children who had lost a parent in the war. Idle spent the next miserable twelve years there, feeling that he had been abandoned. Strangely enough, the boarding school that Idle was sent to had been founded in 1850 by none other than a man called . . . John Leese. Hmm, the plot thickens.

The Wolverhampton boarding school was, typically, about as bad as most most British boarding schools at the time, featuring regular beatings by the headmasters and a rigid hierarchy based on class where younger boys served as "fags" for the prefects, doing them favors and generally acting as unpaid servants. Sexual experimentation was rife and young children tried to hide their tears late at night in bed, so they would not be caught

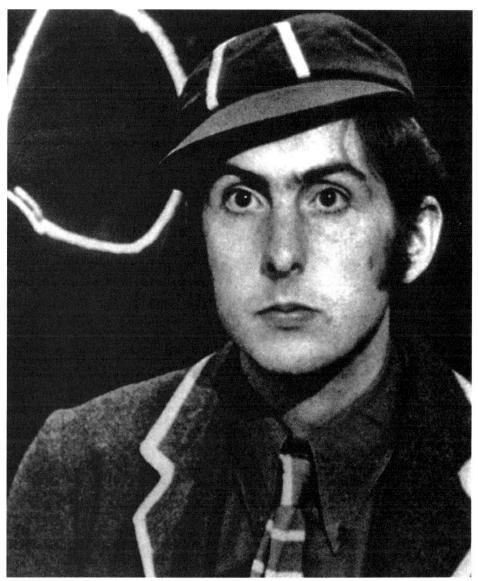

Eric Idle, as he may have looked as a schoolboy.   *BBC/Photofest*

and taunted by their schoolmates. Idle looked back at his boarding school years as a primer in learning to repress your emotions and survive what he called in *The Pythons: Autobiography* a "physically abusive, harsh, bullying environment." Idle played the rebel at school, brazenly sneaking out during the day to see movies; he was finally caught after leaving school grounds to catch *Butterfield 8*, a film that had been given an X rating in Britain. When the headmaster denounced Idle in front of the whole school for this, his reputation as a local hero was firmly cemented. Strangely enough, even the headmaster seemed impressed, later recommending Idle for "Head Boy" in his senior year.

After finally escaping boarding school, Idle was accepted to Cambridge University, where he studied English literature. He auditioned for and joined the Footlights, making president in his last year. Used to isolation from his time at boarding school, Idle started writing on his own, a practice he continued during later years in the group dynamic of Monty Python. Idle revolutionized the Footlights, admitting women for the first time (including noted feminist author Germaine Greer in 1965). And, of course, Cambridge introduced Idle to Cleese, the recently graduated Chapman, and a host of other future BBC comedy legends (including Tim Brooke-Taylor).

After his own graduation. Idle was asked to join a revival of *A Clump of Plinths* at the Edinburgh Festival Fringe. This led to more work on different revues. Idle was also starting to write for the BBC comedy radio show *I'm Sorry, I'll Read That Again*, and the television program *Twice a Fortnight*. Old Cambridge chum Tim Brooke-Taylor then suggested that the two of them start to contribute material to *The Frost Report*, where Idle started working on Frost's interview "ad-libs" and met Cleese and Chapman. Idle's first onscreen roles started out on *At Last the 1984 Show*, where he became better acquainted with Cleese and Chapman.

When Humphrey Barclay recruited Idle for a new children's show he was working on, *Do Not Adjust Your Set*, Idle agreed as long as he could bring in his *Frost Report* friends Palin and Jones.

Terry Jones

Jones was born February 1, 1942, in Colwyn Bay, Wales, making him the only Welsh Python. In terms of the pecking order, this likely left him ranked above the American Gilliam but still subject to razzing from the likes of Cleese (who joked on a talk show in 2009 how Jones never understood that "the Welsh are a servile nation that God put on the planet to carry out menial tasks for the English"). Jones's childhood was relatively tame compared to some other Pythons. His interests were probably the broadest. From his earliest days, Jones juggled academic ambitions with interests in poetry and history and a love of comedy.

Like his fellow Pythons, Jones found the academic demands of school relatively easy; he was accepted by both Oxford and Cambridge. It is worth wondering at this point what would have happened had Jones had gone to Cambridge and joined the Footlights. Would he have teamed with Idle, or even the upper classmen Cleese or Chapman? What would the "Dead Parrot sketch" have been like if it had been written by Cleese and Jones? Would it ever have existed? Fortunately, such speculation is moot: Jones accepted a position at Oxford. They asked him first.

Jones enrolled in St. Edmund's Hall College in 1961, where he majored in history. At first Jones showed little interest in acting and gravitated toward more serious academic pursuits. He worked on the stodgy old student newspaper *Isis*, and discovered that he had the acting bug.

Jones joined Oxford's Experimental Theater Company. There, in 1963, he met and started working with like-minded history major Palin. In the *Loitering Within Tent* revue, they developed the "History of Slapstick" sketch, which first appeared that year in an Oxford Edinburgh Festival performance, was later incorporated by Cleese into the Cambridge Circus's American performances, and was performed by Python most memorably in the 1982 concert film *Monty Python Live at the Hollywood Bowl*. In 1964, Palin and Jones appeared in *The Oxford Review* at the Fringe festival.

After the success of their Fringe debut, the slightly older Jones left Palin behind to move to London and start working as a writer and performer. After a failed attempt at producing *The Love Show*, a play about the history of love and sex, Jones called Palin in for help. The pair worked on another play, this one for television, also unproduced. The two were discouraged enough that Jones almost went looking for a job at Oxford.

At that time, the BBC was hiring new younger writers and actors in the light entertainment division. Although the executives did not necessarily understand the odd-seeming material coming from this new crop of young comics, they *did* understand that shows like *Beyond the Fringe* were increasingly popular and that they should stay on top of this comedy trend. Hired as a script editor at the BBC, Jones secured writing gigs for himself and Palin; the two started writing short bits for shows such as *The Ken Dodd Show, The Kathy Kirby Show*, and *The Illustrated Weekly Hudd* in 1965. Based on this work, the BBC let Jones and Palin appear on a "serious" show, *The Late Night Line-Up*, where they added a dose of silliness for a few weeks, until angry guests forced them off the show. Apparently, even noted author Dennis Potter (*The Singing Detective*) thought their bits a bit *too* silly.

However, the BBC's loss occurred at the same time that David Frost came calling . . . as he had for Cleese and the other Cambridge crew. Their work on *The Frost Report*, where Jones fought for his material with Palin

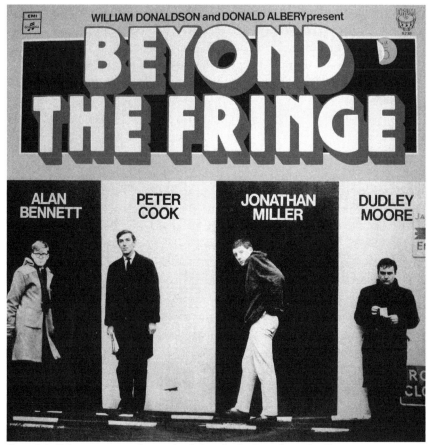

Beyond the Fringe set a comedy standard that the Pythons hoped to live up to.

Lisa Bocchini

against competing writers such as Idle, Chapman, and Cleese, eventually led to the twisted children's show *Do Not Adjust Your Set*, and later *The Complete and Utter History of Britain*.

Michael Palin

Universally known as "the nice one," Palin was born on May 5, 1943, in Sheffield. He got to acting straight off. At just five years old, Palin performed as one of the Cratchit children in a local production of *A Christmas Carol*. Palin appeared in plays throughout his teenage years, while still doing well enough academically to be admitted in 1962 to Oxford's Brasenose College, where he studied history.

But Palin, a fan of Peter Cook and *The Goon Show*, started crafting silly and surrealistic comedy as soon as he arrived at Oxford, even working with the future theater critic Robert Hewison on sketches that were basically Goons retreads. (Many early proto-Python sketches, innovative and radical as they were, owe quite a debt not just to *The Goon Show*, but also to Cook and Dudley Moore's *Beyond the Fringe*, a lineage we examine in later chapters.)

Palin finally debuted his own comedic work at the Oxford University Psychological Society's Christmas party (where else?). A young Jones, one year Palin's senior, watched in amazement. He soon suggested that the two work together. Their first material appeared in *Loitering Within Tent*, before they split up to work separately. Palin had joined the Experimental Theater Group and Oxford University Dramatic Society working on their revues, one of which, *Hang Your Head Down and Die*, played in London for over a month. The next year, Palin and Jones worked on *The Oxford Line*, a comedic review that played at the 1965 Edinburgh Festival Fringe to much acclaim. Clearly, the duo were clicking as actors and cowriters.

Unlike Jones, who was torn between going back to Oxford and working in London after graduation, Palin moved to London to look for work following graduation, hooking back up with Jones. Seen as more televisually friendly, Palin soon became a BBC host on the youth program *Now!* (presumably *When?* was taken). Before long, he was working with Jones full-time on other television shows when David Frost came a-calling. Palin then worked with Jones on *The Frost Report*, which led to *Do Not Adjust Your Set*, leading to *The Complete and Utter History of Britain*, leading to . . . well, you know what comes next. [Don't be coy.—Eds.]

Unlike the other Pythons, Palin seems quite well-adjusted; suspiciously so, for a comic. He himself was legendary for being not just the nicest but also the most stable of the Pythons. Some (such as Palin) have disputed this, but his apparently getting a little cranky if he's hungry doesn't exactly disprove the legend of his niceness.

In 1966, Palin became the first Python to get married. He and Helen Gibbons have by this point been together over a half-century, making theirs the most lasting Python marriage. Even pre-Python, Palin was always a prodigious diarist and some of the most accurate information that we have about the Python years comes from Palin's voluminous diary entries.

2

The Origins of British Silliness

The Goon Show

This chapter is a brief look at the groundbreaking radio comedy show (1951–1960), which drew on the revered tradition of British slapstick and introduced some of English comedy's more anarchic elements—largely thanks to the unbounded antics of Peter Sellers, Spike Milligan, Harry Secombe, and Michael Bentine. The Pythons loved these guys; you should too. There is nothing that more inspired or deeply resembled the work of Monty Python than *The Goon Show*.

Goons on the Radio

The Goon Show was the brainchild of prolific British comedian Spike Milligan. He not only created the show, but is generally credited with writing most of the episodes during its 1951–1960 run. Milligan and Secombe had become friends while serving in World War II. After the war, the two met Sellers, already an established comedian and actor, and then added Michael Bentine as the "fourth goon"; the Goons then became a trio when Bentine left after the second season to work as a writer on various British shows like *After Hours*, *That Was the Week That Was*, *It's a Square World*, and even *The Dave Allen Show* before hosting *Michael*

What's All This, Then?
Head's Up!

Milligan, a veteran who penned a series of memoirs about his experiences in World War II that started with 1971's *Adolph Hitler: My Part in His Downfall*, met Secombe on the battlefield in North Africa. Having lost control of a howitzer that almost killed Secombe, Milligan asked him, "Have you seen a gun?" Secombe replied, "What color?"

Bentine's Potty Time (1973–1980) (we swear, that's the real title: go and look it up on the Interwebs!).

The appeal of *The Goon Show*—like that of *Monty Python's Flying Circus*—is difficult to explain to those who have never experienced it. Their humor was less dependent on plot than it was on the ability of the Goons to deeply inhabit their highly quirky characters. Years later, when Sellers appeared as a guest on *The Muppet Show* and Kermit said that the former Goon could just be himself, Sellers replied, "There *was* a me, but I had him surgically removed." This half-joke gives a hint as to the depth of the Goons' dedication to their craft.

The British Pythons were all avid listeners in their youths. Each of them independently discovered something utterly unlike everything else being broadcast by the stodgy BBC, with its conventional programming and dignified newsmen reading in "Received Pronunciation" (the standard broadcast accent). As Michael Palin recounted in *The Pythons: Autobiography*, *The Goon Show* was "a glimpse of madness . . ." At a time when most sketch comedy shows reflected the prejudices and conventions of the older generation, Palin appreciated how the Goons "saw behind this thin veneer of civilization and pushed these characters to [their] limits." Palin saw in these quasi-anarchists a clear precursor to Python, one that would provide inspiration for his own writing years later.

Jones was also a dedicated fan, as was John Cleese, who said that he was obsessed with the Goons in the same way that the next generation would later be obsessed with Python. Even American Python Gilliam was enamored of the Goons, after he first heard them in the mid-1960s on a New York free-form radio station that played unauthorized recordings. According to a *Goon Show* tribute by Gilliam, "There was nothing in America to compare with it. If Britain could produce nonsense as pure and anarchic as that, then that was the place for me." Clearly, Gilliam would later try to do visually what the Goons were doing with audio.

Years later the starstruck Pythons became friends with their hero Milligan, who had a brief cameo in *Life of Brian*. In his *Diaries 1980–1988: Halfway to Hollywood—The Film Years*, Palin writes that Milligan's answers to his fanboy questions about the Goons "are almost identical to the answers I always give when asked about the Pythons—we did it to make ourselves laugh, to laugh at authority, we always had a love/hate relationship with the BBC, etc." Misunderstood and barely tolerated by the BBC, the Goons and Pythons were nevertheless both given the latitude to change the nature of comedy for a mainstream audience.

A typical episode usually had something resembling a three-act structure, with musical interludes by jazz harmonica player Max Geldray and
singer Ray Ellington (who was replaced by Secombe after the middle of
the second season). Originally, the show's main character was Dr. Osric
Pureheart, played by Bentine. After Bentine's departure, Secombe took
the lead role as the show's intelligence-challenged protagonist, Neddie
Seagoon. In each episode, Sellers and Milligan inhabited a bewildering
array of supporting characters swarming about the lead.

After Bentine left, Secombe came into his own as the comedic lead,
creating what many fans consider to be the best iteration of *The Goon Show*.
Sellers's main characters included Bluebottle, Henry Crun, Major Dennis

This 1974 album contained two episodes of *The Goon Show*, "The Missing No. 10 Downing
Street" and "The Red Fort," which were first broadcast in 1957.   *Lisa Bocchini*

Bloodnok, and the aptly named Hercules Grytpype-Thynne. Milligan's major characters included "the famous" Eccles, snotty foreigner Count Jim Moriarty, and the spinster Minnie Bannister.

But what made the Goons so special that even a young Prince Charles was enamored of them? A typical example of how the Goons worked can be seen in the Season Five episode "The Whistling Spy Enigma." Things start in the usual Goon manner, with boos at the introduction of the BBC Home Service, then Neddie Seagoon announcing the Goons as if they were contenders in a prize fight: "My Lords, ladies and gentlemen, back from the dead, we present half an hour of continuous radio fighting, in both corners—the Goons!"

The episode consists of a combination of puns, surrealistic jokes, and verbal sleight of hand, which lurches forward in the general direction of a plot. Seagoon is summoned to MI5 headquarters, where Hercules Grytpype-Thynne sends Seagoon on a secret mission to Hungary ("via Budapest," of course). There, he is to meet Agent X (pronounced "eeeeex") and procure a secret pouch that will help England recover from a recent humiliating football defeat by Hungary. The "Whistling Enigma" part of the title comes from the secret whistle Seagoon must use to procure the package: "Hungarian Rhapsody" (only "in English"). The only problem: Seagoon can't whistle.

The introductory sketch not only sets up the usual trip around the world the Goons took on a regular basis (some based on Milligan's wartime career), but also points out the limitations of an audio-only medium. In one running gag, Seagoon is constantly asked to "pull up a chair," only the standard accompanying Foley sound effect is missing, both acknowledging the limitations of the medium, and the expectations of the audience. Later, in a further nod to radio conventions, although their objective is stated as being "sixty-three miles away," a whooshing sound effect is followed by the sound of Eccles panting, as if from a prolonged run. While radio has always counted on the audience's expectations of time and space being compressed, this is a tacit acknowledgment of the audience's complicity in fooling themselves to maintain dramatic or comedic continuity.

Indeed, the Goons were known for their elaborate sound effects. So, in the middle of a conversation, for example, the audience might hear the sounds of (as indicated in the script) "[Siren, then bagpipes, then explosion, then clucking chicken]," followed by Crun shouting, "Answer that phone!" After yet another musical interlude and a linked reintroduction to the story (it is BBC light entertainment, after all), the show returns to some

Some Goons (*left to right*): Peter Sellers, Harry Secombe, Spike Milligan   *BBC/Photofest*

older music hall–style jokes (when offering to hit someone with a piano, Seagoon is told "that's no good, it's out of tune") and increasing feats of surrealismsuch as "Hand me that 600-foot factory chimney in the corner!" "I can't, it's our last one!"

While there were variations on this theme, this is a fairly typical Goon episode, with a nominal plot held together by the brilliantly silly Milligan script and the vocal talents of Sellers and Secombe. Sellers in particular would parlay his verbal gymnastics into a lucrative film career, including his three separate roles in Stanley Kubrick's 1964 satire *Dr. Strangelove: Or How I Learned to Stop Worrying and Love the Bomb.* Just as Monty Python would later deconstruct television, the Goons deconstructed radio.

The Goon Show aired for 238 episodes and 12 specials. Many are archived now and broadcast weekly on the BBC7 radio channel. But most of the first four seasons are lost and only about 120 episodes have been released. Partial versions are available online for some of the lost episodes. Go: listen to them. Now.

Goons on the Big and Small Screen

While *The Goon Show* was particularly well-suited to radio (where listeners at home could picture the myriad characters voiced by the three main actors), there were several largely unsuccessful attempts to turn *The Goon Show* into visual media.

The first film, *Penny Points to Paradise* (1951), a light bit of fluff about forgers starring Milligan, Sellers, and Secombe, is mostly forgettable and not really a proper Goon project as they were only there as performers, not writers. All four Goons, including Bentine, appeared in the slightly more successful *Down Among the Z Men* (1952), a lighthearted romp in which the Goons play soldiers guarding a secret formula from enemy agents. Slightly more fun than *Penny Points*, *Z Men* is still nothing like the radio programs, likely because, again, the Goons were just brought on as performers and not writers. The best way to "see" the Goons remains hearing them on the radio.

Now, one would imagine that working with talents such as Sellers, Milligan, and Secombe would lead to an easy transition into television, correct? Ah, astute reader, you are forgetting this is the BBC we're talking about here. This is the same broadcaster that thought, "Great episode of *Doctor Who*, smashing, eh! Well, that's done so let's erase the tape and use it for something else, surely no one will want to see this in the future!" (Don't laugh, it happened to *At Last the 1948 Show* and *Do Not Adjust Your Set*, and nearly *Flying Circus* as well.)

Plan A: The BBC tried the novel approach of *not* adapting *The Goon Show* at all, but instead in 1956 created *The Idiot Weekly, Price 2d*, which starred only Sellers. The show didn't last, but Milligan, never one to throw anything away, resurrected the concept as . . . wait for it . . . an Australian radio show also called *The Idiot Weekly* that Milligan was doing while on holiday sporadically from 1958 to 1963.

Plan B: Puppets! Yes, only the BBC would have the stellar idea of taking half of a half-hour scripted comedy episode and putting it on the air as a fifteen-minute puppet show. *The Telegoons* ran from 1963 to 1964 and can be seen online today, but you'd probably rather watch *The Goon Show: The Whistling Spy Enigma*, a radio episode that was reenacted for Secombe's television program *Secombe & Friends* in 1966. It's a pretty good intro to the Goons' absurdist style of comedy. But the best available video version is 1968's *The Goon Show: Tales of Men's Shirts*, a live reading of the radio program . . . with Cleese as the announcer. The three Goons did one more radio broadcast, *The Last Goon Show of All*, in 1972. After that, their disparate careers (Sellers being particularly busy with the Pink Panther franchise) kept them from a true reunion, which was finally dashed by Sellers's untimely death of a heart attack in 1980.

Sadly, the Goons are no more, they have ceased to be, they . . . well, they're all gone now. Sellers passed away first in 1980, Bentine in 1996, Secombe in 2001, and Milligan in 2002. However, their great influence on Monty Python, Eddie Izzard, the Kids in the Hall, the Goodies, and many others is proof today of their enduring comedic legacy. The Pythons would have not known how much ground a single show could break, and certainly would not have been as bold in taking on both the medium (television) and their employers (the BBC) if the Goons hadn't already knocked down the door with a six-hundred-foot factory chimney. We think Prince Charles would agree.

3

Frost/Python

In Which David Frost Gives Comedy a Go

David Frost (1939–2013) is pivotal to the history of *Monty Python's Flying Circus*, but he's also a hard character to explain to most Americans. There is no real American precedent for a man who worked in so many different mediums and genres, often helping to create them as he went along. Like Cleese, he was a member of the Cambridge Footlights and even performed some Cleese/Chapman material in the revues. After university, he was quickly snapped up by the BBC and by the age of twenty-three had created and was starring in his own program, the television news satire *That Was the Week That Was*. Frost next created the more popular and widely known sketch comedy show *The Frost Report*, which ran for two seasons from 1966 to 1967 and hired almost the entire Python crew (save Gilliam).

Incredibly, Frost did all this *before* becoming Britain's premier interviewer. Frost is best known in America for his blockbuster 1977 interviews with Richard Nixon. Frost was like a combination of Jon Stewart, Lorne Michaels, Mike Wallace, and (at least when it came to self-promotion) Donald Trump, with an unerring radar for tracking the cultural and political zeitgeist. In the 1960s, Frost could tell that the zeitgeist was spinning toward the kind of countercultural absurdity that Monty Python would soon deliver.

That Was the Week That Was and The Frost Report

A revolutionary show that did something never before attempted on British television—parody the news and contemporary British culture—*That Was the Week That Was* paved the way for *SNL*'s "Weekend Update," *Not Necessarily the News*, *The Daily Show*, *The Colbert Report*, and countless other mockumentary shows. *That Was the Week That Was* (popularly known as *TW3*) ran for

That Was the Week That Was delivers the news, sorta. *Left to right*: Elliott Reid, Henry Morgan, David Frost, Nancy Ames.   *NBC/Photofest*

a scant two seasons, from 1962 to 1963, but was soon followed by *The Frost Report*, which ran for another two seasons, from 1966 to 1967.

Both shows were barbed and acerbic attacks on the establishment. Cleese noted in *So, Anyway . . .* that in response to *TW3*, "retired colonels throughout the land bewailed the End of Civilisation as they knew it." As Marcia Landy notes in her 2005 study *Monty Python's Flying Circus*:

> *TW3* became known for its uses of music, topicality, sketches, political lampooning, churchmen, and scandals such as the Profumo affair, which ultimately brought down the Macmillan government. But as Frost pointed out, *TW3* and *The Frost Report* were not there to

take down the government, but rather to express a growing senti-
ment against British complacency. As Frost put it, "We were the
Exasperated Young Men—exasperated by Britain's reoccurring
failures, by hypocrisy and complacency and by the shabbiness of its
politics."

Whatever the writers' and performers' intentions were, *TW3* was certainly seen as a threat to the establishment. Reportedly, the show's 1963
cancellation was due in part to BBC executives worried about pressure from
the government, which was the target of so much of *TW3*'s comedic ire.

Inspired by the enthusiastic reception for *TW3*, Frost recruited Cleese
as a writer/performer for *The Frost Report*; Frost had been Cleese's student mentor at Cambridge, and Cleese was back from his New Zealand
and American tours, looking for an excuse not to pursue a career in the
law. Cleese, who was soon acting as much as writing on the show, in turn
recruited his old partner in sketch comedy, Chapman, to write with him.

The Frost Report parodied the tropes of topical sketch material not
uncommon at that time, but with a new kind of slyly subversive humor
that questioned the foundations of Britain itself, especially the revered but
increasingly maligned class system.

In the tellingly named "Class Sketch," a tall and rather elegant Cleese
(dressed in a recognizably upper-class uniform of conservative suit and
bowler hat) stands next to "regular-sized" Ronnie Barker (representing
the middle class in his similar but less expensive clothing) and diminutive
Ronnie Corbett (more shabbily dressed, as the working class). The sketch's
humor is grounded in physical difference as a metaphor ("High Society,"
class warfare, clear divisions, etc.), but works even better as cogent political
satire. Barker observes that although he is obliged to look up at those in
the upper classes, he, by virtue of his position in society, is nevertheless
privileged enough to be able to look down upon the working class, as
represented by Corbett. Pointedly, Corbett is left to deadpan: "I know my
place." As Cleese and Barker pontificate on what they "get" to do, a visibly
annoyed Corbett cuts off the discussion by noting that while the other two
"get" many things, the only thing he "gets" is "a pain in the back of my neck,"
from constantly having to look up at the other two privileged classes.

While this may seem tame stuff by modern standards, it was actually
quite revolutionary for its time. As Cleese later recalled in his autobiography, "You have to grasp just how deferential, stiff, compulsively super-polite
and excruciatingly cautious British culture was at that time." "The Class
Sketch" (written by Marty Feldman and John Law) is a clear precursor to one

of Cleese's best *Flying Circus* characters, the reoccurring "upper class twit," the stiff-lipped Brit smugly secure of his place at the top of society and oblivious to how pompous and silly he seems to the "lower" classes. In some ways, Barker and Corbett capitalized on that kind of comedic dichotomy for their later show *The Two Ronnies*, but the "Upper Class Twit of the Year" sketch in *Flying Circus* put the sharpest satiric edge on the social commentary begun by "The Class Sketch" on *The Frost Report*.

Cleese, by virtue of his upbringing and height and bearing, could play these upper-class characters perfectly. As Palin later said of his colleague in his *Diaries*, since Cleese looked like a bishop or bank manager, he "was able better than any of us (apart from perhaps Graham) to show this wonderful process of the Establishment character undermining the Establishment." On *The Frost Report*, Cleese looked the part of the Establishment; on *Flying Circus* (and in a few scenes in *The Meaning of Life*) he would take that look further and become, as Palin put it, the headmaster who had gone insane.

Cleese and Chapman were not the only future Python members writing for *The Frost Report*. Frost had also recruited the writing team of Palin and Jones, as well as Idle, leading to all five of the British Pythons working on the same show at the same time. Idle, more used to working on his own, also collaborated with ex-Footlights writer Tim Brooke-Taylor and, perhaps surprisingly, with Chapman.

As Cleese later recalled, while working *The Frost Report*, he began to notice that location shoots were often written by a couple Oxford gents by the name of Palin and Jones who were regulars at the Saturday morning script read-throughs. Some early works by Palin and Jones included a karate champion's birthday party, where he naturally cuts the cake with a fierce karate chop. The blow lands with such ferocity that the neighbor's house collapses from the impact. Palin and Jones and Idle also contributed to Frost's "ad-libs" and throwaway lines. Frost, like Bob Hope and Milton Berle before him, was often accused of stealing jokes, so he probably needed the material. Peter Cook often referred to Frost as "the bubonic plagiarist."

Cleese was so busy as a performer on *The Frost Report*, not to mention keeping up with his other projects, that he reportedly had little time to write material. By the second season, Idle, Palin, and Jones were contributing more of the show's sketches.

Idle was also eventually assigned Frosts CDM's (Continuously Developing Monologues) and contributed some memorable moments, including one bit where Ronnie Barker suggested that Christmas be staggered into several minor holidays in order to avoid traffic concerns and other difficulties.

Idle started coming into his own as a writer and performer and was soon featured in many sketches. It was during this time that Idle developed his fawning, unctuous "interviewer" character as a parody of Frost. In fact Idle often wrote intentionally smarmy links for Frost to read for Idle to study and then imitate Frost reading Idle, then later, Idle performed Idle's version of Frost. Got all that? Good, let's get back to *The Frost Report*.

Season Two was where the five future Pythons dominated the show. Cleese agitated for more work from the Pythons and less from the other writers, sometimes including his own material. (This would not be the case on *Flying Circus*, where the competition was fiercer.) Cleese was also working more to polish his comic persona, and it shows. Unfortunately, most of this season was wiped in another brilliant attempt by the BBC to save a few quid by reusing old videotapes.

In 1967, *The Frost Report* won the Golden Rose of Montreux Prize award for best comedy. However, not everyone was aware of how successful and groundbreaking the show had become. Cleese's father, who lived in a region where *The Frost Report* could not be seen (ah, the BBC!), sent Cleese a letter informing him that there was an open position in the personnel department at British department store Marks & Spencer, and that he should apply for it if his "career was still foundering." Fortunately, Cleese did not take the advice.

While *The Frost Report* had many clever sketches, it can best be looked at as a training camp where the future Pythons could stretch their imaginations outside of the boundaries of conventional British television. Cleese, as usual, was getting bored at the end of the second season. But Frost, convinced by then of the usefulness of Cleese's talents, talked him, Chapman, Palin, and Connie Booth into working on another of his comedy projects.

How to Irritate People and Post-Python Frost

The television special *How to Irritate People* is fascinating in that it shows half of Monty Python (Cleese, Chapman, and Palin) working hard to do something groundbreaking, but not quite making it happen. In one sketch, the three future Pythons play airline captains gleefully menacing a plane full of passengers with vague allusions to danger and sudden jerks of the controls. The "Dead Car" sketch, in which Cleese attempts to return a "dead car" to a reluctant salesman (Palin), was later redone for *Flying Circus*; just add a "Norwegian Blue," and you've got comedy gold. In an unsuccessful attempt to break into the American market, Frost had the special shown in

America as part of a Sunday-night series; it didn't take. *How to Irritate People* lapsed into obscurity until being released on DVD several decades later.

Frost also had a hand in the Cleese and Chapman–written film *The Rise and Rise of Michael Rimmer*, a political satire about a canny advertising executive (Peter Cook) who becomes prime minister, which was at least partially based on the rise and rise of Frost. Although the film wasn't very well received after its release in 1970, it gave Cleese and Chapman an excuse to spend more time with Feldman and Brooke-Taylor, a relationship that led eventually to the Frost-produced *At Last the 1948 Show*.

What's All This, Then?
For a Good Time, Call . . .

Among the many ways in which they took the piss out of David Frost over the years, Monty Python made him the butt of one particularly blink-and-you-missed-it gag: During the "Mouse Problem" sketch in the second episode of *Monty Python's Flying Circus*'s inaugural season, they (very briefly) flashed Frost's home phone number on the screen. It was the least they could do, given that Frost had let Cleese out of his contract to do *Flying Circus*.

By the late 1970s Frost had reinvented himself again, this time as a hard-hitting journalist who most notably interviewed former President Richard Nixon in four blockbuster ninety-minute prime-time specials that aired in May 1977. The interviews and their impact on a post-Watergate America were famously later chronicled in the 2006 play and 2008 film adaptation *Frost/Nixon*. It should also be remembered that Idle parodied Frost interviewing Nixon on an episode of *Saturday Night Live*. After decades of practice, Idle was at his Frosty smarmiest.

After Nixon, Frost continued in his almost miraculous career, hosting numerous specials, appearing on the radio, being knighted by the queen, interviewing every British prime minister from 1964 to 2013, and every American president from 1969 to 2013. Frost, who passed away in 2013, has a memorial stone in Westminster Abbey's Poets' Corner for his "contribution to British culture." While it technically does not mention his "contribution to British culture for bringing five out of six Pythons together in the same writing room and letting them do whatever the hell they wanted," it certainly should.

4

And Now, for Something Oddly Familiar

At Last the 1948 Show

onight, ladies and gentlemen, we bring you the story of a show shot in 1967 but heralding from 1948; a show that tapped into the talent pool of the Cambridge Circus, *The Frost Report*, and the West End; a show that combined the pre-star power of a Goodie, two Pythons, and an Igor; a show that was—until recently—almost entirely erased from history; a show that, quite frankly, is a linchpin in the evolution of Monty Python. That show is, of course, ~~Do Not Adjust Your Set~~ At Last the 1948 Show.

The Show

At Last the 1948 Show (named to reflect the interminable gestation period of most nascent BBC properties) ran for thirteen episodes in 1967 and disappeared almost immediately thereafter, but its contribution to comedy remains indelible: the Pythons, the Goodies, and the Mel Brooks crowd all owe *1948* a debt of thanks. Starring Cleese and Chapman (future Pythons), Tim Brooke-Taylor (future Goodie), Marty Feldman (future Igor), and the lovely Aimi MacDonald (future the lovely Aimi MacDonald), *At Last the 1948 Show* brought the absurd silliness of the Cambridge Circus to a wider audience and helped pave the way for the next stages of surreal British comedy.

At Last the 1948 Show was—like so many other comic properties in the 1960s—"born" from *The Frost Report*. According to lore, Cleese was given the go-ahead from Frost to form a new show, something slightly edgier than *The Frost Report*. They then assembled the new team: Chapman was an obvious choice, as was their old Cambridge chum (and then-flatmate)

Tim Brooke-Taylor; another friend and fellow *Frost Report* alumnus Marty Feldman (then a comedy writer/editor, but not yet a screen name) joined them; and finally, Frost discovered the "lovely" Aimi MacDonald (a multi-talented human interstitial) and added her to round out the troupe.

While on paper it was a traditional sketch comedy with punch lines, terminal fanfares, and a predictable format, *At Last the 1948 Show* featured an array of Pythonesque "anti-conventions" and future Python gags, including

What's All This, Then?
At Last the DVD Show

Long thought wiped from history thanks to BBC austerity measures, various "lost" episodes have since resurfaced over the years: Feldman's wife recovered a few; a compilation in Sweden (totaling about five episodes' worth of material) made its way to DVD; full episodes and other bits arrived from Australia; and British fans and collectors made their home tapes known. In 2014, two episodes were found in the private collection of *1948* executive producer David Frost (who had passed away in 2013). After British fans recovered two additional episodes in 2015, video recordings of eleven of the original thirteen episodes have been more or less recovered or reconstructed by the British Film Institute (BFI). While most of these full episodes have yet to see (legal) public distribution, BFI aired a previously lost episode on "Missing Believed Wiped" (with an introduction by Cleese) in late 2014 and another (with commentary by Brooke-Taylor) in 2015. The search continues for the elusive two missing episodes, but thanks to fan audio recordings of the entire series (and a 1967 LP that featured sketches from the first season), we've got a pretty good sense of the series as a whole. Now that the series is more or less available again, it's enlightening to see how the televisual lunacy of *Flying Circus* evolved—and, in some cases, refused to evolve—from its stage-bound college days.

A 2005 DVD release of five *1948* "episodes" is currently available (packaged in the United States with nine "episodes" of *Do Not Adjust Your Set*), but be warned: it's really a rejiggered Swedish collection of random sketches assembled in no discernible order. As collectors and the BFI continue to scour the lengths and breadths of the land for surviving recordings, one can only hope that the full pre-Monty will be available within our lifetime. Until then: to the Internets!

the magnificent "Four Yorkshiremen" sketch, a witty bit of absurd one-upmanship that many fans assume is pure Python. Frost played more of a background role here than with *The Frost Report*, serving merely as executive producer and not a member of the cast, leaving more room for the proto-Pythons to build the foundation of their future success.

In addition to the directly "incestuous" sketches that both *1948* and *Flying Circus* recycled from Cambridge Circus, *At Last the 1948 Show* delved into many of the general tropes that would soon define Monty Python. You want absurd humor? Here's a man who thinks he's a rabbit, another who attends "mouse parties," and there's a fellow swallowed by a boa constrictor. You prefer rat-a-tat thesaurus wordplay? Enjoy the "Bookshop" sketch. You say you want characters with inexplicably strange names? Let me introduce you to Nosmo Claphanger, Mr. Given-Posture, Wing Commander Bransby Snake-Sinus, and Arthur S. Stoat. Recurring gags tickle your fancy? Have a second helping of Sydney Lotterbys and the ever-lovely Aimi MacDonald. Genre parody? Try not to laugh at the noir silliness of "Mice Laugh Softly Charlotte"! Breaking the fourth wall? Generic mash-ups? False newscasts? Silly experts and vox pops? Glamour stooges? Men in drag? Inexplicable nudes? Chartered accountants? Cleese shouting!?

Yes, *At Last the 1948 Show* has it all. Almost.

Cleese vents spleen, but it's not quite the seething anger of impotent middle-management that made *Flying Circus* so biting. Chartered accountants are targeted, but far more gently than in *Flying Circus* or *The Meaning of Life*. Men appear in drag, but the incongruous erudition of the pedestrian Pepperpot hasn't yet arrived. Characters snigger at weird names, but extended examinations of linguistic futility aren't overtly addressed. The lovely Aimi MacDonald is a hyper-(un)aware bridge between sketches, but she's not half as deconstructively weird as Gilliam . . . or his art. *1948* is certainly clever, but it's not yet the "aren't we clever?" clever of Monty Python.

On the plus side, *1948* had a very "live stage" feel to it, a sense of spontaneity that communicated the infectious joy of the actors (who frequently ad-libbed, corpsed, and flat-out giggled their way through sketches). *Flying Circus* dared its viewers to laugh at themselves; *At Last the 1948 Show* invited its viewers to laugh with them. Ultimately, *1948* may not have had the anarchic venom of *Flying Circus*, but it certainly benefitted from the editorial acumen of Feldman and the toe-tapping talent of Brooke-Taylor: truly, a mild-mannered manifestation of the Terpsichorean Muse.

The Cast

Tim Brooke-Taylor: The Dancing Chartered Accountant

Born Timothy Julian Brooke-Taylor in Buxton, Derbyshire, England (1940), Brooke-Taylor studied law at Cambridge, joined the Footlights Club just before David Frost graduated (alongside Chapman, Cleese, Bill Oddie, Humphrey Barclay, and others), and was named its president in 1963. He toured with the Cambridge Circus in the United Kingdom and the United States, (appearing on *The Ed Sullivan Show* in 1964) and with *That Was the Week That Was* in the United States.

Brooke-Taylor was—like most of the Pythons—a writer for *The Frost Report*, where he first met Feldman, the chief editor for the show. While writing for Frost, Brooke-Taylor appeared on *On the Braden Beat* (1962–1967) as the eccentric E. L. Wisty, a know-it-all character created by Peter Cook (for the Americans in our audience, think of Wisty as Cliff Clavin with less humanity). In addition to his turn in *At Last the 1948 Show*, Brooke-Taylor had a hand in several other hybrid future-Python and future-Goodies collaborations, including *Twice a Fortnight, How to Irritate People*, and—despite Tim's fuzzy memory—even an episode or two of *Do Not Adjust Your Set*.

Beyond his contributions to *1948*, *Frost*, and radio, Brooke-Taylor is best remembered as one-third of the Goodies—Brooke-Taylor, Graeme Garden, and Bill Oddie—a trio of Cambridge fellows who (eventually) all joined the Cambridge Footlights and (more or less) ended up as part of the Cambridge Circus (same group, different name) touring alongside Cleese.

After touring, the three (plus Cleese, David Hatch, and Jo Kendall) formed *I'm Sorry, I'll Read That Again* (*ISIRTA*), a sort of nouveau-vaudeville radio review for the BBC (1964–1973), in which Brooke-Taylor played the memorably loud and outsized Lady Constance de Coverlet. When Feldman became the unlikely star property coming out of *1948* in 1968, Brooke-Taylor joined him on *Marty!* (1968) and *It's Marty!* (1969) before joining up with Garden and Oddie to form the sketch show *Broaden Your Mind*, a self-titled "Encyclopedia of the Air" (1968–1969). After deciding to shake things up by stretching their often surreal sketch comedy into half-hour narratives, *Broaden Your Mind* became *Narrow Your Mind* . . . er . . . sorry . . . we've just been informed that they decided to call it *The Goodies* (1970–1982). How nice.

Brooke-Taylor remains active in comedy, and (with Garden) has been performing on the BBC Radio quiz show *I'm Sorry I Haven't a Clue* since 1972.

What's All This, Then?
The Goodies (1970–1982)

Like the Pythons, the Goodies came out of the David Frost stable of talent: three Cambridge boys who appeared in a series of short-lived shows and revues before clumping together (like plinths) to form a surreal comedy show that broke convention and delighted audiences.

The exceedingly popular series ran for nine seasons (1970–1982) but was curiously never shown in reruns. The general premise of *The Goodies* involved the trio being good: solving folks' problems with—as Oddie notes—"hilarious consequences." Refusing to be pigeonholed as a children's show or an adult show, a satire or a pixelated slapstick, a guest-shot show or musical star vehicle, as a bunch of conservative nice guys or countercultural hippies, *The Goodies* offered viewers low-budget "human cartoons" that held the popular imagination for over a decade.

However, after relations with the BBC grew strained in the early 1980s, the trio took the show to ITV, where—unfortunately—they only lasted one final season (1982). Stuck in an unforgiving contract, the trio was forced to disband and have never "Goodied-up" since . . . save for voice work on the animated *Bananaman* in 1983 and a few recent live "reunion" shows. And that—in a nutshell—is the story of the Goodies— the "Monty Python of Parallel Universe 70B."

In addition to generally small bits in film—he appeared in *Willie Wonka & the Chocolate Factory* (1971)—Brooke-Taylor has appeared on (and has often cowritten) a variety of television shows. He has also written books in a humorous vein on topics ranging from cricket all the way to golf. In 2011, Brooke-Taylor was named Officer of the Order of the British Empire (OBE) for "his services to Light Entertainment."

As far as we can tell, he is not also Michael Palin.

Graham Chapman: Pai gow Winthrop (aka Colin "Bomber" Harris)

Nope: still dead.

John Cleese: "The Tall One That Needs a Shave All the Time"

Yep: still tall.

Marty Feldman: The Third Banana

The London-born Martin Alan Feldman came into this world in 1934, left school fifteen years later, worked in a carnival, then as a music-hall performer and jazz musician, and then finally—in the early 1960s—settled into comedy with his writing partner, Barry Took. The two wrote scripts for BBC Radio, then ITV television, and then created the campy *Round the Horne* for BBC Radio in 1965. *Round the Horne* was a great hit and caught the attention of David Frost, who brought Feldman onto *The Frost Report* as Programme Associate (essentially lead script editor). There, Feldman worked with, at various removes, the young Cleese, Chapman, Palin, Jones, and Idle. Most everyone recalls Feldman's deft advisory hand during this period, and he is universally praised for cowriting the "Class" sketch for *The Frost Report*. When Frost tossed around the idea for what would become *At Last the 1948 Show*, Feldman was tapped by Cleese, Chapman, and Brooke-Taylor to join their new show.

In retrospect, it might have seemed a bit of a risk moving a lowly writer in front of the camera. But Feldman had cut his stage teeth early, not just as a jazz musician (a passion he'd carry throughout his life), but also as part of "Morris, Marty, and Mitch" (as a promotional poster proclaims: "Three Crazy Guys"), a music-hall act with a penchant for physical comedy. While he was greatly respected as a writer/editor, Feldman was only "green" compared to the Cambridge gents who'd worked their way through college under the footlights.

Feldman rarely played the straight man on *1948*, but was outstanding as "the third banana": close-ups of Feldman's wandering eye and vaudevillian expressions often punctuated the ending of a gag. Frost was initially worried that Feldman's protruding eyes (the result of poor corrective surgery for a thyroid condition that manifested in his late twenties) would put off viewers, but as Brooke-Taylor recalls (in his interview on the DVD release of *1948*) "of course, that was his fortune." In addition to his physical comedy and writing chops, Feldman excelled at playing a sort of insistent, needling nudge, what Cleese and the crew often called "Mr. Pest." Feldman's turn as the eccentric Arthur Aldridge in "Train Carriage," and the eccentric (and illiterate) bookshop patron in the "Bookshop" sketch, for example, test Cleese's limits both as a straight man and as an actor (Spoiler Alert: corpsing ensues!).

By the time the second season of *1948* had run its course, Feldman was considered an unlikely standout. Just as Cleese was approached to gather forces for a new show (what would become *Flying Circus*), BBC brass

A couple of future Pythons started making a name for themselves in *At Last the 1948 Show*. *Left to right*: Graham Chapman, John Cleese, Tim Brooke-Taylor, Marty Feldman.
Mirrorpix/Courtesy Everett Collection

offered Feldman his own series. The star vehicle *Marty!* premiered in 1968 as *At Last the 1948 Show* dissolved; the second season (retitled *It's Marty!*) followed in 1969. Feldman asked Brooke-Taylor to join him on *Marty!* and both iterations of the show counted Cleese, Chapman, Jones, and Palin among their writers (and even as occasional bit players). Compared to *Flying Circus*, *Marty!* had a generous budget, the backing of the BBC, and Feldman's mature eye for cinematic television, silent film tropes, and absurd neologisms. Ultimately, *Marty!* went on to win two BAFTA awards and, over the next decade, Feldman would star in another half dozen short-lived shows with similarly eponymous titles: *Marty Amok*; *Marty Abroad*; *The Marty Feldman Comedy Machine*; *The Marty Feldman Show*; *Marty Back Together Again*.

Meanwhile, Feldman parlayed his small-screen success into film, starring in the modest sex comedy *Every Home Should Have One* (1970); soon after, he gained Hollywood immortality as Igor ("That's eye-gore!") in Mel Brooks's

Young Frankenstein (1974), a role that Gene Wilder wrote with Feldman in mind. Other films would follow, notably Wilder's *The Adventures of Sherlock Holmes' Smarter Brother* (1975), Brooks's *Silent Movie* (1976), the Italian sketch comedy *40°C Under the Sheets*, aka: *Sex with a Smile* (1976), and Feldman's own *The Last Remake of Beau Geste* (1977). In 1980, he wrote and starred in a religious lampoon, *In God We Tru$t* (also starring Andy Kaufman, Peter Boyle, and Richard Pryor). But compared to the recently released *Life of Brian* (1979) his was a rather meek satire . . . and the box office reflected as much. Feldman also costarred in an ill-advised 1982 science fiction adaptation of Kurt Vonnegut's novel *Slapstick*, costarring Jerry Lewis and Madeline Kahn (although the less said about that the better).

After his spate of less-than-stellar film outings, Feldman began writing again, and set up a writers' commune (of sorts) in London. Sadly, Feldman died of a heart attack soon after, in December of 1982, during the shooting of Chapman's *Yellowbeard* in Mexico City. He was forty-eight. As many of his friends and costars noted, Feldman drank coffee by the gallon, ate eggs like they were M&Ms, and smoked like a chimney. He was always talented, generally admired, and occasionally lusted after.

At one point, Jones was set to direct *Jeepers Creepers*, a stage play about Feldman and his wife, Lauretta. Terry Jones noted in the promotions for the play that Feldman "was one of those very kind and very funny people who helped all the Pythons along the way. It's lovely to be able to say a belated thank-you by bringing him back to eye-popping life—sort of!—on the London stage."

Blücher!

The Lovely Aimi MacDonald

Born in 1942, the Glaswegian MacDonald trained as a ballet dancer and began her entertainment career in her early teens, performing in both the United Kingdom and the United States. In London, she worked minor roles in cabarets and musicals, but was spotted by David Frost and subsequently recruited for *At Last the 1948 Show*, where she occupied a slight variation on the role of comedic "crumpet" (the precursor to Carol Cleveland's *Flying Circus* "glamour stooge").

The ever-epitheted "lovely" Aimi MacDonald was a multi-threat: she could—according to the lovely Aimi MacDonald herself—sing, dance, play piano, juggle, tell jokes, look lovely, ventriloquize, and perform satirical impressions. Practically speaking, she acted as the interstitial "glue" between the unconnected antics of "the backroom boys" on *At Last the 1948 Show*. The general conceit was clever: the lovely MacDonald rarely interacts with the lads' lunacy, but operates in a sort of parallel show where she is—at least in her own mind—the star. Dressed in glamorous sequined dresses, fur stoles, and feather boas, she and her helium voice and mod hair embodied the contemporary "blond bimbo" role exceptionally well. While she didn't write for the show, as Brooke-Taylor admiringly noted on the *1948* DVD, "if [Aimi] read it first time accurately, she'd always do it well; and if she didn't, you knew it was wrong." Indeed, she pricked the sacred cows of British pomposity with a chirping happiness that foreshadowed the political paint upon *Laugh-In*'s Goldie Hawn.

MacDonald's best bits on *1948* include: an audience sing-along to "I love the lovely Aimi MacDonald"; the metatheatrical "National Make Aimi MacDonald a Rich Lady Fund"; and her absurd "Tap-dancing *Hamlet*" (this latter bit surely inspired the Great Gonzo, who once tap-danced to the tune of "Top Hat" in a vat of oatmeal on *The Muppet Show*). But again, the lovely MacDonald's role was—like Gilliam's cartoon animation—to bridge the gaps, not provide the primary content.

For Python fans, the most important thing the lovely Aimi MacDonald ever did was help get the phrase "And now for something completely different" an airing out. As the *1948 Show*'s resident living interstitial, MacDonald used the phrase to throw to the next disparate sketch "by the boys." Since all the sketches on *1948* were disparate, for MacDonald the phrase simply connected the unconnected. On *Flying Circus*, the phrase—which doesn't really become a catchphrase until Season Two—does that as well, but since the Pythons also ran contiguous (or at least thematically connected) sketches, the phrase served to highlight the moments when the show was about to take a serious (or seriously silly) turn. The catchphrase became, eventually, associated exclusively with the Pythons, who used it as the title of (and running gag in) their first feature film, *And Now for Something Completely Different* (1971). But MacDonald . . . excuse us . . . the *lovely* Aimi MacDonald popularized it first.

After *1948* closed, the lovely Aimi MacDonald appeared in recurring roles on Roger Moore's *The Saint* in 1969, *Sez Les* in 1972 (a variety show starring the comedian Les Dawson with a few appearances by Cleese), and *Rentaghost* (1984). Otherwise, she had a habit of one-shot roles and big-screen moments that were generally of the "attractive woman at bar" type. A stage dancer early in her career, she parlayed her popularity on *At Last the 1948 Show* into a few semi-star turns on the London stage, and even recorded a few records (including a single of "Thoroughly Modern Millie" in 1967), but she never really broke through the way "the backroom boys" on *1948* did. She remains, nevertheless, truly lovely.

The Sketches

In addition to the outstanding "Bookshop" and "Four Yorkshiremen" sketches, other stand-out bits from *1948* include "Mice Laugh Softly Charlotte" (an extended and ridiculously funny parody of poorly acted noir crime drama—rather akin to "Agatha Christie" in *Flying Circus* Episode 11); "The Four Sydney Lotterbys" (a recurring sketch with all four gents sporting squeaky voices and the same name); "The Shirt Shop" and "Clothes Off!" sketches (both examples of escalating absurdity); "The Chartered Accountant Dance" (Brooke-Taylor's clever physical humor); "Train Car" (a surreal "Pest" sketch with Feldman and Cleese); and "Pet Shop" (in which Chapman buys a bank manager . . . for breeding).

The Incest

The British Pythons, who all made their bones in the collaborative arena of college reviews and circuses, had a loose respect for comic copyright . . . if such a thing even existed in their minds back then. What was written once and got a laugh earlier might get one again, and so sketches that first appeared on stage at Cambridge could be revived/recycled/repurposed onscreen for *Flying Circus*. Attitudes on the set of *At Last the 1948 Show* were no different, and in many ways this earlier show acts as a halfway house of ideas, linking the (now lost) live comedy of the Cambridge Circus to the Python sketches.

In any case, here's a short list of some of the better-known "Monty Python" sketches that appeared previously on *At Last the 1948 Show*:

"Bookshop"

A clear precursor to many of the Pythons' thesaurus sketches such as "Cheese Shop" and "Dead Parrot," the "Bookshop" sketch features Feldman as a highly eccentric—and ultimately illiterate—customer who relentlessly badgers a clerk (Cleese) for increasingly esoteric or orthographically unique books. It's a great sketch, one of Cleese's personal favorites from *At Last the 1948 Show*, and manages to get most of its laughs from a combination of absurdity and frustration . . . before wringing one final laugh out of a horrible punch line. Such is the incest of this sketch that in 1970 Feldman recycled it twice: on his own show—*Marty Amok!*—and on *The Dean Martin Show*. Cleese and Connie Booth performed the sketch for *Mermaid Frolics* (the 1977 Amnesty International fundraiser), and Chapman performed it with fellow British comedian Joe Baker on the short-lived NBC series *The Big Show* (1980). Finally, Cleese and Chapman reappropriated the sketch for *Monty Python's Contractual Obligation Album* (1980); in a deliberate act of incestuous double-dipping, Chapman adopts a very Sydney Lotterby tenor while playing the Feldman role on the album. Well worth a listen.

"Man Wrestling Himself"

Chapman athletically plays a wrestler who—"for the first time in this ring"—wrestled himself. Chapman had created the bit while at Cambridge, brought it with him to *1948*, then to *Fliegender Zirkus* (1972). It was a staple at Python live shows (a fine version was recorded for *Live at the Hollywood Bowl*) and in many of Chapman's solo tours. Chapman's physicality and mime work is consistently impressive in these variations, while the creativity and verve of the announcers (whether Brooke-Taylor, Cleese, or Palin) varies widely. For those into deep Python trivia, Chapman's wrestler is named "Pai gow Winthrop" on the *1948 Show*, and "Colin 'Bomber' Harris" in the subsequent Python-verse.

"Four Yorkshiremen"

Perhaps surprisingly, the "Four Yorkshiremen" sketch—often hailed as a "quintessentially Python" routine (full of verbal one-upmanship, absurdity, and social criticism)—was originally a *1948* "joint." Brooke-Taylor, Chapman, Cleese, and Feldman first appeared as the well-to-do, wistfully nostalgic, increasingly complaintive, and verbally competitive blokes smoking cigars and drinking Château de Chassilier on-screen in 1967. But the Yorkshiremen have never stopped complaining, as it were, appearing in various Python live shows ever since. Indeed, the "Four Yorkshiremen" was even performed, with credit to Brooke-Taylor, by the surviving non-Gilliam Pythons in their *Monty Python Live (Almost)* shows in 2014 . . . doubly ironic by then, in retrospect (nostalgia within nostalgia: meta-nostalgia!). Who'd have thought, forty-five years ago, they'd still be sitting there?

So there you have it: *Monty Python's Flying Circus* lifted their catchphrase, their trademark surrealism, and even some of their sketches from *At Last the 1948 Show.* And you try telling that to the kids these days, and they won't believe you . . .

5

The Real Pre-Python

Do Not Adjust Your Set

An important thing to remember about British television in the 1960s was that while much of it was staid, even before *Monty Python's Flying Circus* there were shows that took real risks in form and content. Still, ITV took quite a chance on the "children's show" *Do Not Adjust Your Set*. A daring 1967–1969 comedy series that included about half of Monty Python on staff (Idle, Palin, and Jones) and used Gilliam animation sequences to link the live skits, *DNAYS!* also featured appearances from future Python musical collaborator Neil Innes. Along with *At Last the 1948 Show*, *Do Not Adjust Your Set* was an important precursor to Python in that the comedic sensibility was already in place, but the show still had to work within the stifling constraints of ITV's attitudes toward comedy. Even with these constraints, though, the Python sensibility was apparent.

Producer Humphrey Barclay had initially pitched *Do Not Adjust Your Set* (sometimes punctuated emphatically, and most often abbreviated as *DNAYS!*) as a program for children, a sort of younger version of the Cambridge-inflected comedic material popularized in the radio program *I'm Sorry, I'll Read That Again* (also featuring the ubiquitous Cleese). But in truth the

What's All This, Then?
After *DNAYS!*

It will surprise many American Python fans to discover that for most British television viewers, the future Pythons were *not* the best-known stars to come out of *DNAYS!*. Instead, Jason—better known today as Sir David John White, OBE—takes the prize due to his notable and consistent appearances on higher-rated shows, such as *Only Fools and Horses* and *A Touch of Frost*. For her part, Denise Coffey made many guest appearances after *DNAYS!*, most notably working on the 1980s sci-fi show *The Tomorrow People* and more recently *Alexei Sayle's Merry-Go-Round* in 1998. She has also had a long career writing and directing plays and working as an artist.

show was created in large part as a comedic vehicle for the promising young writer-performer Idle. At Idle's insistence, Palin was quickly recruited as a writer-performer, who in turn recruited Jones. The three pre-Pythons were joined by actor David Jason, as well as comedian Denise Coffey, who had the less rewarding, but still pivotal role as the show's requisite crumpet (the successor to British stage comedy's showgirl trope). Idle, Jones, and Palin wrote the vast majority of the program, while Jason and Coffey were shunted away to film the "Captain Fantastic" sequences off set.

DNAYS! was soon hailed by critics as being far above the typically innocuous BBC children's comedy programming. It became a cult favorite with adult viewers and television critics (sometimes simultaneously!), some of whom praised it as the funniest thing on the telly. Among the show's fans were Cleese and Chapman, who oft found it funnier and more daring than their own program, *At Last the 1948 Show.* While the genre might have proved a hindrance to some, for Idle, Palin, and Jones—who had struggled under the constraints of *The Frost Report*—ITV's "hands-off" approach to children's television enabled them to boldly experiment with form and content . . . free of adult supervision, as it were.

Although Barclay had some misgivings about handing a children's show over to three "intellectual" comedians, he needn't have worried. *DNAYS!* was both groundbreaking and surprisingly fresh, albeit targeted at reasonably bright children and their delighted parents. As Palin would later demonstrate with his favorite Python sketch, the "Fish-Slapping Dance," he was perfectly capable of delivering sketches filled with childlike glee that were silly for the sake of being silly. So *DNAYS!* featured sketches such as two bowler-hatted, stuffy-looking chartered accountants coming over to nervously ask a colleague's wife if their work colleague "could come out and play."

As *DNAYS!* (and, not long after, *Flying Circus*) made clear, the "rules" of television were nothing more than conventions that could be broken by artists with the right mix of daring and invention. By mocking the conventions of a still-young medium—BBC television had only become available around the country since the mid-1950s—and pointing out their absurdity, *DNAYS!* presaged the wholesale demolition of televisual conventions endemic to *Flying Circus.* The children's show was even more low-budget (if that could be possible) than *Flying Circus* would be. Typical for British shows of the time, *DNAYS!* looks as though it was put together by a high school drama club with a few cameras and fewer backdrops. But the seeds of Python are very much apparent even so.

When *Do Not Adjust Your Set!* was on, even the furthest-out comics still had to wear proper suits. *Left to right:* Eric Idle, Terry Jones, Michael Palin, and David Jason help Denise Coffey celebrate her birthday.   *Mirrorpix/Courtesy Everett Collection*

One "seed of Python" obvious in *DNAYS!* is Gilliam's groundbreaking animations. Having recently worked with Idle on the short-lived *We Have Ways of Making You Laugh* (an ill-advised title, according to most critics, but everyone has to start somewhere), Gilliam was introduced to Barclay by Cleese. Although it took a few weeks for the pre-Pythons to warm up to the American from Occidental College, they soon realized that Gilliam was not just a kindred spirit, but someone who could help them break through in new visually comedic ways.

In contrast to the radio comedy that inspired the British pre-Pythons, Gilliam (though also a *Goon Show* fan) learned about visual comedy from the underground comic books of the time. A onetime assembly-line worker at a Chevrolet plant, he also understood the tedium of factory work. The frustration of such monotonous repetition—of mindless predictability and rote convention—bred an anger in Gilliam that carried over into much of his more violent later animation.

Gilliam's hostility toward mindless authority helps us understand his delight in creating works of art and simultaneously deconstructing and/or literally destroying them. Years later, Gillian explained the opening credits of *Monty Python's Flying Circus* (which ends with a Bronzino painting of a

What's All This, Then?
Rules Are for Breaking

A few notes on televisuality. The pre-Pythons were eager to use/abuse the "rules" of the British television's legendarily sporadic broadcast signal. The first sketch of the very first *DNAYS!* episode features most of the cast performing *King Lear*, before cutting to not-quite-glamour stooge Denise Coffey watching the previous scene on a television set and adding lines as other actors are frozen whenever the signal stops working; a very familiar occurrence for British television viewers in the mid-1960s.

Another early sketch that plays with the conventions of television was "Science for Sixth Forms." Idle appears inside the frame of a television set, delivering a lecture on the theory of gravity, and dropping a pencil several times to make his point. The pencil drops the first and second times, but the third time it mysteriously floats away into a music interlude in which the Bonzo Dog Doo-Dah Band performs "Monster Mash," complete with *Frankenstein* costumes and props, including a segment where the "monster" plays electric spoons, before shorting out and ending the song. Ah, British TV of the 1960s!

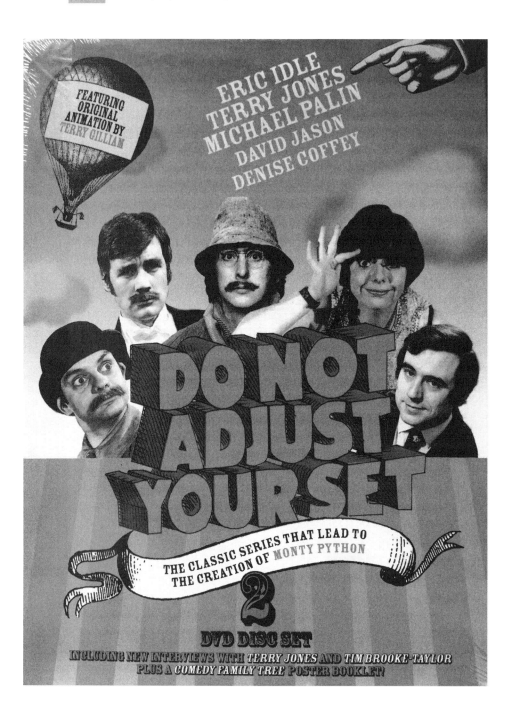

giant foot smashing down into the frame) this way: "You create something beautiful and then you crush it." Gilliam's art was far less violent for *DNAYS!*, but the impulse towards deconstruction was there.

Another element that marked *DNAYS!* as a proto-Python show was its house band: the surrealistic musical revivalists the Bonzo Dog Doo-Dah Band, one of whose primary songwriters was Neil Innes, who would go on to become a contender for the position of "Seventh Python."

While initially meant to be a children's show by the lightest of the light entertainment division of the BBC, *Do Not Adjust Your Set*, by adding Gilliam's animation and introducing the Pythons to their chief musical collaborator, put the Pythons one (very) silly walk from *Flying Circus*. Jones wrote in a 2005 column for the *Guardian* that Monty Python was essentially "*At Last the 1948 Show* meets *Do Not Adjust Your Set*." While this may not be 100 percent true, we'll go with it.

As usual, ITV, like the BBC, *desperately* needed videotapes, so only about half of *DNAYS!* survived austerity measures. The extant material is mostly from Season One, including episodes 1, 2, 5, 6, 9–13, which are available on DVD. Saving one episode and the "Do Not Adjust Your Stocking" Christmas special, the rest of Season Two was erased.

After two seasons, it was clear that the show had run its course. Idle, Jones, and Palin were chafing at the bit to do more surrealistic comedy and the network was unsure of what that would do to the already popular show. Ultimately, Idle, Jones, and Palin did not want any more contributions from Coffey or Jason, who were eager to have more say in the program, and an impasse was reached. Luckily, the show was ending just as Cleese and Chapman were free from their *1948* obligations as well. Excepting a brief 1969 detour for Jones and Palin into their historical comedy show *The Complete and Utter History of Britain* (more about that in the next chapter), the end of *DNAYS!* led directly into *Flying Circus*. And there was much rejoicing.

6

Whither the BBC?

Monty Python's Flying Circus
and How It Began at the Beginning

The Situation in 1969

1969 was not a frivolous time for Britain, which was struggling with a severe identity crisis born out of an ironic twist of historical fate. They had helped the world beat back the Fascist threat. But everything about the postwar order, in which the Soviet and American blocs dominated the world stage, signaled that the United Kingdom, with its dramatically contracting empire, was an increasingly irrelevant power.

The country was also transforming internally. The British Nationality Act of 1948 gave every citizen of the Commonwealth the right to enter the United Kingdom. The following years saw the arrival of large numbers of South Asian and Caribbean immigrants. This didn't sit well with a segment of the white population already dismayed at the perceived loss of national power and respect. Enoch Powell, Conservative MP for Wolverhampton (a place Idle once reluctantly called home) gave voice to the ethnic backlash in a scorching 1968 anti-immigrant diatribe that became known as the "Rivers of Blood" speech. Powell and his fellow xenophobes were exactly the type of "blinkered Philistine pig-ignorance" that Python would soon cherish lampooning.

Meanwhile, on the Telly . . .

Richard Nixon ordered the secret bombing of Cambodia, Westminster deployed troops to Northern Ireland, and to top it all off, Levi's started selling bell-bottom jeans. 1969 was a rough year. However, popular culture was catching up with the times, albeit in very hit-and-miss fashion.

Idle theorized in *The Pythons: Autobiography* about the 1960s: "Light entertainment was totally changing, it was no longer these terrible . . . end of the pier-style shows." He was referring to the cheeseball variety shows that were once the staple of holiday season at the kind of dreary, rain-sodden England seaside resorts where a character like Graham Greene's Pinkie in *Brighton Rock* would be driven starkers.

But help was on the way.

In 1969, British television was as much at a turning point as the society at large. The country needed it.

At that point, the most consistently top-rated shows on the telly were the apparently unkillable soap opera *Coronation Street*, sitcoms like *Dad's Army*, and the just-as-racist-as-it-sounds variety program *The Black and White Minstrel Show*. The medium wasn't exactly groundbreaking in the middle of the decade, showing little of the "Swinging London" panache exemplified in films like *The Knack* (1965) or *Alfie* (1966); the much-touted "Angry Young Men" attitude of British theater and film that had been viciously cutting down the Establishment (see John Osborne's *Look Back in Anger* and Lindsey Anderson's *If . . .* , in particular) since the mid-1950s; or even the psychedelic silliness of the Beatles' 1967 album *Sgt. Pepper's Lonely Hearts Club Band* (a precursor in tone and arrangement to *Flying Circus*).

But by 1969, the post-*Goon* sketch shows scattered over British television were becoming particularly irreverent. This mirrored a general shift in American television; although *TV Guide* was packed with shows like *Gunsmoke* and *Bonanza*, the top-rated series was the anarchically goony (even *Goon*-y) *Rowan & Martin's Laugh-In*, which occasionally jabbed at politics, albeit lightly.

Inspired sketch comedy shows in the Frost and *Goon* mold were a large part of the British television diet, if generally not its highest-rated series. Due in large part to the busy efforts of David Frost—whose various shows had nurtured the Pythons' talents and padded their resumes—by the time 1969 rolled around, the pre-Pythons were as geared to hit it big as any collection of comics ever could be in such a cutthroat industry.

Interregnum: *The Complete and Utter History of Britain*

In January and February of 1969, ITV broadcast Jones and Palin's six-episode *The Complete and Utter History of Britain* miniseries. This sketch show imagined what past events like the Crusades might have been like had television cameras been around. Inspired by a short, *The Battle of Hastings*, that Jones and Palin had done for a series called *Twice a Fortnight*, it's the comedy equivalent of Peter Watkins's *Culloden* (1964), which recreated the 1746 battle as though for a modern-day documentary.

Ostensibly, Jones and Palin wanted to reveal history as it actually had been rather than package history as most popular shows did: as patriotically glossy entertainment. But their ultimate goal was less Watkins-esque historical-political investigation than past-tweaking comedy that called to mind the historical spoof shorts made by Fred and Joe Evans all the way back in the 1910s (*Pimple's Charge of the Light Brigade*, *Pimple's Battle of Waterloo*).

For *The Complete and Utter History of Britain*, the oh-so-serious host Colin Gordon promised to bring viewers "history as it actually happened," then introduced sketches. In one typical sketch, a premodern real estate broker tries to convince a couple to buy Stonehenge ("It's a bit drafty, isn't it?" they complain).

The series looks now like a pretty decent, albeit rough, prefiguration of the way in which *Monty Python's Flying Circus* would highlight the absurdity of modern television tropes by juxtaposing them with historical figures like Robin Hood and Oliver Cromwell. In terms of execution, though, it leaves something to be desired, even when compared to the not-precisely-big-budget *Flying Circus*.

Once *Complete and Utter* ended in February 1969 and *DNAYS!* broadcast its twenty-seventh and final episode in May, Jones and Palin were out of full-time work, along with Idle and Gilliam. That didn't mean the lads were completely unemployed. In March, the TV special *It's Marty Feldman* included material by Cleese, Chapman, Jones, and Palin. Meanwhile, Idle was writing for Ronnie Barker's *Hark at Barker*, which ran that April and May. But none of these was a long-term prospect.

Clearly, the universe would not let this turn of events go unanswered for long. Good thing for the Pythons that by playing in seemingly every comedy revue in England and grabbing every writing and performing opportunity they could, the ever-overlapping gang of six had also spent the last few years making themselves essentially ubiquitous on the comedy scene. It also helped that *Do Not Adjust Your Set* had a deep base of support among slightly cracked adults.

Just as later generations of supposed grown-ups found a guilty pleasure in watching *Pee-Wee's Playhouse*, Cleese and Chapman made a point of catching Palin and Jones's wink-wink children's show each week. Cleese thought that he and Chapman would mesh nicely with what they had seen of Jones and Palin on *Complete and Utter History of Britain* and *Do Not Adjust Your Set*.

At first, David Frost had wanted to create a show combining Cleese and Chapman with the *Do Not Adjust Your Set* gang. But it wasn't to be. In April 1969, Palin recorded in his diary that Frost had called him in something of a panic, worried that the future Pythons weren't interested in working with him anymore. "How are the mighty falling," Palin wrote. It turns out that Frost was right: the Pythons weren't interested.

But somebody else was.

Baron von Took's Flying Circus

Starting in 1969, the BBC had a comedy consultant (which only sounds like a glorious position) named Barry Took. Another comedy legend who found success as part of a pair, Took was a failed solo performer whose career took off once he teamed up with writing and performing partner Marty Feldman, whose credits overlapped with the Pythons' on shows like *At Last the 1948 Show* and *The Frost Report*. Took and Feldman's radio sketch

The BBC's Television Centre, where all the *Flying Circus* magic happened.

Wikimedia Commons

show *Round the Horne* (1965–1968) is today considered one of the decade's comedic masterpieces.

All of which is to say that Took knew his way around the particularly unique style of British comedy fomenting in the late 1960s. Took's appreciation for and understanding of both the older *Goon Show* school and the newer Oxbridge comics was unique at the time. At the BBC, he would prove essential to creating *Monty Python's Flying Circus*, which distilled both styles into a uniquely surreal soufflé.

The coming together of the Pythons at the BBC in 1969 has an air of random happenstance to it. The comparison has been made before between the Pythons and the Beatles, and not just because George Harrison and HandMade Films would play such an important role in the Pythons' later history. Both groups were of roughly the same age and came to artistic maturity at a time when Britain was transforming from staid imperial conservatism to a more open-minded, Technicolor, jittery anxiousness. Critic Robert Lloyd posited that "If the Beatles were a rock band with the instincts of a comedy troupe, Python was a comedy troupe with the dynamics of a rock band." As with the Beatles, momentous art was created almost by accident.

There was no preordained air of mystery in 1969 as the troupe was slapping together the first season of *Monty Python's Flying Circus*. They were simply a band of like-minded complementary comics with a desire to work together and enough credits that the network suits considered them reliable enough not to drop the bag.

For today's audiences, much less aware of the comedic ecosystem that *Flying Circus* grew out of, it can look like a revolution in comedy: a shot across the bow at convention and tradition. But just as the Beatles didn't exactly invent Brit-rock, the Pythons didn't create their trademark style of off-the-wall surrealism out of whole cloth.

The inaugural season of *Flying Circus* was part of a continuum of everything that had been changing in British comedy from Spike Milligan's work to the 1962 *Beyond the Fringe* revue to all the Frostian current events satire and faux-documentary skits that the various members had already been perfecting. The formation of the Python troupe simply allowed all these like-minded comics to merge their instincts for boundary-breaking and taboo-smashing and push it just a little bit further. In the documentary *Monty Python: Almost the Truth (The Lawyer's Cut)*, Cleese talks about Monty Python presenting a universe of new possibilities: "It was really like somebody opening the gate to a field of flowers, none of which had been picked."

This 1968 David Frost television special was one of the last projects that John Cleese worked on before *Flying Circus*.

Took initially approached Cleese about spearheading a new show in early 1969. Cleese wasn't crazy about doing it all on his own. That's where the idea of bringing in the *Do Not Adjust Your Set* gang appeared. In short order, the six got together—possibly at a flat, or in a park, or at an Indian restaurant in Hampstead, depending on who's telling the Python origin story—and decided that yes, they were going to work together on something new.

The original plan was to call it *The 5 Show*, a structure that sidelined Gilliam as a mere animator and not full writer-performer. That idea was dropped, even though Gilliam was certainly the odd man out as the least experienced writer and performer and the only non-Oxbridge graduate.

What were the six left with, then? All they knew was that they wanted to do a show. But what was it going to be?

In March 1969, Milligan's *Q5* went on the air. It was madcap and surreal, nearly bereft of punch lines, and strung together by antic wordplay and caricatures of stuffy BBC announcers. In fact, *Q5* looked something quite like what the future Pythons had been planning to do. Gilliam put it neatly in *Almost the Truth* when he pointed out that all the comedy sketch groups they loved had one glaring flaw: great, edgy, hilarious material, with a propensity toward weak punch lines that killed the good memories. "Just chop 'em out" was the consensus. And so they did. But in the eleventh hour, the Pythons worried that Milligan (whom Cleese once said was "the great God to us") had stolen their thunder.

Despite their misgivings, on May 23, the Pythons had a meeting at the BBC. Took was present, along with future directors Ian McNaughton and John Howard Davies. It couldn't have been less momentous.

Michael Mills, the head of comedy for the BBC, asked the comedians what their show was going to be.

They had no idea.

He asked what it was going to be called.

They weren't sure.

He wanted to know whether there would be music or guest stars.

A shrug.

Surprisingly, presented with a new show that was positively *Seinfeld*-ian in its lack of defined structure, Mills relented. The BBC wanted to work with rising star Cleese in some capacity, and Took was pitching hard for the future Pythons.

In a casual agreement that would give heart palpitations to any modern network executive, Mills told the Pythons that they had thirteen episodes and would air on Saturday nights. In Palin's memory, Mills said it plain: "All right, I'll give you thirteen shows, but that's all!"

That was it.

Oh, and production was going to start in just three months.

Now all the boys needed was a name. And a bunch of scripts.

Around the hallways of the BBC, the long-gestating and never titled project was informally known as *Baron von Took's Flying Circus*. The list of potential names sprawled out over the next several weeks, ultimately achieving a legendary length rivaled only by that of Toad the Wet Sprocket, perhaps.

For all the excitement about the show that the six were about to christen, though, nowhere in the Pythons' recollections of that time can you find any sense that they were making history. This is probably a good part of the reason why they *were* able to make history.

What's All This, Then?

A not-complete list of considered names for *Monty Python's Flying Circus*:

- *The Algy Banging Hour*
- *Arthur Megapode*
- *Bunn Wackett Buzzard Stubble and Boot*
- *Gwen Dibley's Flying Circus*
- *A Horse, a Spoon and a Bucket*
- *It's . . .*
- *Ow! It's Colin Plint*
- *Owl Stretching Time*
- *Sex and Violence*
- *The Toad Elevating Moment*
- *Whither Canada?*

Boldly Going and Going and Going . . .

The first episodes of *Monty Python's Flying Circus* were produced in a manner just as unceremonious and unfussy as it was conceived. Maybe this is how revolutions and superheroes are born.

The recollections of the various Pythons about this period make for opaque reading, especially for those looking to find a *Flying Circus* origin story. The six never quite sat down and definitively laid out what the show was going to be, beyond the earlier-stated stipulations about eschewing punch lines and pushing their Milligan-esque style further down the road. Not long before, after all, they had all just been recently unemployed comedians looking for a gig. That was particularly true of Palin, since he had a son to support as of the previous year. Each had been hopping from one televised lily pad to the next for some time, and this show without a name seemed at first to be just the next relatively dry patch.

But that doesn't mean that *Flying Circus* came about due to dumb luck. The performers all shared a certain sensibility. Cleese could see that Jones's and Palin's work would nicely complement his and Chapman's—or at the very least help take up some of the writing slack left by his famously deadline-averse partner. None of them was that comfortable with shtick. All were adept at skewering British cultural norms and were keen not only to flout taboos but to bust the fourth wall. They all loved the same comic heroes, crafting silly sketches, and challenging audiences.

One of the more standout elements of the new show was that it followed the style of the animations Gilliam produced for *Do Not Adjust Your Set*. His famous *Christmas Card* piece, a stream-of-consciousness flow through a series of Victorian Christmas cards that Gilliam found at the Tate, was very influential for Jones, who used it as a touchstone for the aesthetic he thought the Pythons should embody.

Also, using animated segments as interstitials helped relieve the show of the pressure for punch lines, no matter how much the oft-confused studio audiences might have missed them.

The Pythons started work in earnest during the summer of 1969. Since the team were nearly all working writers, everybody had a bottom drawer of unused sketches and bits (some rejected for being too beyond the pale) to contribute. "Nudge, Nudge" from Episode 3 of Season One was in fact originally written by Idle for *Hark at Barker*. The first sketch of Episode 2—in which Jones and Chapman discuss the problems of a flock of sheep that think they're birds, all due to the pernicious influence of Harold, "that most dangerous of creatures: a clever sheep"—had originally been written by Cleese and Chapman for *The Frost Report*, which rejected it for being too silly. That reaction, of course, would become a *Flying Circus* mainstay, with various colonels or police officers bringing a halt to things when they threatened to get "too silly."

As a result, the material accumulated quickly. Then it was just a question of hashing out how to string everything together into an episode, without the interference of producers.

Idle later described on his website just what a unique situation the creative process for the start of *Flying Circus* was: "For the first and last time in Showbiz history, the Writers were in charge." It's not difficult to see the results of that once the show hit the small screen, both in terms of the out-on-a-limb daring that another collaborator might have nixed, and its tendency to occasionally get lost in creative culs-de-sac that an outsider could have helped get them out of.

Nevertheless, at some point, words needed to be put on paper and images seared onto celluloid, not to mention all the other folderol that was involved with creating a show, even one operating under the starvation-level resources typical of the era's British television.

The Pythons started fast, writing the first episode by mid-June. They plowed through the remainder in quick succession, stringing much of it together with previously existing material (as well as Gilliam's animated interstitials) to get to each episode's contracted length of twenty-nine minutes, fifty seconds.

Although the newly minted troupe had been given what amounted to near complete artistic autonomy at the start—that would change later on—the same freedom hardly extended to their budget. Postwar Britain didn't exactly have the funds to splash out for glossy TV shows; and let's be honest, even the bigger-budget A-list shows that were on in America at the time look pretty grimy by today's standards. Allotted only around £5,000 per episode, the Pythons had to strictly ration how much time they could spend filming on location instead of shooting in the studio. In practice, having to plan this far ahead meant that all of Season One had to be written before they could start production.

By July, the Pythons were ready (in a way) to begin production.

It's . . . "That Bloody Weird Show"

On July 8, 1969, the creative team and production crew responsible for *Monty Python's Flying Circus* gathered in the gardens of Ham House, a seventeenth-century Jacobean home southwest of London. They were there to film "the Wacky Queen" sketch that would appear in the second episode.

While the disciplined BBC man John Howard Davies (a favorite of Cleese, who later collaborated with him on *Fawlty Towers*) helmed the first few episodes, the chaotic Glaswegian Ian MacNaughton (more on the other Pythons' wavelength, due to his temperament and work on *Q5*) took over afterward.

During the start of Davies's period, though, the show's working title was *Bunn Wackett Buzzard Stubble and Boot*—which, for the record, at least one and no more than six and one-third of this volume's authors believe would have been a perfectly acceptable title. [Leave the maths to the experts.—Eds.] Later that month, the BBC finally prevailed on the troupe to choose a name for this thing they were already producing.

During a meeting of the half dozen, Cleese suggested "something slimy, like a python." Idle liked the idea of a sleazy agent named Monty. Plus: *Baron von Took's Flying Circus* still had some currency around the network

What's All This, Then?
Words, Words, Words

Jones and Palin were sometimes mocked by the other Pythons for their tendency to start every sketch with a majestic pan over beautiful countryside. For their part, Jones and Palin thought that Chapman and Cleese's word-happy writing often sounded like a thesaurus. As a joke, Jones and Palin once wrote a sketch in which each character used so many synonyms that they could never get around to saying anything. Chapman and Cleese loved it, of course, leaving Jones and Palin to tell them it was just a gag. But it got on the show, anyway.

since many memos about the show already referred to "Flying Circus," and the always parsimonious BBC was certainly *not* going to print everything again with a different name. Took said in *Monty Python Speaks* that all of this led his boss to say, "I don't give a damn what it's called . . . make them call it *something Flying Circus*."

Thus, through a somewhat arbitrary cutting and splicing method not unlike Gilliam's animation style, *Monty Python's Flying Circus* was born.

Finally, in late July, Palin, Gilliam, and Jones met at the BBC to listen to some possible music. They settled on a recording of Sousa's "The Liberty Bell (March)" performed by the Grenadier Guards. It had just the right combination of pomp and circumstance that they were looking for. Just as importantly, the number was in the public domain, and thusly free. To quote the late great Garry Marshall in *Soapdish*: it was "peppy and cheap."

On August 30, Studio 6 at BBC's Television Centre complex was slotted for the first live recording of *Monty Python's Flying Circus*. The audience for what became "Sex and Violence" was a standard-issue gathering of middle-aged folks who'd requested tickets to any random BBC show, some perhaps hoping to see a circus. This went on for some time. Listening to the first few episodes, there are very few moments of full-out laughter (the Pythons took pride in never laying on a laugh track), except for Cleese's wife, Connie, whose laugh is often the loudest on the soundtrack.

However, once the word got out, a dedicated cadre of surrealist comedy fans began showing up on a regular basis to make the audience for studio shoots sound far more appreciative.

Still, even though much of the studio audience was likely baffled during the shooting of that first episode, Palin wrote later that the reception "was very good indeed . . ." apart from their initially very unimpressed agent.

"Sex and Violence" was actually the second episode to be shown. The first to be broadcast, "Whither Canada?," was recorded on September 7 and shown to London and the regions that hadn't opted out of broadcasting it on October 5, a Sunday. It was presaged by a gnomic announcement in the *Radio Times* that stated the show was designed to "subdue the violence in us all."

Although *Flying Circus* can seem like sheer chaos to the uninitiated, in the same way that seemingly improvisational comics dating back to Groucho Marx plotted out their supposedly off-the-cuff remarks, the Pythons fully scripted every splunge, albatross, and "stop that!" The Pythons had several days of rehearsal—unless they felt it was done right, in which case they'd spend their time goofing off and playing football, so that it wouldn't get *too* planned out—and one day on the technical run-through before putting each episode on in front of the studio audience. So it went, week after week, at a fast clip. At least, the mornings were quick . . . MacNaughton having a reputation for being less wired for work after lunchtime drinks. Still, things got done generally on time. The first season's thirteenth and last episode, "Intermission," was recorded on January 4, 1970, and broadcast a week later.

The audience wasn't large at first, and was considerably cut into by the BBC's habit of continually moving the time slot around and keeping the show on late (think of the children!). But the reviews were mostly, and surprisingly, positive at first. Positive attention from publications like the *Observer* made *Flying Circus* palatable to some of the smart set. The BBC's own internal audience research reports contain reactions from viewers to the first episodes that October. They range from "funny, witty, and refreshing" to "a load of rubbish."

Before the end of 1969, though, the word started to get out to audiences, no matter how difficult the BBC made it for viewers trying to find the show. Idle's frequently recounted anecdotal metric for how the show was doing came from the chaps he played football with Sundays in Hyde Park. At first

What's All This, Then?
Not Funny!

To put it mildly, not everybody got *Flying Circus* at first. That included not just the audience but some BBC staff. According to Jones, during Season One, the BBC's director of light entertainment Tom Sloane begged director Ian McNaughton "to do something about this dreadful program. It's simply not funny. There is nothing remotely comical about a man walking out of the sea and saying 'It's . . .'"

they'd tell Idle, "That was a weird show of yours," and later, "That's rather good, that bloody weird show."

Many fans later asked the Pythons about BBC censorship. Astonishingly—particularly considering that, according to Jones, their first season included (reportedly) the first appearance of a woman's breasts on the network: "The Dull Life of a City Stockbroker" (Episode 6: "It's the Arts")—it appears that nobody at the BBC even *watched* the episodes before broadcast, much less tried to censor them.

Several Pythons later discussed their great luck in arriving at the BBC when they did. It was a particularly anarchic time at the network, with many people more eager to get off to the pub at five o'clock than burn the midnight oil worrying about what those Oxbridge goons and the runty American with the big weird coat were shooting down in Studio 6. According to *From Fringe to Flying Circus*, Cleese (the Python most comfortable with keeping up *some* standards) said that no less an authority than David Attenborough said to him at a party, "'Use shock sparingly,' which was the best advice we ever had. I don't think we actually stuck to it."

Ironically, problems with the network began later . . . once the BBC realized that people were watching, some three or four million each episode by the end of the year. Critics were noticing, too. The *Observer* approved of its "inspired lunacy," while an early review by the *Evening Standard* noted how the show "pushes jokes beyond the merely illogical into the realm of dream-like impossibility." But as long as just enough people were watching *Flying Circus* to keep it on the air, the Pythons had free rein to push every boundary of comedy they could find.

7

Under the Big Top

Monty Python's Flying Circus: Season One

hile the four seasons of *Monty Python's Flying Circus* vary in content, quality, and even format—we're looking at you, Season "so-called" Four—there are often binding thematics and running gags that give the proceedings a sort of newly minted generic unity.

Each episode of Season One, for example, opens with Palin's castaway croaking out "It's . . ." following by the rousing chords of "The Liberty Bell (March)," and Cleese announcing the series title over Gilliam's florid animation. Many of the first season's episodes feature background gags or themes (sheep, cats, undertakers), and nearly all of them include a fully armored knight (an anonymous Gilliam, according to legend) lumbering onto sketches and hitting characters with a plucked chicken.

While the Pythons eschewed easy skit closure and punch lines, they doted on metatheatrical self-references like directly addressing the audience, breaking the fourth wall, referring to sketches as sketches, and so on. It doesn't take long, really, for an audience to catch on to the Pythons' disregard for narrative and generic expectation. In fact, their disregard for convention becomes a convention itself by the end of Season One, something the audience comes to expect (demand, even).

Although eight of the first nine episodes of *Flying Circus* are tagged with particular titles (which include "failed" names for the overall series, significant sketches within episodes, or baffling non sequiturs), episode titling becomes exceedingly sporadic until the fourth and final season (1974), when episode-long narrative threads make such titles almost . . . almost! . . . relevant. Each season hewed to its own particular intro sequences, although "The Liberty Bell (March)" remained a constant throughout the series and the It's Man popped up in episodes until the fourth season; some seasons would abandon running gags (so long, Knight of the Chicken!), but the early comic patterns in Season One offered viewers an anchor against a general disregard for narrative and generic expectation the show strove to present. In short, Season One may not feature the densest assortment of Pythonesque sweetmeats, but it has its memorable moments and sets the stage for the heights of quotable comedy to follow.

Episode 1: "Whither Canada?" (original air date: October 5, 1969)

Episode 1 introduces viewers to several future Python staples: highbrow/lowbrow incongruity, false starts and non-finishes, fourth-wall bashing Pepperpots, absurdist animated interstitials, generic and temporal mash-ups, obsession with minutia, creative linguistic gymnastics, and an overt self-awareness regarding comedy as intentional creation. This episode's running gag: sheep!

Early on, the Pythons establish their fondness for the kind of temporal mash-up that Jones and Palin explored in *The Complete and Utter History of Britain*, but take it to new heights: Wolfgang Amadeus Mozart hosts a modern-day television show called *Famous Deaths*, and gleefully announces the death of Genghis Khan (among others).

Absurdity and language are brought to the fore in the "Italian Lesson" classroom, populated by native Italian speakers (and one mistaken German in lederhosen) who speak more fluent Italian than their earnest teacher (Jones). In "It's the Arts," an interviewer (Cleese) is more interested in what to call his guest (Chapman)—Edward, Ed, Ted, Eddie-baby, Sweetie, Sugar-plum, Pussycat, Angel-drawers, Frank, Frannie Knickers—than in discussing the director's latest film, ostensibly the whole reason for the interview to be taking place. Once "It's the Arts" dies (no need for punch lines here!), the "name gag" is taken up in the subsequent sketch, as Arthur "Two Sheds" Jackson (Jones) struggles to direct conversation away from his nickname and get his interviewer (Idle) to discuss his career as a composer.

Speaking of art and incongruity theory, in the "Picasso/Cycling Race" sketch, Pablo Picasso is made to paint while riding a bicycle in heavy traffic, with full "back to you!" sports-announcer enthusiasm. Also evident in this sketch is the Pythonic penchant for lists . . . and erudite lists, at that. At one point, the race-caller (Cleese) announces, seemingly in one breath, the passing of the following celebrated artists (on bikes): Wassily Kandinsky, Georges Braque, Piet Mondrian, Chagall, Max Ernst, Moro, Duffy, Ben Nicholson, Jackson Pollock, Bernard Buffet, Brâncusi, Géricault, Fernand Léger, Delaunay, Willem de Kooning, Kokoschka, Paul Klee, and Kurt

Schwitters. Such mash-ups of high-end art figures and low-brow sports conventions became a Python staple, culminating in Episode 11's outstanding "Literary Football Discussion" and "The Philosopher's Football Match" in their 1972 two-parter for German TV, *Fliegender Zirkus*.

In short, the Pythons' interest in upending expectation (who would/should take an intro Italian class, what is the purpose of an interview, how does one talk about art/sports, where are the demarcations of "sketch comedy") are all here in abundance. While Episode 1 may not contain any of the Pythons' most quotable bits, it does a fine job of leading viewers into this new world of deconstructivist comedy and establishes many of the soon-to-be-expected motifs going forward.

If there is one standout sketch in this inaugural episode of *Flying Circus*, it is the final (and lengthy) "The Funniest Joke in the World." The sketch involves Ernest Scribbler, a Brit who pens a joke so funny that anyone who reads it, Scribbler included, dies laughing. Naturally enough in the logic of the Python-verse, the Killer Joke is weaponized and put to use in the trenches of World War II. The World's Funniest Joke thus becomes, via the compartmentalized weaponization/translation process, an easy metaphor for the Manhattan Project, or yet another atomic bomb parable, like Godzilla with a British accent. As expected in a sketch that parodies the conventions of war films (archival images and dubbed Hitler footage establish the genre), the Nazis attempt a counter-joke (a play on the old "assaulted peanut" gag) that proves ineffective. Ultimately, the deadly effect of The Joke—read by English Tommies traipsing about the Ardennes—raises comedy to levels of destruction typically reserved for nuclear weapons. According to this first salvo from a fledgling comedy troupe, British humor wins the war. It's a weird world, this Python-verse: cruel, satiric, absurd . . . and oddly hopeful. Sometimes.

And finally, in a nice bit of closure that became the pattern throughout Season One (excepting Episodes 2, 5, 6, and 7), we witness Palin as the It's Man again, this time staggering back out to sea, a man adrift in comedy. Ah, symbolism.

Episode 2: "Sex and Violence" (original air date: October 12, 1969)

Episode 2—shot first, aired second—starts to really show the Pythons' ability to construct earworms of comedy. The It's Man establishes a sense of continuity (punctuated by a squealing pig from the previous episode) by appearing before the title animation—this time, he traipses over sand dunes toward camera to utter his one line. Sheep are the overtly stated theme this episode, and two early sketches combine sheep and aviation to absurd effect: in the first, a rabble-rousing instigator—Harold the sheep—convinces his brethren they can fly (they can't); and in the second, two Frenchmen (Cleese and Palin) lay out schematics—in outrageous jabberwock French—for a massive flying sheep. The sheep thematic then turns philosophic with the interruption of unexpectedly well-educated Pepperpots (Chapman, Jones, and Palin).

As if to punctuate the absurd frumpiness of the Pythons-cum-Pepperpots, Carol Cleveland makes her first appearance in this episode as the . . . sexually inspiring Deirdre Pewtey, the wife of timidly suspicious Arthur Pewtey (Palin). Palin first shows off his milquetoast chops in this episode as a spineless cuckold (he is rather good at being deferential), while Cleveland shows off her, well, Cleveland.

In other bits, Queen Victoria and William Gladstone engage in newsreel-style Laurel and Hardy slapstick during a temporal mash-up that echoes the temporal tomfoolery of *The Complete and Utter History of Britain*. Gilliam

What's All This, Then?

When the Python boys went in drag, they transformed into frumpy housewives in day frocks who were middle-aged and middle-class (generally), shrill (certainly falsetto'ed), oddly well educated, and foul-mouthed. The Pepperpots were mad harridans who stood in stark contrast to *Flying Circus*'s stable comely glamour stooges and crumpets. While most Pepperpots were simple comic crones, one should always be on the lookout for that most dangerous subspecies of Pepperpot: Hell's Grannies!

Of course, the Pythons weren't the first blokes to don the old frock and wig: English men have been dressing up as women for as long as there's been theater in England (possibly even before). And in the 1960s, female impersonators—like Barry Humphries (Dame Edna Everage) and Flip Wilson (Geraldine)—played "straight" . . . ish. The Pythons just added their particular spin to theatrical transvestism, as did the Kids in the Hall (the Canadian Pythons of the 1980s and '90s) and more recent Pythonesque comedy duos like *Mr. Show* and *Key & Peele*. Of course, none of these can hold a candle to Bugs Bunny. For a two-dimensional rabbit, the dude made an uncomfortably attractive coney. Grrooowl!

transforms a pram into voracious monster and turns Rodin's *The Kiss* into a tooting flute. The episode's most ambitious sketch, "Working-Class Playwright," upends British class structure by questioning what a "full working day" is for a prodigal coal-miner son whose lifestyle is demeaned by his judgmental playwright father: "What do you know about getting up at five o'clock in t'morning to fly to Paris, back at the Old Vic for drinks at twelve . . . That's a full working day, lad, and don't you forget it!"

As in many other sketches to come, "Working-Class Playwright" both highlights the Pythons' natural antiauthoritarianism and underlines the inherent silliness of the British class system. Oh, the writer's cramp!

Also of note in this episode is Jones as Arthur Ewing, who—with his Musical Mice—provides an example of animal cruelty humor par excellence, malleting his squealing "Mouse Organ." Jim Henson paid homage to this gag (repeatedly) a few years later on *The Muppet Show* (whose cracked surrealism was more ecstatically received in the United Kingdom than the United States) with the mallet-wielding musician Marvin Suggs and his "ow!-ing" Muppaphone. Fun fact: Henson was a mega-fan who—as Jones recalls in *Monty Python Live!*—literally stopped traffic in New York to greet his idols in 1976.

Graham Chapman explains "The Mouse Problem" to Michael Palin.   *BBC/Photofest*

And finally, the episode ends with the extended and wryly surreal "furies" sketch: "The Mouse Problem," which owes a great deal to the animal shenanigans of *At Last the 1948 Show*. In a lampoon of televised confessionals, an anony*mous* (hah!) Mr. A (Cleese) meekly offers the interviewer insight into his life as a man-sized mouse, supported by secret footage "taken at one of these mouse parties by a BBC cameraman posing as a vole." It's exactly as silly as it sounds.

The episode ends with an overt nod to the show *qua* show, as an earnest television journalist (Palin) notes, "Perhaps we need to know more about these mice men before we can really judge them. Perhaps not. Anyway, our thirty minutes are up." And so they are.

Episode 3: "How to Recognise Different Types of Trees from Quite a Long Way Away" (original air date: October 19, 1969)

Stride is duly struck in Episode 3! Bicycle Repair Man, Cardinal "so-called" Richelieu, the Seduced Milkman, Mr. Nudge Nudge—the hits begin bubbling up in this one. As memorable as many sketches became, the range of sketches in Episode 3 is similarly impressive.

The "Court Scene" gives us Pepperpot Chapman spouting verbal diarrhea—such breathless rambling recurs everywhere in the Python oeuvre, really, but Chapman and Idle seemed particularly keen on it—and introduces us to Palin as Cardinal "so-called" Richelieu. While the full assault of the Spanish Inquisition won't be felt until Episode 15 (and who would have expected that, eh?), running gags need to start somewhere, even if only in traffic court. "Bicycle Repair Man" is another genre-bender, presuming a world in which the extraordinary is ordinary, and in a world full of caped wonders, someone still has to do the mundane jobs. Really, the understated sketch implies that in an extraordinary world the ordinary would be extraordinary: take that, *Incredibles*!

There are other quickies in this episode that stay with you: "Children's Stories" is a delightful/creepy mash-up of traditional fairy-tale plots and subculture fetishism ("With a melon?!"); "Seduced Milkman," wherein Palin superbly showcases his pre-Galahad innocence, is a silent sketch straight out of the *Benny Hill* playbook that allows us another glimpse at Cleveland (always a bonus); and "The Larch" is absurdly quotable.

The hyperbolic reactions of the waitstaff in the "Restaurant Sketch" recall the overreactions of the "Shirt Shop" sales staff from *At Last the 1948 Show*, with Chapman once again in the "innocent customer" role; but the

Pythons distance themselves from traditional comic closure by ending with an intentionally clichéd (and metatheatrically delivered) punch line.

But perhaps most memorable of all is "Nudge Nudge," a wordplay sketch that takes circumlocution to unparalleled distances vis-à-vis the relative upward dimensions of, well, heights. Starting with "I want to see a sketch of Eric's" (meta!), Jones and Idle engage in a dialogue of frustration and pantomime that certainly ranks among their most famous examples of—as Led Zeppelin would say—"communication breakdown." While the "Parrot" sketch may be the most fully quoted (and fully misquoted) Python sketch, "Nudge Nudge" has to be a close informal second. I mean, when was the last time you were at a pub and someone *didn't* quote at least part of this sketch? Say no more!

Episode 4: "Owl-Stretching Time" (original air date: October 26, 1969)

After Palin's It's Man is hurled off a cliff, Idle opens the episode as a schmaltzy American singer/show-host (is there any other kind?), who sings of teeth briefly (foreshadowing!) before throwing to the next sketch: "Art Gallery." There we see two *astoundingly* erudite Pepperpots (Cleese and Chapman) who opine at length upon the Great Masters while slapping their unruly (off-screen) children silly. The "Art Gallery / Art Critic" sketches— which both devolve into the critics "eating" art and are guilty of employing punch lines themselves ("I don't know much about art, but I know what I like"), turn the tables metatheatrically upon the corny humor of art puns: Palin's critic scolds his wife (occasional crumpet Katya Wyeth), who delivers him a tray of liquid refreshment and puns "Wateau, dear?" After being told "What an awful joke!" by Palin, Wyeth responds, crying, "But it's my only line!" to end the sketch. Similar exchanges—typically uttered by Cleveland—may, perhaps, signal the troupe's awareness of the limited roles allotted to the glamour stooge or their inherent 1960s sexism. The joke is echoed in this very episode by Gilliam (as a Viking?), who does, in fact, utter his first *Flying Circus* line here.

Chapman's Colonel also appears for the first (and second and third) time in this episode, breaking into the show shouting to the camera, "Right, cut to me!" It will be one of his most frequent roles on the show going forward.

Then there's more *Benny Hill* silent slapstick with a semi-naked Jones at the beach, followed by a memorably absurd bit in which Cleese teaches a room of cadets how to defend themselves against attackers bearing fruit, and a trip to the bookshop that turns into a spy thriller . . . about dentistry. This last bit of brilliance draws heavily upon the genre parody "Mice Laugh Softly Charlotte" from *At Last the 1948 Show*, but adds several layers of absurdity with its constant dental puns. I mean, really: Who *hasn't* conflated dentistry with German torture?

Fun fact: the sixteen-ton weight—recalling the destructive silliness of Warner Bros. cartoon (anvils/weights/ton of bricks)—makes its *Flying Circus* debut in this episode.

Episode 5: "Man's Crisis of Identity in the Latter Half of the 20th Century" (original air date: November 16, 1969)

The fifth episode is the most self-consciously self-conscious of the lot so far. It directly draws audience attention to genre conventions and performance as performance: in short, "Man's Crisis of Identity in the Latter Half of the 20th Century" is *metatheatrical AF*. It's not as chockablock with memorable quotes or popular sketches as some episodes, but the general Pythonicity (is that a word? [Hardly.—Eds.]) of the episode lingers long after the credits roll.

The "Confuse-a-Cat" sketch—with its wacky Shakespearean stage-upon-a-stage performance augmented by manipulating film via jump cuts designed to, well, confuse a cat—allows the Pythons to be more baffling than ever. In another timey-wimey metatheatrical moment that approaches the reality-bending sensibility of a Philip K. Dick short story, Idle's newsman announces (in front of a screen showing him being escorted from his desk by police) that police interrogated a suspect in a jewelry heist before turning their attention to "a newsreader in the Central London area," whereupon he is led off by police and the news concluded by his "second self" on the screen. Got all that?

Jones and Cleveland, a romantic couple locked in a passionate and semi-clad embrace, tease the audience with conventionally implied "intercourse cut-scenes" (stock footage of towers rising and falling, waves crashing upon a beach, fountains, fireworks, and rocket ships, trains chugging through tunnels, and so forth) . . . which turn out—as an exasperated and smoking Cleveland laments—to be Jones actually showing her film clips. Of course, by the time it is revealed to the audience that the two were *not* in fact having sex, the images have been planted, and the Pythons have had their way with the viewer.

Gilliam then throws in a Charles Atlas cartoon . . . of sorts. Boxes in boxes, people.

Other future Python tropes are briefly in evidence throughout the episode: Palin and Cleese both border on corpsing during their exchange at Her Majesty's Customs and Excise (Palin as an incredibly nervous traveler/smuggler opposite Cleese's disbelieving officer). The two would go on to crack one another up repeatedly in the series and on stage. Cleese appears as a proto-Gumby (to be hit with a plucked chicken by Gilliam's knight from Episode 1) and as an Upper Class Twit—two staples of the Pythons going forward. These are small moments, but the steam is building, as it were.

Episode 6: "It's the Arts" (original air date: November 16, 1969)

Episode 6—which technically has no title, although it's sometimes referenced as "The BBC Entry for the Zinc Stoat of Budapest" or "It's the Arts" (and is often titled "The Arts" on later DVD compilations)—is a grab-bag episode. The Pythons return to obsess over names again (this time as an interviewer struggles to make any substantive progress while repeatedly invoking the name of his subject: Johann Gambolputty de von Ausfern-schplenden-schlitter-crasscrenbon-fried-digger-dingle-dangle-dongle-dungle-burstein-von-knacker-thrasher-apple-banger-horowitz-ticolensic-grander-knotty-spelltinkle-grandlich-grumblemeyer-spelterwas-ser-kurstlich-himbleeisen-bahnwagen-gutenabend-bitte-ein-nürnburger-bratwustle-gerspurten-mitz-weimache-luber-hundsfut-gumberaber-shöne-danker-kalbsfleisch-mittler-aucher von Hautkopft of Ulm . . . quite literally the greatest name in German Baroque music.

Stereotypes loom large: a group of fast-talking film gangsters led by Palin plan to "legally" buy a watch (before their plan goes sour); and Idle—sporting skin-tone makeup and syntax that reads rather racist nowadays—plays a "Redfoot tribe" warrior with a deep appreciation for theater (Cicely Courtneidge, especially). In "The Dull Life of a City Stockbroker," Palin vacantly treks across town to work, oblivious to the thrilling adventures occurring around him (an African warrior spears his neighbor; a topless model sells him his morning paper; Frankenstein's monster throttles those waiting behind him at the bus queue; a squad of soldiers engages in a firefight during his bus ride, and so forth). The stereotypes—including the bland stockbroker—are legion. In retrospect, Palin's commute reminds one of Simon Pegg's utterly oblivious trek through his zombie-infested neighborhood to buy his morning soda in *Shaun of the Dead* (2004). Given Pegg's vocal Python fandom—he appeared on stage at their O2 concert in 2014—it's not a stretch to suggest some sort of inspiration, despite the disparate genres at play here.

And finally, in "Twentieth Century Vole," Hollywood stereotypes—six yes-men and a megalomaniacal studio head (Chapman)—collide during a writers' meeting. SPLUNGE!

But the gem of this episode is really the "Whizzo Chocolates" (Crunchy Frog) sketch. Like many of their incongruity sketches, "Whizzo" plays with and against expectation, as the "chocolate-covered crunchy frog" is, literally, a chocolate-covered frog . . . and not a "mock frog" as expected. Chapman, as a constable who has eaten most of the increasingly vile confections in the Whizzo assortment, repeatedly exits to vomit. The Pythons were fond of comic vomit. [As they should be.—Eds.]

Dessert entrepreneur Terry Jones (*left*) guides policemen John Cleese (*right*) and Graham Chapman (*center*) through the gastronomic joys of the "Crunchy Frog" sketch.   *BBC/Photofest*

Episode 7: "You're No Fun Anymore" (original air date: November 30, 1969)

In some ways foreshadowing their final season, Episode 7 attempts a common narrative for most of the half hour, with less-than-stellar results. The show starts off on familiar genre-busting ground: Cleese interviews a "Camel Spotter" (Idle) who turns out to be a train-spotter; Palin's chartered accountant embezzles a penny from a multimillion-pound corporation; there are multiple throws to folks uttering the running gag "You're no fun anymore!" as scenes fold back into previous sketches, and so forth. Typically atypical Python fare.

Then the "Science Fiction Sketch" begins, and traditional narrative rears its ugly head. In a lengthy parody of B-film science fiction, we encounter a flying saucer that turns "ordinary people" into Scotsmen! Aware of the mass exodus of nouveau-Scots north, the police and a local scientist (Chapman) get involved; meanwhile, Angus Podgorny (Palin) receives an order for forty-eight million kilts from a blancmange hailing from the Andromeda Galaxy. Or is he really Riley, a blancmange impersonator and cannibal? Nope: it's really a pudding-based ET with a predilection for tennis! To be honest, this all looks better on paper than onscreen.

What's All This, Then?
The Rowling Connection

The first man to be turned into a Scotsman in this sketch is a character named "Harold Potter." This is *clearly* the inspiration for all J. K. Rowling's multibillion-pound success, and thus the answer to all of Cleese's financial divorce woes. You're welcome, John.

It's not that the parody isn't effective; it's just that it's hardly Pythonesque (blancmanges aside). It feels, honestly, like something the Zucker brothers would write in a few years. There's nothing wrong with that; it's just not what we've come to expect from the Pythons (which is the unexpected).

Oddly enough, the highlight of the "Science Fiction Sketch" may be the vacuous glamour stoogery of Donna Reading, who relentlessly vamps for the camera while (intentionally) fumbling her lines; she's a great foil to Chapman's staid scientist, and the two make a nice couple of science fiction stereotypes.

Episode 8: "Full Frontal Nudity" (original air date: December 7, 1969)

Aaaand . . . we're back! Back to form, to Gilliam goofiness, to quotability, to running gags. Thanks for bringing the sexy back, "Full Frontal Nudity"!

Opening non sequiturs lead to "Army Protection Racket," with Palin and Jones as the Vercotti Brothers, who put the muscle on the British Army until the Colonel breaks the fourth wall and ends his own sketch ("the whole premise is silly and it's very badly written. I'm the senior officer here and I haven't had a funny line yet"). We nearly see animated full-frontal nudity; we return to old characters like Palin's Art Critic, who Freudian slips his way through "The Place of the Nude" before glamour stooge Katya delivers a pun (as she did in Episode 4); she is again reprimanded and again cries, "But it's my only line!" (repeated by Cleveland later in this episode as well).

We then move on "to pastures new" and a newlywed couple (Jones and Cleveland) who are "Buying a Bed" from some mathematically and verbally quirky salesmen (including Chapman's Mr. Lambert, who puts a bag over his head every time someone says the word "mattress"). Also of note in this episode are some rather sociable hermits and a gang of "senile delinquent" Pepperpots: Hell's Grannies!

But the gem of this episode—and the season, and perhaps the series—is the "Dead Parrot" sketch: the most (mis)quoted and popular of all Python sketches. "Dead Parrot" is one of the Pythons' many "thesaurus" jokes—these include the "Bookshop," "Cheese Shop," and "What the Stars Foretell" sketches, as well as Chapman's litany of "Red Sea Pedestrian" synonyms in *Life of Brian*—most often (but not exclusively) written by the wordplay-loving Chapman and Cleese. It is an erudite investigation into circumlocution and euphemism, a paean to verbal muscle memory, and a pretty morbid bit of humor, when you get down to it. Beautiful plumage notwithstanding, of course.

Senile delinquents, baby snatchers, mafia shakedowns, glamour stooges, a Norwegian Blue, and repeated interruptions by the Colonel: Episode 8—which aired just as Python was garnering a wider viewership—likely did much to ensure their continued popularity.

Episode 9: "The Ant, an Introduction" (original air date: December 14, 1969)

Predictably, there are no ants in this episode. The episode does open with a clever—if entirely misleading—Spanish song about llamas (llamas

What's All This, Then?

The "Dead Parrot" sketch is, by most counts, the most popular sketch in the Python milieu. It began as a resurrected thesaurus sketch inspired by an earlier "Car Salesman" bit that Palin and Chapman performed in *How to Irritate People*. Cleese and Chapman reworked the sketch, briefly trying out "toaster return" in place of "car trouble," until hitting upon the surreal Norwegian Blue pining for the fjords. Granted, similarly morbid jokes may have been in circulation since the fourth century, but the Pythons seemed to have hit upon a particularly timeless version. In fact, the Parrot Sketch (if not the parrot itself) refuses to die, having inspired various "Dead Parrot Societies" and the following:

- In 1989, at Chapman's memorial service, Cleese eulogized his writing partner by invoking elements of the "Dead Parrot" sketch before adding: "Good riddance to him, the freeloading bastard. I hope he fries." Chapman would have approved.
- In 1990, Prime Minister Margaret Thatcher mocked Liberal Democrats in England by quoting bits of the "Dead Parrot" sketch. Chapman would *not* have approved.
- In 2014, as both advertisement and homage before their airing of the Pythons' final O2 performance, a fifty-foot fiberglass Dead Parrot (Norwegian Blue, of course) was laid to rest in Potters Field, London, by UKTV Gold. Chapman would have ridden the damn thing down a ski slope somewhere shouting hallelujah.

do not—despite what the subtitles or Internet may tell you—have fins, live in Amazonian rivers, or possess a beak for eating honey; they are, however, larger than frogs). Surreal moments include Sir George Head, OBE (Cleese) interviewing Idle(s) for an expedition of the twin peaks of Mount Kilimanjaro. Like the "Buying a Bed" sketch, numerical perception underlies this sketch.

Palin's subsequent performance as a conflicted, muttering, bloody barber suggests a *Sweeney Todd* parody, until the sketch unexpectedly morphs into the "Lumberjack Song"—complete with the Mounties Choir (the Fred Tomlinson Singers) and a swooning ingénue (Connie Booth). Far from craving blood as the previous sketch suggested, Palin's barber-cum-lumberjack embraces his feminine side, eating scones, pressing wildflowers, wearing high heels and a bra . . . hardly the "rugged" chap one expected. The "Lumberjack Song"—certainly one of the Pythons' most

What's All This, Then?
The Fred Tomlinson Singers

Episode 9 marks the first appearance of the Fred Tomlinson Singers (as Mounties and miners); they will return on occasion throughout the series. According to Palin, Tomlinson did not just arrange much of their music; he was almost a co-collaborator. After Tomlinson's death in 2016 at the age of eighty-nine, Palin wrote on the Python website that when he and Jones had written the "Lumberjack Song," they weren't sure how it would sound, so he called Tomlinson up late one night and sang it to him to solicit advice. By the next morning Tomlinson had written the song's score. His singers then formed the chorus when *Flying Circus* first performed it. Tomlinson may be gone, but his cheery versions of twisted Python lyrics are still sung across the globe today.

memorable—upends gender and lyrical expectations, and has become a hallmark performance piece.

Chapman gives us a more articulated (if not articulate) Gumby—complete with glasses, headkerchief, rolled sleeves, and suspenders—bashing himself in the head with bricks. (Various Gumbys, individually or in a yowling group, would recur throughout the series henceforth.)

"The Visitors" sees a good night go terribly wrong, in part due to polite British sensibilities and decorum. We open as Iris (Cleveland) and Victor (Chapman) begin to realize their love on a dimly lit couch, when suddenly the doorbell rings. Victor answers, only to find Arthur (Idle), a brash fellow he met at the pub some years ago, here to make good on a drink once promised in passing. Increasingly impolite and uncouth folks pour into the apartment (at Arthur's invitation), telling off-color jokes, making lewd comments, shouting at one another, wetting themselves, ushering in a goat, and so on. Iris runs off, Welsh miners rush in, and Victor finally attempts to see his unwelcome "guests" out . . . only to be shot dead by the boorish Mr. Equator (Cleese, who, when you think about it, does a good bit of shooting in this series).

Episode 10: (no title) (original air date: December 21, 1969)

A bit of a piecemeal episode, tied together by nothing more than a strain of metatheater; a few of the sketches—including the opening "Bank Robber

(Lingerie Shop)" sketch, "Vocational Guidance Counsellor," and "The First Man to Jump the Channel"—were shot for use in earlier episodes.

Episode 10 begins with an in-your-face bit of metatheater, as a plumber (Palin) receives a letter from the BBC asking if he'd like "to be in a sketch on the telly." Pop culture references to Marlon Brando and Paul Newman are casually dropped, cuts to actors (Cleese and Idle) in a lingerie shop are inserted, and eventually we see—on a telly—Palin's plumber walk off the lingerie set as the next scene (Cleese robbing Idle) begins. It's all very meta.

A talking tree—no, really, it has moving lips and everything!—interviews a piece of laminated plastic and a block of wood, until an animated Chippendale does impressions (and bad puns). Surreal.

"Vocational Guidance Counsellor" gives us another look at Palin's milquetoast nebbish (Mr. Anchovy, close cousin to Arthur Pewtey from Episode 2), a chartered accountant who desperately wants to be a lion tamer . . . even if he's a tad unclear about what a lion, in fact, is. Between Anchovy and Homicidal Barber (Episode 9), Palin nails man's desire to change what he is . . . maybe. Plus, the Pythons seemed to have it in for chartered accountants (pirates, the lot of them!).

Into the annals of *Flying Circus* "absurd sports" enters Ron Obvious (Jones), who intends to jump the twenty-six miles across the English Channel to Calais while carrying half a hundredweight of bricks and his passport. It ends as expected (about four feet in), but leads to ever sillier and impossible (failed) "athletic" endeavors: eating Chichester Cathedral, tunneling to Java, splitting a railway carriage with his nose, and running to Mercury. After this last attempt—and thanks to the constant encouragement of his manager, Mr. Vercotti (Palin), the now-dead Ron has a go at breaking the world record for remaining underground. It's a darkly silly sketch, but one that comments upon the ludicrous nature of sports records. Or—as two off-screen Pepperpots opine after Ron's death: it's "a bit sad"/"satire"/"zany madcap humour."

Then, in what appears to be a revisit to the "Dead Parrot" sketch, Palin and Cleese barter in a pet shop over "Pet Conversions"; their subsequent matter-of-fact negotiations regarding animal vivisection would make Dr. Moreau giggle uneasily. Again, a pet shop serves as the site of a ridiculously dark premise, one that urges audiences to reflect upon the awful things we do that—because they are part of our daily routines, part of our daily jobs—become mundane. (Patton Oswalt—a stand-up geek-lore comic who has never been afraid to confuse his audience or to name-drop Proust or

Spam—explores similar habitual dark places more directly in his "Piss Drinkers" bit, c. 2003.)

In "Gorilla Librarian," a job interview goes very well for Idle (in a gorilla suit), until he confesses that he is not, in fact, a gorilla. Finally, in "Strangers in the Night," a slew of men (including Biggles, star of British children's lit) climb through a matron's bedroom window to profess their love, while her oblivious husband (Palin) snoozes through the shenanigans until he leaves the sketch (to visit the loo and his own lover). The episode trails off as a series of animated animals discuss the merits of originality in comedy while eating one another; as the credits roll, we see Palin's It's Man carried off his meat hook to one end of a slaughterhouse; our last image is of a butcher walking out the other end of the slaughterhouse carrying a mass of bloody victuals. The Pythons are fully embracing self-reflexivity at this stage of the game, albeit at the price of quotability.

Episode 11: "The Royal Philharmonic Orchestra Goes to the Bathroom" (original air date: December 28, 1969)

Gallows humor and self-reflexivity continue in Episode 11, which opens with complaint letters and animations directed at the show (too "lavatorial," too "athletic," too many "cheap jokes about poo-poo"). It then somberly cuts to Professor R. J. Canning (Cleese), who starts lecturing on "The Black Death, typhus, cholera, consumption, and bubonic plague" before a group of top-hatted undertakers sitting on a coffin languidly comment: "Ah, those were the days . . ." More gallows humor follows, as undertakers happily picnic near a busy "Accident Black Spot" corner, and one (Jones) winks to the camera, encouraging viewers who are "tired of life" to "Keep it up." The recurring interruption of the undertakers throughout the episode, a growing pile of dead investigators, and the slapstick treatment of the Battle of Pearl Harbor make this the darkest *Flying Circus* episode to date.

The first extended sketch of the episode, an Agatha Christie murder mystery parody, keeps the episode's darkly comic tenor rolling, as a series of verbally challenged and oddly named Inspectors ("Tiger . . . where?!") seek to find the murderer in the room . . . even if there's no corpse evident (at least initially). As a succession of inspectors enter the room, and their corpses pile up, we cut *Benny Hill*–style to some pallbearers ditching a corpse by the side of the road, and then move on to football(?!).

The unheralded "Literary Football Discussion" represents the height of high-brow/low-brow interaction, of learned erudition and natural sport talent, and the classical brain/body dichotomy as embodied by an exchange between a sports analyst and a sports figure. Here, an erudite and effeminate analyst (Idle) rhapsodizes upon the previous night's "Proustian display of modern existentialist football" during Jarrow United's match against Bologna; Idle's florid diction echoes the then-current penchant for over-intellectualized sports analysis (culled in British papers like *Private Eye*; epitomized in the United States by Howard Cosell). Unfortunately for Brian, the "arch-thinker" behind Jarrow's win is less than articulate, capable of two responses, really: "I'm opening a boutique" and "I hit the ball first time and there it was in the back of the net." Despite Brian's game prompts at eliciting a suitably "smart" answer from his guest, the sketch ends in mid-conversation (such as it is) when an undertaker throws us back to "the state of play" in the "Detective Sketch" (more corpses). This short but packed sports interview—crammed between sketches about death—is sharp evidence of a recurring motif in Python, what Andrew Stott described in *Comedy (The New Critical Idiom)* as "the discussion of quotidian topics in an elevated register, exploiting discontinuity between form and content." It's also a reasonable satire on the modern intellectual's idolization of the physical over the intellectual. But don't believe us: go watch *Bull Durham* again.

Then it's back to undertakers expiring, one by one, while bearing a coffin. This live-action (heh) sketch evolves into a stop-motion sketch (as the coffin transports itself to a grave), then morphs into an animation of coffins (cutaway view as seen underground), and then—THEN—in a move that would confuse all but the staunchest of Freudians, a series of Gilliam animations involving full frontal female (and police) nudity. The move from live action to animation, from death to life, segues into a sketch on "Eighteenth-Century Social Legislation," wherein a lingerie-clad Cleveland gyrates on a bed while lip-synching a lecture on world history voiced by Cleese . . . punctuated by a fast-motion striptease and a German Professor (Palin) being fondled by "an amorous siren." Honestly, it's like a Van Halen video for the intellectual crowd.

But the episode ends—as all episodes should, really—with "The Batley Townswomen's Guild Presents the Battle of Pearl Harbor." Here, an obviously self-pleased local dame, Rita Fairbanks (Idle), demurely gushes about her guild's previous exciting dramatic productions—"Camp on Blood Island" and "Nazi War Atrocities"—before she and her fellow Pepperpots launch into something "in a lighter vein": "The Battle of Pearl Harbor." After a whistle blows, the Pepperpots launch into battle, smacking one another with handbags in the middle of a muddy field. It's silly, it's irreverent, it's in bad taste, it's an indictment of provincial ignorance, and as far as physical humor goes, it's no "Fish-Slapping Dance." Still, one cannot help recall Homer Simpson's critique of the offerings at the Springfield Film Festival: "Barney's movie had heart, but *Football in the Groin* had a football in the groin!"

Episode 12: "The Naked Ant" (original air date: January 4, 1970)

Speaking of "offending everyone," Episode 12 takes a reasonably direct approach to satirizing politics and class and introduces us to a group of "Upper Class Twits" and those dickie old chums, Mr. Hilter and Ron Vibbentrop.

After a full-stop non sequitur to open (man mauled by bear in signal box), two businessmen (Idle and Cleese) watch a series of men fall past their office window. Their blasé response to these deaths—evolving into a "fiver bet" on who will jump next—marks a cynicism about the "business as usual" world that informs many Python attacks on the middle class (and accountancy in particular).

Gilliam's subsequent animations of sideward-falling suicides, a promulgation of flowers, and a nudist beach baller crushed by the earth shift viewer attention quickly, however. The next bit, "Spectrum," promises to answer the age-old question "What is going on?" It doesn't, of course, thus further underscoring the futility of human existence that was thrown out the window as the show opens. Then a train careens out of control, crashing . . .

Man, we hope something happy happens soon.

Oh, look, it's a lovely boarding house in Somerset. This looks promising. And there's Jones, all Pepperpotted up. How nice! Oh, and here's an early example of inane verbal diarrhea pouring forth from Idle (which he'll perfect in his "Watney's bleedin' Red Barrel" spiel in Episode 31's "Travel Agent" sketch). And there are the rest of the boarders. And Adolf Hitler in full military regalia. Crap.

No, wait . . . it's not Hitler, it's that nice Mr. Hilter (Cleese) and his chums, Ron Vibbentrop (Chapman) and Heinrich Bimmler (Palin)! And they're just planning a hiking trip to Bideford, *not* a march to Stalingrad. Oh, this is jolly fun, thank goodness. Ooh, this National Bocialist Party they're planning sounds like a blast. Not sure about their plans to annex Poland, or those "boncentration bamps," but that's Conservatives for you. Next thing you know, Joris Bohnson will be planning a Brexit holiday.

We're sorry: that was very silly. Back to the program!

Other sketches include "Police Station (Silly Voices)" (really just a conceptual rehash of Episode 8's "Buying a Bed" sketch), "Ken Shabby" (Palin is cast against type and plays the gob-hacking eponymous letch, Shabby), and "How Far Can a Minister Fall?" (Chapman—Minister Warbeck of the Wood Party—attempts to deliver a public address after falling into a very deep hole).

Political commentary is never far down the menu in this episode, and in addition to the *very* lightly veiled satires on Nazis and Conservative British politics, the Pythons turned their attention to culling of Upper Class Twits: those chinless, overprivileged, undereducated, loud, obnoxious, and generally spastic homegrown British boobies (think nasty versions of Bertie Wooster) whose sense of class-based superiority so irked the troupe. Cleese is on record as hating Upper Class Twits in particular, since a real-world version of them—a group he dubbed the "Sloane Rangers"—frequented a local drinking parlor near Sloane Square where he lived, disrupting his peace.

In the lengthy "Upper Class Twit of the Year" sketch, we are treated to an estates satire (think Chaucer) in which assorted aristocratic twits vie to win a kind of Darwin Award. And so, in what proved to be one of the Pythons' more memorable concept sketches, a quasi-Olympics / dog show of idiocy ensues, narrated at breakneck pace by Cleese, who treats the entire event with the enthusiasm normally reserved for a football match. Twit-challenging events range from jumping over matchbooks to kicking a beggar, stopping for a photo op with ingénues, backing over an old lady, waking the neighbors, insulting a waiter, removing the bra from a mannequin, and finally shooting themselves with a pistol. Happily, all the contestants eventually complete their tasks, and the world is less five massive twits. As Cleese notes at the close of the sketch, "There'll certainly be some car door slamming in the streets of Kensington tonight!" It's all rather satisfying, really.

Between "Mr. Hilter" and "Upper Class Twit of the Year," the Pythons proved once again that death and satire oft march hand in hand. Perhaps even as far as Bideford.

Episode 13: "Intermission" (original air date: January 11, 1970)

The final episode of the first season (and at the time of its filming, there was certainly no guarantee that there would be a second) opens with

Palin's It's Man peeking out from a casket borne by the pallbearers from Episode 11. We cut from the grave-bound It's Man straight to a sign reading "INTERMISSION"—self-reflexive metatheatrics once again—and then on to the opening animation . . . and another "INTERMISSION." If the Pythons weren't sure about their future on television, this was certainly an epic way to go: open *en medias res* and then on to an implied demise. And— not knowing whether there would be a tomorrow next year—they stuffed this episode with Cardinal Richelieu, Gumbys, Luigi Vercotti, Twits, *Benny Hill*-esque chase scenes, recurring intermissions, Carol Cleveland (asserting herself!), overly self-aware thesaurus humor, and a host of metatheatrical self-reflection. Some of it even worked as comedy.

The show begins, properly, with "Restaurant (Abuse/Cannibalism);" Idle is a buxom Pepperpot in full vapid chatterbox mode, while Cleese plays her husband, a man who cannot seem to conjure a complimentary comparison to save his life. The two take a reasonable amount of abuse from two waiters at a smug vegetarian restaurant, but the sketch is largely formless, peppered with a few painful one-liners and a series of unconnected walk-ons. Oh, did we say "vegetarian"? We mean "no animal meat": humans are on the menu (mind the vicar, however, he's hardly fresh).

But before the cannibalism can begin, we cut to another "INTERMIS-SION," a few short commercials, and then return to one of the Pythons' more avant-garde (and oddly popular) sketches: "Albatross." Wearing an ice-cream girl uniform, Cleese is flogging not choc ices but a large, dead alba-tross, to the initial confusion of his confection-hungry patron (Jones). The sketch, as performed in this episode, is very brief, and the humor mostly derives from its incongruous premise and Cleese's appearance.

In later stage performances, as at the Hollywood Bowl shows, the exchange between the two becomes a tad more involved, but the skit still rests on the massive cross-dressed shoulders of Cleese. Any intellectual frisson brought about by the audience's recognition of Coleridge's *Rime of the Ancient Mariner* is just gravy (no wafers!).

Another "INTERMISSION" appears and is promptly blown up. Various characters in various sketches shout out "Albatross!" for no apparent reason. Nearly every sketch is tied to another. Shots of an audience clapping punc-tuate scenes. Gumbys make sketch requests, like fans at a rock concert. Temporal mash-ups (various historical figures impersonating modern celebrities and events) abound. The television audience for this last episode is constantly reminded that they are watching a performance, that the Pythons are—above all else—aware of genre and form.

"Come Back to My Place," a silent bit with the "Special Crime Squad," the mockumentary "'Probe-Around' on Crime," and "Attila the Hun" all focus on the British police. Surprisingly, these authority figures are neither satirized nor demonized; instead, situational humor arises from the mash-up of police employing magic in their duties (foreshadowing the religiously empowered constabulary in Episode 29's "Salvation Fuzz" sketch). This is hardly the sharp political criticism leveled at Twits and Conservatives in the previous episode.

The episode more or less ends with the surreal "Operating Theatre (Squatters)" sketch, in which—upon slicing open Palin—Chapman's doctor finds a trio of squatters (frizzy-haired hippy Idle, naked *Nova* reporter Cleveland, and David Ballantyne in a Sikh turban) living in his stomach. It feels a bit like the "Reptile Keeper" sketch from *At Last the 1948 Show*, really, which featured Cleese berating Brooke-Taylor . . . who had been swallowed by a giant boa constrictor.

Of course, the Pythons couldn't just end the season on a recycled boa constrictor gag. Instead, they toss to Gilliam's autocritical animation, which opines: "What a terrible way to end a series!" After a bit of animation that pleases the animated commentator, the Bronzino foot comes down, squash-ing him with a fart. So that's the end, then.

But wait! As the credits roll, the It's Man flees for his life from undertakers, which seems at least a slightly more optimis-tic way to end the series than the crushing foot or art.

But wait! There's more! A final (final!) "INTERMISSION" sign pops up, and Cleese's voice-over intones: "When this series returns it will be put out on Monday mornings as a test card and will be described by the *Radio Times* as a history of Irish agriculture."

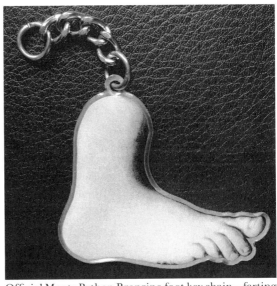

Official Monty Python Bronzino foot key chain—farting noises optional.

What's All This, Then?
The It's Man

Palin's "The It's Man" has a hard life. He opens and closes every episode of Season One, ragged and exhausted, arriving on Britain's shores at the start of Episode 1 and running from death at the end of Episode 13. Along the way he introduces the show by: crawling out of the sea; trekking over the heath; escaping a lion; being thrown off a cliff; rowing up river; answering a phone; running down a mountain (and forgetting his line); getting bombed; avoiding bombing; hanging from a meat hook; crossing a street; pin-balling through a copse of trees; and rising from a pallbeared (pall-borne?) coffin. That's life in a nutshell, innit?

Even in its final throes—past them, really—the last episode of the first season of *Monty Python's Flying Circus* reminds the viewer that this is, after all, a television show, subject to the whims of programmers and reviewers, not just audiences.

8

Spam, Spam, Spam, Spam, Wonderful Spam!

Monty Python's Flying Circus: Season Two

B y the time Season Two of *Monty Python's Flying Circus* began in 1970, Python had hit its stride. While the first season had been brilliant, the second upped the ante in terms of sheer anarchy and comedic deconstruction. Season Two was more focused, and showed all the Pythons breaking new comedic ground. Most comedians would have been content to have merely created the Ministry of Silly Walks and the Spanish Inquisition in one season. But Season Two not only had those two classic sketches, but also equally strong material in "Blackmail," "The Society for Putting Things on Top of Other Things," "Bruces," "Spam," and the "Dirty Hungarian Phrasebook."

In this season, *Flying Circus* tore down the walls of conventional comedy. Like a bad Hungarian phrasebook, this was an act that intentionally caused all kinds of confusion.

Episode 14: "Face the Press (Or Dinsdale)" (original air date: September 15, 1970)

The first episode of Season Two starts with what looked to be a conventional critique of British bureaucracy. A woman (Jones) has ordered a new cooker for her kitchen, but of course the deliverymen have got the order wrong. In conventional sketch shows like *Benny Hill* or *The Two Ronnies*, the new cooker sketch would have been an excuse for the deliveryman to seduce the housewife (Python themselves parodied this in the "Milkman" sketch, where

Ministers of Silly Walks. *Left to right*: Terry Jones, Eric Idle, Graham Chapman, Michael Palin, and John Cleese.   *BBC/Photofest*

a poor milkman is imprisoned by a lovely young housewife). But instead, the only logical way to get the cooker connected turns out to be a gas leak, and by the end of the sketch the deliverymen help Jones's housewife inhale gas to get the process going quicker.

In the phenomenal "The Tale of the Piranha Brothers" sketch, a faux-news documentary tracks a criminal pair based on infamous real-life London criminal celebrities Ron and Reggie Kray. The actual Kray brothers had terrorized London for years and were convicted in 1969, making this a fairly topical sketch by Python standards. It also includes some fairly sharp satire of the public's tendency to celebrate homicidal criminals with good media relations; witness the parade of interviewees who profess what great blokes the Piranha Brothers were, even when they were getting their heads nailed to the floor ("Well he did do that, yeah. He was a hard man. Vicious but fair"). Several movies have been made about the Kray brothers' exploits, but none were as funny as the Piranha Brothers—and none contain Spiny Norman (we'd explain this last bit, but well, we don't want to . . . also, it would be difficult). An allusion to Ronnie Kray's bisexuality comes in the form of Cleese, who proclaims that they "knew how to treat a female impersonator."

A highlight of the episode is, of course, "The Ministry of Silly Walks." The long-limbed and comically flexible Cleese's amazing display starts as he walks to work in the morning, high- and silly-stepping his way down the sidewalk like a wind-up toy whose parts are not all working correctly. At the ministry, he meets Palin, who is a supplicant looking for a grant but does not have the "legs for it." Cleese then proceeds to demonstrate his walk with astonishing physical dexterity. The dialogue is funny, but it's really an excuse for Cleese to bend his legs in extraordinary ways as he walks around the office declaiming on how underfunded Silly Walks is compared to other ministries (a mere £348 million for silly walks!). Luckily, this makes sense in the context of Python and even Cleese's secretary has a silly walk that leaves her splashing coffee everywhere. There's more to it, but those few minutes alone of Cleese walking as though he had all of his bones amputated and replaced with rubber bands is comedy gold.

Episode 15: "The Spanish Inquisition" (original air date: September 22, 1970)

Of all Python's deconstructionist bits of comedy, none is more justly lauded than the "Spanish Inquisition" sketch. The idea of interrupting a sketch or abandoning it completely and moving on to a new topic was a technique that Python had already explored in Season One, but the Spanish Inquisition took the idea to a new level, where the fearsome Spanish Inquisition appears in modern times to interrupt a sketch. In the beginning of the sketch, Chapman's character Reg, dressed as a Victorian-era mill worker, informs Lady Mountback that the "treadle has gone askew." When asked what this means, Chapman, acknowledging that he's in actor in a sketch, informs her that he has no idea what the line means and that he hadn't "expected a sort of Spanish Inquisition."

At that moment, the music leaps an octave and into the room springs the ferocious trio of Cardinal Ximmenez, (Palin), Cardinal Biggles (Jones), and Cardinal Fang (Gilliam). After gleefully announcing that "No one expects the Spanish Inquisition!" Palin's maniacal bishop attempts to proclaim what their three major weapons are ("surprise, fear, and an almost fanatical devotion to the pope") without much luck. After consistently mangling his lines, he hands them off to a befuddled Bishop Biggles—named for a British children's book character who became a running gag in many Python episodes—who is clearly not prepared for the responsibility. Eventually, the sketch is disrupted by a BBC announcer who asks Reg to come with him to read a quick announcement. The Spanish Inquisition returns later in the episode in a new twist, this time as part of a movie about the Spanish Inquisition. However, while the real Spanish Inquisition was quite good at torture and wringing confessions out of supposed heretics, the Spanish Inquisition in Python has to make do with a comfy chair (which Lady Mountback clearly enjoys) and instead of the expected torturous rack a kitchen sink rack, which proves to be particularly ill-suited as a torture device. The Inquisition returns one final time in the episode, during a courtroom scene where after the classic line "I didn't expect a sort of Spanish Inquisition" is uttered the scene cuts to the members of the Spanish Inquisition running frantically from a house, boarding a bus and finally arriving in the courtroom just as the credits roll, ending with them bursting into the room at the last second and Palin crying out, "No one expects the Spanish . . . oh bugger!" as "The End" flashes across the screen.

What's All This, Then?
The Real Spanish Inquisition

"The Spanish Inquisition" sketch is another example of Python's historical bent leading back to their largely Oxbridge roots. Python would have known the *real* Spanish Inquisition was created in 1478 by Pope Sextus XII at the urging of King Fernando and Queen Isabella of Spain, who were worried about a rise of heresy in Spain and apparently just killing time until Columbus dropped in a few decades later looking for some travel money.

The main function of the real Spanish Inquisition was to ferret out *conversos*, Jews who had converted to Catholicism in name only and still observed their Jewish faith in secret. After a few decades, the Inquisition grew in power and gained the authority to punish heretics of all kinds, sometimes using torture (the Spanish Inquisition did not always use torture as they suspected it would lead to false confessions) and later ritualistically killing the heretic in public at an auto-da-fé. (Ask Mel Brooks for the exact translation.) The Inquisition was a blot on the Catholic Church and its last vestiges did not end until 1834. Python, as usual, played with history out of context, thus defanging the fearsome inquisitors by putting them into the context of modern times (except for Cardinal Fang, of course).

Python's tendency to play within the medium of television and viewers' expectations is vividly illustrated here: they first interrupt a sketch (not a first for Python) to introduce the concept, and then reintroduce it again, this time in the context of a movie that the viewer has presumably stumbled upon while idly changing channels from BBC1 to BBC2 (people got bored in Britain back in the day), and then finally acknowledge that the Spanish Inquisition are merely characters in the show, subject to the time limits and final credits that ended every episode. In Python's world, the Spanish Inquisition wasn't disbanded by the vagaries of the modern world, but by the constraints of time.

Other highlights include a semaphore version of *Wuthering Heights*. What could make the plight of doomed lovers Heathcliff and Catherine more evocative, than the use of semaphore? What's that, you say? Almost everything else would? Quite, quite. Wait, how about *Julius Caesar* with an Aldis lamp? But in Python's hands, the ship-to-ship communication device leads to comedic gold. One of Season Two's most solid episodes, it shows Python breaking new ground and deconstructing television again.

Episode 16: "Déjà Vu (or: Show 5)" (original air date: September 29, 1970)

One of the highlights of "Déjà Vu" is the story of beloved Scottish poet Ewan McTeagle (Jones), a caricature of poets such as Dylan Thomas who perpetually squandered away what money they did make on drink and dissolute lifestyles. The difference here being that McTeagle's poetry is awful. Just wretched. Also, he's Scottish, which is automatically humorous in the Pythonverse.

The episode begins at the beginning, with a woman seen in a window about to strip, only to be blocked by Cleese rising up on a window washer's platform to announce "and now for something different," whereupon we are interrupted by a stuffed animal exploding. Cleese tries to start the show a second time, at which point we cut to the It's Man and the opening credits, after which another animal explodes. Because that's what they do.

Meanwhile, a bishop (Palin) is practicing lines from a script ("Oh Mr. Belpit, your legs are so swollen") only to be interrupted by a suit-wearing Mr. Chigger (Jones). He asks the bishop about flying lessons, only to be informed that the bishop isn't actually in this episode ("I'm not in until show eight"), so, sorry.

Chigger is directed to a desk in the woods, womaned by a receptionist (Carol Cleveland), who has him follow her. The following string of scenes has them walking through a series of office vignettes (a coffee cart, businessmen with papers, coworkers chatting) displaced to various outdoor settings. Chigger ultimately arrives at an actual office where a Mr. Anemone (Chapman), hanging from the ceiling, offers to teach Chigger how to fly. After some classic Chapman verbal abuse, Jones points out that Chapman is actually not flying himself, but suspended by wires. An outraged Chapman demands "an 'oop" (a hoop) to demonstrate that he's is indeed flying and pulls it apart to put it around him, fooling no one. Luckily, Chapman is in rare abusive form, shouting, "Pardon me, I'm off to play the grand piano!" The sketch soon becomes "pointless bickering," which was the point after all.

We then cut to two years later, where a caption says that Jones is now fully qualified as a pilot, followed by an interruption from Idle playing a spokesperson for the British Airline Pilots Association (BALPA), who wants to point out mistakes in the current episode as well as other programs. Back on the plane, a passenger (Chapman) thinks the cockpit is a bathroom and bursts in, much to the pilots' surprise. He acts embarrassed (possibly because in *How to Irritate People*, the cockpit looked just the same, and Chapman was the pilot). Naturally, instead of returning to his seat, he walks out the door into the air, but luckily lands by a toilet.

Back on the plane, a hijacker (Palin) bursts into the cockpit with a gun and hijacks the plane Luton, even though the plane was going to Cuba. They drop the hijacker off near a bus to Luton. He is stymied yet again when the bus is then hijacked to Cuba. Incidentally, many planes *were* hijacked to Cuba in the late 1960s and early '70s, but very few to Luton. Fewer palm trees.

The camera pans across a river to reveal the immortal poet Ewan McTeagle, the author of such beloved lines as "to my own beloved lassie, lend us a couple of bob until Thursday." All of this is presented as great poetry, although his greatest work, "Can I have fifty pounds to mend the shed?" is acted out on stage by Idle in Shakespearian regalia (the authors' favorite remains, "What's twenty quid to the bloody Midland Bank?").

The episode returns to the great outdoors and another stuffed animal explodes. "A highland spokesman" (Cleese) complains much as the BALPA spokesman had earlier as a pilot. We then cut back to Idle, who corrects him, before the camera pulls back to reveal Palin at work below Cleese's kilt; he's a gynecologist, but on his lunch hour.

This leads to a classic Gilliam animation of a little girl eating a Scotsman and then being eaten herself by giant floating teeth, followed by hands growing like trees, as other hands fly by like birds. Then a cowboy on a giant hand rides up, his lasso extending out to some naked women and then indoors to where Pepperpot Mrs. Ratbag (Chapman) is knitting. A milkman/psychiatrist (Idle) shows up at the door and asks Mrs. Ratbag to take a word association test. As the two head to the dairy for psychiatric help, a stuffed cat hidden by a fence explodes.

Then we're back to complaints! Psychiatrist Dr. Cream (Jones) butts in to complain, but the BALPA spokesman corrects him, only for Cleese to complain about "people who make rash complaints without waiting to see if those complaints are justified," leading to the BALPA spokesman who corrects them and "complains about shows that have too many complaints in them." Palin, as the last complainer, is crushed by a sixteen-ton weight. Well, you can complain too much we guess.

Mrs. Ratbag enters the psychiatric dairy, where Mr. Cream is psychoanalyzing a cow, then back to forest office where the bishop is still working on his lines. Another stuffed animal explodes. This doesn't have to make sense.

Finally, a new program begins. We see an introduction to a science program called *It's the Mind*, which examines the phenomenon of déjà vu. The presenter (Palin) starts to repeat himself and the show starts over. He is a bit shaken and wonders if this has happened before, when all of a sudden, the program starts again. This time, the phone rings, he answers, he is given a cup of water, and the program starts again. The phone rings again, he again gets a cup of water, and this time he panics and runs off set. As the presenter flags down Idle's milkman/psychiatrist, *It's the Mind* starts again, he panics and runs off to the cart again. This repeats again as the two of them drive off past the (still) rehearsing bishop, arrive again at the dairy, and go again to see Jones. The credits roll, as the presenter, stuck in some sort of temporal loop, arrives for the fourth time, before the program finally fades to black. For all we know, he may still be reliving those moments today.

Episode 17: "The Buzz Aldrin Show (or: An Apology)" (original air date: October 20, 1970)

The episode starts with a Gilliam animation of a man who crawls into bed and comes out the next morning as a flamboyant, Liberace-type butterfly. Then we are back to "normal" as Cleese's announcer appears at a desk set against an animated background, apologizing for the next announcement, followed by the It's Man, and the opening credits.

Is there any program that couldn't be improved by an influx of Gumbys? The Gumbys struggle to make an announcement about an "ARCHI-TECTS sketch" in which a firm is looking at designs for a new block of flats and are shown two versions of a building, one of which is a slaughterhouse (heavily soundproofed), and the other a tower that bursts into flames. The first is turned down as "we wanted a block of flats and not an abattoir," while the second is accepted despite its flaws because the architect is a fellow Freemason. The architect of the first building (Cleese) is then filled with rage, mostly because they will not let him join. It's a classic example of Cleese unfurling abuse with great gusto, yelling about "You black-balling bastards!" After a humorous illustration of how to cure a man "of these unfortunate masonic tendencies" (whack them with a massive hammer: sorry about that, Chapman), we are back with the Gumbys in the "insurance sketch" where Chapman (captioned as "straight man") is trying to buy motor insurance from a certain Mr. Devious (Palin, hair slicked back in full minor criminal mode). Before their exchange is concluded, the Rev. Morrison (Idle) arrives concerned about a letter he received from the insurance company. Chapman, hopping out of character, asks if "he has any more lines." Palin checks the script to see that yes, he indeed is done and Chapman leaves. After the sketch concludes with the reverend wheeling a naked woman away in a shopping cart, Devious is confronted by . . . "The Bishop!"

The "Bishop" sketch features Jones as the hard-boiled cleric with the snarling demeanor of a mob enforcer and *Peter Gunn*–type theme music. "The Bishop" is a parody of police and private eye shows popular in the mid- to late-1960s, such as Roger Moore's *The Saint*. (Strangely, the jazzy and evocative opening titles bear strong resemblance to the opening credits of *Elmer Gantry*, the Burt Lancaster–starring 1960 film adaptation of Sinclair Lewis's novel about a flimflam man posing as a reverend.) *The Bishop* "show" starts over a few times during the episode, reminiscent of the previous "Déjà Vu" episode with the constantly restarting *It's the Mind* program.

A couple (Chapman and Palin) leave the theater to go home, which consists of couches out on the street. A BBC news presenter (Idle) arrives, changing the sketch to a documentary on housing. Then we cut to an animated advertisement for a "poet in every home." After the animation, a meter reader (Palin) shows up at a house to "read your poet," which is a "Wordsworth." As the resident Pepperpot (Jones) tries to seduce him, he rambles about weather and becomes a BBC weatherman with weather charts before cutting to the BBC logo. (During the 1960s, the BBC logo would often appear onscreen while a voice provided programming information to viewers.)

We cut back to Jones (as a more voluptuous Pepperpot) trying to seduce Palin with "I've got Thomas Hardy in the bedroom," to which Palin responds, "I can't check him, he's a novelist!" We pull back to see that this has been occurring on television and the sketch now involves a panel with a nude man (Chapman), who rails against filth on television. When the host (Cleese) asks the Bishop for his opinion, it restarts *The Bishop*. This goes on until the BBC apologies "for the constant repetition in the show." (We, however, apologize for nothing!)

After some animation and vignettes, the episode gets back to sketch-time: A blunt chemist (Cleese) distributes prescriptions by shouting, "Who's got the pox?" or "Who's got a boil on the bum?" After a few more like-minded jokes, the censors take over and the chemist is dragged off by the police. A customer (Idle) then walks into "A NOT AT ALL NAUGHTY CHEMIST'S" and asks the chemist (Palin) for a "fishy"-type aftershave. As some are in the basement, Palin's chemist runs out of frame to find them and bring them up. This leads to yet more acknowledgments of the show's artificiality, as Palin is caught by a camera backstage waiting to reenter the sketch.

After a shoplifter (Gilliam) enters, some semblance of order is restored in the form of Constable Pan Am (Chapman this time; Cleese plays him in a later episode), who, after being informed he needs to say "What's all this, then?" proceeds to get just about everything wrong and acts generally loony while talking about Buzz Aldrin. The chemist says he "didn't expect a Spanish Inquisition," but because Palin is still in the sketch and unable to play Cardinal Ximenez, they do not burst in. Pan Am threatens to charge the customer with possession of "whatever we have lying around the station," and then the program ends with a photo of Buzz Aldrin, who apparently also did the script, makeup, and other tasks. American astronauts, is there anything they *can't* do?

Episode 18: "Live from the Grill-O-Mat" (original air date: October 27, 1970)

"Live from the Grill-O-Mat" is a primer for Cleesian characters who desperately want to be accepted but can never truly fit in. After a brief introduction announced over the BBC logo, the camera cuts to inside a Grill-O-Mat diner where Cleese's announcer tries to (painfully) introduce the show as if it was a large dinner with different courses. He asks for the titles and the It's Man appears, followed by the opening titles and a quick segue into *Blackmail*!

One of *Flying Circus*'s finest straight parodies, "Blackmail" stars Palin in fulsome, unctuous game-show-host mode. Weaving sinister threat with smarmy plays for audience approval, Palin calls people and shows them embarrassing film footage, all the while promising things like to "not reveal the name of your lover in Bolton" if the victims pony up cash. *Blackmail* never did become a major television show, though given the modern ubiquity of gotcha tabloid media (*TMZ* and others), that may just be a matter of time.

Another masterful sketch that reoccurred throughout the episode was "The Society for Putting Things on Top of Other Things." This looks at first to just be a commentary on British eccentricity, but it is actually a subversive gag about televisual formalism. After the society discovers that they have been "wasting their time" on a useless project for years, they try to leave their banquet, only to realize they were on film when outdoors, but on video indoors. The sketch's characters are literally trapped by the BBC's internal televisual logic. (The BBC insisted that shooting on film was useful for outdoor shots as it looked "more realistic," but that videotape was more effective—and cheaper, especially when you could erase the tapes and use them over again later—for interior shots.)

The society members plan to tunnel under the building (and therefore below the film), presumably into another building where they will again be on video. The sketch then shifts to a full parody of a World War II POW film, complete with men assigned to various tasks to lull the Nazis into not noticing their escape efforts. Two stereotypical Nazi officers wonder, "Where's the traditional cheeky and lovable Cockney sergeant?," who then appears in all of his lovable Cockney glory to reassure them that the conventions of genre are being observed. They finally sneak away, only to end up in a Gilliam animation, which leads to more cutout buffoonery (various headless figures, the hand of God, and such).

Idle arrives at a friend's mansion where the house begins to crumble around him, while the servants basically blame him for the carnage. First a mirror falls off a wall, followed by a bookshelf. Cleveland as a maid comes in and asks him to hold a ceremonial Brazilian dagger, which of course she then falls on and is killed. Jones next comes in as a handyman, but falls out a window accidentally; Palin as a copper comes in and promptly has a heart attack and dies. Chapman, as the butler, has the ceiling fall on him.

As Idle flees, the rest of the house collapses around him, and then blows up. People come walking through the rubble, including the bishop from last episode still practicing his lines outside. The Society for Putting Things on Top of Other Things now arrives at a rather bad school performance of *Seven Brides for Seven Brothers* done by schoolkids with Chapman as a strict headmaster disappointed that only three out of seven brothers come out when he calls, and worse still, only two girls come out as the seven brides. Nonetheless the show must go on and the padre marries the five of them to a few desultory claps.

We then cut to Gilliam animation of two large military figures who want to hunt "piggy banks," then to a Gilliam animation of piggy banks trying to escape hammers, but they are caught and cracked open to find they are filled with sirloin steaks and that what we thought were the contents of the piggy banks are actually a meat chart in a butcher's shop.

Following that, we are ever so gently deposited inside a decently funny shop sketch that's more along the lines of a *Do Not Adjust Your Set* sketch than Python. We return to Cleese, who is still at the Grill-O-Mat. The last item "on the menu" is a training boxer (Cleese) so dedicated and so incredibly stupid that he needs to be woken up by a steel peg driven into his skull.

Meanwhile, back at the Grill-O-Mat, Cleese is leaving on the top of a double-decker bus, and not at all sure if he will be back as his parts were "not well received." He sadly rides the bus home over the closing credits, finally asking plaintively that they just show "the end."

A final note: this episode starred all three of Python's primary glamour stooges, Cleveland, Connie Booth, *and* Lyn Ashley (aka Mrs. Idle, Eric's then-wife).

Episode 19: "It's a Living (or: School Prizes)" (original air date: November 3, 1970)

For this episode, Cleese's announcer announces from behind a desk in a blacksmith's shop that he is unable to say "and now" because he cannot appear in the show this week. Despite the fact that he just did. General chaos ensues. Jones, as a man whose tooth hurts, interrupts and is chastised for it. At a school awards ceremony, a bishop (Palin) is assaulted by another bishop (Idle), who insists the first one was an imposter. Then, the second bishop is himself attacked and replaced, this time by a man in a Mao jacket (Chapman, identified in the script as "Chinaman" and delivering his lines in a Chinese accent that was offensive even in 1970) seizing the prizes for the

People's Republic of China, who is himself (it just goes *on*, don't it?!) taken down by a detective (Jones), who is himself shot as suddenly soldiers enter the room and a firefight erupts.

After the school-set combat scene, complete with students being shot, we cut to a talk show where the host (Chapman) is talking to indie film director Mr. Dibley (Jones), who made the segment just concluded. The thing about Dibley is, like many guests on *Flying Circus*'s ersatz interviews, he's a near or complete imposter. As it turns out, Dibley is a serial maker of cheap imitations, from the *If . . .* knock-off we just witnessed to a silent version of *Rear Window* that consists solely of just a man looking out a window, and a take on *Finian's Rainbow* "starring the man from the off-license."

Following a string of bits involving people getting tossed into the river, next up is a fancy dinner party, interrupted by a deliveryman (Cleese) with the latest dung delivery from the book of the month club: "with every third book you get dung." Following the *Flying Circus* habit of escalating madness, another deliveryman (Chapman) arrives with a free dead Indian ("as advertised") who is not *quite* dead, a precursor to a certain sketch from *Monty Python and the Holy Grail*.

The concluding sketch centers on Timmy Williams (Idle), a particularly vicious caricature of David Frost. The shallow and narcissistic Williams prattles on about how "lovely" and "super" everything is, ignoring the plaintive entreaties of the desperately miserable Nigel (Jones) who ultimately shoots himself, after which Williams wonders whether he still came off as human.

Though he only appeared twice, one of the great Python minor characters was Raymond Luxury Yacht (Chapman). He pops up in this episode as a (another) talk show guest, informing the host (Palin) that his name is only *spelled* Raymond Luxury Yacht, but is in fact pronounced "Throat-Wobbler Mangrove." The host immediately loses patience and tells him that "you're a very silly man and I'm not going to interview you." Raymond complains that he simply "wants to be on television" ("Well, you can't," the host responds). His disappointment is palpable. If only he could have waited for reality television!

One of this episode's few negatives is Gilliam essentially reusing an animated sequence from the previous episode with a large bikini-clad woman bouncing men off her stomach. But it's nevertheless one of Season Two's most solid episodes.

This is evidenced most strongly in the final sketch: "Election Night Special." Later immortalized on the *Monty Python Live at Drury Lane* album, the sketch spoofs the kind of American-style hyperventilating TV political coverage then becoming more common in the United Kingdom. Cleese's linkman is coordinating the coverage of an election showdown between the Sensible Party and the Silly Party. Things start off in a basic dichotomy between the Sensible candidate (Alan Jones) and the Silly candidate (Tarquin Fin-ti-lin-bin-whin-bim-lin-bus-stop-F'Tang-F'Tang-Ole-Biscuit-barrel) before diving into schismatic complication with the introduction of candidates from the Slightly Silly (Kevin Phillips-Bong) and Very Silly (Malcolm Peter Brian Telescope Adrian Umbrella Stand Jasper Wednesday . . . [No room for it all here, paper isn't free.—Eds.]) parties. The Silly Party takes Leicester, with the frantic announcers gabbling on at a frenetic pace, even when they have no new information (sound familiar?). The credits roll over last results. Considering the state of American politics today it is clear that the Pythons knew more about the future state of politics than most modern pundits.

Episode 20: "The Attila the Hun Show" (original air date: November 10, 1970)

"The Attila the Hun Show" starts out as a supposedly straight historical re-creation of the life of Attila the Hun. But things soon devolve into a sitcom version wherein Attila the Hun and family are living in a suburban home and getting involved in all manner of punch line–ready shenanigans, complete with an over-the-top laugh track. A typical intentional groaner is when Cleese as Attila gives his children severed human heads as he wants them to "get a-head" in life. Hah!

This episode is another example of how Monty Python employed television conventions to point out how restricted and conventional most programming was in the 1960s. The parody goes on to include (obviously) Attila the nun, before we end up watching Carol Cleveland in all her glory being seen to by a doctor, and several shabbily clad men who are "students" there to examine her. This naturally shifts again, leading us to a strip club, where the Secretary of State for Commonwealth Affairs (Jones) states the government's position on agricultural subsidies, all the while stripping.

Sheep, a favorite Python topic, reoccur in this episode, first infesting a family's house and then later turning out to be both hyperintelligent and deadly. In fact, they have infected other animals, who are now also intelligent and in need of their own news programs. That development sprawls into another Python surreality torrent, including news for parrots, news for gibbons, and eventually news for wombats, including a brief mention of those "yummy eucalyptus leaves, yum yum." Humans get their due, as the Pythons dip back into scatological humor including a Parliament session that involves bestiality and cries from the back benchers, including "postcards for sale" and "hello, sailor!" (Fun fact: The latter is also the title of Idle's first novel, published five years later.)

Python was keen on the traditions of rural England, and this came through in a sketch about the village idiot, which is an apparently time-honored tradition that involves rigorous training and education. The sketch even has a punch line, in which a village idiot (Idle), after being revealed to be in bed with two young nubile women, cracks, "I may be an idiot, but I'm not a fool!" Luckily, the sketch demonstrates that this was actually not the punch line at all, just a transition as the scene then switches to the city where other idiots, mostly Upper Class Twit of the Year contenders, are revealed. Lastly, Python parodies a game show in which Mrs. Scum (Jones, who reprised the role in the "Mr. Neutron" episode of Season Four) proves particularly inept at answering the simplest questions, but nonetheless receives the coveted prize of "a blow on the head."

While "The Attila the Hun Show" gets a lot of laughs out of its mockery of TV conventions, the whole thing is a bit scattershot for the Pythons.

Episode 21: "Archaeology Today" (original air date: November 17, 1970)

At this point, the BBC was getting increasingly upset about *Flying Circus* keeping on with their parody using the BBC logo, followed by "today on the BBC" announcements. This, of course, made Python only too willing to continue using the BBC logo whenever they could, as in this episode.

Also here: the other Pythons finally noticed how tall Cleese was. In a supposed "sport" program *Archaeology Today*, the interviewer (Palin) makes the interview with two noted archaeologists all about Sir Robert's (Cleese) height, to the detriment of Professor Kastner (Jones), who somehow is deluded enough to think they might actually start talking about real archaeology, instead of the height of the two men. Sir Robert eventually takes offense at the interviewer's humiliation of Kastner and slugs him, leading the interviewer to vow revenge. Then we shift genres to a Western-influenced title sequence and a title card that informs us that the scene is now taking place in "Egypt 1920," whereupon things turn into an awkward six-person battle royale of combatants standing on one another's shoulders. Naturally, they all end up dead.

A lengthy sketch that seems designed as a challenge to the BBC standards (and a precursor to *Life of Brian*'s "Biggus Dickus" and his wife "Incontenentia Buttocks") involves a family named the "Gits" who have surnames such as "Dreary Fat Boring Old" and "Sniveling Little Rat Faced."

After a few minor skits, including one on mosquito hunting, the two camp judges (Idle and Palin) appear. Another classic example of Python's antiauthoritarian bent, this sketch mocks and undermines the stoic, butch image of British governance. The sketch has stood the test of time and was frequently redone on stage, including the 2014 reunion shows. After some lively business with Cleese as a very Germanic Beethoven, the show ends with a reappearance of the camp judges in a coda, usually skipped when performed live.

Episode 22: "How to Recognise Different Parts of the Body" (original air date: November 24, 1970)

"How to Recognise" would have been a wonderful episode even if it only contained "The Bruces." But it also had a very short audio piece that serves as an exploration of the limits of various mediums: a radio play about the "Death of Mary, Queen of Scots." As this is Python, instead of the polished BBC radio drama that one might have expected, we hear minimal dialogue ("Are you Mary, Queen of Scots?" "I am") before Mary is brutally beaten, shot at, exploded, and whatever else one's imagination can supply in the way of off-screen gruesome deaths. After a minute of implied audio gruesomeness, a voice announces, "I think she's dead," followed by Mary's rejoinder, "No, I'm not." Then we're off to the races again.

Another classic and one often performed live was "The Bruces," a tightly written bit by Cleese and Idle, which exemplifies their love of wordplay and contrast. The Bruces sound like stereotypical Australian rednecks at first. Then we discover that they're all the members of the philosophy department of the Australian University of Woolamaloo (hear, hear!), and want to rename their newest faculty member Michael Baldwin (Jones) Bruce, just to keep things clear. Their division of labor is clear: "Bruce here teaches classical philosophy, Bruce there teaches Hegelian philosophy, and Bruce here teaches logical positivism, and is also in charge of the sheep dip." As for the faculty rules, these involve basically four distinct admonitions against homosexuality ("No Pooftas!") as well as a rule about drinking after hours, not mistreating the "abos" (aboriginal peoples of Australia), and the mysterious rule six, which is simply "there is no . . . rule six!" "The Bruces" sketch is one Python sketch that actually works better live than on television, as live it is concluded by the "The Philosophers' Song."

In this episode, Raymond Luxury-Yacht/Throat-Wobbler Mangrove reappears, visiting a very credentialed doctor (Cleese) who, despite Raymond's desire for a nose job, points out that Raymond's nose is in fact a false nose and that his real nose "is a beaut." Despite that, Raymond still wants the surgery, which the doctor agrees to "only if you go on a camping holiday with me!" As they happily frolic hand in hand in the woods, the next sketch reveals that the British army is just as camp as they "camp it up!" with precision.

The episode is full of great bits, including a pair of Pepperpots watching as the penguin on top of their television explodes. Throw in a Eurovision Song Contest parody where Inspector Zatapathique sings "bing tiddle tiddle bong!" and this ranks as one of the best episodes of Season Two.

Episode 23: "Scott of the Antarctic" (original air date: December 1, 1970)

This episode starts with the Pythons parodying French New Wave cinema in a short film where a man (Brian Distel) and a woman (Brianette Zatapathique) talk in listless laconic French, featuring dialogue such as *"Je vois que vous avez un chou"* (not only does he observe that she "has a cabbage" but refers to her in the formal *vous* instead of the less formal *tu*, indicating of course the existential despair of life). They reappear in a second short film where the cabbage explodes, killing them both. The presenter (Idle) intones, "pretty strong meat from Longeur" (the director), a phrase the Pythons reuse for the "Sam Peckinpah's Salad Days" sketch in Season Three.

There were quite a few British epic films in the 1960s, but most were (almost by definition) filmed on location outside of Britain. However, for the *Flying Circus* mock epic sketch that opens this episode, *Scott of the Antarctic*, the lads at Twentieth Century Vole decided that it would be fine to film on the beach at Paignton, the "queen of the English Riviera," despite the utter lack of, well, snow. Their solution? Paint the sand white and tack up incredibly unrealistic fake snow around the area. One problem with the film is that Scott (Palin) and his love interest Evans (Cleveland) are badly matched in terms of height, and also that Evans is uncomfortable reading her lines in a trench, which she has been placed in to make the leading man look taller.

A larger problem is that the director, McRettin (Cleese), doesn't appear to have a clue. Though he can confidently report that the film is "basically pro-humanity and anti-bad things."

Another issue with *Scott of the Antarctic* is that Scott wants to fight a lion, leading to the film being retitled *Scott of the Sahara*, in which Palin fights a ludicrously fake lion, intercut with shots of a real lion. Later, Ensign Oates (Jones) fights a giant tentacle-clad robot penguin and Miss Evans is pursued by a "man-eating roll-top writing desk" which chases her until her clothing is torn off by three strategically placed cacti.

As she runs out of frame, she passes Cleese as the announcer, who intones, "And now for something completely different," leading to the It's Man and finally, twenty very odd minutes in, the opening credits, a typical Pythonesque confusion of linear order. The episode has only two more sketches, the great fish license bit that manages one of the troupe's best Marcel Proust references and appeared on *Monty Python's Previous Record*. Also: increasingly ludicrous soccer matches (including gynecologists vs. immobile Long John Silver impersonators) and an unctuous presenter (Palin) who is crushed by a sixteen-ton weight. As in the French film, the closing credits roll over scenes of destruction and explosions.

Episode 24: "How Not to Be Seen" (original air date: December 8, 1970)

If ever there was a *Flying Circus* episode that could be safely skipped, "How Not to Be Seen" is pretty much it. The jokes are solid and the acting first-rate, but the episode seems more like a collection of B-sides or bottom-drawer leavings than the usual A-grade Python material.

There's an Agatha Christie sketch about a train schedule being the main impetus for a murder. Another sketch about a religion that openly admits it's there just for the cash descends into a maelstrom of intertextuality. Familiar faces dominate and a procession of different, but familiar bishops evokes old Python characters—talk about speed, the series is just over a year old and already *Flying Circus* is circling back in a self-referential spiral—including "Bishop Nudge ("Peace? I like a peace. Know what I mean, know what I mean?"), Bishop Bruce the Australian, Bishop Shabby (Palin reprising his all-out disgust totem Ken Shabby from Episode 12), Bishop Gumby ("I believe in peace and bashing two bricks together"), and even Bishop Lennon (Idle), who intones, "I'm starting a war for peace" as a precursor of Idle's post-Python Beatles project the Rutles.

The titular piece, "How Not to Be Seen" (reprised in *And Now for Something Completely Different*), works better as a sketch . . . although it also seems as though the Pythons just liked to blow things up. The animating principle here is that if you are seen, you will be blown to pieces, so hiding is one's best bet. In the end, things blow up real good, as they would say on *SCTV*.

The best part of the episode comes after the closing credits, where a voice intones, "In case you missed *Monty Python's Flying Circus*, here it is again," after which the show is shown in fast-forward in about twenty seconds. It's not a bad episode, but for this one, the fast-forward might be warranted.

Episode 25: "Spam" (original air date: December 15, 1970)

If "How Not to Be Seen" was a mere blip on the Python radar, "Spam" stands out as a high point of their entire oeuvre. [Lay off the French, we said.—Eds.]

Things begin on a high note with one of the Pythons' singular achievements: "Dirty Hungarian Phrasebook." Bewildered immigrants navigate London using a phrasebook that seems deliberately designed to cause trouble. They meet confusion and bafflement when trying to navigate the streets or buy cigarettes by saying, "My nipples explode with delight!" or "My hovercraft is full of eels." The man behind the fake phrasebooks, Alexander Yahlt (Palin), is arrested and hauled off to court, whereupon the trial is interrupted by the stock footage of old women applauding, leading the judge to angrily announce that he will clear the court "if there's any more stock footage of women applauding." The trial continues to be a meta-commentary on the media, as a Page 3 girl cutout is called in as a witness, leading to leering depictions of most of the characters until we exit on a Gilliam animation of a judge at an airport.

"World Forum" is next, another classic that could have held an entire episode together. The brilliant premise situates Karl Marx, Lenin, Che Guevara, and Mao Tse-Tung on a TV quiz show where the host (Idle) peppers them with questions about British football. Marx (Jones) somehow makes it to the final round, where to win a beautiful lounge suite he must answer questions on "workers' control of factories," which is, admittedly, a little more up his alley. He does very well on questions about class struggle and the development of the urban bourgeoisie, but is stumped by the final question, "Who won the English football cup final in 1949?" (The Answer? Wolverhampton beat Leicester 3–1.)

A sketch involving soldiers at the battle of Ypres drawing straws to see who will kill themselves rather than use up scarce rations ends with Cleese as an armless padre giving a long, evocative speech, before being brought via ambulance to a hospital for patients suffering from "severe overacting," which then feeds into a Gilliam animation of various Hamlets.

Another classic Python bit ends the episode. A Mr. Bun (Idle) and Mrs. Bun (Chapman, doing one of his best, screechiest female characters) are lowered by wires into a restaurant full of Vikings that only serves dishes with a high proportion of Spam (playing off the ubiquity of the canned meat product, which the United States sent by the shipload in relief packages, to postwar England). While the proprietor (Jones) rattles off the specials, like "Spam, bacon, sausage, and Spam" and "Spam, Spam, Spam, Spam, Spam, Spam, baked beans, Spam, Spam, Spam." (Of course, as the beans "are off," thankfully, Spam can be substituted instead.) Alas, Mrs. Bun does not care for Spam, even the special of the day: "Lobster Thermidor au Crevette with a Mornay sauce served in a Provençale manner with shallots and aubergines garnished with truffle pâte, brandy, and with a fried egg on top and Spam." Meanwhile, as the ordering negotiation continues, the table of Vikings (amazing how much some resemble the Fred Tomlinson

What's All This, Then?
Words, Bloody Words

On *Flying Circus*, there was often more below the hood than most people could get even upon repeat viewings. Even the "Dirty Hungarian Phrasebook" sketch has a lengthy backstory. In 1883, Pedro Carolino published a guide to the English language most commonly referred to as *English as She Is Spoke*. The book, which tried with all of its might to be a conventional Portuguese to English phrasebook, ended up a bewildering but hilarious compendium of malapropisms and absurd mistranslations. A typical example is "the walls have hearsay" instead of the correct (but much more boring) "the walls have ears." Mark Twain wrote in an introduction to a reissue (this time acknowledging its comedic prowess), "Nobody can add to the absurdity of this book . . . it is perfect." While not quite as witty as "my hovercraft is full of eels," it is clear that as long as phrasebooks are made, mistranslation is possible and sometimes even lovely.

Singers!) keep bursting out into glorious choral renditions of "Lovely Spam! Wonderful Spam!"

A stray Hungarian comes in and, thanks to his phrasebook, says, "Great boobies, honeybun. My lower intestine is full of Spam, egg, Spam, bacon, Spam, tomato, Spam" before being rushed off by a police officer. A historian tries to explain the "great Viking victory at the Green Midget Café in Bromley," but at that the backdrop disappears and we return to the café where the Vikings are conducted in their "Spam chant" by the historian. The closing credits include actors such as "Graham Spam Spam Spam Chapman" and "The Fred Tomlinson Spam Egg Chips and Singers."

Spam returned as a throwaway line in *Holy Grail*, and of course as the title of the Python musical *Spamalot*.

Episode 26: "Royal Episode 13 (or: The Queen Will Be Watching)" (original air date: December 22, 1970)

Season Two's final episode is predicated on the possibility that the Queen might be watching *Flying Circus* and thus the troupe needs to be prepared. The announcer (Cleese) can barely contain himself as he breathlessly intones that viewers at home should stand when the Queen switches over (she's currently watching *The Virginian*).

The newly redone "regal opening titles" caption indicates that the "first spoof" takes place in a "coal mine in Llanddarog Carmarthen." There, Welsh miners are furiously arguing about the "Treaty of Utrecht" as well as the "name of the section between the triglyphs of the frieze section of a classic Doric entablature." A "management man" (Cleese, of course) arrives, but has "no idea" and the miners walk out.

When the Queen finally changes her channel to the "royal episode," it is in the middle of an insurance sketch where a man has brought in twelve gallons of "wee" to show he is serious about wanting life insurance. The sketch is interrupted by "God Save the Queen" playing in the background while the Pythons stand at attention. A voice-over intones that the Queen has just tuned in and that one of the actors is "about to deliver the first great royal joke here this royal evening." Then they are informed that the Queen has now switched channels and is watching *News at Ten*. The scene immediately switches to the real *News at Ten* set where anchorman Reginald Bosanquet hears the national anthem and stands in the middle of reading the news.

The episode also features a clever Gilliam animation for "Crelm toothpaste" and a reappearance of Spiny Norman (the source of nightmares for Dinsdale Piranha in the season's first episode). A commentary on the British health system shows patients engaged in ART (Active Recuperation Techniques, of course), which include building the doctors a holiday home and wheeling them around in wheelchairs. Unsure of how to get out of this sketch, the scene cuts to St. Michael's Hospital for Linkmen, where a doctor (Cleese) explains that at the hospital they "try to help people who have to link sketches together."

After some shorter sketches, Python pushes the envelope further. After a sketch about cannibalism in a lifeboat and some more grotesque Gilliam animation on cannibalism, they up the ante even more in a sketch where a man (Cleese) brings his recently deceased mother to an undertaker (Chapman). After dismissing cremation and burial, the undertaker recommends eating her "roasted with a few French fries, broccoli, horseradish" and that if the son feels guilty about it, "we can dig a grave and you can throw up in it." After this, "the audience" rushes the stage to end the sketch.

This was done to appease the BBC, who had apparently by this point actually started to watch *Flying Circus* and were duly horrified. The network would only allow the sketch on air if there was audience outrage at the end. As the credits roll, the national anthem resumes as the Queen has apparently tuned in again and the show fades out with the cast standing at attention. A royal exit for Season Two.

9

The First Rip-Offs

And Now for Something Completely Different and Fliegender Zirkus

What Else to Do?

Monty Python's Flying Circus wasn't a hit right out of the gate. But by the end of the first season in January 1970, it was clear that there was something going on with this whacked-out collection of sketches, non sequiturs, cutout animation, and screeching Pepperpots. The question was, though, where to go next? Within about a year of Season One's conclusion, the Pythons forayed into just about every other medium there was at the time.

Some took more time than others.

Except for Gilliam, the Pythons were all veteran performers even before they began the show. But still, taking what worked on Flying Circus, which had film and animation clips and editing to move things along, and adapting it to live theater was hardly a surefire thing. It would pay off handsomely for the Pythons later, but they didn't attempt a live performance with Flying Circus material until doing three midnight shows in Coventry in early 1971.

Likewise, simply putting Python words and the occasional still image on a page was no guarantee of success. Their first foray into publishing, Monty Python's Big Red Book, didn't come out until November 1971, in the interregnum between Seasons Two and Three.

Other offshoots, like their album with the multiple grooves or the fourth wall–busting elements of Monty Python and the Holy Grail, came later. Immediately after Season One, the easiest thing to do was just take what they had done on the TV show, replace the video element with sound effects, and put out a record. That is what they did, with relative speed: Monty Python's Flying Circus, an LP of material culled from the show and recorded before a live audience in May 1970. It was released that fall.

Even though it was familiar stuff to British audiences, *And Now for Something Completely Different* was the first chance Americans had to experience Monty Python.

The next most obvious step was motion pictures. This was something easier said than done, of course. There is a long list of British comedy legends who had transitioned easily from radio to television but were stuck at the moat separating those genres from film; for every success like Dudley Moore or Peter Sellers, there was a Spike Milligan or Peter Cook. But theoretically, moving from television to film should have been a relatively easy thing: both are highly similar sound-and-vision mediums; one is just generally longer than the other.

On the film front, things moved with relative speed. The last episode of the *Flying Circus*'s first season was broadcast on January 4, 1970. Already by January 14, Palin was recording in his diary that one Victor Lownes, who ran the Playboy Club in London, was back in Chicago trying to sell Hugh Hefner on the idea of a Monty Python film.

Let's Make a Movie!

One might imagine that the appeal of *Flying Circus* to the Playboy business empire would have had something to do with the show's sex-positive vibe and generous usage of the buxom blond self-described "glamour stooge" Carol Cleveland. But even though Cleveland had worked at the London Playboy Club for a few months in 1966, Lownes's interest in the show was more straightforward: he thought it was funny. Originally, in fact, Lownes had tried to purchase American broadcast rights to *Flying Circus*. But American networks were reluctant to take a shot on something so British, so odd, and as yet so far from a big hit even on its home turf.

So Lownes rang up Cleese, who was the most recognized Python and the one most people assumed was in charge (that looming height and in-character bossy bearing!), and had him to the Playboy Club for lunch. Lownes's proposal was simple: *Flying Circus* wasn't meant for the American mainstream. But there were a couple thousand college movie theaters that might be interested in a kind of greatest-hits package of the first season's material, reshot on film.

Compared to the more tortured preproduction issues of later Python films, *And Now for Something Completely Different* came together with relative ease.

A small budget of about £100,000 was quickly secured. Cleese put together a selection of sketches to film, a decision that irked some of the other Pythons, who grumbled that they would have chosen different sketches to present as their showreel to the youth of America. The general

John Cleese contemplates the dangers of a banana in *And Now for Something Completely Different*.
Columbia Pictures/Photofest

sense of unease with which most of the Pythons speak about the film now likely has something to do with not just that idea—Palin has said that he would have liked to have shot new material instead of just reusing existing material—but the fact that this was primarily Cleese's deal, instead of something that the group came up with on their own.

As was usual in the Pythons' early, hyper-productive years, after agreeing to the film deal, work proceeded on multiple projects simultaneously. They filmed and recorded Season Two of *Flying Circus* from May through October 1970. At the end of October, only about a week and a half after finishing work on the show, the Pythons reassembled at a dank old milk depot on London's north side to start production on *And Now for Something Completely Different*.

Things didn't proceed without hiccups. But the Pythons were pleasantly surprised by all the accoutrements of shooting a movie instead of a TV show: crew to look after them, drivers, the opportunity to shoot on luxurious

35mm instead of 16mm. Ah, the heady world of Playboy-sponsored milk depot Hollywood.

Five weeks later the Pythons had finished shooting their first movie. Success in the all-important American market was sure to follow!

And Now for Something . . . Kind of the Same

There are a few reasons that when fans speak of Monty Python films, *And Now for Something Completely Different* is usually mentioned last, if at all.

The first is that it was directed by *Flying Circus* director Ian MacNaughton, whom Palin referred to affectionately as "a bit of a wild Scotsman." MacNaughton's experience assembling Python bits and pieces into half-hour television episodes didn't translate to the demands of feature filmmaking. It also didn't help that MacNaughton had cranked his alcohol intake up to eleven during filming. So had Chapman at this time, but an ensemble can carry an underperforming member through the rough patches easier than they can function under an increasingly besotted director. MacNaughton's firm, if sometimes chaotic, grip on the directorial reins caused further friction at a time when both Gilliam *and* Jones wanted to be more involved in the editing booth and behind the camera.

But most crucial to the film's inability to hold up as more than a curiosity these days is the simple fact that it's a generally style-free revue that doesn't add anything to the television presentation and sometimes actually detracts from it. The film's name comes from Cleese's recurring BBC announcer bit. That useful interstitial flicker helped more than a few *Flying Circus* episodes from one sketch to another without having to bring on so and so of the Yard to arrest everybody for being silly. Here it serves as the closest thing to a spine that the film has. It also offers the sight of Cleese in a pink bikini. So, yay?

And Now for Something Completely Different opens with a literal bang, the "How Not to Be Seen" sketch, in which the announcer (Cleese, cheerfully sadistic as ever) intones quietly about how well the film subjects are hiding themselves behind trees or bushes. When he asks them to step out of hiding, twice in a row, they are instantly shot. The third one refuses to show themselves; the announcer solves the problem by detonating a bomb in their hiding place and describing his actions in a blithe, tut-tutting voice. (Even though the film was planned as a greatest-hits show, this sketch and a few others weren't actually broadcast until Season Two.)

The second piece up is "Man with a Tape Recorder Up His Nose" from Season One, Episode 9. Never a top-line sketch, this plinky bit is an odd transition here, and leads in poorly to the downbeat "Dirty Hungarian Phrasebook" that would appear in Season Two, Episode 25.

Things don't pick up until "Hell's Grannies," the gleefully silly upending of finger-wagging television documentaries about juvenile (here senile) delinquents: "Theirs . . . is a harsh existence." A little over halfway through, the Pythons spike the ball with a couple of pieces—the "Dead Parrot" and the "Lumberjack Song,"—that they likely knew even then were going to be among their greatest hits. Unfortunately, the momentum quickly flags with a tiresome sketch like "The Dirty Fork" and doesn't pick up again until a series of classics like "Blackmail," "The Battle of Pearl Harbor," and "Upper Class Twit of the Year" finish things off.

What's happening with old people today? It's like they have no respect for the young! "Hell's Grannies" tear it up in *And Now for Something Completely Different*.   *Columbia Pictures/Photofest*

It's perhaps not fair today to write off *And Now for Something Completely Different*. At the time, there was simply no other way for people outside the United Kingdom to see anything of *Flying Circus*. Even within the United Kingdom, the impermanence of the show itself (no VCRs, very few repeat broadcasts, and a network that nearly erased the tapes) meant that access to the material was highly limited. In other words, if it was 1971, odds were your only chance to see a pocket-sized classic like "People Falling Out of Buildings" (almost exactly what it sounds like) was this film.

But even though a few pieces stand out, like "The Funniest Joke in the World," the format distances the audience from this television-crafted material. Padded with multiple Gilliam animations when half as many would have sufficed, the film suffers from a slower pace and more traditional structure than *Flying Circus*. Whereas the show kept things antic and Dadaist, continually subverting its own gags and storylines, the film clunks along in linear fashion from one bit to the next.

From a production standpoint, the dank surroundings at the milk depot made for a dreary palette. MacNaughton's ostentatious camera is always shooting from attention-grabbing skewed angles or indulging in long and slow pans, further distancing the film from the material at hand. The lack of a studio audience's laughter adds to the tepid energy. These sketches were designed to play off a live audience. Jones and Idle do a perfectly fine "Nudge Nudge" in *And Now for Something Completely Different*. But it doesn't compare for a second to the one they do in *Live at the Hollywood Bowl*. Why? For one, the live version doesn't have all those extras mucking up the mise-en-scène [Nix the film-school bosh.—Eds.]. Also, the people hooting and howling in response encourage the viewer to howl along as well; Python, as a burgeoning cult, practically demanded communal appreciation.

What Happened Then

On-set conveniences aside, the Pythons had little good to say about the finished product. Some liked having the chance to have another shot at some of their sketches, but also wished that they had written some original material. Jones told David Morgan that he thought the sets "a bit tacky" and that the film itself wasn't any improvement on the series.

And Now for Something Completely Different was cut into several different edits, the troupe looking for the best possible shuffling of material. But no matter how many things the Pythons shifted about, test screenings went the same. Inevitably, the audience would laugh for about fifty minutes. Then silence. Then a little more laughter at the end. Cleese said in *The Pythons* that no matter how they reedited the film, people would go quiet about halfway because it was just sketch, cartoon, sketch, and no story: "comedy"—as Steve Martin used to say—"is not pretty," but comedy fatigue is deadly.

Nevertheless, *And Now for Something Completely Different* served as a useful training ground, and it might not have been worth wast-ing good material on. Given that

What's All This, Then?
Dead Parrots Equals Dollars

According to Darl Larsen's encyclo-pedic *A Book about the Film* Monty Python and the Holy Grail, *And Now for Something Completely Different* had something of a second life after its truncated initial feature release. Larsen notes that the film was being used as a fundraiser for American high schools in 1976 and 1977. One must wonder how the PTA reacted to the "Battle of Pearl Harbor" or "Dirty Hungarian Phrasebook" sketches.

comedy troupe films are a notoriously tricky business (just ask the Upright Citizens Brigade or the Kids in the Hall), the Pythons were unlikely to suc-ceed their first time out, particularly with Lownes controlling the format.

So maybe it was better that they learned all their lessons on a quickie rehash of their *Flying Circus* material. In the more traditionally narrative-based films that followed, not only did they keep directing duties in house with one or both Terrys, but they made sure to have a story that would keep the audience engaged. Nobody was going to nod off halfway through *Monty Python and the Holy Grail.*

The American fate of *And Now for Something Completely Different* was prob-ably sealed from the moment after the film's distributor, Columbia Pictures, informed the Pythons that nobody understood "Upper Class Twit of the Year" and the Pythons refused to take it out. Unsure of what to do with this violent, surreal, and occasionally scatological anthology film from comics nobody had heard of, Columbia sat on it. Apparently, nobody ever passed along the memo from Lownes to open it wide on college campuses.

Meanwhile, the Pythons moved on.

Nine months after wrapping, *And Now for Something Completely Different* finally had its London premiere in September 1971. Ironically, even though the film wasn't even designed for the United Kingdom market and was mocked there for being a crass redo with a title that suggested new material, it ended up a decent success.

What's All This, Then?

Not So Wealthy, After All

The Pythons were initially assured that they'd be raking in great profits on *And Now for Something Completely Different*. The reality was different. In September 1972, after the film had been out for several months, the Pythons were told that in fact so far they were only netting about £1,000 each. Palin wrote in his diary later that this revelation had an "incredible" effect: suddenly everybody wanted to work.

In August 1972, Columbia finally threw *And Now for Something Completely Different* onto a few American screens. With an unknown cast pushing a wildly eccentric British style of humor and confused advertising (the poster made it look like a kids' film), it didn't have much of a chance.

Reviews ranged from enthusiastic—Roger Ebert approvingly noted its similarity to *The Goon Show*, while the *New Yorker* called it "battily funny"—to the flummoxed—the *New York Times* said "compared to this, *The Beverley Hillbillies* seems downright Shakespearean." Interestingly, *New York* magazine, noting that the show was a cult hit in England, thought that "the film might start something similar here."

Writer Hendrik Hertzberg, who became fast friends with the Pythons on the trips to New York, related in the May 12, 1975 *New Yorker* this possibly apocryphal reaction:

> [*Monty Python's Flying Circus* is so funny] it once caused a man in a theater watching "And Now for Something Completely Different" . . . to catapult himself out of his seat and over the armrest, and to roll head over heels clear down to the front of the theater, pounding the floor with his fists all the way.

Unfortunately, that wasn't a common reaction from American audiences, which generally had little idea the film was playing and strenuously ignored it when they did.

Nancy Lewis sent a copy of the film to various radio stations to promote the Pythons in general. But as a commercial matter, the film was a disaster, possibly not even earning back its advertising budget.

Python Goes to Germany

And Now for Something Completely Different failed in its mission to establish a Python beachhead in America. Meanwhile, in Germany, sinister forces were at wor . . . apologies. Wrong script. Meanwhile, as *Flying Circus* began to gain a following in the United Kingdom, the show was garnering attention on the Continent. In April 1971, the show was the BBC entry at the prestigious Montreux Television Festival and it played beautifully, taking home the Silver Rose. This attracted the attention of certain Germans concerned that their country had a humor deficit. But knowing their countrymen's affection for most things British at the time, they saw an opportunity.

German television producer Alfred Biôlek reached out to the Pythons in early 1971. This was the right time because, as Palin explained to BBC Radio 4 in 2011, the Pythons were at the height of their conjoined productivity. They were working on *Flying Circus*, albums, books, "anything that came along, really." It didn't take much for Biôlek to talk them intro traveling to Deutschland and filming some funny stuff for a country legendary in Britain for how unfunny it was. The two forty-five-minute shows were to be (creatively) called *Fliegender Zirkus!*

It remains unclear why exactly the Pythons agreed to write in English but shoot in German (Palin has claimed the first he heard of it was when they were in Germany and he was handed a script). Cleese, of course, had a smattering of German under his belt, but the rest of the troupe were in Deutsch, as it were. This proved tricky in certain scenarios—there did not, for example, appear to be any German equivalent for "scare the shit out of you."

But language problems were overcome by the warm friendship that sprouted between Biôlek and the Pythons, not to mention the endless steins of pilsner at night. Most of the Pythons speak glowingly of the production, as though being away from Television Centre lent an air of vacation to the usual workaday grind. The troupe spent July 1971 shooting in Munich and the Bavarian mountains, including the glorious Nymphenburg Palace. They returned the following year for another three-week production; this time the dialogue was in English and dubbed into German.

The first episode, broadcast on January 3, 1972, is first-rate Python, particularly noteworthy for how little-seen it is. Sharp and hilarious, layered with that extra frisson of the Pythons' varied attempts at German pronunciation, the episodes operate as essentially bonus-size *Flying Circus* episodes with a Teutonic slant to the cultural references. In case you were wondering, however, there is NO mention of World War II in *Fliegender Zirkus*. None.

The first episode begins with German newsreader Claudia Doren, a stunning Bavarian scene behind her, introducing the audience to these English comics they're about to witness. Two men in scuba gear clamber out of the water and drag Doren away in a manner that's as funny as it is slightly menacing.

Like some of the better *Flying Circus* episodes, the first *Fliegender Zirkus* has a theme. In this case, it's a seemingly straight television documentary on Albrecht Dürer that keeps getting interrupted by everything from cows performing Shakespeare, to a certain lumberjack experiencing a sexual identity crisis in song, until we witness a tangled sketch that references a Frenchman who hasn't gone to the bathroom for five years while throwing in clips of Richard Nixon, Moshe Dayan, and West Germany's then chancellor Willy Brandt. Cleese, who along with Idle seems the most comfortable mouth-gargling German, appears to apologize for the inaccuracies: "Dürer *never* operated a car hire service."

The second *Fliegender Zirkus* was shot in English and later dubbed into German. It's a more traditional *Flying Circus* hodgepodge, jumping from sketches on chicken mining and sex-maniac economists to a longer piece, "The Tale of Happy Valley." The latter sketch prefigured several members' post-Python interest in medievalism and fairy tales and was later repurposed for *Monty Python's Previous Record*. Not as strong as the first episode, the second is still one for the ages, including as it does "International Philosophy."

Filmed at Munich's Grünwalder Stadion, the sketch's transfiguration of German and Greek philosophers into competing soccer teams, with Confucius as the referee, still serves today as the perfect distillation of the troupe's comic slurry of high/low influences, or what Jones later termed "the clash of opposites." The sketch was regularly included in the filmed interludes at their live shows.

Unfortunately, *Fliegender Zirkus* wasn't warmly received by most of the German public. Except for a 1973 British broadcast and a 1989 retrospective at the Museum of Broadcasting in New York, it remained mostly unseen until its release on video in 1998.

Since it was broadcast after Season Three of *Flying Circus*, it was also the last time that Cleese would perform as part of Monty Python on television.

10

Blood, Devastation, Death, War, and Horror

Monty Python's Flying Circus, Season Three

By Season Three of *Flying Circus*, Cleese was growing tired of Python, and he was wondering what else there was to do in terms of deconstructing comedy and commenting on the medium of television. One result of this was the tendency to try a different tack, one where the entire episode could be seen as a complete narrative, albeit with diversions. Season Three is a mix of classic Python, experiments in surrealism, and attempts to blend traditional narrative with the techniques they had perfected the previous two seasons. In the best episodes, it works; in the rare misfires, it shows the limitations of constant deconstruction.

Episode 27: "Whicker's World (or: Njorl's Saga)" (original air date: October 19, 1972)

One of the driving elements of the first episode of Season Three, "Njorl's Saga" is another historical sketch from Python, only this one has trouble getting off the ground. (Perhaps reflecting the almost two-year delay since the end of Season Two.) The first attempt comes before the opening credits as a caption reads: "Njorl's Saga" and "Iceland 1126," where an "Icelandic man" attempts to read a scroll. Then Jones plays the organ naked and the announcer gets no further than "And now . . ." before the It's Man chimes in just before the credits, redone since last season, roll.

The first sketch takes place in a courtroom where a gregarious defendant (Idle) apologizes profusely for killing twenty people. He is so complimentary of the judge, police, and jury for doing their job that everyone is thoroughly charmed. After he receives just a six-month suspended sentence, the entire courtroom sings, "For he's a jolly good fellow." In some ways, the sketch is a little pedestrian for Python—it could almost be a *Two Ronnies* bit—but Idle's near-perfect performance elevates the material.

The next sketch tries to return to "Njorl's Saga," but after a few futile minutes that include corrections, the documentary grinds to a halt. After pleading for assistance to restart it, the saga begins again, this time tied into the attempts of the village of North Malden to promote tourism and economic development, including Viking shields emblazed with "M.A.L.D.E.N." and a flash frame of "invest in Malden." While the sketch is silly, it also demonstrates the struggle between corporate sponsorship and historical preservation, where tourism often leads to commodified versions of history.

The next sketch takes place in a courtroom where a Viking so heavily bandaged he resembles a cast more than a human being is put on trial for conspiring to "publicize a London suburb in the course of a BBC saga," among other charges. Sadly, the bandages turn out to be empty and only a Gilliam animation can end the sketch.

What's All This, Then?
Whither Whicker?

Alan Whicker was a real-life British reporter and presenter, who did indeed host a program called *Whicker's World* on the BBC from 1959 to 1988, after which he continued to write and report up until his death in 2013. Perennial nice guy Michael Palin called him "a great character, a great traveler, and an excellent reporter" and clearly, an inspiration whether acknowledged or not for Palin's later work as a travel presenter.

After that, Python tackled philosophy as Mrs. Conclusion (with a cameo from "Mrs. Cut-Out," a life-size Gilliam cut-out from the previous sketch) goes to visit Jean-Paul Sartre and asks: "Your famous trilogy, *Rues a Liberte*, is it an allegory of man's search for commitment?" Sartre, being a man of few words, simply answers, "*Oui.*" The show ends with "Whicker's World," an island inhabited entirely by "ex-international interviewers in search of the impossible dream." Which ends up being "too many Whickers" and "not enough rich people to interview."

Episode 28: "Mr. and Mrs. Brian Norris's Ford Popular" (original air date: October 26, 1972)

Strangely enough, the highlight of the second episode is among the troupe's shortest bits, but one that is pure Python: There is simply nothing that better epitomized their sense of humor than the beautifully silly "Fish-Slapping Dance." More on that below.

The episode's titular heroes, the Norrises, are unfortunately part of (presumably) Palin's attempt to milk comedy out of "ordinary" people. The dull quest they embark on to prove that the inhabitants of Hounslow could have been descendants of people from Surbiton who had made the trek north is unfortunately a slog.

However, there's a lot more to the episode, which also introduces the completely unlovable Mrs. Niggerbaiter, who treats the Minister for Overseas Development (Cleese) as a child, until she ultimately explodes, to the relief of Cleese and the audience.

Another Gilliam animation picks up the by now well-established Python obsession with the limits of the television medium. A walking skeleton tumbles off his frame of celluloid into blank space, leading to a shout of "He's fallen off the edge of the cartoon!" and the response, "Well, so much for that link." If Python fans were not well aware of televisuality and the tropes of comedy shows by now, they just weren't paying attention.

The "Trim-Jeans Theatre" sketch is one of Python's shortest, but best allusions to how advertising could make any major work of art that much sillier. In this case, T. S. Eliot's play *Murder in the Cathedral* is mashed up with trim jean-wearing knights who have been sent to kill Archbishop Thomas Beckett, while losing "inches off your hips, thighs, buttocks, and abdomen!" The Trim-Jeans Company can apparently also help you lose weight to Chekhov's *The Seagull* and Shakespeare's *The Trim Gentlemen of Verona* (as presumably the Bard's best play, *Gay Boys in Bondage*, had yet to be become part of the canon).

Shot the previous year for a television special called *Euroshow 71*, the short, wordless "Fish-Slapping Dance" has Cleese and Palin dressed in full safari gear and pith helmets standing on the side of a canal. As light music plays, Palin dances back and forth in front of Cleese, slapping him in the face with two small fish. After his dance concludes, Cleese responds, but not in the same way: he produces one much larger fish, with which he clobbers Palin, sending him plunging into the canal (by the time they had set up the sketch and rehearsed, the water had receded by quite a bit, making for a much longer fall for Palin and a much funnier end to the sketch).

Python has had some interesting celebrity cameos, but the end of this episode features two of the biggest names in English music at the time: Ringo Starr and Scottish singer Lulu (who recorded the theme song for *The Man with the Golden Gun*) on stage waiting for the host, who turns out to be the It's Man, looking very happy for once. He finally gets a longer line, "Hello, good evening, it's . . ." but at the end of his catchphrase, the credits start all over again and his guests walk out in disgust.

Episode 29: "The Money Programme" (original air date: November 2, 1972)

If the "Money Programme" only contained "The Argument Clinic" sketch, it would be enough. One of Python's most famous sketches and among the most endlessly repeated by rabid fans, its popularity is well justified.

Its premise is situated in one of those alternate universes that Python specialized in where absurdity is rife yet controlled by a certain logic. A man (Palin) arrives at a nondescript office looking for an argument. A mistaken detour leads the man to a room where he's furiously berated by Mr. Barnard (Chapman), who stops the fusillade of insults and apologizes ("Sorry, this is Abuse") before directing him to Mr. Vibrating (Cleese, in one of his singularly officious roles).

At first, the argument centers on whether Palin has been told if he's in the right room for an argument, but soon degenerates into a back and forth of "No it isn't / Yes it *is*" exchanges until Palin argues that they are not having an argument, only exchanging contradictions. He explains to Vibrating that the purpose of an argument is a "connected series of statements designed to establish a definite proposition" as opposed to just contradiction. To which Vibrating replies with an infuriating smoothness, "It can be."

As they get into it again, Cleese announces the argument was over because he was only paid for five minutes, and then refuses to continue even after Palin pays up, denying reality in that superbly serene Cleese manner, ultimately positing that he might be only arguing "in my spare time."

As one of the primary elements of the episode involved various inspectors breaking into the narrative, (including Leopard of the Yard, only "more violent"), "Argument Clinic" is broken up by Inspector Fox (Chapman) of the "Light Entertainment Police, Comedy Division, Special Flying Squad."

Fox arrests Palin and the others for a violation of the "Strange Sketch Act," i.e., willfully participating in a strange sketch. The episode ends with an infinite loop of inspectors arresting other inspectors.

Other highlights of "The Money Programme" include the "Money Song" from Idle, who was beginning to write more songs for *Flying Circus*. There is also "Dead Bishop on the Landing," which continues Python's—or at least costume designer Hazel Pethig's—obsession with clerical outfits, and was also used many times for the live shows. The episode also features an interesting "Explorer Sketch" that ends up, like "The Society for Putting Things on Top of Other Things," with the characters noticing they are on film. And, if they are on film, there must be a film crew nearby, so when they discover the film crew, they are saved from starvation. Of course, by *that* logic, who is filming the film crew? If you guessed an Antonioni impersonator, you guessed correctly and win a blow on the head!

Episode 30: "Blood, Devastation, Death, War and Horror" (original air date: November 9, 1972)

The program starts with the titular show, *Blood, Devastation, Death, War, and Horror*. It's introduced by stock footage of explosions and war, but then shifts to a rather conventional mix of two *Flying Circus* tropes by setting an Idle wordplay conceit (he plays a man who only speaks in anagrams) inside another oddball talk show. Interestingly, it ends on something like a punch line, after Idle's anagram-spouter is called out by Palin's presenter for lapsing into a spoonerism—for all you non-English majors out there, that's defined by the good folks at Merriam-Webster as being when the sounds of words are transposed by accident, such as "blushing crow" for "crushing blow"—at which point Idle stalks off after telling Palin, "If you're going to split hairs, I'm going to piss off!"

After some more playing with words, including an anagram version of the show's title and a game-show parody that ends with a large comic hammer crushing Jones's Pepperpot, the topic switches to high finance. A Mr. Ford (Jones again, having thankfully recovered) attempts to solicit contributions from "a City Gent" (Cleese) for an orphan's home. In a proto-Trumpian twist, the City Gent is unable to comprehend the idea of charity for its own sake, only conceiving of a gift for its tax dodge purposes. Finally the City Gent grasps the concept, and thinks asking people for money is a wonderful business idea. But, as Ford gave him the idea before getting the money, "that's not good business," off Ford goes through a trapdoor.

The next visitors to the City Gent are two pantomime horses, familiar to British viewers of the annual holiday "pantos," or holiday pantomime shows that include badly costumed characters and lots of cross-dressing. The horses are told that the company can only afford to keep one and that the two should fight to the death. When they protest, they are informed that the management consultants had "actually queried the necessity for us to employ a pantomime horse at all!" While they fight to the death, we see another nature show featuring more fights, including a fifteen-year battle for supremacy between a wolf and an ant.

The episode then returns to a theme from last season, i.e., the increasing opportunities for creative types of all gender identities, including regiments that are "more effeminate then others." What seemed to be a happy situation for the potential army recruit soon goes south when he realized that the recruiter has all of the good lines, but in that sketch on a bus, his only line ("Five penny, please.") fails to get laughs. But, perhaps it's his delivery?

Later on, the BBC World symbol is shown (once again to the network's chagrin) while a voice-over reflects the existential despair of a BBC announcer whose home life is falling apart. Egged on by other announcers, he is finally able to announce the start of the nine o'clock news, read by Richard Baker, which then goes to the credits of the real nine o'clock news. Knowing that their use of real newsreaders and the BBC logo annoyed the BBC, the Pythons continued using the logo and the BBC tropes at any opportunity.

The end of the episode shows one pantomime horse lying with Carol Cleveland, presumably after a vigorous bout of lovemaking, when they are attacked by the other pantomime horse, leading to an exciting car chase. There's also more commentary on the struggle for survival in the world during the end credits. As there should be; *Flying Circus* was, if nothing else, well attuned to the state of geopolitics.

Episode 31: "The All-England Summarize Proust Contest" (original air date: November 16, 1972)

Python specialized in absolutely horrible yet fascinating game shows, a mini-genre that *SNL* has done their best to run into the ground over the past few decades. Needless to say, the Pythons did it more smarterer.

In the "All-England Summarize Proust Contest" (the best *Flying Circus* game show spoof since "Blackmail" from Episode 18), contestants try to summarize Marcel Proust's seven-book masterwork, À *la recherche du temps perdu* (which Cleese referenced so effusively in Episode 23's "Fish License" sketch), first in a swimsuit and then in an evening gown. The contest is in its latter stages and the tension is growing. Who will best summarize Proust *this* year? The first contestant Harry Bagot (Chapman), dressed in a rather

Marcel Proust, circa 1895. Proust's masterpiece, *A la recherche du temps perdu*, prominently referenced in two major *Flying Circus* sketches, sprawled over seven volumes and approximately 4,000 pages.

Otto Wegener/Wikimedia Commons

fetching evening gown, valiantly attempts to sum up the wildly prolix Proust, even using the term "extra-temporal" correctly.

But alas! Proust's work is too difficult to summarize in a few sentences, and he's out. The second contestant, Ronald Rutherford (Palin), is a bit confused and doesn't get much further than "It's the morning . . . no, it's the evening" before he's out. The Bolton Choral Society (the Fred Tomlinson Singers) try their best to sing the answer in a "round" style, but they have no success either. Ultimately the decision is made to just give the prize to "the girl with the biggest tits." While this is a bit salacious for Python, it does make the case that television, with its bias toward the visual as opposed to the literate does not easily lend itself to analyzing works of great literature.

We then take a 180-degree to hairstylists trying to conquer Mt. Everest only to cut their losses and open a salon. Next, the fire brigade is working on various projects that have nothing to do with fighting fires, which segues into a home where Mrs. Little and her son Mervyn are desperately trying to save their pet hamster (mostly by playing the cello for him), but to no avail. He is an ex-hamster. But their sorrow is alleviated by the second son, Eamon, in full tribesman gear and blackface, just arriving home from Dublin. Apparently, Dublin is somewhere in the wilds as Eamon constantly intones that "well, things is looking pretty bad, but there does seem to be some hope for a constitutional settlement." But with Eamon home, the fire brigade finally answers their phone and shows up for dinner. A happy ending, well, not for the hamster, but for everyone else.

Another sketch involving prolonged monologues featured a tourist called Mr. Smoke-Too-Much (Idle) who wants to go on a holiday, instead of "going upstairs," which was receptionist Carol Cleveland's initial offer. (In *Live at the Hollywood Bowl*, she ups the ante to "Would you like a blow job?") After deciding he'd rather have a holiday, Idle goes off on a wonderfully infuriated and lengthy rant about miserable package tours filled with provincial Brits just eager to find some place "you can even get Watney's Red Barrel and cheese and onion," as the travel agent desperately tries to get him to shut up.

The scene then shifts to yet another talk show, where this time an interviewer (Chapman) queries Anne Elk (Cleese, imitating Chapman's longtime companion, David Sherlock) on her theory on the brontosaurus. She is rather possessive of a theory that all brontosauruses "are thin at one end, much thicker in the middle and then thin again at the far end, ahem!" which causes to Chapman to walk off, Mr. Smoke-too-Much to reappear, and the Fred Tomlinson Singers to launch into another round of the Proust song as the show ends.

Episode 32: "The War Against Pornography" (Original air date: November 23, 1972)

The literal war against pornography starts with some Pepperpots rampaging around England as pre-Thatcherite Tory enforcers, forcing loafing factory laborers back to work and cleaning up the arts scene (including removing Othello from his marital bed with Desdemona). While her name is not mentioned, the image of notorious anti-anything-fun crusader Mary Whitehouse (immortalized by Cleese in the "Election Night" sketch: "Mary Whitehouse has taken Umbrage") is ever-present as the rampaging Pepperpots attack liberal society with military-grade weaponry, leaving only the nude organist, the announcer, and the It's Man to start the show.

If there was a male yang to the Pepperpots' yin, it is the Gumbys. We now find them at their most difficult task yet, conducting brain surgery in a hospital. Returning to "Pornography," a door-to-door documentary salesman (Cleese) has come to see Mr. and Mrs. Jalin (Jones and Chapman) with a special offer of a documentary about mollusks, who are apparently very, *very* randy. We learn that the randiest is the limpet and that the whelk is "nothing but a homosexual of the worst kind!" It is subsequently smashed by the Jalins.

Genre hybridity comes into play again as BBC newsreaders' stories soon become a BBC serial, involving Mr. D'Arcy, which then morphs into the Tuesday documentary and then the children's story and then back into the Tuesday Documentary, a Party Political Broadcast, Religion Today, Match of the Day, and finally an attack on politicians masked as an apology. It's all a fantastic showcase for the Pythons' ability to embed extended satire of their network within a sketch. Things wind down with an extended (and less funny) bit about a British naval expedition to Lake Pahoe.

The episode concludes with a brief sketch in which Mr. Badger

What's All This, Then?
I . . . AM . . . A . . . BRAIN . . . SURGEON!

After Palin's wife had to undergo brain surgery, he repaid the specialist who operated on her by taking a picture with the doctor dressed as a Gumby—apparently, all brain surgeons, or at least British ones, are enormous Gumby fans. Which should be cause for trepidation among users of the National Health Service.

(Idle) has a theory (does Anne Elk know this?) that the Magna Carta was actually a "piece of chewing gum on a bedspread in Dorset," which he then mimes to the host (Cleese). As a reward for this, the host takes him to dinner where Mr. Badger orders a whisky for each course while the waiter (Palin) bemoans his paucity of good lines.

Episode 33: "Salad Days" (original air date: November 30, 1972)

Sam Peckinpah's Salad Days, the Cheese Shop, *and* Biggles! What more can one want from a *Flying Circus* episode?

In this thrilling episode of "The Adventures of Biggles Part One—Biggles Dictates a Letter," Biggles (Chapman) dictates a letter to his secretary Miss Bladder (Nicki Howorth), who keeps calling him "Señor Biggles" for some reason. Biggles is informed by Miss Bladder that his best mate Algy is now "a bleedin' fairy. Mincing old RAF queen." When asked, a cheerful Algy rejoins, "I should bally well say so, old fruit!" He is quickly shot dead by Biggles. Then, Biggles's other best pal, Ginger (Gilliam), comes in dressed as "a terrible poof in camp flying gear." When asked by Biggles if he is gay, Ginger shouts (in camp outrage), "I should say not!" and storms out.

After sketches about climbers trying to climb a completely horizontal Uxbridge road, and a lifeboat that's actually an ordinary suburban house, we cut to a Gilliam animation about how television is bad for your eyes. In this case, arms reach out from a television set and literally pull a viewer's eyes out of his head, then play with them as if they were balls on strings. The televisual nature of the show is commented on again as Jones sums up the "show so far" ending with a bit he doesn't remember in which "a great hammer came and hit him on the head." Naturally, a big hammer then appears and hits him. Bad luck

What's All This, Then?

Biggles?

While a cultural institution in Britain, the character Biggles is relatively unknown in America. In England, he is the star of dozens of action-packed books pitched to school-age boys, and several movies for teenagers. He was seen as rather old-fashioned by the 1960s. While Biggles never crossed over to a US audience, the stories are reminiscent of many "Scouting for Boys"–type tales where young men brave the rugged outdoors without any girls (ewww, icky!) to slow them down.

for him, but at least the It's Man reappears and gets a chance to say "lemon curry," which unlike his catchphrase does not start the credits rolling again.

"The Cheese Shop" sketch, while similar to "Argument Clinic" and "Pet Shop," is near-definitive Monty Python wordplay lunacy. The contest is between a customer (Cleese) and the proprietor of the "finest cheese shop in the district" (Palin), which only lacks one item: cheese. The sheer number of cheeses that Cleese requests ranges from the ordinary (Stilton, Gruyère, Cheshire, Danish Blue, Camembert, Gouda, Gorgonzola, Parmesan, mozzarella), to increasingly rare and ultimately nonexistent cheeses (Danish Fimboe, Czechoslovakian sheep's milk cheese, and Venezuelan beaver cheese); all to no avail. There's not even any cheddar, despite it being the most popular cheese in the world. In the end, as suspected, there is no cheese in the cheese shop and the proprietor admits that he was "deliberately wasting your time" before being shot dead by the annoyed customer. The sketch is not just memorable for the repetition, but for it being a game that Cleese plays even though he knows full well there will be no winners. A perennial favorite, "The Cheese Shop" was wildly cheered at the O2 Reunion shows in 2014.

The last sketch, "Sam Peckinpah's Salad Days," is a genre mash-up that starts with an unctuous film critic (Idle, riffing on British film critic Philip Jenkinson) pontificating about American film director Sam Peckinpah's usage of "utterly truthful and sexually arousing" violence, before showing a clip from Peckinpah's version of the sentimental British musical *Salad Days*. A group of straw hat–wearing upper-class British men and woman chat merrily in a field on a bright summer day. Lionel (Palin) proposes a game of tennis, at which point Julian (Chapman) very gently tosses a tennis ball at him and everything goes to hell. The ball hits Lionel's head, causing blood to come spouting out, at which point he tosses his tennis racket, which eviscerates a woman. The following sequence shows the other picnickers dying horrendously in slow motion, severed limbs flying and gore spattering their sprightly outfits. After Idle's critic pops back in to comment, "Pretty strong meat there, from Sam Peckinpah!," he is summarily gunned down, also in luxuriantly violent slow motion.

Python is first referencing the 1954 quintessentially British musical *Salad Days*, a massively popular (and just as massively reviled) nostalgic look at the last vestiges of the British upper class. Python's British members knew this particular rose-colored vision of undergraduate life from their time at university. Python's audience would certainly be familiar with Peckinpah's

Ernest Borgnine and William Holden get shot to pieces in *The Wild Bunch*, the inspiration for Python's "Sam Peckinpah's Salad Days" sketch.   *Warner Bros./Photofest*

infamous revisionist western *The Wild Bunch* (1969), whose controversial use of over-the-top, slow-motion bloodshed demonstrated the period's cultural cynicism and undermined the moral certainties of the typical western. The skit's uneasy merger of two wildly different genres, Peckinpah's ultra-violence and good-old-days British nostalgia, is a typical Python mash-up of radically different sensibilities, styles, and genres.

Episode 34: "The Cycling Tour" (original air date: December 7, 1972)

An unusually plot-driven part of the increasingly frenetic Season Three, "The Cycling Tour" is based around a throwaway story about Mr. Pithers's (Palin) attempt to take a bicycling tour of north Cornwall. While some of the situations that Pithers runs into are amusing, the character tests your patience with his disinterested cluelessness about those situations.

The episode's only bright bit is a charming turn by Jones as Gulliver, a man with a head wound who thinks he is Leon Trotsky, although he is often confused for the singer Clodagh Rogers as well. Eventually they end up in Russia, as Gulliver morphs steadily into Trotsky. Pithers and Gulliver are captured and nearly executed, but somehow the soldiers miss. The Russians later try to execute them with fixed bayonets, but miss as well.

At least the episode ends with an amusing animation of two monsters dancing to Clodagh Rogers's version of "Jack in the Box." The Pythons might have been trying for "something completely different," but overall "The Cycling Tour" is the biggest miss in the third season.

Episode 35 "The Nude Organist (or: The Nude Man)" (original air date: December 14, 1972)

A collection of sketches that is a definite improvement on "The Cycling Tour," "The Nude Organist" seems to prove Cleese's point when he said that Monty Python was starting to go around in circles.

One of the episode's more memorable sketches is "Housing Project Built by Characters from Nineteenth-Century Novels," which works on the usual Python level of meta-commentary. But other sketches do not fare well. One bit about different radio stations and a mortuary quiz drag on, and a competitive men's hide and seek championship is cute, but again overly long. Presaging his death by heart attack in *Holy Grail*, Gilliam makes an appearance as himself creating his animation for the show while explaining to someone, "You see, it's very simple—I just take these cut out figures and by putting them together . . . oh, do you mean we're on?" before popping his head in for a quick cameo.

The episode ends with a sketch about the "Cheap-Laughs" family next door, as well as an extended bit about the planet Algon, where inflation is rampant. Mr. Badger (Idle), who has been interrupting sketches since the start of the program, appears and offers to read the closing credits for forty pence. As he finishes, we see a sixteen-ton weight hanging above him. While this would have been a good episode in most seasons, it seems as though the Pythons were trying for a mishmash approach as a deliberate contrast to the (relatively) linear nature of "The Cycling Tour." It wasn't necessary.

Episode 36: "E. Henry Thripshaw's Disease" (original air date: December 21, 1972)

Python was always playing with storytelling forms and at times introduced characters immersed in worlds that were simultaneously fictitious and factual at the same time. Characters such as Michael Ellis in Season Four found themselves the heroes of stories where they seemed prisoners instead of being willing participants. So it goes at the beginning of this episode.

In the "Tudor Job Agency" sketch, the unemployed line up to find work as Tudors, even though the agency has not had any success since in placing anyone since 1625, and now works as a front for a pornography store. When a Tudor-dressed Detective Gaskell (Palin) arrives on a raid, he is identified as Sir Philip Sydney, the famous British Renaissance man of letters. Another assistant identifies him as Sir Philip Sydney as well and soon Gaskell realizes that his assistant, Sgt. Maddox, has disappeared. Trying to find an exit, Gaskell emerges in Tudor times, where others recognize him as Sir Philip Sydney as well. Soon, Gaskell has adapted to life as Sir Philip Sydney and is entertaining a Tudor-era dinner party (his amusing story is about busting the Harry Tony mob, "who did seek to import Scandinavian filth via Germany . . .") when he is informed that the Spanish have landed. When he gets there, he is intrigued to find that they are not invading, but trying to smuggle porn into England, including *Toledo Tit Parade*, the latest work by Lope De Vega. After arresting the "dago dustbin(s)," Sir Philip returns home to London a hero. His return was not diminished by the fact that his wife was reading William Shakespeare's new play *Gay Boys in Bondage*, which she reads aloud much to Sir Philip's pleasure; as he remarks, "'Tis like *Hamlet* . . . what a genius!" But, just as Gaskell has completely embraced his new life four hundred years before his own, the smut police burst in and arrest them both. As they are dragged off in the paddy wagon, a Gilliam animation shows us what *Gay Boys in Bondage* would have looked like, in the finest Shakespearean fashion.

The other major sketches in the program both involve vicars, one disturbing and the other an overenthusiastic fan of the sherry. The sketch ends with a return to selling pornography and credits that have less-than-subtle allusions to pornography throughout. Overall, the episode is an amazing mixture of the Pythons' historical and literary bent, fused with their deconstructive storytelling approach and commentary on the often-tenuous connection between fact and fiction.

Episode 37: "Dennis Moore" (original air date: January 4, 1973)

While Dennis Moore is not a single-story episode like "The Cycling Tour," it does have a connecting force, the confused highwayman Dennis Moore (Cleese), who continually robs people of their lupins (a flowering plant to all you non-gardeners out there) to give to the poor. ("Stand and deliver, give me, all of your lupins!") The trouble is that the poor really don't want lupins; they want the money and possessions that the rich have. Over the course of the episode, Moore realizes that he had made the poor rich (and oh, so snobby) and the rich now so poor that they have nothing left to rob.

Dennis Moore even gets his own song, a parody of the Richard Green theme song for ITV's 1950s show *The Adventures of Robin Hood*. While Cleese, who is a bit "Cleese-ian" in his apologetic Dennis Moore persona, may be off-base in trying to steal lupins for the poor, the rich actually *are* hoarding lupins in anticipation that they may be stolen.

The Dennis Moore sketch is interrupted several times, first, and most notably by Jones and Palin essentially sending up the wordplay-heavy sketches that Cleese and Chapman specialized in. Mrs. O (Idle) and Mrs. Trepidation (Chapman) discuss "what the stars say," leading to a cavalcade of synonyms. Cleese and Chapman loved the sketch, possibly not even knowing at the time that Monty Python was sending up Monty Python.

Another sketch, supposedly a BBC drama about the life of Queen Victoria, starts with heavy-handed exposition only broken up by Moore swinging in on a rope to steal lupins, which he happily delivers to a poor couple who exasperatedly inform him they need material goods instead of lupins. A sketch on "loons" morphs into an off-license where a man starts to tell the tale of Moore, circling back to his quest to redistribute (plant) wealth, which is being judged by sports commentators. But what would Karl Marx or Che Guevara have thought? Moore is more or less Cleese's last major contribution to the third season, and ends on a typically ambiguous note.

Episode 38: "A Book at Bedtime" (original air date: January 11, 1973)

Strangely enough, "A Book at Bedtime" began with Cleese and Idle as Conservative and Unionist party candidates showing the voters their new ideas through dance. The sketch was cut after the election in 1979 and is still not a part of that episode on the re-releases. Pity.

Instead, the episode starts with Jeremy (Palin) reading a story to children in the "A Book at Bedtime" show. In the very same *Do Not Adjust Your Set* sketch, Jeremy stumbles over ordinary words and different readers come on to help, each of them stymied by ordinary language. From there we cut to the best military idea Python has ever had: Kamikaze Scotsmen, who end up doing their job too well and killing themselves even before their mission has begun (a precursor to the suicide squad of *Life of Brian*). A lengthy and somewhat pointless digression on the phrase "no time to lose" follows, but it leads to an excellent Gilliam animation of French painter Toulouse-Lautrec as a gunfighter in a western called *No-Time-Toulouse: The Story of the Wild and Lawless Days of the Post-Impressionists!* This is followed by a lengthy digression on penguins and IQ, before briefly cutting back to the Kamikaze Scotsmen.

The episode sews thing up with a bit of current shows being mocked in intertextual terms, including several send-ups of *Dad's Army* (1968–1977), a British sitcom about middle-aged men in England preparing to defend the country in case of an invasion. The show spoofed most memorably was "Dad's Pooves," in which a delightfully camp Gilliam in women's underwear spanks a judge (Jones) with links of sausages. While this chaotic intertextual send-up seemed like an ideal place to end Season Three, Python had one more trick up their sleeve.

Episode 39: "Grandstand (or: The British Showbiz Awards)" (original air date: January 18, 1973)

Season Three ends, probably fittingly, with something of a middle finger to the medium. The final episode is built around the "Light Entertainment Awards" sketch, a full-on parody of British broadcasting hosted by Dickie Attenborough (Idle), an amalgam of David Frost and Sir Richard Attenborough, constantly crying and adding maudlin over-sentimental bits to all of his appearances. Dickie introduces the remains of the late Sir Alan Waddle, an urn apparently full of ashes (voiced by Palin), which introduces the Light Entertainment Award nominations, including the "Third Parachute Brigade Amateur Dramatic Society for the Oscar Wilde Skit."

"The Oscar Wilde Sketch" is perhaps one of Python's most interesting commentaries on class and comedy. The intriguing premise has James McNeill Whistler (Cleese) and Oscar Wilde (Chapman) being celebrated as the premier writers and public intellectuals of their time period. In the sketch, Wilde and Whistler attempt to outdo themselves with bon mots at a party hosted by the Prince of Wales (Jones). At first, both make jokes that are "very witty." But Wilde goes too far and blames an insulting joke on Shaw (Palin), who blows a giant raspberry, the wittiest rejoinder of the evening.

In sports, we see a version of Pier Paolo Pasolini's film *The Third Test Match*, in which cricket players turn into cowled monks, people make love on the match field, and the umpire turns into a cardinal judging the match. Two Pepperpots both named Zambesi (Chapman and Jones) are disgusted with what's on the telly and go to get one of the Zambesis a new brain.

We return to the awards show, where Dickie is now pumping away at a fake tears device in order to show emotion. He presents an award for best credits sequence (the real-life Monty Python closing credits, which just went by), inadvertently outing the credits designer by waking him up at home in bed with another man. After that, Dickie announces the "moment you've all been waiting for," as "The End" flashes onscreen. Dickie soldiers bravely on, giving the final award of the evening, the "Mountbatten Trophy, Show Business's Highest Honor" to the cast of the "Dirty Vicar" sketch, who then come on stage to accept their reward.

As obvious as any Python had done, "The Dirty Vicar" can as such be seen as a sketch about sketches. The lecherous new "Dirty Vicar of St. Michaels" (Jones) arrives and cannot help but throw himself on two ladies. While molesting the second lady (Caron Garden), the first lady (Carol Cleveland) admonishes him for his behavior. The vicar momentarily restrains himself, joining in mundane conversation about the new parish. After rhapsodizing about how he "finds the grounds delightful and the servants most attentive, especially the little serving maid with the great big knockers . . ." the vicar loses control again and wrestles the first lady off camera.

At this point, Dickie walks on set and announces the end of the awards show, saying "I think none more than myself can be happier at this time than I . . . am." The script notes that then "the cast of the sketch stand in a line looking awkward and smiling. Fade out." And with that, Season Three of *Monty Python's Flying Circus* ends, not with a bang but an ambiguous whimper, leaving it unclear if Python would return for another season.

All That's Left

Monty Python (sans Flying Circus): The Final Season

The fourth—and final—season of *Flying Circus* often gets a bad rap from fans and critics, and some of that valuation is merited. At the time, Cleese was popularly considered the "star" of the show; he'd had the widest appeal before *Flying Circus* and had maintained that distinction reasonably well while the series was rolling. But he'd recently announced to his peers that he'd be quitting the show to work on a new comedy with Connie Booth: the outstanding *Fawlty Towers*. He barely appears in Season Four. Without the looming presence of Cleese, the series seemed smaller, somehow. And, in fact, it was: unlike the previous three seasons, Season Four contained only six episodes (rather than thirteen) and the title of the show was shortened to *Monty Python* (sans the *Flying Circus*).

Of course, even with Cleese on board, the Pythons were already struggling in Season Three to satisfy the expectations of not just the audience but themselves. When your primary shtick is to present counter-narratives to convention, you need to continually change your own format, lest you become conventionally counter-conventional. So perhaps they were intentionally counter-punching their own counter-conventional conventions in Season Four by presenting viewers with more of the same: repeated characters, slight tweaks to old concepts, and plenty of excretory humor. Instead of utterly disparate sketches stitched together—somehow!—by Gilliam's trippy animation, Season Four attempted running continuous narratives throughout episodes . . . small-screen Pythons with a plot?! Was nothing sacred?

As a reward, perhaps, for increasing viewer accessibility, the BBC brass began pushing for favorable "repeat" slots for the show, and Python's name recognition grew even as Season Four faltered. Shot over the course of five weeks (soon after *Monty Python and the Holy Grail* was completed), and screened in shooting order, the last six episodes of *Flyi* . . . sorry, sorry . . . of

Monty Python often feel a bit rushed, and—as other critics have noted—seem to miss Cleese's editorial hand. But they are definitely weird; surreal, even. Also on the plus side, we see more of Carol Cleveland. *Say no more!*

Although ratings dropped to new lows, the BBC still offered the Pythons (less Cleese) a renewal for the second half of the season. Although the troupe was somewhat divided, they declined. *C'est fin.*

Episode 40: "The Golden Age of Ballooning" (original air date: October 31, 1974)

Something's not right here . . . you can tell from the get-go. For starters, Episode 40 doesn't open with a patented Gilliam animated title sequence, but launches straightaway into documentary-style animations for "The Golden Age of Ballooning" (you know, balloons and such, with a florid title). It's a bit disconcerting, really, like walking into the theater to see a nice medieval film and instead seeing an advert for Breem toothpaste. Within the guise of a BBC documentary, old tropes are soon trotted out: we first see the Montgolfier brothers Jacques (Idle) and Joseph (Jones) staring out a window (directly into the camera) at their flying balloon, just as Jones and Chapman stared over a fence (into the camera) at the flying sheep in Episode 2. The historical Mongolfiers—pioneers of balloon aviation—are deflated as the Pythons dwell, with scientific precision, upon their bathing habits. Temporal intrusions abound (the Montgolfiers talk of their place in future history; two members of a film crew set up a projector and screen in the eighteenth-century parlor; three singing "Ronettes" arrive at George III's throne room). This is all fine, but we've seen these jokes before.

More important, perhaps, than the story of the Montgolfiers are the many ancillary products one can buy accompanying the BBC series on ballooning: books, videos, bedspreads, commemorative toilet-seat covers, and so forth. Consumerism—which will be the primary focus of the next episode—is obviously on the minds of the Pythons this season. If they only knew what the future of Monty Python™ would bring.

Returning (without random animation or oddly disjointed interruption!) to the next installment of "The Golden Age of Ballooning 2: The Mongolfiers in Love," we find Antoinette (Cleveland) suspended in a harness complaining at length about her husband Joseph's balloon obsession as he measures her suspended breasts with a pair of calipers. Honestly, it all feels a bit sitcom at this point, although it is nice to hear Cleveland chew on substantial dialogue for a change. Then come more implications about

The *actual* Montgolfier brothers launched the world's first manned hot-air balloon in Paris on October 19, 1783.   *Wikimedia Commons*

Joseph's body odor, followed by a few chuckles at Louis XIV (Palin), who stammers in a Glaswegian accent . . . which makes sense, really, since he's not really Louis XIV but a Scot who absconds with their balloon plans (a close cousin of Palin's Ron Higgins, professional "so-called" Cardinal Richelieu impersonator, perhaps). "The Golden Age of Ballooning 2" ends in a mock cliffhanger ("Will Louis XIV get away with the Mongolfiers' plans?"), but it soon returns only to collapse in a mass of anachronisms: black divas sing in sequined dresses while pseudo-Frenchmen in tam o'shanters head-butt English royalty; meanwhile a modern stage crew sets up another screen with the placard: "Meanwhile, in France."

Thus, the narrative doesn't die, as we return to Jacques one last time before audience applause prompts O'Toole the butler (Chapman) to take a bow, then repeat his (unfunny) lines to increased canned laughter and a final bow as other actors (in costume) come on "stage" to congratulate him . . . as if it were the end of a *Saturday Night Live* episode. Sadly, despite breaking about seventeen different conceptual walls (television-film-theater), it's not all that funny. It's certainly not subtle.

Credits for "Monty Python" then roll (with Cleese notably absent), followed by another pitch to buy ballooning-related merchandise from the BBC and an advert on behalf of the Norwegian Party (Idle, reading jabberwock-Norwegian over racy English subtitles). And then, in case you were hoping the show would get creative again, it's back to ballooning. Er, "zeppelining." Definitely not a balloon!

A last pair of sketches finds an irritable Ferdinand von Zeppelin tossing German dignitaries out of his balloon . . . excuse me, his zeppelin . . . where they land in the sitting room . . . excuse us, the drawing room . . . of an old German couple (Jones and Palin). As elsewhere in this episode, there's humorous mileage to be had from vocabulary confusion, but overall it's rather tame. Even with the German government piling up like cordwood in the sitting . . . oh, never mind.

Episode 41: "Michael Ellis" (original air date: November 7, 1974)

As if to deny that the "new" season of *Monty Python* had become more "consumer friendly," the target of this week's righteous wrath is . . . consumerism! As a sustained narrative, it's rather weak. But the lads certainly stick to their guns, as it were: if you don't leave this episode thinking that the middle class can purchase anything but power, you're fooling yourself. And if the episode reads like an extended version of the "Constitutional Peasants" scene in *Monty Python and the Holy Grail*, that's because it is. Much of this episode is leftover scraps from early drafts of *Holy Grail*, which was initially to span the medieval and modern periods more evenly, with Arthur finding the Holy Grail at the "Grail Counter" in Harrods; see the *Monty Python and the Holy Grail (Book)* for the whole story. Mmmm . . . reconstituted leftovers . . . CONSUME!

"The Liberty Bell (March)" and Gilliam's opening title animation are back (newly done for Season Four, with some confusion regarding the title of the show), followed immediately by the end credits (including Cleese back among the "conceived and written by" crowd). Then it's off to Harrods, or a reasonable facsimile thereof ("Fourth Floor: Granite Hall–Rocks . . . Tenth Floor: Fresh Air, Clouds"). Some quick slapstick and oddly self-referential signage signal that the Pythons' dual loves for wordplay and physical humor are still in effect.

Within, a posh Cleveland purchases a flamethrower, and Chris Quinn (Idle)—seeking to buy an ant from an eccentric sales assistant (Chapman)—is mistaken for Michael Ellis. And not for the last time! Idle plays it straight, mostly, and his exasperation at the *ant*ics (heh) of the staff offer the new viewer a sort of "in" to the surrealism. In yet another "Pet Shop"–style bit, Quinn and another assistant (Palin) haggle over the adv-*ant*-ages of owning ants, which are treated both as if they were purebred dogs also like utterly disposable commodities (it's cheaper to let them die and purchase another than to feed them). More important than the ant itself, however, is the purchase of useless *ant*-cillary items: an ant-cage, an ant-wheel, ant-swing, a two-way radio, and, of course, a book on ants (squish). Total cost: £184 (plus 11/2 pence for the ant). It's cruel, silly, and a pointed indictment of both mindless consumerism and animal slavery. Both indictments are further underscored by the piles of television sets and hordes of animals Quinn has amassed at his house and then duly neglected: a baboon, polar bear, dromedary, trout, tiger (live and onscreen!), an orange-rumped agouti, and a dead sperm whale (now serving as the family's garage).

And then the Michael Ellis confusion kicks in again, tying the whole show together: a mix of *The Third Man*, *North by Northwest*, and *The Man Who Knew Too Little* (although that last might be a tad chronologically challenging). In his home—sitting before with a wall of television sets (more stacked outside: consume!)—Quinn watches shows on ant communication (what a stroke of luck!) and ant homeopathic medicine (via Gilliam animation). Realizing something is wrong with his ant (missing legs), Quinn returns to the store to complain and is sent (loudly) to the "toupee hall," but accidentally enters the "Victorian Poetry Reading Room," where Wordsworth, Shelley, Keats, and Tennyson all sit to recite their poetry on ants. Parodies of established poems are in erudite evidence here: Shelley (Gilliam) reads "Ozymandias, King of Ants" (a real crowd-pleaser) and Keats (Idle) scares the bejeebers out of the audience with his emotional description of a

voracious anteater. But the formici-
dophilic fun is interrupted by Queen
Victoria (Palin), who—standing
alongside Albert's coffin in a deeply
Germanized accent—decrees that
"ants is verboten!"

Quinn is then secretly drawn
to the "Electric Kettles (Toupees)"
department where three salesmen
(Jones, Chapman, Palin) wearing
very obvious toupees greet him con-
spiratorially, until he outs them for
wearing toupees and runs into the

What's All This, Then?
Toupees

For those interested in Python's lasting impact on surreal comedy (and
toupees), please see the *Kids in the
Hall* sketch "My Horrible Secret," a
noir short starring Bruce McCulloch
and his squirrely hairpiece (Season
Three, Episode 13). But shhhh . . . no
one must know . . .

actual "Complaints" department. Sadly, Cleese is conspicuously absent; one
has to wonder what his brand of supercilious arrogance could have added.
Happily (?) the episode ends abruptly when, over the intercom, we hear the
following announcement: "It is now the end of 'Michael Ellis' week. From
now on it is 'Chris Quinn' week."

Quinn finally says what we're all thinking: "What a rotten ending." He
then complains at the "End of Show Department" where Jones offers him
several film-school alternatives: the long, slow pull-out, the chase, walking
into the sunset, the happy ending, the summing up, the slow fade, and so
forth. Each is teasingly enacted, briefly, until we finally come to the absolute
end: a "sudden ending" . . . and the show cuts to black.

See? And you thought the finale of *The Sopranos* wasn't funny.

Episode 42: "Light Entertainment War" (original air date: November 14, 1974)

While the title may be the Pythons' mild jab at the BBC division that produced their show and the brief "Programme Titles Conference" caricatur-
izes the condescending idiocy of television executives (who seek to rename
existing repeats), the bulk of the episode is more concerned with linguistics
than ought else, and the Pythons' typical disconnected sketch format is
embraced once again. The opening credits appear midway through the
show, for those keeping track of such things.

Opening this so-called war on light entertainment is a jaunty, if short-
lived, send-up of conventional sitcoms (this one a jab at *Steptoe and Son*,

the British precursor to the American *Sanford and Son*) called "Up Your Pavement." But once the two "happy-go-lucky" stars (Palin and Jones) are run over by Alex Diamond (Chapman), the opening bounces from sitcom to spy film, then to infomercial, to war autobiography, to college exposé, to, well, a long series of "another things." It's a clever bounce, with enough false payoffs to confound even the Python faithful, who'd have become accustomed to such sudden shifts of focus. Again, perhaps the Pythons thought that one way to counter their own counter-conventions was to simply magnify them: a "more is more" kind of thing (a tactic that had worked wonderfully in their "thesaurus" sketches, but doesn't work as effectively when applied across an entire episode . . . or season). In any case, the series of intros eventually stops at "RAF Banter," one of the more linguistically challenging of the Python oeuvre.

Given the genre-specific expectations of a war film, the audience expects the banter bandied back and forth between the RAF (Royal Air Force) pilots to be full of jargon, just as any police procedural or hospital drama employs terminology specific to their common occupation to establish verisimilitude ("Roger, that's a 10-19, over;" "Nurse! Get me 50ccs of hemoglobin, stat!"). But almost as soon as this sketch begins, the jargon and slang spouted by the Squadron Leader (Idle) becomes so dense, so convoluted, that the officers (Jones and Chapman), who should share this patois, can't understand him at all. Mixed in with "authentic" jargon and slang, the Pythons add a heap of neologisms and nonce words, and while some make a modicum of contextual sense, most leave everyone (officers and audience) in a state of confusion, even when repeated slowly and loudly. As Idle—the master of the machine-gun patter—says: "Banter's not the same if you say it slower, Squiffy."

Later in the episode, we get another dose of verbal gymnastics, as "Woody and Tinny Words" offers a rather forward-facing lesson in phonaesthetics (the study of how the sounds of words make one feel). As a bored upper-class patriarch (Chapman) in 1940s England explains, all words can be divided into two categories: woody (euphonic, or pleasant-sounding) or tinny (cacophonic, or unpleasant-sounding). His obsession with the phonaesthetic value of words is so insistent that his linguistic dissection becomes the primary focus of all discussion in the house. Such is the familial sensitivity to sounds that Daughter (Cleveland) runs offstage repeatedly after hearing too many tinny words, Father becomes dangerously overexcited after reciting too many woody words (and is doused with cold water as a corrective), and Mother (Idle) dies upon hearing the overloud song "She's Going to Marry Yum Yum" (a slight variation on "He's Going to Marry Yum Yum" from *The Mikado*, which Idle would star in twelve years later).

A series of interconnected sketches in "Light Entertainment War" focus on comedy and warfare, beginning with the insight that the Germans "are not only fighting this war on the cheap, but they're also not taking it seriously." The stereotypical British stiff upper lip reaction, of course, is for the military to "double down" on seriousness and punish anyone not treating the war seriously, paradoxically culminating in a rousing sing-along of Cole Porter's "Anything Goes" during a court-martial. Compare, perhaps, this late treatment of war with the Pythons' earliest war sketch, "The Funniest Joke in the World" (in which humor wins the war), or contemporary war-based comedies like *Dad's Army* (1968–1977) and *Hogan's Heroes* (1965–1971), both exceedingly popular television shows, even if they didn't treat the war—or history, or *comedy*—seriously.

In other bits, Palin provides voice-over for "Film Trailer": a melodramatic war film using stock/mixed footage; a Pepperpot (Jones) proves—in a silent montage—that she is an idiot; her friend (Chapman) electrocutes an "Arab boy" (Gilliam) repeatedly with her television remote; and finally, in an unusual bit of non–Python Six casting, Peter Woods (a real BBC newscaster, in on the joke here) reads a short newscast before Neil Innes closes out the show with an overtly sentimental (and instantly forgettable) serenade, "When does a dream begin?"

Episode 43: "Hamlet" (original air date: November 21, 1974)

ACT I

Scene 1
The Watch: G-G-G-G-GHOST!

Scene 2
Claudius: Nephew, I married yo mama.
Hamlet: Ewww.

Scene 3
Laertes: I like Hamlet too, sis, but watch yourself while I'm gone.
Ophelia: Oh, what's the worst that could happen?

Scene 4

Horatio: Hamlet, your dad's a frickin' ghost!

Hamlet Jr.: Hwah?!

Scene 5

Hamlet Sr.: Son, your uncle Claudius killed me. Grant me revenge!!!

Hamlet Jr.: G-G-G-G-GHOST!

ACT II

Scene 1

Ophelia: Daddikins, a naked Hamlet just groped me.

Polonius: Excellent! I'll tell the king.

Ophelia (aside): I have the worst dad in Early Modern history.

Scene 2

Rosencrantz and Guildenstern: Yo, Hamlet, whazzup?

Hamlet Jr.: I'm crazy. Maybe. Never mind: I'm going to put on a show!

ACT III

Scene 1

Hamlet Jr.: To be or not to be.

Ophelia: I'm sorry—I came in late. What was the question?

Hamlet Jr.: Get thee to a nunnery!

Ophelia (aside): I have the worst boyfriend in Early Modern history.

Scene 2

Players: Ladies and gentlemen, kings and queens, Damen und Herren, it's with great delight that tonight on this very stage-within-a-stage, we'll be performing that classic Spanish revenge tragedy, "*Mousetrap, Buzzard, Stubble, and Boot!*"

Claudius: G-G-G-G-GHOST!

Scene 3

Claudius: Shit, I am in way over my head.

Hamlet Jr. (aside): I'll kill him! Or not. I am in way over my head.

Scene 4

Hamlet Jr.: What ho! A rat!
Gertrude: Eek!
Polonius: Ack!

ACT IV

Scene 1

Gertrude: I hate to say it, snookums, but my dear boy is cray-cray.
Claudius: That's it! He's grounded! Better yet . . . what's the opposite of grounded?
Gertrude: Exiled?
Claudius: Yeah, let's do that thing.

Scene 2

Hamlet Jr.: You two are idiots.
Rosencrantz and Guildenstern: 'At's a' right, boss.

Scene 3

Letter: "Dear King of England: Kill whomsoever delivers this letter unto you. Sincerely, Claudius"

Scene 4

Fortinbras: I—Fortinbras of Norway—am a fine, active, and decisive fellow!

Scene 5

Ophelia: That's it: I'm out. <splash>

Scene 6

Pirates: AAARGH!
Hamlet Jr.: Say, fellows, mind if I hitch a ride?

Scene 7

Claudius: That son of a bitch (sorry, dear) just won't stay dead! Ah well, if you want something done right . . .

ACT V

Scene I

Hamlet Jr.: Alas, poor Yorick! I knew him, Horatio.

Horatio: Well, I do feel a bit peckish . . . and we can always throw him back up into the grave afterward, amiright?

Scene 2

Osric: A hit, a hit, a very palpable hit!

Gertrude: Cheers! <gack!>

Laertes: Owie! <gack!>

Claudius: Glurg! Owie! <gack>

Hamlet Jr.: <gack>

Fortinbras: I'm sorry—I came in late. What'd I miss?

The Colonel: Rosencrantz and Guildenstern are dead.

Episode 44: Mr. Neutron (original air date: November 28, 1974)

The most sustained of the single-theme episodes, "Mr. Neutron" is broken into three major scenes: "Postbox Ceremony," which provides a segue to the main narrative and is subsequently woven into it later; "Teddy Salad (CIA Agent)," which is the primary narrative (largely about Mr. Neutron); and "Conjuring Today," a very short post-credits bit of confusion. As far as themes go, the science fiction parody is memorable, but the jokes are not. Even the surreal moments (man as dog, for instance) are feeling watered down at this point, and there's an increasing reliance on the "more is more" method of comedy. Ultimately, the episode feels like an overextended *SNL* skit.

"Mr. Neutron" opens with Gilliam's animation, the Bell, and then live-action to Jones upon a horse-drawn scrap cart (odd echoes of "Bring out your dead!" in retrospect); various ladies and Pepperpots (including new quasi-Python Douglas Adams) throw scrap—missiles, a bazooka—onto the cart as he passes. An example of "beat the idea to death for comedy" follows, as a GPO official (Palin) dedicates a new postal box(!) at great length and in three languages. It may be self-consciously overdone, but that still doesn't make it suddenly funnier.

Happily, we fade from Palin and the primary narrative begins, via voice-over, as we focus on . . . MR. NEUTRON! (Chapman in two-tone

"Superman" wig, muscular shoulder pads, yellow tights, and matching cape): "Mr. Neutron! The most dangerous and terrifying man in the world!" Wise! Strong! Powerful! Extraterrestrial! Dangerous!!! A man waiting "for his moment to destroy this little world utterly!"

After some fine comic-style graphics by Gilliam and a melodramatic voice-over from Palin, generic incongruity follows; we see the flashy Mr. Neutron exit a mundane train (Sainsbury's grocer bag in hand) and join in tedious conversation with Mr. and Mrs. Entrail (Jones and Palin) over tea in the garden.

Meanwhile . . . the secret American agency F.E.A.R. (aka F.E.E.B.L.E.)—having lost track of this most dangerous alien—seek out the brilliant Teddy Salad, retired CIA agent. After a series of "salad" jokes, Captain Carpenter (Idle, disguised as a member of the U.S. Ballet Forces) finds Salad in Canada: but he's become . . . dum-dum-dum . . . a dog!

Meanwhile . . . at 10 Downing Street (which looks remarkably like an Italian restaurant), the prime minister (Idle) hears news of the F.E.E.B.L.E. attempts to counter Neutron and their M.A.D. plans to bomb London. Maybe.

Meanwhile . . . Teddy Salad (Palin's voice over a live dog actor) declares that he needs more walkies!

Meanwhile . . . bombing ensues around the world . . . but never in the right place. "Sorry!"

Meanwhile . . . Mr. Neutron has fallen in love with local cleaning woman Mrs. Scum (Jones); he has also, incidentally, won a Kellogg's Corn Flake Competition worth £5,000 (or as much ice cream as you can eat). A swooning Mrs. Scum agrees to be his helpmate and "dominate the world."

Meanwhile . . . in the Yukon, Salad (Palin's voice over a puppet dog) is about to reveal the location of Mr. Neutron when a bombing run by F.E.E.B.L.E. destroys them.

Meanwhile . . . the Commander of F.E.E.B.L.E. (a naked Palin), having run out of places to bomb, orders his office to be bombed. It is. So too is the Gobi Desert, where the GPO official (Palin) from the opening scene is dedicating yet another mailbox.

Meanwhile . . . Neutron "magically" transforms Mrs. Scum into the most beautiful woman in the world (surprisingly, not Carol Cleveland, but simply Jones in new clothes). As she rhapsodizes, the (animated) world is blown into bits and Palin's voice-over asks: "Has Mr. Neutron escaped in time?" Stay tuned!

And in a way, we do. A quick cut to Idle as a BBC TV announcer reading a *Radio Times* newspaper as he encapsulates the most thrilling and expensive(!) scenes ever funded by the BBC . . . none of which is seen, of course. What the Pythons have presented, really, is the cheap intro to a B-grade science fiction film with none of the payoff. Ironically (following Idle's complaint that Cotton should "give us another minute"), after the credits have rolled, we are treated to fifty seconds of "Conjuring Today" and a voice-over for "World Domination" T-shirts (available through the BBC). Then, Idle's announcer gets laid out by a fifteen-foot hammer. See? Could have been expensive extravaganza, but noooo . . . this is what you paid for, Cotton.

Episode 45: "Party Political Broadcast" (original air date: December 5, 1974)

The last episode—EVER—of *Flying Circus*. Sigh. If only we knew then what we know now, eh? Ah well.

Happily, the final show returns to the Pythons' multiple sketch format, interstitial animations are back, and we are treated to "The Most Awful Family in Britain," which truly lives up to its title. It is far from the best episode in the series, but it has its moments.

In an oddly topical move, the Pythons have a Halloween mask version of Jeremy Thorpe (then Liberal Party leader) pop up in the background of various sketches as a running gag. For all their political and social commentary, the Pythons generally avoided topicality (sticking to historical stand-ins for current concerns), and the lack of audience reaction to "Thorpe" in this episode suggests why. Still: funnier than the inexplicable "Chicken Knight" from Season One. Maybe.

The episode opens pre–title animations by promising "A Party Political Broadcast on Behalf of the Liberal Party," but instead cuts to the Garibaldi family kitchen: a dingy and crowded set where Mrs. Garibaldi (Idle) irons everything, slovenly Mr. Garibaldi (Jones) eats his breakfast of "Ano-Weet" cereal while sitting on a toilet, a clumsy and pimply Ralph Garibaldi (Palin) reads the morning tabloid paper, a fat-suited Kevin Garibaldi (Gilliam) shovels beans down his gullet while lying on the couch, and a foul-mouthed and trampy Valerie Garibaldi (Chapman) primps before a mirror. Jokes about laxative cereals, Parliamentary snogging, and bean-spilling ensue as the radio announces a football match in the background (Idle). It's hard to do the visually packed scene justice really, but it's all terribly (albeit intentionally) lowbrow. It's only when Tarzan the postman swings by that we realize the Garibaldis are contestants on *The Most Awful Family in England, 1974*, hosted by a sequined Palin before a distinguished panel of judges . . . who are not entirely impressed by the Garibaldis' grossness. Ahead of them are an upper-class family of twits, the Fanshaw-Chumleighs, whose primary awfulness appears to be their loud and vapid chatter over dinner . . . and the fact that they're all upper-class twits. But in first place is a family whose awfulness cannot be shown onscreen (recalling the "expensive" ending of Episode 44) thanks to implied BBC standards. Given the struggles over censorship that the Pythons had experienced over the years with the BBC, it's hard not to see this as another biting-the-hand-that-feeds-you moment. The sketch also recalls the vile "Aristocrats" gag that had been a popular inside joke among comedians since the Age of Vaudeville: the sort of taboo gross-out humor that could never really be staged.

The rest of the episode is a scattering of loud yelling, gushing blood, and—generally—physical humor. Chapman—who, lest we forget, was very

What's All This, Then?
The Comics' Joke

"The Aristocrats" is a joke—a tradition, really—told by comedians to comedians, a sort of "dirtiest one-upmanship" contest predicated upon the following formula: A talent agent is approached by a family of perform-ers who pitch their vile, disgusting, and immoral extravaganza in lengthy detail. Every comic describes the act differently, but the joke always ends with the same punch line, in which the agent is told the name of the act: "The Aristocrats!" (or, alternately, "The Sophisticates," or "The Debonaires").

However it is told, the joke is based on simple incongruity humor; the "joy" is in the creative description each comic brings to the filth-ridden table. Penn Jillette and Paul Provenza gathered one hundred comics—including Idle and Gilliam—to tell their versions of the joke in the documentary *The Aristocrats* (2005). Idle performs his version of "The Aristocrats" in full-bore jabberwock German accompanied by wild panto-mime; he ultimately falls on his couch, laughing hysterically at his own joke. Gilliam offers his own version of the joke—heavily invested in production values and setting—but since there was (as the director notes) some error with the sound equipment, his voice has been completely dubbed. Somehow that seems entirely appropriate.

nearly a physician before the Queen mum steered him wrong—gets to malign the callous greed of private medical practice in "A Doctor Whose Patients are Stabbed by His Nurse." Elsewhere, the tutu-wearing Brigadier (Idle) dictates a letter to his secretary/bishop (Palin), who intones pseudo-sermons (as he would in *Monty Python and the Holy Grail* and again in *The Meaning of Life*) until the two awkwardly profess their attraction to each other and lament that there's not much that the two can do about it . . . not on television, anyway. The Pythons had long danced around (and occasionally with) homosexuality on the show, but this is as overt a protest against homosexual censorship as they'd yet posed (or ever would, until Idle penned the gay-friendly *Spamalot*: "Just think, Herbert, in a thousand years' time, this will still be controversial").

Before the episode—and the series—is over, everyone gets their moment in the spotlight:

Gilliam (who had a fine turn earlier as the bean-eating Garibaldi son) animates an opera singer who is shot by a missile so slow that he has time to finish singing "Ride of the Valkyries" before exploding; Chapman offers a scathingly understated reverse-minority report in "Appeal on Behalf of Extremely Rich People"; Idle returns (yet again) as a fast-talking speech pathologist in "The Man Who Finishes Other People's Sentences"; a Pepperpotted Jones strides purposefully through town and field (to the strains of "Ride of the Valkyries") toward Stonehenge; and Palin offers a travelogue (of sorts) as a confused—and sweaty—David Attenborough chasing "The Walking Tree of Dahomey" through the African jungle.

The episode then ends, more or less, with "The Batsmen of the Kalahari," a sketch that combines cricket commentary with colonialist pseudo-documentary; the all-black Batsmen (with a deliberate nod to "Bushmen") play a mean game of civilized cricket, you see, but remain savages since they throw spears and machetes into the opposing (white) players. If there's a saving grace to this rather uncomfortably racist sketch, it's that the white cricketers are A) all named Pratt ("dumb-ass"), and B) die cowardly deaths. The audience in 1974—largely whites, one gathers—seemed to like it, however.

On the plus side, the episode (and series) wraps up with an intentionally amateurish rendition of "The Liberty Bell (March)" theme on guitar (Innes). Not with a bong, but a whimper, as it were. Then on to another set of false ends, post credits, where Idle reads the news, Cleveland dances on a tabletop, and—in a series of quick throws—we see Palin (as generic newsman) on a pier, Chapman (in swim trunks holding a harpooned cat),

Palin again (in sequins from "The Most Awful Family in Britain" earlier), back to Idle (as newsreader), and then, at the last possible moment before the screen goes to black, Jones pops in as a second reporter.

And finally-finally, in the last seconds of the last *Monty Python* television show ever, we hear Pythons laughing off-screen.

There are worse ways to go.

12

What Hath We Wrought?

The Pythons Storm America

Whither America?

When it comes to successful British cultural imports to the United States in the postwar years, music was the thing. First, of course, was the British Invasion: the Who, the Beatles, the Rolling Stones, and the like. Following in their musical footsteps were glam outfits and rockers and every kind of alien in between—David Bowie and Led Zeppelin stomping their way through heartland arenas filled with screaming adulation. Rock and roll might have been an American invention, but for years British bands made good bank by selling it right back to the colonies.

Comedy was a far less certain product. Go ahead: ask the average American about some great British comics of the postwar years. We'll wait. Maybe Benny Hill will ring a bell. *Maybe*. But even hallowed classics like *The Goon Show* never made much of an impression in the States, though Peter Sellers later would, sneaking himself into the country by way of his roles in films like *Lolita*, *Dr. Strangelove*, and the *Pink Panther* series.

Nevertheless, like any rock band worth its salt, British comedians wanted access to the American market. All those radio and TV stations and record stores and concert halls between the Atlantic and Pacific meant a far greater revenue stream, not to mention a louder cultural megaphone and just plain more relevance, than could be had by playing just to the punters in ol' Blighty.

Monty Python was no different. But it wasn't easy for the lads to crack the market.

The first serious attempt to introduce Python to American audiences, *And Now for Something Completely Different*, failed rather spectacularly upon release in 1972, due in large part to the distributor's halfhearted distributing and marketing campaign.

Somewhat more successful were the albums. Nancy Lewis, at the New York–based Buddah Records, which released Python's albums in the States, flogged their work relentlessly. Instead of marketing the Pythons' albums like the next Bill Cosby or George Carlin release, though, Lewis took the rock 'n' roll approach. She targeted the same kingmaking FM radio DJs who in the 1970s set the pace for that intersection of popular music and subversive comedy that had been bubbling up from the counterculture since the 1960s.

It made sense to go after the rock crowd. After all, rock gods from Elvis to Led Zeppelin were already fans. Elvis was known to recite Python bits (people must have wondered why he was always calling them "Squire"), and Cameron Crowe referred (in his liner notes to a Zeppelin box set) to John Bonham "thundering down the aisle" of their tour bus "performing Monty Python routines." Paul McCartney would supposedly stop recording sessions when *Monty Python's Flying Circus* was on. Elton John delivered Python lines from the stage. George Harrison famously sent a fan telegram to the Pythons at the BBC; the network never delivered it.

Comedy troupes like Firesign Theater and oddity grab-bag shows like Dr. Demento had carved out a home for themselves on the freakier stretches of the FM dial by the early 1970s. Starting in November 1973, many stations also started carrying the *National Lampoon Radio Hour*, which featured the edgier, darker (and honestly funnier) work of future *Saturday Night Live* players like Harry Shearer, Christopher Guest, and John Belushi. At the time, *National Lampoon*'s usage of shock humor and non sequiturs, while more outwardly rebellious and less intentionally surreal, made them probably the closest thing that the American audience had to Monty Python.

So, Lewis made sure that DJs had all the new Python records. She had plenty to work with. Starting with 1970's *Monty Python's Flying Circus*, the troupe would put out about one record a year for most of that decade. They eventually became enough of a music industry staple that none other than industry mogul Clive Davis (Janis Joplin, Patti Smith, the Kinks) hosted a listening party for *Matching Tie with Handkerchief* at Sardi's.

Palin later told *Mojo* magazine:

> . . . it was the albums that broke America. That FM stoner crowd was quite important. US television was very commercial and safe but with a lot of rock DJs Python was exactly the sort of stuff they were looking for.

With John Cleese, Michael Palin, Graham Chapman, Eric Idle, Terry Jones, Carol Cleveland

Released in 1970, the first Monty Python record helped spread the word with ideologically friendly rock and rollers and FM DJs.   *Lisa Bocchini*

But until *Flying Circus* had a TV station that would take a risk on it, Monty Python would have a hard time breaking out of the cult oddity ghetto.

First . . . We Conquer Canada

Just as the Allies took the long road to Berlin by invading Italy before France, to get to the United States, first the Pythons had to establish a beachhead in Canada.

This was not as hard as it might sound. Remember that in the 1970s, the Great White North was even more culturally somnolent than today. There was a reason that nearly the entire crew of *SCTV*—the oh-so-Canadian sketch comedy show that started in 1976 and was to *Saturday Night Live* what *Cracked* is to *Mad*—bolted to the United States at just about the first opportunity.

But still, the land of Molson, hockey, and good-hearted normalcy was hip to Monty Python well before their American neighbors. The Canadian Broadcasting Corporation (CBC) started showing *Monty Python's Flying Circus* very early, in the fall of 1970. The response was strong enough that when the CBC took the show off the schedule the following February, fans protested in several cities. The second season followed on CBC on May 25, 1973.

Just a week afterward saw the start of the Canadian leg of *Monty Python's First Farewell Tour*. For this cross-continental cavalcade, the Pythons used mostly the same material as their just concluded and very successful month-long tour of Britain.

The troupe landed in Toronto on June 3, 1973, and were greeted at the airport by about 150 fans who had been alerted by the local media. Some showed up wearing Gumby T-shirts. The two-week barnstorm across Canada from Toronto to Vancouver, intimate theaters to three-thousand-seat auditoriums (the latter necessitating what Cleese grumpily termed "opera acting"), was a surprise hit. Idle believed the audiences were highly stoned. The Canadian reception was so positive, in fact, that Nancy Lewis proposed to the Pythons that they soldier on for a few more days after they were done. She wanted to send them down the West Coast of America, doing press and appearances as a way of priming the audience and flogging their albums for the inevitable Python conquest of the States.

However, fissures were already showing in the troupe. They had completed Season Three but not yet embarked on the fourth and most fraught season. Chapman's drinking was reaching epic proportions. Cleese thought they had started to repeat themselves and was itching for the exit. He was not exactly keen to tack on yet more travel time to an already lengthy tour.

Nevertheless, after the last show in Vancouver (a sell-out), the Pythons, minus Cleese, headed for California. There, after knocking about in the Bay Area, they showed up on *The Midnight Special*. This mostly forgotten late-night variety show sprinkled comics like Andy Kaufman and Bill Cosby in between rock bands and pop stars that NBC hoped would attract a younger demographic too groovy for Johnny Carson. The Pythons' set, which included "Nudge, Nudge" and "Gumby Flower Arranging" went over quite well with the kids.

You can read all about the Pythons' first Canada tour in *Monty Python Live!*

Next up was the far more mainstream *Tonight Show*, with staggeringly unenthusiastic guest host Rat Pack-er Joey Bishop, no less. This was the big-time, with tens of millions of American viewers. But instead of performing a surefire water-cooler hit like "The Parrot Sketch," the Pythons performed "Putting Down Budgies," which few of even the most dedicated fans would call a favorite. Whether strategized or intentionally sticking a thumb in the eye of an audience that would never probably get them, it all went over about as well with uninitiated viewers as one can imagine.

Nevertheless, the Pythons weren't done with the New World.

Remember the Dallas PBS Affiliate!

In 1974, the BBC told the Pythons that Lewis was still doing her best to sell *Flying Circus* in the States but having as yet no luck. According to Palin's diary that January, some of the sales people at Time-Life Films, heartened by brisk sales of Python's albums and books, had even taken the challenge of selling *Flying Circus* to the masses as a dedicated mission.

Finally, in October, the first episode of *Flying Circus* was broadcast on American television.

Not surprisingly, it appeared on a public television affiliate. Much like today, a good part of PBS stations' schedules was filled with British imports like *Upstairs, Downstairs* and *Masterpiece Theater*; what can we say, they didn't have Bob Ross's *The Joy of Painting* or *Antiques Roadshow* yet. At a time when the commercial networks were filled with Americanized versions of British shows like *Sanford and Son* and *All in the Family*, the PBS audience preferred their Britishness straight, no chaser.

The freedom provided by being non-commercial and not needing to placate advertisers or investors allowed PBS stations to take more creative risks. What was surprising was that the PBS affiliate to show *Flying Circus* on a Sunday night was KERA Channel 13 in flat, conservative Dallas, Texas: *very* far in both distance and mentality from the bohemian fleshpots on the coasts.

What it came down to was that KERA's vice president of programming, Ron Devillier, had requested tapes of *Flying Circus* from the BBC, who, somewhat typically, tried to insist that he wouldn't like it before reluctantly sending them over. He binge-watched them over a weekend, recalling to *Current* that hours later he had to be jolted back to reality by his wife throwing gravel at the window of the screening room. Devillier's conversion to the

Even lumberjack dolls prefer to sleep all night and work all day.

Lisa Bocchini

Python cause was later singled out by Idle as "the catalyst that led to Monty Python quietly subverting America."

Devillier used the "Lumberjack Song" and "The Argument Clinic" to bring station president Bob Wilson (father of actors Luke and Owen Wilson) on board. The two men convinced a very not-amused board, and several other stations (who had to pool resources to afford the then-expensive transfer from British to American tape formats) to take a shot on the very odd, very very British, very very very risky show. *Flying Circus* premiered on KERA in October 1974. It was a nearly instantaneous hit.

That fall, *Flying Circus* was added to the schedule of stations in crucial media markets like New York and Washington, DC, and smaller affiliates from Scranton to Erie and Buffalo. Whether the show was plugging into an anti-establishment zeitgeist, the country just needed a laugh after the exhaustion of Watergate—President Richard Nixon resigned on August 8, 1974—or this was simply the first time that most Americans had had the opportunity to see it, *Flying Circus* became a ratings bonanza.

Supposedly, once *Flying Circus*'s numbers—even in the graveyard slot of 10:30 p.m. on Sunday—outdid *Masterpiece Theatre* and produced hundreds of pledges, an executive at WNET in New York who previously had said he would only ever air the show over his dead body came around.

By 1975, over 130 stations were showing *Flying Circus* around the country. On February 24, 1975, Palin wrote in his diary about hearing that the show was becoming de rigeur viewing in some quarters. He was pleased in an ironic fashion, given that Monty Python appeared to be catching on in America "whilst back in little old quaint, provincial London it has finally run its course."

What's All This, Then?
Thank You, Public Television

"If it hadn't been for PBS," Terry Gilliam says in David Morgan's oral history *Monty Python Speaks*, "we wouldn't be sitting here." That point was underlined by Jones when the Pythons appeared on KERA for that fundraiser evening in March 1975. In response to a question about censorship, Jones explained that public television probably was the only place for a show like theirs on American television, because commercial television stations are run by corporate interests and executives who "think they know what other people like." To Jones's way of thinking, Python didn't know what people liked, they just knew what *they* thought was funny. Fortunately, the viewers of KERA emphatically agreed.

Possibly due to their rising profile on American television screens, in February 1975, the Pythons signed a US deal for two of their albums (*Matching Tie and Handkerchief* and *Live at Drury Lane*) with Arista Records.

On March 7, 1975, Chapman, Gilliam, Jones, and Palin flew over to the States for a two-week stretch promoting *Flying Circus* and *Monty Python and the Holy Grail*. The film's world premiere took place at the Filmex, or Los Angeles International Film Exposition, on March 14. The following day they flew to Dallas to start a PBS promotional tour.

There, the true scale of the Pythons' American fandom was revealed when they arrived at the KERA station. The Pythons were interviewed live in the station by their Texan cheerleader Devillier in front of a great audience of local Python fans who showered them with questions and enthusiasm

What's All This, Then?
Suing ABC

Not everything went smoothly while the Pythons were conquering the States in the mid-1970s. The first three seasons of *Monty Python's Flying Circus* were broadcast on PBS. But the fourth season was sold instead to ABC. In its inimitable wisdom, the network decided not to show all six episodes but to whack them all together into two ninety-minute specials for late-night broadcast. Once the Pythons had a chance to review the tape of the first episode, broadcast in October 1975, they discovered that ABC had slashed and burned their way through the material. The network had deleted not just curses they thought would be offensive, but entire characters and plot points, rendering the material well-nigh indecipherable. The Pythons brought ABC to court in New York (courtesy of Gilliam's American citizenship) to block the broadcast of the second special. As part of their presentation, the Pythons showed their edit of the "Light Entertainment War" sketch (which got laughs) and then ABC showed their edit (which didn't). Gilliam implored the judge to understand that the network's commercial intrusions had damaged the integrity of their show, which "does extraordinary things, takes all sorts of chances, is not out to sell corn plaster or anything else." (Several Pythons would do plenty of commercial work, of course, but that was separate from *Flying Circus*.) ABC broadcast the second episode, with a disclaimer, before the case was resolved, but ultimately the Pythons reached a settlement with the network, the BBC, and Time-Life, that awarded the troupe complete rights to every episode of *Flying Circus*.

while the station showed *Flying Circus* clips and raised money. Chapman apologized for being a poor interview, Palin walked away with a stuffed armadillo, and the phones rang off the hook.

Most of the rest of the tour involved the Pythons showing up at the various PBS stations that had been showing *Flying Circus* and helping the stations pass the hat. In Chicago, they taped fund-raising spots that included Chapman kneeing Jones in the groin when he doesn't contribute, and what appears to be Jones in full Gumby gear standing in a fountain off Michigan Avenue and bellowing "*subscribe! SUBSCRIBE!*"

Back in New York on April 25, the Pythons showed up for a photo session that required that they be wearing only socks and shoes, plus the odd hat, and Chapman's pipe, of course. But since it was Richard Avedon taking the photographs, they went along with it.

Just two days later, the touring Pythons attended the New York premiere of *Holy Grail* at Cinema II on Third Avenue. Coconuts were handed out to a few (hundred) lucky fans, and film funders Robert Plant and Jimmy Page of Led Zeppelin showed up for the 8:00 p.m. show, just to throw the gathered throngs into more of a frenzy.

What with *Flying Circus* a hit from coast to coast, a new film garnering rave reviews, as well as furious incomprehension—which the Pythons sometimes preferred to positive feedback—their fancy near-nude black-and-white photo spread, and a Manhattan coconut riot, it was clear that by 1975, the Pythons were successfully exposed to America.

13

Of Course It's a Good Idea!

Monty Python and the Holy Grail

efore they began shooting *Monty Python and the Holy Grail* in 1974, the Pythons were beginning to unravel, like woolen chainmail on a wet Scottish night. They'd wrapped Season Three of *Monty Python's Flying Circus* (1972), shot *Monty Python's Fliegender Zirkus* (1972) for German television, and just completed *Monty Python's First Farewell Tour* (1973) when fatigue and creative concerns arose: Cleese was making noise about leaving the group.

And yet . . . ever since the release of their first film—*And Now for Something Completely Different* (1971)—they'd been throwing around ideas for a "real" movie (rather than a glorified clip-show). By early 1974 they'd hammered out a rough script for *Holy Grail*: the legendary story of King Arthur, the Knights of the Round Table, and their quest for the most important MacGuffin in medieval history . . . as well as some coconuts, rude Frenchmen, a shrubbery, and a rabbit with a vicious streak a mile long. Ni!

Origins

In the 1960s and '70s, stories of the once awe-inspiring *rex quondam rexque futurus* (the "Once and Future King") of all England were generally seen as silly kiddie fare thanks to watered-down versions of medieval legends popularized by Howard Pyle, T. H. White, and Hollywood; potentially worse, Arthuriana had been linked to silly "musical faire" thanks to the hugely popular 1960s Broadway musical *Camelot* (which had been made into a hugely popular film in 1967). And yet, Arthur remained a legendary figure, a touchstone for "the good old days" of British nobility, moral superiority, and political dominance; in short, as the most recognizable

Years before *Mystery Science Theater 3000*, Monty Python talked over and commented on movies; only with this soundtrack album, it was their own movie. *Lisa Bocchini*

"authority figure" to ever walk the lengths and breadths of England, Arthur was still due for a good drubbing.

Cleese recalls that all the Pythons "did a bit of reading" to get in the "fanciful" medieval spirit, but it was Jones—just starting his groundbreaking academic investigation into Geoffrey Chaucer's *Canterbury* knight—who acted as the group's resident medievalist. As a result, *Monty Python and the Holy Grail* both subverts and supports historical and literary medievalism, in much the same way that Palin and Jones's earlier endeavor *The Complete and Utter History of Britain* took liberties with history while simultaneously projecting history. As comic theorists oft posit, parody must occupy the space of its primary material before comically distorting it: parody puts forward what it puts down. Much of *Holy Grail* (and popular Arthuriana) may seem downright silly, but as Gilliam has noted, their film (like *Flying Circus*) "demands intelligence" of its audience.

The first few drafts of the script initially jumped between the medieval and modern eras, with Arthur ultimately finding the Holy Grail at the "Grail Counter" in Harrods of London, the five-acre upscale department store that famously touts *"Omnia Omnibus Ubique"* ("Everything for everyone everywhere!"). But by 1974, the boys had focused the script more squarely in the "medieval" period (something like the 1350s, according to Jones; the opening date of 932 AD reflects the medieval period's own penchant for back-dating legends), with a few intrusive and befuddling modern intersections. Rather than include the grand panoply of Arthur's life, from his birth to his death (as collated by Sir Thomas Malory in the late-fifteenth-century *Le Morte d'Arthur*), the Pythons take a truncated approach to Arthuriana, focusing almost exclusively on the exploits of the Knights of the Round Table during their Grail Quest. Gone, for example, is the pulling of Excalibur from the anvil and stone; gone is Arthur's half-sister Morgan le Fay and their bastard son, Mordred; gone too is any mention of Queen Guinevere or the "courtly love triangle" between Arthur, Guinevere, and Lancelot that brings about the fall of Camelot; heck, Camelot itself is practically "written out" of the script. In short, *Monty Python and the Holy Grail* is a well-informed but select parody of Arthurian legend that mocks history, pop culture, musicals, science, religion, heroism, genre, and—above all else—authority.

Production

Troubles plagued the film before it even began. Days before shooting, Jones and Gilliam learned that the Scottish National Trust had denied their use of pre-scouted castle locations, noting that the film was "incompatible with the dignity" of their national landmarks. But years on low-budget television shows had trained the troupe to be creative and penurious; so with one primary castle (the privately owned Doune Castle in Stirling) for interior shots, and another (the likewise privately owned Castle Stalker in Argyll) for a climactic shit-storm, they set out—with some plywood, a few coconuts, and a cast that included the film's carpenter, costume designer, production designer, and the students of a local college—to create an epic medieval comedy out of modest modern means: reportedly £229,575 (funded largely by their mega-fans: rock stars, the lot of them).

The six-week shoot was exhausting for all involved. The four non-directing actors complained bitterly of the cold, wet Scottish environs, exacerbated by the necessity of wearing "chainmail" armor throughout the shoot (in reality, knit wool, but once wet, it got heavy and stayed wet . . . all day) and the lack of hot water at their local lodgings. The two actor/directors—Jones and Gilliam shared the directorial load—had different shooting styles, concerns, and duties that lasted well after the final cut was shouted each day. The demands of production—lighting, framing, and maintaining "excretory verisimilitude"—required of Jones and Gilliam sometimes seemed at odds with comedy itself (SFX smoke being not, on the whole, funny). Meanwhile, Chapman was struggling with alcoholism and the DTs on set, forgetting his lines or getting the hiccups (which the troupe played up in "The Tale of Sir Lancelot"). Most of the Pythons agreed, afterward, that production was less fun than had been hoped; it was exhausting, frustrating, but—in retrospect—pretty damn good, all things considered. For a group of comedians who'd never made a long-form film before (and few TV properties had, back then), *Monty Python and the Holy Grail* was a successful quest.

Reception

Unlike the mixed British and nixed American reviews of *And Now for Something Completely Different*, *Monty Python and the Holy Grail* was an almost instant success, both critically and popularly. Without denying the film's inherent genius, part of its American success was simply due to improved timing, as discussed in the previous chapter. When *Holy Grail* hit the screen, the Pythons were confirmed comedy rock stars . . . in America, at least.

Aftermath

Of course, success is not always skittles and beer. Due to an oversight, the television rights to *Holy Grail* were first sold to CBS, which aired a radically edited version of the film in early 1977. The Pythons protested, of course, and upon regaining the rights to the film, sold it to PBS, who had helped them get a foothold in America with *Flying Circus*. PBS subsequently aired *Holy Grail* uncut . . . and it's suddenly funny again. The film gained cult status in the early days of VHS (bootlegs abounded), and it has since been

released in various forms, including laser disc (1993), DVD (two-disc in 2001 and three-disc in 2006), and Blu-ray (2012). It was also re-released in US theaters in 2001. Toys and swag—from Killer Bunny slippers to Holy (Gr)ail Ale—have reflected the enduring popularity of the film, and *Monty Python's Holy Book of Days* (a day-to-day chronicle of the shooting of *Holy Grail*) was released as an iPad app in 2012.

The Film

Main Titles

The jabberwock-Danish opening credits—with inappropriate øs and umlauts and escalating moose jokes—arose from a combination of penury, arty education, and Swedish erotica: three deep drives among the Pythons, to be sure. Without the funds to create "fancy" credits, Palin thought to mock, both musically and orthographically, the uber-seriousness of "Norwegian movies" commonly heralded as genius among undergraduate creative types; linking such high-brow fare with contemporary low-brow "Swedish erotica" (which had proliferated in Europe since the 1950s) before the film even starts was an inspired juxtaposition. Of course, in another typical *Flying Circus* move, the Swedish/Danish/Scandinavian credits are metatheatrically deemed too silly (here "the management" stands in lieu of "The Colonel") and so—naturally—they're replaced by something even sillier: high-energy Spanish music, strobing colors, and llama references. It's all absurd and cheap. And speaking of cheap . . .

Coconuts

The film proper opens in proper Bergman fashion: amidst smoke and haze a Catherine wheel juts up from the morbid Scottish terrain; in the distance, hooves approach. Hark! King Arthur (Chapman—playing it deadly serious throughout, despite the mustachioed sun upon his tabard) approacheth!

However in lieu of horse, Patsy (Gilliam, acting as both horse and page) trails Arthur, banging two empty halves of a coconut together as his lord pantomimes riding on horseback. This opening visual and auditory juxtaposition of serious and silly (of expectation versus presentation) sets the stage, really, for all the many temporal mash-ups, outright anachronisms, and genre-bashing to follow. While coconuts may have been inspired by penury, and their BBC radio days, they carry the narratological weight of a Clydesdale.

Soon enough, Arthur's authority as king, something presumed in nearly all versions of his legend, is challenged. He ends up trapped in a pointless argument with two local chaps (Cleese and Palin) about swallows, migration patterns, and coconuts. Early on, the Pythons establish that while Arthur and his knights may take their quest seriously, those around them—whether contemporary medieval characters or modern police—will undercut their generic and political authority. Ultimately, the two soldiers ignore Arthur completely—turning to each other to discuss avian aerodynamics and lift ratios—so he rides off unanswered and unsatisfied.

Plague Village

Known to many as the "Bring out yer dead!" scene, Arthur plays a "drive-by" role that allows the audience to witness one of the hallmarks of medieval history: plague. Well, we assume that it's plague, really. There's a cart full of corpses. Must be plague, right? Anyway, everyone knows the Middle Ages were full of filth and death. And buboes: ick. But rather than focus on the unfunny aspects of the Black Death (the death part), the Pythons focus on the practical aspects of pandemic, like the day-to-day postal routine of the Dead Collector (Idle) and the burdens of annoyingly healthy pensioners on their descendants (Cleese).

This scene also underscores the "excretory verisimilitude" that Gilliam and Jones sought to achieve throughout the movie. That is, the medieval settings are nothing but muck and straw and the characters are filthy: muddy, pock-faced, black-toothed, low-hygiene folks, the lot of them. As Jones admitted, medieval cleanliness was never *this* bad, but it "feels authentic" to a modern audience, and that's what counts here. When the Dead Collector (Idle, ad-libbing) sagely notes that Arthur must be the king because "he hasn't got shit all over him," he's simultaneously reflecting upon popular Hollywood representations of the Middle Ages and the physiognomic expectations (stereotyping) of the British class system.

Constitutional Peasants

Easily the most academically referenced scene in the film, "Constitutional Peasants" presents a classic Python temporal mash-up: modern Marxist theory meets medieval feudalism. Arthur—as the chivalric embodiment of divine authority—again runs up against two plebeians who fail to recognize his privilege as king ("Well, I didn't vote for you!"). Full of political terminology and medieval tropes, the result is a typical failure in communication for the Pythonverse. The apparent serf, Dennis (Palin), employs modern political jargon—"anarcho-syndicalist commune," "mandate from the masses," "self-perpetuating autocracy"—while Arthur counters with mythical medieval referents: "The Lady of the Lake," Excalibur," "Divine Providence." As neither speaks (or acknowledges) the other's vocabulary, communication fails.

Dennis clearly wins this bout of medieval flyting (verbal one-upmanship) and Arthur trots away, once again stymied by the lower classes.

The Black Knight

After the intellectual sparring of "Constitutional Peasants," Arthur finds himself in a much more familiar medieval milieu: the old "defeat the big guy / cross the river" trope which is famous in fairy tales, medieval romances, and every Robin Hood tale from Errol Flynn to Daffy Duck.

Arthur and Patsy witness a bloody (bloody!) fight between two helmeted knights blocking a small bridge spanning a tiny rivulet. The Green Knight

One of these knights is about to lose, well, all of his limbs. Careful, though . . . he's a biter.

Columbia Pictures/Photofest

and the Black Knight (Gilliam and Cleese, respectively, who took sword lessons and do their own "stunts" here) give each other quite a pounding. Eventually, the Green Knight receives a flying sword through his visor slit: blood gushes bright red upon the ground (this is Gilliam's first death in the film: he dies quite a bunch, really, for those interested in such things). While the old "sword through the visor slot" may seem a bit outlandish, even cartoonish, there is medieval precedent: the Red Knight suffers a similar demise in Chrétien de Troyes's rather-more-serious twelfth-century romance *Perceval: The Story of the Grail.* Still: ick.

Arthur is impressed with the Black Knight's puissance and asks him to join his court. Rebuffed by the Black Knight's silence, Arthur attempts to cross the ridiculously small bridge, only to be told, "None shall pass." Left without verbal recourse, Arthur fights the good sir knight, Excalibur in hand. The ensuing melee is far more lopsided (heh) than the previous: Arthur is clearly, even perfunctorily, superior in battle. As the fight goes on, Arthur dismembers the Black Knight—arm, arm, leg, and leg—all while the Black Knight repeatedly refuses to yield . . . or pass out, as one might, watching the streams of "Kensington gore" spigot from the knight's wounds. Really, it's over-the-top live-action cartoon violence, the sort of a darkly comic splatstick that underscores the unreality of so much onscreen violence nowadays (but again, not without medieval precedent). Ultimately, while we may admire the Black Knight's "never say die" attitude, he ends up a limbless torso, as empty a threat as he had been when the fight started.

Communication is useless and combat is terminally silly. Kind of wonder where the Pythons are going to go with this film, eh?

Witch Village

Leaving behind politics and chivalry for the moment, we turn to debunking/supporting religious superstition.

The scene starts with a procession of hooded monks (led by Neil Innes) engaged in a somber Latin chant (that proto–heavy metal dirge *Dies Irae*— "The Day of Wrath"). The self-destructive monks punctuate their chant by hitting themselves on the forehead with planks of wood . . . a slightly more slapstick version of the medieval self-flagellation/whipping/scourging imagined in films like *The Seventh Seal.* After the monks pass, Arthur and Patsy look upon a trial of sorts, led by Sir Bedevere (Jones) who—seen tying a coconut to a swallow—stands for "forward thinking medieval science" throughout the film.

On trial today: a woman with a parsnip nose and funnel hat (Connie Booth) who is accused of being a witch—apparently, she had previously turned a local peasant (Cleese) into a newt. And she looks like a witch. Well, she has got a wart.

Anyway, over the course of some truly tortured logical correlation/causation, Bedevere posits that if A) we burn witches, and B) we burn wood, then C) she must be made of wood. And since wood floats, she must also float on water. And since ducks float, if she weighs the same as a duck, she must be made of wood and therefore will float.

What's All This, Then?
Bedevere's Visor: The Drinking Game

Hey kids! Are you 18?* Do you like *Holy Grail* and hate your liver? Then do we have a game for you! Grab a case of Holy (Gr)ail Ale and throw in the film. There are five rules (three, m'liege!), so write them down: Every time Sir Bedevere either raises or lowers his visor, take a drink. When the film is over, take a nap. You're welcome!

*The legal drinking age in the US in 1975.

Setting both Booth and a duck upon Bedevere's "largest scales," we see that she does, in fact, weigh the same as a duck, and is thus, logically, a witch! As the burn-happy lynch mob celebrates the verdict, Booth admits, staring into the camera: "It's a fair cop." Arthur is also impressed with Bedevere's knowledge of science and dubs him his first knight of the Round Table.

The Book of the Film

We then cut to a brief interstitial intrusion by *The Book of the Film*, which speedily introduces the audience to some of the other knights Arthur gathers: Sir Lancelot the Brave (Cleese), Sir Galahad the Pure (Palin), Sir Robin the Not-so-Brave-as-Sir-Lancelot (Idle), and Sir-Not-Appearing-in-This-Film (Palin's then-infant son, William). We also get a cameo of a woman's hand . . . and a gorilla paw. Clearly, this is all Gilliam's doing, the scamp.

Knights of the Round Table

Having gathered his knights, Arthur spies a castle in the distance: Camelot!

In one of the film's subtler metatheatrical moments, as Arthur points off to the distant plywood cutout, Patsy mutters the wry rejoinder "It's only a model," only to be shushed by Arthur. For fans who recognized Gilliam as the troupe's animator and model-maker, the joke is doubly funny. For the cast who had to endure multiple takes of this scene as the plywood castle collapsed repeatedly in the background, perhaps it was less funny.

In any case, we (and presumably Arthur and company) are offered a quick peek inside Camelot, where knights frolic and sing a jaunty musical number (proclaiming their affinity for sewing sequin vests, doing chorus

Consult the Book of Armaments!

routines, pushing prams, and, of course, eating "ham and jam and Spam a lot"). The scene was shot in one day, inside Doune Castle (of course), and showcases Jones's talent as a musical director: it's compact, frenetic, and even a bit Marxist (Harpo, not Karl). Yet as Arthur dourly notes, this exceedingly *Camelot* version of Camelot is indeed "a silly place," and so he and his knights set off to find adventure elsewhere. Ironically, of course, the Pythons—or at least Idle—would return to embrace this scene in the megahit musical *Spamalot* thirty years later (but more on that in another chapter).

God

Eschewing Camelot, the Knights of the Round Table (where do they keep it?) are fortuitously visited by God, or at least an animated version of renowned cricketer W. G. Grace as voiced by Chapman (who booms imperiously at himself). Like many of the animated bits in the film, this scene speeds the story along: God gives them their quest, shows them the Grail (which, as Palin notes in the DVD commentary, looks a good bit like a Football Cup), and off they go . . . manuscript illuminations and flatulent fanfares pursuant.

French Taunters

Right out the box, Arthur and his "silly English kuh-niggets" run afoul of a group of French "taunters" (yes, a real thing in medieval warfare) led by a highly eccentric Cleese copping a highly eccentric French accent. Outrageous, even. Like the earlier "Constitutional Peasants" scene, Arthur is rebuffed by the "lower classes" (and *French*, adding insult to injury) who refuse to respect his *auctoritee*. Despite his polite pleas, Arthur is rudely, albeit creatively, insulted; when he and his knights resort to a futile show of force, the French hurl animals down upon them from the parapets (another

The *Monty Python and the Holy Grail* card game released in 1996 contains 22 "Taunt cards."
Lisa Bocchini

reasonably medieval practice). Even after they've "run away," the French taunters shout, "Fetchez la vache!" and catapult a cow upon them, crushing a page (Neil Innes, seen earlier as a monk hitting himself with a board. And no, that's not the last abuse he'll see in this film). Fun fact: while there was a life-size practical model of a cow on set for close-ups, the "flying" cow was actually a four-inch model from a model railroad set.

The Trojan Rabbit

Not content to walk away from this encounter entirely, Arthur—led by Bedevere's classically inspired brainstorm—and his crew noisily construct a twenty-foot-tall "Trojan Rabbit" on wheels, which they leave at the gate of the castle, awaiting their moment to spring out upon the French, totally unawa . . . never mind.

Fun fact #2: unlike the four-inch flying cow from the previous scene, the Trojan Rabbit was a full-sized construct that needed to be winched up to the castle gate (out of shot). And when it is hurled back by the French taunters (to terminally land upon poor bandaged Neil Innes), the Pythons suspended it, via crane, and let it literally fall to pieces . . . in one take. As the (im)mortal Daffy Duck once said: "It's a great trick, but I can only do it once."

[A Famous Historian]

We get the first modern intrusion upon the medieval narrative at this point, and what seems like a simple "exposition dump" by a bespectacled professor (John Young, who also played the "not dead yet" old man earlier). However, in mid-lecture, the Famous Historian is practically beheaded by a knight riding by on horseback. Wait? There are horses in this movie? Since when?

The Tale of Sir Robin

After having been gob-smacked, heifer-dropped, and rabbit-crushed, Neil Innes finally gets his (verbal) revenge. Here we follow Sir Robin (Idle) and his minstrels (led by Innes) as they trot through the dark and scary forest. Minstrels have a long medieval history, of course, recording and promulgating stories of real and imagined knights. Here, the irony is that Robin—"the not-so-brave"—is treated to "minstrelsy on the fly" as it were, real-time reportage (in song!) that underscores his pants-wetting cowardice.

Robin—after casually passing the "Constitutional Peasants" en route out of the forest—encounters the Three-Headed Knight (Jones, Chapman, and Palin, playing it close and camp). Now, meeting with and slaying giants, ogres, and multiheaded monstrosities was part of medieval romances, and this should be no different . . . except Robin is a coward, and the giant Three-Headed Knight gets caught up bickering with himself. It's quite a bit like the squabbling of the three trolls in J. R. R. Tolkien's *The Hobbit*, when you think about it. But very, *very* camp.

In any case, before their conflict comes to a head (sorry), Robin has—in the singsong reportage of Innes—"bravely turned his tail and fled."

The Tale of Sir Galahad

A complex illuminated manuscript animation of monks diving into a pool (one getting diddled upside-down by a nun) foretells "The Tale of Sir Galahad," an exploration into spirituality, hospitality, and the (potential) pleasures of the flesh. As the scene opens, the mood has taken a turn: it is dark, stormy, and wet; Galahad is hard-pressed, alone (no coconut horsemate for him!), until he sees, above a distant castle, the Grail, glowing like a beacon! Galahad hies himself hence, and is greeted within Castle Anthrax by the fair maid Zoot (Carol Cleveland). Despite his straitlaced pleas to see the Grail, he is rebuffed; instead, Zoot describes for him the loneliness of the castle's occupants: eightscore young blondes between the ages of sixteen and nineteen-and-a-half (fifteen Glasgow "girlies," as the script notes), bored, sexually curious, and lonely. So, so lonely.

So, on the one hand, Galahad the Pure seeks only the Grail (not "the feminine")!

On the other hand . . . this is the 1970s, man! Down with repression! Free love is where it's at!

Fortunately/unfortunately, just as it seems that milquetoast Palin is

What's All This, Then?
Get On with It!

Holy Grail DVDs since 2001 have come with an "extra twenty-four seconds" of footage, a bit of hyper-meta-self-referentiality and fourth-wall bashing in which Cleveland questions whether her scene (as Dingo) is very good. The camera then cuts to various characters from the film (including those we've not yet encountered!) urging her to just "get on with it!" Jones and Gilliam yanked the scene from distribution at the last minute, only to find that they—and preview audiences—loved it. So look: it's back! And there was much rejoicing.

about to relent and give in to the pleasures of the flesh ("Well, I suppose I could stay a *bit* longer . . ."), Lancelot and company arrive to whisk him away to "safety." Because there's nothing like your father showing up just when the orgy is about to start.

"Shit."

Scene 24

After some brief shtick with *The Book of the Film* and a gorilla hand, we cut to Arthur and Patsy in a hovel being fed exposition by the Soothsayer (Gilliam, who reprises the role later as the Bridgekeeper). In short: Arthur must seek an enchanter, a cave, a gorge, and a bridge. If the Soothsayer had thrown in "six cc's of rat's blood and some dribbly candles," he'd have described every Dungeons & Dragons quest and RPG plot since 1976.

Without further explanation, the Soothsayer and his hovel disappear in a hail of echoing laughter. Onward!

The Knights Who Say Ni!

Words have power. Even silly ones.

After the Soothsayer disappears, Arthur encounters the Knights Who Say Ni!, a group of bizarre otherworldy folk who demand favors of Arthur in return for their cooperation: it's a scene right out of the Joseph Campbell quest fiction handbook, really. Here, the helmeted wild men—led by a ten-foot-tall horned Palin (bewhiskered, helmeted, and on a tall ladder throughout)—demand a shrubbery from Arthur, who wishes to pass through their woods. In the parlance of role-playing-games, this is a "fetch quest," but it is also a legendary adventure deflated by the shrubbery's addition of mundane, middle-class reality. As Idle notes in the film commentary, the overall concept and particular verbiage in the scene is "very Goon-y": absurd and verbal. Tasked with his ridiculous mini-quest, off Arthur goons. Er, goes.

The Tale of Sir Lancelot

Another genre-bashing scene, this one poking fun at Errol Flynn-esque swashbuckling films, which are really quite violent if you stop and think about them (but you didn't, did you?) and at period musicals, which are indeed quite silly (but you knew that already). There's also some gender-swapping, hiccups, communication breakdown, and more "not quite dead" nonsense.

Admittedly, the rather tall Cleese makes an imposing traditional knight, and he inhabits the swashbuckling "idiom" with violent aplomb as Sir Lancelot the Brave (a knight who, in medieval lore, was known as the doughtiest of fighters).

The Rescue of Prince Herbert

The chief genre joke here is that Lancelot is not, as is typical, saving a "fair maiden" from incarceration, but a "fair maid" (in the technical sense of the term: an "unwed youth"). But stealing the show, Jones's impressive pantomime notwithstanding, are Idle and Chapman as two guards who alternately hiccup and stammer their way through compulsively misunderstanding their lord's simple command. Ah, language: is it ever simple? <HIC!>

The Wedding Guests

We get a second (or third) dose of "not dead yet" as Lancelot and Herbert's father return to the scene of Lancelot's earlier carnage and—after some renewed heroic violence from Cleese ("Sorry! Sorry!"), Palin attempts a violent merger between Camelot and Swamp Castle. It doesn't quite work, as Herbert—the creep!—returns from the dead. Somehow.

The scene ultimately just peters out on two levels: Lancelot is literally left hanging in mid-escape (heroic!), and the camera fades even as Herbert—finally—begins to sing (theatric!). It's almost as if the two competing genres cancel each other out. Almost.

Roger the Shrubber

And we're back to Arthur, who fortuitously finds a professional Shrubber (Idle) in a nearby town. What a co-inky-dink.

A Herring

And we're back to Arthur (again), presenting his shrubbery to the Knights Who Say Ni. It's very nice.

Of course, this being a quest and all, there's a wrinkle or two: Palin and company are now no longer the Knights Who Say Ni, but the Knights Who Say Icky Icky Icky Ptang Zoop Boing . . . and so they require yet another shrubbery . . . and a tree to be cut down with a herring. Really: as much as "three is the magic number" in quest fiction (see *Sir Gawain and the Green Knight* for ample evidence of the tradition), at this point the knight's requests have gotten so silly that even Arthur has had enough.

Fortunately for Arthur, the Knights Who Until Recently Said Ni are betrayed by their own verbal weakness: the word *it*. Unwittingly aided by the recently arrived Sir Robin (and by the bizarre knights themselves, who keep saying it), Arthur passes through the forest to his next adventure. A great bit of linguistic nonsense, that.

[Dead Historian / A Year's Worth of Animation]

Meanwhile, back in what appears to be the modern day, that historian slashed dead by the passing knight is still dead, and the coppers have shown up, adding an ever-so-slight secondary plot to the medieval proceedings.

Also meanwhile, we are treated to some more Gilliam animation that quickly (and cheaply) brings all of Arthur's knights back together over the course of a compressed year. Oh: and they eat Robin's minstrels. Yay.

Tim the Enchanter

Somehow finding themselves among the rocks of a Scottish quarry, the gathered knights meet Tim the Enchanter (Cleese, absorbing a local Scottish brogue and in the process doing an excellent, if accidental, impression of a similarly tall Billy Connolly), who impresses them with his pyrotechnic skills and points them in the direction of Caerbannog—the site of their next mini-quest.

As Jones notes in the commentary, there's a point in many Python films where the bam-bam-bam pace of their comedy begins to build audience fatigue. This is one such point. Tim's a cool character, but the scene is mostly exposition, fiery SFX, and spit.

The Cave of Caerbannog

Aw, look at the cute li'l bunny. Upending the traditional "boss-monster" of many medieval quest fictions (and modern RPG games) by replacing the fearsome dragon with a wolf in sheep's clothing, the scene gives the Pythons another chance to ridicule traditional models of heroism and narrative expectation. After Sir Bors (Gilliam, who ends up dying quite a bit in this film) is unexpectedly beheaded by the flying lepus (portrayed by a combination of live shots, hand puppetry, and suspended models), Arthur and his men enter the fray, only to meet a frenetically bloody—indeed "Peckinpah-ish"—defeat at the "nasty big pointy teeth" of the vicious rabbit; a full five (er, three) knights are killed, and Robin soils his armor. Again.

The Holy Hand Grenade

Of course, the quest must go on, so against this unnatural foe Arthur calls for supernatural (and seemingly anachronistic) aid: the Holy Hand Grenade of Antioch! Led forth with pomp by Brother Maynard (Idle) and described with great verbosity by Maynard's Roommate (Palin), the Holy Hand Grenade and its instruction manual—*The Book of Armaments*—offer another moment of thesaurus humor and enable them to ridicule the semi-castrati monotony of typical Church of England services endured by the British Pythons in their youth. Throw in one more "three for five" gag, and the Holy Hand Grenade doth snuffeth the killer rabbit. Amen.

[A Shot Rings Out!]

Meanwhile, two policemen—bagging evidence at an abandoned shrubbery—and a trench-coated investigator (the film's production designer pulling double duty) hear the bunny explode and dash off to, uhm, investigate.

What's All This, Then?
Monty Python and Dungeons and the Holy Grail and Dragons

In the Dungeons & Dragons tournament module, *Expedition to the Barrier Peaks*, adventurers encounter a "cute little bunnyoid" that morphs into a fearsome tentacle beastie, which rips into unwary heroes. Written by D&D cofounder Gary Gygax for the second Origins International Game Expo in 1976, the module—which unusually mashes together traditional "medieval" and science fiction elements—seems a very likely homage to the Pythons and reinforced the early geek cred of the troupe. As your authors can attest, many a young geek ran away—a lot—in that module. >sigh<

Must-have for every serious *Holy Grail* fan: Killer bunny slippers. Comfortable and homicidal.

Black Beast of Arrrghhh

Leaving the bunny-borne carnage behind them, Arthur and his knights enter the Cave of Caerbannog and Brother Maynard reads the last words of Joseph of Arimathea (a "real" Biblical figure who was apocryphally credited with bringing the Holy Grail to England way back when; no, really, if you don't believe us, read Dan Brown. Go ahead: we'll wait) carved upon a cave wall. But before the group can make sense of the saint's scrawl, the Vicious Black Beast of Oooh . . . sorry . . . of Arrrghhh attacks the troupe and swallows Maynard (Idle's second full death).

Did we mention that the Black Beast is an animation? Ah. Well, it is. Lots of eyes, big maw—we saw him back in an earlier cut scene, actually. Oh, do pay attention, Wadsworth. We may very well set an exam this term! Right. So, anyway, a lovely animated sequence involving medieval illumination, photo realism, and airbrushed monstrosity follows, and things look to be dire for the knights until, suddenly, the animator (Gilliam as himself) suffers a fatal heart attack and keels over melodramatically; the Black Beast—like Bambi's mother—was no more.

[Hot Fuzz]

Quick shot of the policemen and the investigator examining the carnage outside the Cave of Caerbannog; it's starting to feel like two plots are converging. Hmmm . . .

The Bridge of Death

Exiting the cave (into what was the first scene shot for the entire movie), the knights (including a king with the

The actual Black Beast of Arrrghhh was far more terrifying than this adorable impersonation by young squire Massey.

DTs) work their way along a precipice to the Bridge of Death, where the Soothsayer from Scene 24 awaits to test their mettle with riddles. Yes, riddles are a medieval quest "thing" (see any tenth-century Anglo-Saxon codex, like *The Exeter Book* . . . or just read *The Hobbit*).

The Bridgekeeper/Soothsayer (still Gilliam) poses the following five (three!) questions to each knight in turn:

1. "What is your name?"
2. "What is your quest?"

3. and (alternately) "What is your favorite color?" or "What is [random Final *Jeopardy*–level trivia question]?"

Failure to answer any of the questions incorrectly results in immediate, seemingly magical, catapulting into the Gorge of Eternal Peril; as the boys note in the film commentary, the 250-foot-deep gorge in Glencoe was no joke, and—although well constructed—the bridge "no fun to cross." Add to this natural ravine smoke and diabolic under-lighting, and it does "read" as menacing: the last divide for the knights on their quest. Maybe.

Lancelot answers the Bridgekeeper's questions first and makes it past (favorite color: blue), but Robin and Galahad meet their demise here (Idle's third death; Palin's first). Arthur then steps forward and turns the tables on the Bridgekeeper, who is stumped by a follow-up question regarding sparrows (information learned by Arthur in the first scene of the film; that's called a narrative causality loop, folks, a sort of intellectual Chekhov's Gun: it was bound to go off). As the Bridgekeeper plummets to his death (Gilliam's fifth and final demise), Arthur and Bedevere cross the bridge— the tension cut by a sudden [INTERMISSION] sign flashing onscreen briefly—and head off to meet Lancelot. Or so they think.

[All right, what's all this, then?]

While Arthur and Bedevere call for Lancelot, we see he is indisposed: jacked up against a police rover getting frisked.

The Castle Arrrghhh

Standing at the edge of a loch, Arthur and Bedevere look out upon a water-locked "Sacred Castle" (Castle Stalker in Argyll) when a dragon-headed Viking ship appears through the fog; triumphant music swells and the two cross to the island, their quest nearly at an end: Avalon awaits!

It's a great mood piece, serious and dramatic, magical and quasi-religious; Chapman is at his straight-man best here, and the directors are firing on all verisimilitudinous cylinders.

The Holy Grail

Unfortunately, the French taunters who so badgered Arthur earlier have beaten him and his "knees-bent creeping about advancing behavior" to the castle. Cleese is cruelly creative with his verbal jabs in this round ("electric donkey-bottom biters"?), while Chapman is utterly out of patience. To add injury to insult, the taunters hurl ordure upon Arthur from high above, covering the English king in French shit. Historically, there can be no greater insult. Arthur—besmirched, befouled, and bedeviled—has been defeated.

Prepare to Attack

Yet wait! As Arthur and Bedevere trudge out of the loch with the castle behind them (it's now low tide, apparently), Arthur steels himself and calls out: "Stand by for attack!" Suddenly—without preamble (well, if you discount two seconds of the cut scene from Castle Anthrax)—an "enormous" army of medieval soldiery appears behind him. Although only about two hundred extras are in the shot (students from nearby Stirling University, the film's crew, their families, and so forth), the frenetic filming, intermixed close-ups, and fast edits make the charging army seem as impressive as anything in *Braveheart*. Unfortunately, the entire charging army is halted by a police car and paddy wagon that suddenly pull up before them: the second plot has finally caught up with Arthur.

The End of the Film

As the wife of the dead historian IDs Arthur, our hero is thrown against the car, frisked, and unceremoniously relieved of Excalibur. Bedevere and the Stirling army mill about, confused, and police break up the throng. As Arthur is taken away in the police car, an officer roughly throws his hand over the camera (!), breaking the fourth wall (again) and ending the film. The film visibly unspools onscreen; and slushy organ music pipes in. *Hic iacet Arthurus, rex quondam rexque futurus.*

Coda

The abrupt ending of *Monty Python and the Holy Grail* tends to surprise first-time viewers: for anyone invested in Arthur's narrative, it's a bit of a slap, really, a cheat, a WTF? moment. Of course, in retrospect, it's a pretty predictable non-ending from the Python crew, who made a habit of not ending sketches on *Flying Circus*. It's also not a stretch from a medieval perspective. One of the traditional themes in Arthurian literature is Arthur's "not-quite-dead" ending. In many versions of his "death" (Malory included), Arthur is carried off on a barge (maybe even a dragon-headed one) to the

Isles of Avalon, where he may or may not be dead, whence he may return in time of need. Heck, Chrétien de Troyes's version of the Grail Quest also ends abruptly, before anyone actually finds the cup of Christ. Of course, in that case, the story ended because the author died while writing it (take that, Gilliam-animator!).

In short, *Monty Python and the Holy Grail* ends as it should: abruptly.

14

Moving On

John Cleese Checks into *Fawlty Towers*

awlty Towers is a bit of a miracle. After deconstructing comedy and genre for both television and film, what were the individual Pythons to do with their comedic gifts after Monty Python had run its course? For Cleese, the answer seemed obvious: return to the discredited form of the sitcom and approach it in a new way, one that acknowledged the genre's intrinsic limitations but also injected new life in what seemed (at the time) a cultural dead end.

The result was *Fawlty Towers*. Cleese's reinvention of the sitcom was as new and startling as anything Python had done, even if it seemed just a little bit more . . . *familiar* to most TV viewers. *Fawlty Towers* ran for just two seasons: six episodes in 1975 and another six episodes in 1979. This seems incredibly brief in retrospect, but each episode was a finely hewn comedic gem, and arguably the single best post-Python project conceived by any member.

The origin story for *Fawlty Towers* involved an actual B&B, Gleneagles Hotel, where the members of Python stayed during the filming of *Monty Python's Flying Circus* in 1970. The Pythons were shooting exteriors in Torbay and the owner, Donald Sinclair, was astoundingly rude. At one point, he chastised Gilliam for switching his fork back to his right hand after cutting some food, saying, "We don't eat like that in this country." At another point Idle found that the bag he had left downstairs had been tossed over a wall, because Sinclair had had "some problems with the staff" and thought it might be a bomb. This caused all the other Pythons to decamp, except for Cleese, who was as bemused as he was appalled and stayed to take notes, even inviting wife Connie Booth to join him. Cleese did a dry run with a character inspired by Sinclair's unique style of customer interaction on a 1971 episode of the sitcom *Doctor at Large*, which he still wrote for at times during the *Flying Circus* years. A few years later, Booth and Cleese were hard at work on the new sitcom.

The fan anticipation for *Fawlty Towers* ran high, as no one knew (in those long-lost pre-Internet days) exactly what to expect. Rabid Python fans were tuning in to see what Cleese's new show would be like, but wondered: What would it be like watching Cleese interact with non-Pythons?

A 2000 poll by the British Film Institute declared *Fawlty Towers* the greatest British television program of all time; four slots ahead of *Monty Python's Flying Circus.*   *BBC America/Photofest*

Starring as the comedically terrible hotelier Basil Fawlty, Cleese was a familiar commodity, and the most alert Python fans might have recognized Booth from her Python appearances (especially as the "witch" in *Holy Grail*), or might have known that she was married to Cleese. As Basil's wife, Sybil, Prunella Scales was a better-known commodity in general, as was Andrew Sachs (playing Spanish waiter Manuel), at least to most BBC viewers, but *Fawlty Towers* was still a risk. The BBC certainly thought so, and decided to give Cleese "notes" indicating they wanted to move the action out of the hotel and, as usual, did not find the initial scripts "funny" (a similar situation to Python), but assumed that Cleese would make the scripts funny via his usual magic touch. This was accurate in many ways, as Cleese and Booth labored over each script for multiple drafts to polish their comedic gold.

Fawlty Towers was set in Torquay, Devon, although no exteriors were shot there. Booth and Cleese initially split writing duties based on female/male characters at first, but after a while simply wrote the episodes in tandem, with Cleese writing most of Basil's trademark angry outbursts. The show was shot in the BBC studios, with exteriors at the Woodburn Grange Country Club in Buckinghamshire, which alas is no more; the Country Club has ceased to be . . . [None of that!—Eds.] Well, it burned down in 1991.

The first season aired in 1975, and after some initial public and critical trepidation, it soon became a critical favorite, winning the BAFTA award for best comedy series. Cleese was also awarded the Royal Television Society Programme Award. Despite Cleese and Booth getting divorced in 1978, a second and final series appeared in 1979, also for six episodes.

But enough about the show in general; let's look at what happened during the episodes.

Season One

Episode 1: "A Touch of Class" (original air date: September 19, 1975)

The first episode starts with Basil squabbling with Sybil about hanging a picture and trying to micromanage Manuel, their new trainee waiter from Barcelona. Basil's manic energy, inherent anger, and simmering frustration at his circumstances are established within the first few minutes as he turns from unctuous to smiling evilly, sometimes mid-sentence. Manuel is a source of particular frustration for Basil, who though he says he speaks "classical Spanish," really is not conversant in the language. We are also introduced to waitress Polly (Booth), who is a budding artist and not afraid to stand up to Basil, although many times she gets sucked into his elaborate schemes.

Cleese's Basil Fawlty is a simmering ball of fury, both desperate to suck up to the upper classes and resentful of his position. Basil's fawning over the Major (Ballard Berkeley), a permanent resident of the hotel, is contrasted with his seeming inability to understand why he's supposed to be cordial to his guests. The episode revolves around Basil's wish to associate himself with people like the Major, of "better class" and economic status. Basil has even bought an advertisement in the local paper to "attract a better class of person." Basil is pleased to see that Sir Richard Morris and his wife have booked a room and also appalled that a new guest, Mr. Brown (who does *not* seem like "a better class of person" to Basil) has just checked in.

When a man who introduces himself as Lord "Melbury" arrives, Basil's sycophancy leaps to exponential levels, as his eyes gleam with thoughts of serving such a noble personage. The lord leaves a valise with "just a few valuables" for Basil to hold, and the awestruck Basil is soon moving guests from table to table to seat the presumptive Lord Melbury, leading to Basil's both unseating his lordship and tripping Manuel at the same time. Two points for Basil!

Basil is so happy he even tries to be nice to Sybil by kissing her on the cheek, leading to the classic exchange of:

Sybil: "What are you doing?"
Basil: "Kissing you."
Sybil: (annoyed) "Well, don't!"

Naturally, a peer would not soil his hands with actual cash, and the Lord asks Basil to cash a check for two hundred pounds. While going in to cash the check for Basil, Polly stumbles upon Brown, who is part of a police stakeout at the local jeweler's.

Later, Melbury tries to con Basil out of his rare coin collection, while Polly reveals that Brown is in the CID and that "Lord" Melbury is a con man, which Basil refuses to believe, until Sybil opens Melbury's case, which is filled with bricks.

At this point the actual Sir Richard Morris and his wife arrive, just as Basil, now disenchanted with the fake lord, breaks out in a fit of rage, unleashing his inner frustration. He starts off by softly asking, "Any valuables to deposit, any . . . *bricks?*" before shifting to a (soon-to-be) classic Basil outburst, shouting, "You bastard!" while the fake lord is arrested by the police in the hotel lobby, causing the real "better class of people," Sir Richard Morris and his wife, to leave in a huff as Basil shouts abuse in their wake. Within half an hour we have already been introduced to not only the main cast, but also one of the key themes of the show: Basil's pretensions and ambition to associate with people in the upper classes.

Episode 2: "The Builders" (original air date: September 26, 1975)

The second episode opens as Basil and Sybil are off for a holiday, leaving Polly and Manuel in charge. Basil tries to explain in his pidgin Spanish that Manuel should clean the windows, before finally picking Manuel up and carrying him to the window. O'Reilly, a local builder mentioned in the previous episode, calls to say that the builders are on the way to finally "put up the garden wall." In reality, they are doing major renovations to the building, which Basil has hidden from Sybil, despite knowing that the builders are incompetent and against Sybil's wishes.

Polly decides to take a nap, leaving Manuel to wait for O'Reilly's men by himself, informing him he is supposed to wake Polly when they arrive. A deliveryman drops off a large garden gnome and calls Manuel a "dago twit" before leaving. Next to arrive are three workers from O'Reilly's firm, but Manuel feels bad and does not wake Polly, and of course, the men have the wrong information. Fawlty calls back and arranges for Manuel to insult a workman, leading to his being hit.

When Basil arrives the next day, the workmen have walled off the dining room. Polly feels guilty and, naturally, Basil panics, demonstrating the wonderful physicality of Cleese, who ends up being slapped repeatedly by Polly and ultimately tries to strangle the garden gnome. Frantically, Basil calls O'Reilly, who shows up to fix the door. But alas, for Basil, Sybil has arrived early. Basil follows his natural inclination (hide and then lie), but his ruse is quickly discovered by Sybil, who proceeds to pummel Basil and O'Reilly with an umbrella. In the end Basil leaves with the gnome to "see O'Reilly,"

What's All This, Then?
Each Second Counts

Among the reasons that *Fawlty Towers* is considered such an incomparable example of the British sitcom are its verbal density and taut structure. This isn't by chance. Cleese told the Onion's *AV Club* in 2009 that filming was manic due to the length of the scripts, which were about double the length of the average sitcom. He also said that they would spend easily twenty hours editing each episode to make each moment count: "So for every minute you see on your DVD, forty minutes were spent editing it."

having previously threatened to do an anatomically inappropriate action with the gnome on O'Reilly.

Episode 3: "The Wedding Party" (original air date: October 3, 1975)

When Manuel has a night off for his birthday, Basil and Sybil are squabbling as usual. (As an indication of how well he and Sybil get along, Basil asks a guest, "Did you ever see *How to Murder Your Wife?* I saw it six times!") Polly's date, Richard Turner, stays at the hotel. Basil catches them kissing, which upsets his natural prudishness. But he is even more enraged when he suspects a couple checking in of being unmarried (they have different last names) and will not rent them a double room. Sybil, however, relents and gives them a room. Basil expresses his "disgust!" when one of the couple asks where the local chemist's is, assuming the guest wants to purchase condoms.

The episode is structured not unlike a French farce, heavily predicated on mistaken identity and people running though doors. This influence is given a tip of the hat in the character of Mrs. Pegnoir, a French guest who hits drunkenly on Basil, leading to a classic Cleeseian infuriated monologue as he tries to explain what's going on.

In their room—where Basil and Sybil sleep in two single beds, what did you expect?—Manuel arrives back from a night of drinking, honking a horn and covered in streamers. He ends up rolling on the floor with Basil as the other guests look on, assuming it's a gay liaison (Manuel *does* keep repeating how much he loves Basil).

The next morning, Manuel is too hungover to serve breakfast and keeps falling around the dining room. Further complications ensue when Basil tries to fire Polly and kick out the guests after misinterpreting another situation, but after Sybil explains the whole situation Basil is forced to apologize (well, as much as Basil can).

In the last scene, Basil, thinking there is a burglar downstairs, hits Manuel with a frying pan—the padded prop pan that Cleese was supposed to use for the scene was mistakenly replaced by a real one, injuring Sachs. As the French farce ends, the viewers are left with one burning question: Why on earth would Mrs. Pegnoir try to seduce Basil Fawlty? We may never know.

Episode 4: "The Hotel Inspectors" (original air date: October 10, 1975)

Two guests check into Fawlty Towers. The first one, Mr. Hutchinson, sounds a bit like Cleese in the "Cheese Shop" sketch, talking circuitously in a very

Cleeseian manner and (ironically) thoroughly annoying Basil. The second guest, Mr. Walt, is the polar opposite, as taciturn as Mr. Hutchinson is gregarious. He is inadvertently insulted when Basil writes "P. Off" as an abbreviation for "Post Office."

Sybil informs Basil that hotel inspectors are in town, leading Basil to panic over how poorly he's been treating the guests. Basil soon suspects that Mr. Hutchinson is the inspector, and begins kissing up to him in his usual unctuous manner. When Basil changes his mind, and is convinced that Walt is actually the hotel inspector, he is torn between his natural urge to be completely horrible and to flatter the person he's now convinced is the real inspector. Basil's solution ends up with him insulting both men and throttling Hutchinson into unconsciousness.

After a fight with the now-awakened Hutchinson, Basil tries to bribe Walt and is then horrified to find out that Walt is not the hotel inspector, either. But, as revenge is one of Basil's specialties, he then attacks Hutchinson with pies and, with the aid of Manuel (who also put cream in Hutchinson's briefcase), they eject him from the hotel. Watching the scene are three men who turn out to be the real hotel inspectors. Basil emits a bloodcurdling scream as the show cuts to the credits.

The "Hotel Inspector" is another example of Basil turning on someone when he is not who he thought he was, as with the fake "lord" in "A Touch of Class," a reoccurring motif in *Fawlty Towers*.

Episode 5: "Gourmet Night" (original air date: October 17, 1975)

In his constant attempts to surround himself with a "better class of person," Basil has planned a "no riff-raff" gourmet dinner night, for which his new Greek chef, Kurt, is promising an elaborate menu with a large variety of gourmet dishes. Kurt's secret is that he's an alcoholic who has fallen off the wagon because his crush on Manuel is unrequited, naturally leading him to drink to the point of passing out before the gourmet dinner. Their friend Andre, who had recommended Kurt in the first place, volunteers to send dishes from his restaurant instead; the only caveat, in the words of Basil, "If you don't like duck . . . you're rather stuck."

Basil makes two attempts to get the duck dinner, the first time dropping it in the kitchen, and Manuel aids in its destruction by getting his foot stuck it in it. A second attempt goes wrong when Basil's car breaks down while en route to pick up the second meal. Basil heaps the car with abuse, and promises to give it a "damn good thrashing," which he proceeds to do with a tree

What's All This, Then?
Sign Anagram

One of the running gags in *Fawlty Towers* can be spotted in the opening credits. The establishing shot of the hotel includes its sign, which for reasons unknown changes its wording ever so slightly from one episode to the next, as a kind of light anagram. Our personal favorite shows up at the start of "Gourmet Night": "WARTY TOWELS." Runner-up is the sign for the "Waldorf Salad" episode: "FLAY OTTERS."

branch. After Basil finally arrives back at Fawlty Towers, things go even worse when a "bombe surprise" dessert is accidentally substituted for the duck dinner. Naturally, Basil then proceeds to tear it apart, finally announcing, "Ducks off!" before the credits roll.

One episode highlight has the supporting players taking center stage while Basil is off trying to get the duck dinner. The staff attempts to entertain the guests, with Sybil telling an "amusing story," Manuel playing (unsurprisingly) inept flamenco guitar, and (surprisingly) Polly singing "I Cain't Say No" from *Oklahoma!* Booth, a veteran of the West End and Broadway, shows how sometimes you need a highly talented performer to play somebody without any talent.

Episode 6: "The Germans" (original air date: October 24, 1975)

With Sybil in the hospital—her ingrown toenail procedure is leaving her bedridden and in great pain for three days, something that causes Basil no end of pleasure—Basil is tasked with running the hotel by himself, a job at which he proves to be (of course) spectacularly inept.

Basil attempts to put up a moose head, which falls on his head, causing a masterfully comic chain reaction. Later, while waiting for Basil to start a fire drill, Manuel accidentally starts a real fire in the kitchen, after which Basil of course locks Manuel in the kitchen. The scene peaks when Manuel hits Basil on the head with a frying pan, knocking him out. (No information is available on whether Sachs used a real pan for this scene in revenge for getting whacked by Cleese in Episode 3.) Basil is hospitalized with a severe concussion and awakes to see Sybil, who naturally has no sympathy for him.

Racism was a theme throughout this episode, as the Major tells a story of having to correct a woman on a date on her use of the term "niggers," which she had applied to Indians. The Major informed her that the term was more appropriate for "west Indians" and that Indians should be called "wogs." While this gross and horribly racist comment is meant to show how out of touch and racist the Major is, it is still shocking in the context of modern television. The Major, who was presumably in World War II, also reveals unsurprisingly that he "hates Germans." This may have been subtly imprinted in Basil's brain, if the next sequence is to be believed.

In the hospital, Basil's concussion is making him ruder and more hyperactive than ever, insulting the nurse without realizing how far he is going. He later slips out and back to the hotel just after the German guests have arrived.

The episode's manic energy builds and builds to a crescendo of Basil's madness. He first informs Polly that while around the Germans, "don't mention the war," and then proceeds to work the war into every question and conversation. Basil asks them if they want something to drink "before the war." Then while taking their food orders, he elevates the absurdity to such a high pitch of obnoxiousness ("When I said prawn, I thought you said war," mistaking other orders for a 'Herman Goering," and so on) that he drives one of the Germans to tears. When they finally shout at him in exasperation to "stop mentioning the war!" befuddled Basil replies:

Basil: "Well, you started it!"
German Tourist: "No we didn't!"
Basil: "Yes you did, you invaded Poland."

Basil, now clearly revealed as mad, starts imitating Hitler and goose stepping / silly walking Hitler-style through the dining room. Eventually the doctor arrives and recaptures Basil, but not before some of the most hysterical moments in a modern sitcom. In the DVD commentaries for the episode, Cleese reveals that the Major's racist comments were intentional to show the casual racism of the British, as well as the "kind of person that never forgets the past." Political commentary aside, "The Germans" contains some of Cleese's best work as a comic, and some of Cleese and Booth's greatest writing.

Season Two

The second season of *Fawlty Towers* was filmed and aired in 1979, four years after Season One and after Booth and Cleese had finally divorced. Despite the acrimony that must have gone on behind the scenes, Season Two is perhaps an even greater example of excellently performed and written television comedy than Season One.

Episode 1: "Communication Problems" (original air date: February 19, 1979)

Somewhere in the world, *could* there be someone more obnoxious than Basil Fawlty? In "Communication Problems," the answer turns out to be the utterly horrific Mrs. Richards, a woman with severe vision and hearing problems (she has a hearing aid, but leaves it out). Naturally, she proceeds to complain about her room, the view, and her radio, all of which try Basil's patience.

Despite Sybil's orders, Basil has secretly bet money on a horse, and amazingly enough has won the bet, which paid off £75. Basil, being Basil, naturally tries to hide this from Sybil, eventually giving the money for safekeeping to the Major, who, being the Major, promptly forgets that he has the money in the first place. When Mrs. Richards comes down to complain about a missing £85, Sybil becomes suspicious. When the Major claims to have "found" some money, Sybil assumes it belongs to the evil Mrs. Richards and gives it to her, much to Basil's chagrin. Eventually, the mystery is sorted out when a deliveryman arrives with a vase for Mrs. Richards and the money she had left on the counter in the shop. As Basil counts his money, the Major blurts out that he was holding the money for him after all! Naturally, Basil is so startled he drops the vase, and has to pay the odious Mrs. Richards most of his gambling money.

Episode 2: "The Psychiatrist" (original air date: February 26, 1979)

If "The Wedding Party" was partially influenced by French farces, "The Psychiatrist" doubles down on the premise that most prudes (like Basil) are secretly obsessed with sex. When stereotypical 1970s playboy Mr. Johnson (compete with shirt unbuttoned and gold medallions around his neck) arrives at Fawlty Towers, Basil dislikes him from the first glance, comparing him to an ape (Sybil does seem quite smitten).

Other new guests include a married physician couple, Dr. and Dr. Abbott. She's a pediatrician (which Basil has never heard of and thinks she is some kind of foot doctor) and he's a psychiatrist, which alarms Basil who (correctly) thinks the man will try to diagnose him. There's also Raylene, an attractive young woman whom Basil develops an infatuation with.

Further plot complications ensue when Basil suspects Mr. Johnson is hiding a woman in his room. The prudish Basil goes to comedic lengths to find the woman and expose her. After utterly embarrassing himself in a series of miscalculations that include falling off a ladder and leaving handprints on Raylene's bosom, the episode ends with Basil, irritated by having only discovered Mr. Johnson's mother in his room, pulling his coat over his head and jumping up and down in frustration.

Episode 3: "Waldorf Salad" (original air date: March 5, 1979)

In Britain during the 1960s, '70s, and '80s, there were few stock characters considered funnier than the boorish American tourist who refused to adapt to local customs (the British version of which the Pythons memorably satirized in the "Travel Agent" sketch from Season Three). "Waldorf Salad" is an episode about just such an obnoxious wanker—several episodes of *Fawlty Towers* try to make it clear that for all of his faults, there *are* worse people than Basil out there—but also about the way in which Americans and the British interact. Americans are usually represented in British television as brash, obnoxious, and demanding, particularly during the 1970s. This portrayal is meant as a contrast to the repressed, uncomplaining British (just think of how many Python sketches involved stiff-upper-lip Brits keeping calm and carrying on while horrible things happened all around and sometimes even to them); Basil aside, of course. It is interesting to wonder it this was also an inside joke from the British/American couple of Cleese and Booth. But armchair psychology is not what this book is about, or is it? Well, never mind. [It's not.—Eds.]

"Waldorf Salad" is a very contained episode, only involving one consistently deteriorating situation instead of several. A Mr. and Mrs. Hamilton are checking into Fawlty Towers on a day where several diners are already complaining about the quality of the service, but in a very restrained British way. Basil is delighted to see Mrs. Hamilton, a proper British woman, but appalled at her extremely pushy American husband, who does nothing but complain about his journey.

Basil is his usual appalling self, but when he realizes the two are a couple, he backtracks and turns into a model of sniveling servility. Hamilton bribes Basil to keep the kitchen open. Naturally, Basil tries to pocket some of the

What's All This, Then?
The Anti-Cleese

It is interesting that Basil, prudish, afraid of judgment, and correctly assuming others will see through him, is in some ways the opposite of Cleese, who by this time had been in therapy for years. He worked for a long time with therapist Robyn Skinner, eventually writing two books with him, including *Families: How to Survive Them*. If only Basil had a copy!

money, instead of giving it to the chef, Terry, who was leaving for a night out with Polly, Manuel, and his girlfriend (wait, Manuel has a girlfriend?!). After realizing he can pocket the entire £20 if he lets Terry go, Basil does so, but is mystified by Mr. Hamilton's requests for a screwdriver (he has never heard of the drink) and a Waldorf salad (the nerve!).

Basil's inability to make the salad infuriates the Hamiltons. Mr. Hamilton and Basil get into a prolonged argument, whereupon Basil blames the (now-absent) Terry for the mix-up. When Sybil finally presents them with a Waldorf salad, a furious Basil returns to the kitchen to yell at a nonexistent chef. When the "rare steaks" the Hamiltons ordered begin to burn, Fawlty again attempts to blame the long-gone Terry, but this time Mr. Hamilton walks into the kitchen and discovers the ruse. By this point, Basil has had enough, and after trying to convince himself his customers are satisfied, stalks off when some say they are not. Realizing he has nowhere else to go, Basil returns to Fawlty Towers, checking himself in as the epitome of a loathsome and demanding guest.

While this episode was not the only one to involve a culture clash, it was the most sustained example of how a sense of being British vs. being an American was reflected in cultural conflicts. Also, it provides a nice explanation of what a Waldorf salad is.

Episode 4: "The Kipper and the Corpse" (original air date: March 12, 1979)

Finally, Cleese gets back to some of the more morbid humor that darkened many an episode of *Flying Circus*. In this episode, Basil is his usual ingratiating and cheap self, trying to pass food that's gone "off" as fresh. Basil is convinced that a guest, Mr. Leeman, has died because of bad kippers that Basil has served him for breakfast. When a visiting Dr. Price determines that is not the case, most people would have called the coroner and been done with it.

Most people are not Basil Fawlty.

He and Polly decide to hide the body. Along the way they run into Miss Tibbs, who screams in panic and is then knocked out by Polly, who's over-enthusiastically trying to quiet her down. At this point, most people would have said, "Let's just call the coroner, eh?" Not Basil, as his logic dictates that the body be hidden, this time in the cupboard of Mr. and Mrs. White, two other guests, who are naturally concerned to see an arm sticking out of their cupboard. Basil tries hiding the body in the kitchen and then in a laundry basket, eventually exposing the corpse to the horrified residents. Naturally, Basil has no real solution to the problem other than to hide in the laundry basket (subsequently taken away by the laundrymen) and leave Sybil with the mess. Years later *Weekend at Bernie's* tried the "lugging the corpse around" trick with inferior results. [Cinematic blasphemy!—Eds.]

Episode 5: "The Anniversary" (original air date: March 26, 1979)

One would imagine that Basil and Sybil would have been divorced long ago, but if every battling couple split up, where would the sitcom be? Nonetheless, the episode begins with Basil planning an elaborate ruse to convince Sybil that he forgot their anniversary. Strangely enough, he is planning a surprise party with her best friends waiting for her at the hotel. Sybil, who naturally is furious at Basil, leaves in a huff (her usual form of conveyance) just as the party guests start to arrive.

Rather than try to solve this dilemma, Basil informs everyone that Sybil is ill and substitutes Polly for Sybil in her bed upstairs. After several guests are hurt tripping in the dark, Sybil returns, only to find Manuel and Terry fighting over who can best make paella in the kitchen. Basil quickly ushers the guests out, completely ruining what must have been a last-ditch attempt to keep the marriage going.

Episode 6: "Basil the Rat" (original air date: October 25, 1979)

If the faithful *Fawlty Towers* viewers forget how incredibly inept the character of Manuel was supposed to be—after all, he *is* from Barcelona, the likes of Basil might add—and how incredibly obnoxious Basil could be, the final episode spells all that out quite nicely.

Manuel has adopted a rat (though he imagines it a "Siberian hamster") and names it Basil. Hotel inspector Mr. Carnegie informs Basil and Sybil that unless numerous infractions are cleared up right away, the hotel will be closed. Human Basil agrees that rat Basil can stay with a friend of Polly's, but Manuel instead hides it in the shed, whereupon it returns to the hotel and is almost shot by the Major.

Naturally, Mr. Carnegie returns to Fawlty Towers (sign for this episode: "FARTY TOWELS") and is so pleased by the progress that he decides to stay for lunch. Human Basil, who had left out a poisoned piece of veal to catch rat Basil, accidentally mixes it with the other veal they are serving and almost kills the inspector. Carnegie asks for cheese and biscuits for dessert. Naturally, the rat is hidden in the biscuit tin brought to the table, confusing Carnegie and leading Manuel to drag a now-fainted human Basil out of shot.

The slapstick ending is a natural closing to the series, which ends with the usual chaos that marks Fawlty Towers as the single worst B&B in all of Britain.

Conclusion

There had been discussions of a Season Three or reunion special. But luckily it never came to pass, most likely because of Booth's retirement from acting. Sadly, the Americans (always wanting their Waldorf salads!) attempted four times to remake the program for their audience.

The first was a 1978 pilot, *Snavely*, with Harvey Korman and Betty White (which does sound interesting), that was never picked up for a series. The second was a gender-reversed 1983 version, *Amanda's*, starring Bea Arthur, that managed thirteen episodes but was promptly forgotten. *Over the Top*, starring Tim Curry and Annie Potts, with Steve Carrell as the Greek chef, was attempted in 1997 and mercifully did not last beyond one season. *Payne*, with John Larroquette, gasped out a few episodes in 1999 before saying good night.

Even stranger, a German version, *Zum Letzten Kliff*, (which we think translates as "Don't Mention the War") was given a shot, but didn't quite make the grade. Just like the Germans in World War II, those Bas . . . [Get on with it!—Eds.], well, anyway, a new version mercifully never happened.

Cleese and Sachs *did* revive their characters for commercials and Cleese did by himself for a novelty song "Don't Mention the World Cup" in 2006. (It might have been more appropriate in 2014, when Germany

What's All This, Then?
Please, Make It Stop

Fawlty Towers remake *Over the Top* was so despised that one critic wrote of it: "The truth is, I have never seen anything like I saw last Tuesday night. I stood in a freezer full of dead people at the morgue. I have seen a man's scalp pulled back over his nose. But I can now honestly say that until Steve Carell's turn in *Over the Top* I have never known true horror." Years later, Carrell (who finally had his big break on a more successful British remake: *The Office*) got a kick out of reading this review on *Letterman* and elsewhere.

beat Argentina for the championship.) Scales also reprised her role as Sybil for a charity fundraiser.

Most recently, Cleese appeared as Basil Fawlty in a series of television ads for Specsavers, a British optical chain. In August 2016, Cleese traveled to watch an Australian stage version of three *Fawlty Towers* episodes put together in a continuous storyline.

Today, *Fawlty Towers* is widely available on all your fancy modern media formats and is graded as one of the greatest sitcoms of all time by numerous critical authorities . . . like us. Many of the themes of class consciousness, physical abuse, horrible marriage, and petty bickering are universally relatable. For those Americans who didn't get the particularly British class consciousness, they could at least laugh at the pratfalls.

15

"I'm Not the Messiah!"

The Very Naughty *Life of Brian*

hile many television shows have tried to break into movies with little success (*Entourage, Sex in the City II*, anyone?), other shows make the transition easily. After their tepid rehash of previous sketches, *Now for Something Completely Different*, Python bounced back with the brilliant *Monty Python and the Holy Grail*, which more clearly reflected their sense of humor and encouraged them to try again.

Following that success, the Pythons started searching for the subject of their next film. When asked during an interview what their next project would be, Idle blurted out, *"Jesus Christ: Lust for Glory!"* The reporters laughed, but after the interview, the Pythons sat and thought. While this "idle" comment had been intended as a joke, it quickly intrigued the Pythons and became the key topic of conversation when they next met to discuss plans for future projects.

After agreeing that there was some merit in working on a film about the life of Jesus Christ, the Pythons dove into the project with their usual meticulous research; never forget that for all their Gumby affectations, these were at heart all serious students. By the time the Pythons met again they all were still keen on the project, but shared the caveat that they didn't want to satirize Jesus Christ (historical or mythological), but instead satirize religion itself.

The Pythons came away from their voluminous research—unique in itself, and not exactly the sort of thing one imagines Judd Apatow (or really any other modern comedy filmmaker) doing—with a newfound respect for Jesus as a person and fount of wisdom. They also had a renewed contempt for what would be the real target of the film: organized religion. According to *Monty Python Speaks*, Idle called *Life of Brian* "an attack on churches and pontificators and self-righteous assholes who claim to speak for God, of which there are still too many on the planet."

While many did not get this (more about that in a moment), the Pythons *did* feel just a bit better when Terry Gilliam's mother, the most religious of the Python relatives, saw the film and did not have a problem with it. But before the film was even made, the production was in serious trouble. Whether consciously or not, the Pythons were picking a fight and as they were the premier comedy team in the world in those days, the fight was shaping up to be quite the brouhaha.

Production

The pre-production and production of *Brian* were tumultuous at best. While finishing up the script, there was an initial dispute that had been bubbling since the production of *Holy Grail*: Who was going to direct? While both Terrys had shown promise as directors during the making of *Holy Grail*, their constant fights over control led to a compromise: Jones would serve as director and Gilliam would be art director and essentially in charge of the overall look of the film. Based (correctly, it would seem) on their *Holy Grail* experience, the Pythons presumed that Jones would work better with actors and Gilliam with the design and look of the film. In addition, Gilliam created the opening credits and short animated pieces; he also filmed a short scene where Brian is abducted by aliens before being dropped back off in Judea. Because, you know: extraterrestrial verisimilitude.

The Pythons decided to shoot in Monastir, Tunisia, where the climate was correct and the huge sets built for Franco Zeffirelli's epic miniseries *Jesus of Nazareth* could be reused for *Life of Brian*. (It helped that Tunisia was more receptive to outside productions and less onerous in terms of civil rights violations than other countries in the area.) A final script was completed in January 1978; three days before going into production in Tunisia, the Pythons, who had initially agreed with EMI for a funding deal, found out that EMI's head, Bernard Delfont, had pulled funding at the last second, afraid of the controversy. The Pythons' subsequent and immediate pleas fell on deaf ears. Delfont's unwelcome surprise left them scrambling for backing at the last minute.

Life of Brian would have likely been canceled before it happened, had it not been for the timely intervention of a Beatle. George Harrison—a rabid Monty Python fan, good buddy of Idle, and, apparently, an all-around mensch—formed a production company called HandMade Films to raise enough money to resume production. "It was a bit risky," Harrison later told *Film Comment*. "But as a big fan of Monty Python my main motive was to see the film get made." HandMade would go on to work with the Pythons on *Live at the Hollywood Bowl* and various Python solo films (including *Time Bandits*) for years to come. With funding secured, production took place in Tunisia between September and November 1978, with a first cut of the film completed by January 1979.

While pre-production had been hectic, one positive note was that leading "straight" man (pun intended) Chapman had sobered up before production started and arrived fresh, in great shape and eager to participate. Chapman, remembering his medical training, also loaded down his bags with numerous medicines, salves, ointments, and even antibiotics so that he would end up acting not only as Brian, but also set medic: clearly a welcome change from his withdrawal symptoms on the set of *Holy Grail*.

The Pythons arrived in Tunisia eager to make their film. Aside from a few setbacks due to cultural differences—Chapman's nude scene caused such consternation among the extras that the mixed gender crowd had to be switched out for a mostly male crowd—the production ran smoothly. Rather incredibly, given the last-minute financial emergency and (given his later record) Gilliam's involvement in a complex foreign shoot, *Life of Brian* was completed on time and more or less on budget.

The only question then was what would the critics, and more importantly, the Python fans, think?

Life of Brian: The Movie

Let's get this over with right away: Jesus Christ *does* appear in *Life of Brian*. But the film is not about him. Just as important to remember: Jesus is never the target of any joke, nor does the film try to attack or even question his teachings in any way. The first two scenes of the movie directly involve Jesus, but not as a source of ridicule. The film presents Jesus (played by Kevin Colley) as a respected prophet, one with numerous followers, and the actor playing him is lit from behind in the manner that many older films tried to show Jesus as lit by an "aura" of holiness. When Jesus is shown delivering the Beatitudes, he is speaking the actual New Testament text. Again: *Not in mockery*. All that clear? Good. Because somehow all the nattering nabobs of negativity who protested *Life of Brian* never seemed to understand. (Fun fact: it helps when one has actually *seen* the film one is protesting.)

Prior to this scene, the film's first gag involves the Three Magi ending up at the wrong manger, where Brian's mother, Mandy (an especially horrid Pepperpot in a masterful performance by Jones), eagerly tries to accept their wrongly delivered gifts. Unfortunately for her, they quickly see their error, retrieve the gold, frankincense, and myrrh, and deliver them to the next stable where the holy family were actually staying.

This establishing sequence then segues to the James Bond-ish version of the theme song from *Life of Brian* (complete with Sonia Jones doing her best Shirley Bassey impression). Just a few minutes into the film, and we've already been shown that Jesus does exist and that Mandy is horrible. (*Blasphemy quotient: 0%. Jesus is shown, but respectfully; Mandy and Brian, not so respectfully. Besides, even when following a star, all mangers start to look alike in a new country.*)

The next time we see Jesus, he is preaching to the crowds at the Sermon on the Mount. While a gathered crowd (including Brian) tries to make out Jesus's words from a long distance, an argument erupts over what is actually being said. Their interpretations of some of his admonitions don't exactly mesh with the written Bible—"Blessed are the big noses?" "Blessed are the *cheese makers?*"—and it ends as badly as you can imagine. (*Blasphemy quotient: 10%; if we are to believe that Jesus had not yet learned to project his voice while speaking to a very large crowd.*)

Meanwhile, not far away, a man found guilty of uttering the name of God is about to be stoned to death. Some women, who as a gender were banned from attending such religious ceremonies, are dressing as men to gain attendance (a remarkable shift from the usual male crossdressing that the Pythons specialized in). Brian is there with his mother, Mandy (disguised as his father). When the official in charge of the execution—the condemned man was accused of telling his wife "that piece of halibut was good enough for Jehovah!"—keeps mistakenly uttering the name of the Lord himself, he in turn is stoned to death by the crowd of mostly women in beards. Well, tough luck, but maybe next time the next official won't be so quick to judgment. (*Blasphemy quotient: 50% for taking the Lord's name in vain and an additional 5% for reverse cross-dressing, which was as banned then as it is funny now.*)

As Brian and Mandy go home, we notice that Judea during this time is not that different from the England of *Holy Grail*, i.e., filled with lepers and other beggars beseeching passersby for coins. Brian meets a remarkably spry beggar (Palin) who explains that he is now an *ex*-leper because of a chance encounter with Jesus, who had healed him. Despite his disease being gone, he is decidedly not happy with his healing. Although the hideous deformity is gone, so is his livelihood. That "bloody do-gooder!" he complains about the man who healed him. (*Blasphemy quotient: 50% for the gratuitous half insult to Jesus but take back the 50% for acknowledging Jesus's miracles. Our tally, 0% Blasphemy!*)

Back at home, Brian meets a Roman centurion waiting in the living room to have sex with Mandy. She informs a deflated Brian that he is not completely Jewish, but half-Roman. Startled at this news, Brian angrily denies it, claiming, "I'm not a Roman, Mum, and I never will be! I'm a Kike! A Yid! A Hebe! A Hook-nose! I'm Kosher, Mum! I'm a Red Sea Pedestrian, and proud of it!" before running off to his job at the local coliseum. (*Blasphemy quotient: 0.5%. Although this may have referred to some heretical theories that Jesus was the son of a Roman centurion, the script makes it clear that this accusation is about Brian, not Jesus.*)

At the coliseum, Brian is selling the usual tat: larks' tongues, wrens' livers, chaffinch brains, jaguars' earlobes, wolf nipple chips, dromedary pretzels, and Tuscany fried bats. There, he meets Judith (Sue Jones-Davies), whom he had previously met at the Sermon on the Mount. She's with the "People's Front of Judea," who are initially put off by Brian's asking if they are in fact the "Judean People's Front" (splitters!). Apparently, Judea was rife with different anti-Roman separatist movements at the time of Christ. But Python ups the ante by using their bickering and infighting to satirize the typical divisions of the splintering British left during the 1970s.

Hoping to impress Judith, Brian asks to join up. He is given a job writing anti-Roman graffiti. Sadly, Brian's Latin is not up to snuff—he is writing "Romanes Eunt Domus," which translates to the "People called Romanes they go the house." But rather than hauling him off to jail, the Roman centurion who confronts him grabs Brian by the ear and gives him a refresher on Latin grammar as though he were a slow schoolboy and not a proto-revolutionary. The centurion (Cleese, who took this bit from his pre-Python teaching days, causing PTSD flashbacks for many a British viewer) then orders him to write the correct phrase a hundred times before dawn. Although the next morning Brian is chased by furious centurions, his mission was a success, having left the building covered with anti-Roman graffiti and thusly proving his bona fides to the Popular . . . er, People's Front of Judea. (*Blasphemy quotient: 0%, unless crimes against Latin count. Some of the authors would argue that this is indeed the case.*)

Back at their hideout, the People's Front of Judea bicker and gripe about the most minute aspects of their agenda. After dithering about how to

John Cleese's centurion gives Graham Chapman's Brian a lecture on the finer points of Latin grammar. *Orion Pictures/Photofest*

take action, they finally plot to kidnap Pilate's wife. But while doing so, the question "What have the Romans ever done for us?" comes up for debate. The answer, surprisingly, appears to be: the aqueducts, sanitation, the roads, irrigation, medicine, education, and public order, to name but a few modern advancements. Ah, the ironies of imperialism. (*Blasphemy quotient: 0%; the Romans may have been a fighting force equaled by none at their time, but they did construct roads, keep the peace, and bring better **wine with them**.*)

In any case, back to Judea! Brian agrees to go along, but the raid is bollixed by a simultaneous raid by yet another dissident group, the Campaign for Free Galilee. Amidst the ensuing chaos, Brian is arrested. In the prison, Brian is "comforted" by the improbably cheerful long-time prisoner Ben (Palin), who states that Brian will probably be facing "only crucifixion," as it's a "first offense." Ben, who is hanging on the wall most

What's All This, Then?
Sure, But Apart from That . . .

The continuing relevance of the "What Have the Romans Ever Done for Us?" scene was highlighted during the 2016 Brexit campaign, when it was appropriated by the Stay forces to argue against the Know-Nothings of the Leave bloc, who insisted that membership in the European Union had done *nothing* for the United Kingdom. In March 2016, Prime Minister David Cameron even referenced the scene in a speech where he sarcastically responded to "What Has the EU Ever Done for Us?" carping by saying, "Well, apart from the market of five hundred million people, the regional grants, the access to the market, the support for our universities," nothing much.

of the day, thinks of Brian as "the jailers' pet" and argues that he would love to be in his place. (*Blasphemy quotient: 50% as crucifixion is a serious matter, but then again it is not mentioned in terms of Catholicism, just as a particularly brutal punishment the Romans did to try to prevent further insurrections.*) One frequent critique of *Life of Brian* was that it trivialized crucifixion, and indeed it does. But it also trivializes all the other brutalities of the Roman occupying force and many of the customs of the time. Python might be making fun, but they were also being historically accurate (more or less) about the methods used for execution.

Brian is then dragged before a lisping Pontius Pilate (the near-ubiquitous Palin). He is startled to learn from his men that the name "Biggus Dickus" is a joke, which is surprising to him as Pilate has a friend with that very same name! Pilate asks the centurions if they find the name of his good friend "amusing." While the centurions double over with laughter (Pilate also informs them, "He has a wife, you know. You know what she's called? She's called . . . 'Incontinentia.' 'Incontinentia Buttocks'"), Brian uses the confusion to escape. (*Blasphemy quotient: 10% for all the giggling; these are British actors and they knew that Palin was to trying to get them to giggle.*)

Brian then lands on (of course) an alien spaceship and flies off into space before being returned home—the best argument for this nonsensical interruption (which feels like a forced attempt at *Flying Circus* Dadaism) is that it gave Gilliam something else to do.

Back in Judea, Brian hides from the Romans by joining a band of street preachers. After buying a fake beard, Brian begins to preach as well. He soon attracts followers, who pursue him seeking wisdom. Brian, confused that people would listen to anything that he had to say, is then reunited with Judith. The pair escape to his mother's home where they consummate their relationship. (And there was much rejoicing.)

The next day, multitudes proclaiming Brian the Messiah are massing outside waiting for Brian's appearance. Despite Mandy's excoriating the crowd that "He's not the Messiah, *he's a very naughty boy!*" they continue to follow him and even declare Mandy, of all things, a virgin. (*Blasphemy quotient: Either 100% or 0%, depending on if you think this is a direct allusion to Christ. There were many people who were convinced the Messiah was imminent and many others who were declared the Messiah at that time.*)

Brian is recaptured and brought again before Pilate, who is coincidentally being visited by his old friend Biggus Dickus and his wife. After some more humor based on both Pilate's and Biggus Dickus' speech impediments, Brian is sentenced to crucifixion (after all, it was a first offense). As it is a venerable tradition, Pilate addresses the crowds and much to their laughter announces that "To pwove our fwiendship, it is customawy at this time to welease a wongdoer fwom our pwisons." The crowd shouts out *R*-named prisoners (including "Woger," "Woderick," "Weuben," "Weginald," etc.) before eventually calling for Brian's release. Pilate agrees to send a pardon to "Bwian" in a show of his magnanimity. The crowd could not have had a better time, regardless of whom they wanted to have released. (*Blasphemy quotient: Either 115% if you think that Pilate is a tricky subject, or 0%, depending on your tolerance for speech impediment humor. This is a tough one.*)

We return to Brian, who was on his way to be crucified and is about to be freed, but in a nod to *Spartacus*, another prisoner (Idle) declares that *he* is Brian and is duly released. All the other prisoners also declare themselves to be Brian (with one saying, "I'm Brian and so is my wife!"). As a result, Mr. Cheeky takes Brian's pardon and Brian is left up on the cross. (*Blasphemy quotient: 15% for so directly quoting a Hollywood classic, and for cheating the audience of a happy ending.*)

In the last scene, Brian is hanging on the cross along with all the other prisoners, looking rather hopeless when fellow crucifixee Mr. Frisbee (Idle again, cheery as you like) breaks into a rousing song. It's a jarring moment, of course. But it isn't long before all the other prisoners join in. After all, it's next to impossible to resist an "Always Look on the Bright Side of Life" sing-along, even if you were on the verge of a horribly long-suffering death.

Life of Brian, which was produced with the cooperation of far fewer llamas than *Monty Python and the Holy Grail.*   *Orion Pictures/Photofest*

As the song ends, Mr. Frisbee urges the audience members to buy a copy of the album version of the film, noting, "It's the end of the film. Incidentally, this record's available in the foyer" before we cut to the credits. (*Blasphemy quotient: 13.5% for making light of crucifixion, life, death, and the meaning of life, and for putting in a plug for the cast album.*)

So, how to judge the film? Is it hilarious? By all the standards of Monty Python, Life of Brian shows them in peak form. Bringing together the history-specific detailing of *Holy Grail* with the sharp wit of the best *Flying Circus* material, it remains not just a classic piece of Pythonia but very likely their creative peak. While *Life of Brian* certainly took chances, and risked being misinterpreted, it was also a very simply hilarious film that did not directly criticize Jesus, but did take on religious intolerance and hypocrisy with a vengeance.

While the members of Python were used to controversy, however, they were completely unprepared for the firestorm that ensued once the film was released. For a while, it seemed *Life of Brian* would be the last film Python would ever make.

Life of Brian—The Controversy

Even before *Life of Brian* was released, controversy was swirling. When it was finally released, the Pythons found themselves assailed as never before. While many critics praised the film as a comic masterpiece, it was picketed from the first day of its American release (which came before the British release). Protest groups included Catholic priests and nuns, evangelicals, and even some Jewish groups. Python, who should have known they could have been misinterpreted, ended up fighting for their show business lives.

Never forget that the Pythons were among the most intelligent and well-researched comedians ever to make a film. Amidst the firestorm, the Pythons were invited to debate the merits of the film on the BBC late-night talk show *Friday Night Saturday Morning*, with Bishop of Southwark Mervyn Stockwood and British writer and public intellectual Malcolm Muggeridge. The Pythons accepted. Cleese and Palin appeared on the show to defend *Life of Brian.*

The mood at first seemed cordial, with the affable bishop trading jokes backstage. But once the cameras were on, the bishop and Muggeridge, both of whom had arrived at least fifteen minutes late to a screening of the film (therefore missing completely the context that Brian *was not meant to be Jesus*), pronounced it blasphemous and attacked the Pythons' stance on religion. The exchange grew increasingly testy. At one point, a visibly annoyed Muggeridge asserted that Christianity has been responsible for more good in the world than any other force in history, leading Cleese to ask in return, "What about the Spanish Inquisition?" Needless to say it did not go well, but later on, God was said to exist by two falls to a submission. (Much of this foolishness was re-created in the 2011 BBC docudrama *Holy Flying Circus*.)

Despite the Pythons' best attempts at damage control, the controversy endured. Noted British busybody and occasional target of Python lampoonery Mary Whitehouse (look her up, trust us . . . or don't, really, it's depressing) tried her usual shenanigans to get the film banned (it was banned in a town in Torbay!), but had to settle for passing out pamphlets and picketing local cinemas to no avail, and possibly giving the film even more free publicity. At least thirty-nine British town councils banned the film outright, even though several didn't actually have any movie theaters in their district. Presumably, one could have been built just so that the film could have been banned, but that would have been a bother. Other town councils imposed the dreaded X (eighteen and over) certificate, which dramatically reduced the number of cinemas available since many towns couldn't show anything without a AA (fourteen and above) certificate. (This would be the American equivalent of a PG rating at the time.)

Despite the protests, the film did good business. It grossed nearly $20 million in America, making it the year's highest-grossing British film there in 1979. Which is better than Ireland and Norway, both of which banned the film altogether.

Another problem was that many people thought that *Life of Brian* was trivializing the concept of crucifixion. This could be argued, since the film does minimize the idea of crucifixion as a punishment. For instance, Mathias, the old man working for the People's Front of Judea, argues that being stabbed would be far worse, while longtime prisoner Ben practically longed for execution. In one of his angrier tirades, Jones went so far as to argue that "any religion that makes a form of torture into an icon that they worship is a pretty sick sort of religion."

Ultimately, the Pythons sent out a public letter arguing that people should see it themselves before rushing to judgment. The letter argued, "The film is set in biblical times, but it is not about Jesus. It is a comedy, but we would like to think that it does have certain serious attitudes and things to say about human nature." Tellingly, before signing off on the letter, the Pythons go on to write that the film "does not ridicule Christ, nor does it show Christ in any way that could offend anyone, nor is belief in God or Christ a subject dealt with in the film."

Life of Brian in Retrospect

One would be hard-pressed to find a Python fan who does not today consider *Life of Brian* not just a classic but one of Monty Python's best projects, just as one would be hard-pressed to find someone not friendly to Python who could articulate exactly what the fuss was about. While the film itself led to angry pickets and fervent debates on television and in the press, the DVD copy of the film and frequent screenings have been met with no opposition. Could it be that the critics who cried blasphemy at the time (mostly those who could not have been bothered to watch the actual film itself) realized that the film was *not* actually about Jesus, or in any way an attack on Jesus, but was a full-fledged critique of how both politics and religion can be used for the wrong purpose?

Theological controversy aside, *Life of Brian* also contains some all-time classic Python lines, with many a young fan memorizing the exchange about Pontius Pilate's good friend "Biggus Dickus" (he has a wife, you know . . .).

Other "must memorize" parts include Cleese's pedantic Roman centurion/schoolmaster collecting Chapman's poorly phrased Latin graffiti ("The Romans are the ones to go home?") and especially the Judean People's Front's "What have the Romans ever done for us (well, there's the roads . . .)." But the one part of *Brian* best known to non-Python types is Idle's closing song, "Always Look on the Bright Side of Life." The ironically cheery missive that ends the film with a chorus of crucified prisoners whistling was initially criticized for cheapening the agonizing experience of the crucifixion, but later the song took on a life of its own. The song with full orchestration and the ubiquitous Fred Tomlinson Singers on the chorus soon became an inspirational song that touched the British imagination.

During the Falklands War, groups of sailors sang the song while awaiting rescue on two different sinking British ships, the HMS *Coventry* and the HMS *Sheffield*. (Spoiler Alert: they were rescued.) The Pythons themselves revisited the song at Chapman's 1989 memorial service; it soon became a ubiquitous song at British funerals. By the 1990s, it had become a football chant, primarily used by fans of Championship League team Sheffield Wednesday. In 1991, the single was re-released, going into the Top 10 British pop charts (it went to number one on the charts in Ireland, where the film had been banned for a year). Later, the song was reused in *Spamalot* and still later recycled in *Not the Messiah (He's a Very Naughty Boy)*. (More on that in Chapter 25.)

16

A Fish Film

The Meaning of Life

Following the success of *Life of Brian*, the Pythons set about writing another film. This time, however, they had no definite framework in mind . . . not even a *Jesus Christ: Lust for Glory* kernel. As they toured and performed in various benefit concerts (en masse and in cliques), sketches and ideas were bandied about; as Terry Gilliam recalls, *Monty Python's World War Three* was in the running at one point, as was the hyper-meta *Trial of Monty Python* . . . but the troupe just couldn't settle on one solid theme for their next film. So, they did what any mega-popular British comedy troupe in the 1980s would do: they went to Jamaica for January holiday.

And on the Seventh Day . . .

There, they desperately came up with the "Seven Stages of Man" format—a loosely chronological survey of the "big moments" in every human life: birth, sex, death, and all the fiddly bits in between; this framework gave the Pythons just enough of a through-line to avoid another full-on sketch-show like *And Now for Something Completely Different*, but still capitalized upon the anarchic non-format of *Flying Circus*. After the success of *Life of Brian*, there was an in-house concern that they were growing conventional; yet with *The Meaning of Life*, the Pythons managed—in what would be their last full-length film together—to create something they hadn't done yet: a reasonably coherent partial narrative sketch film. On top of the central narrative, they (eventually) crammed Gilliam's short film *The Crimson Permanent Insurance* (more below), an utterly random bit on "Live Organ Transplants," a Dada-esque "Middle of the Film," and some talking fish.

The film was not, on the whole, an immediate success; preview audiences were particularly unkind. At the film's US preview screenings (in Yonkers, New York), eighty people reportedly walked out. Cuts were

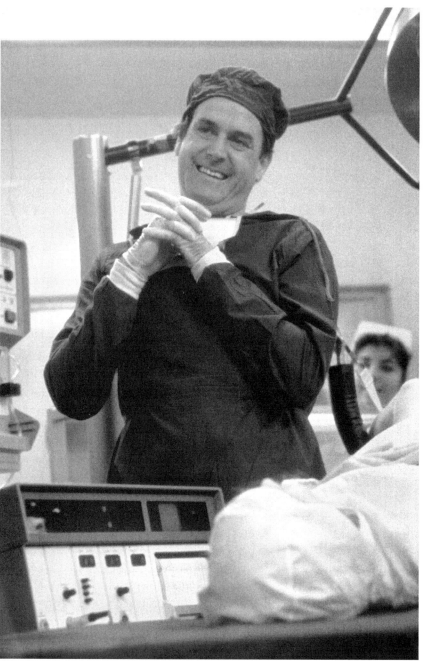

Who doesn't like the machine that goes "bing"?   *Universal Pictures/Photofest*

made, including Jones's turn as a sex-crazed Martin Luther (!) and Carol Cleveland's condom-slapping waitress (!!!) in the Hawai'ian Dungeon Room (never fear: both sketches were made available almost immediately afterward in the book of the film, and have since been included on the 2003 "Special Edition" DVD release).

Fortunately, critical reviews and box-office takes were far more kind upon the film's official release on March 30, 1983. Many critics (but certainly not all) hailed *The Meaning of Life* as the best Python film so far. The consensus was that it was intentionally vulgar, savage, and ground-breaking; most admitted it was funny. The film won the Special Jury Prize at Cannes that year and a BAFTA for Best Original Song ("Every Sperm Is Sacred"). *The Meaning of Life* performed decently but not spectacularly in the United States, ending up at number forty-nine in the year's box-office results, just behind *Cheech & Chong's Still Smokin'* but ahead of Woody Allen's *Zelig* and Mel Brooks's *To Be or Not to Be*. It was—of course—released on DVD repeatedly, and a video game tie-in was produced in 1997.

The plus/minus artistic tally for *The Meaning of Life* is more complicated. The Pythons are certainly on the top of their acting game here: Palin and Cleese, in particular, transcend their stereotypical characterizations, and the "First Zulu War" sketch is particularly deft on all sides. *The Meaning of Life* is also their most "hummable" film. *Holy Grail* might have its *Camelot* parody, and *Life of Brian* kills with the "Always Look on the Bright Side of Life" ending, but *The Meaning of Life* has not just its eponymous theme and "Galaxy Song," but "Every Sperm Is Sacred," and even "Christmas in Heaven." On the other hand, the relative dearth of Gilliam interstitials (replaced by formal chapter headings and more traditional segues) distances the film, visually, from *Flying Circus* (and even *Holy Grail*).

The humor in *Life* is often more violent, and the slapstick more morbid, than in their previous films (the bloody Black Knight in *Holy Grail* being a possible exception); there is certainly more vomit here than ever before. The religious satire is, if anything, more pointed than in *Life of Brian*. But there is still an abundance of "thinkerly" humor in the film (lessons in Protestantism and universal geography stand out), and the almost-coherent narrative enables the troupe to take full advantage of their hallmark highbrow/low-brow juxtapositions.

The central narrative is divided into seven slices, more or less: The Miracle of Birth; Growing and Learning; Fighting Each Other; [The Middle of the Film]; Middle Age; Live Organ Transplants (!?); The Autumn Years; and Death. It opens with fish talking from behind the glass of a tank and ends with a television playing the opening animation from *Flying Circus* as it drifts off into space. The fourth wall of "television" is repeatedly toyed with throughout film, as cameras pan to (and into) televisions, through windows, and adopt a fish-eye lens. The Pythons may not have known that this would be their last cinematic collaboration, but they certainly managed to produce something with a reasonable sense of self-reflexive closure.

The Film

The Crimson Permanent Assurance

The film opens gently enough, with a "complete" narrative: the sixteen-minute *The Crimson Permanent Assurance* featurette, a Gilliam-directed mash-up of pirate tropes and business settings, in which a Dickensian firm of aged British accountants unmoor their chains of bondage (and their building), then set off to plunder the glass-and-steel towers of "multinationals, conglomerates, and fat, bloated merchant banks." The "desperate and reasonably violent men" lay siege to the modern business world inventively, snapping off fan blades to make scimitars, and turning filing cabinets into cannons. It's funny, anarchic, and a bit nostalgic, really, ending with the rousing "Accountancy Shanty" by Idle and John Du Prez. Initially intended as a very brief metatheatrical "interruption" to the main film, *The Crimson Permanent Assurance*—like many an anti-modernist Gilliam film thereafter—ran long and over budget during its filming; it was subsequently pulled from the middle of the film and set as an opening featurette (a then-outdated film practice). This featurette was very well received, however, and was nominated for a BAFTA ("Best Short Film") in 1983.

The main film subsequently opens and closes with the bouncy anthem "The Meaning of Life," which promises to answer three eternal questions: "Why are we here?" "What's life all about?" and "Is God really real?" The film does, indeed, offer myriad quasi-philosophical answers to these questions. As we go, see which you prefer.

Part I: The Miracle of Birth

The Miracle of Birth: The Delivery Room

In this on-the-nose criticism of the artificiality and profitability of hospitalized "first-world" birth (contrasted to the wholly "natural" birth in the subsequent scene), an anxious pregnant woman—on a gurney and already in stirrups—is rolled out before a sea of interns and tourists (notepads and cameras ready!), surrounded by extraneous medical machinery, and subjected to an incredibly antiseptic (and quick!) labor before her baby is tagged, typed, isolated in an incubator, and rolled away. It's all about "the set," really, not the mother, the father, or the baby; when the doctors (Chapman and Cleese, who will appear as two similarly unsympathetic medical professionals—"organ repo-men"—later in the film) call out, "Show's over!" to the gathered crowd as soon as the baby's wheeled away, leaving the mother alone and confused, we know where modern attention lies.

In short, the opening sketch is cold, rather brutal, and feels rather a bit like *Brazil*, really. "Ping!"

The Miracle of Birth: The Third World (Yorkshire)

Following the antiseptic first world version of birth, we get a sharply contrastive (and satiric) depiction of "natural" childbirth in the third world (cheekily epitomized by a Yorkshire slum). There, a downtrodden Roman Catholic worker (Palin) watches in exhaustion as a cartoon stork drops a bundle down his chimney; a bloody baby subsequently—and unceremoniously—falls out from between the legs of his chore-laden wife (Jones), adding one more to the number of children in the house already. And the house is quite literally "full" of children: they're stacked like cordwood, sitting on mantels, popping out of cupboards . . . everyone a sympathetic Dickensian urchin.

Once inside, Palin explains to his massed progeny that, because the Catholic Church won't let him wear a rubber thingie on his cock (or "sock," as they said pre-dubbing), he's been forced to sell them all for medical experiments. Sadness ensues, of course, but it's punctuated (and temporarily shunted) by a magnificent *Mary Poppins*-meets-*Oliver!* dance number, "Every Sperm Is Sacred." To the choral strains of angelic children, the song rolls merrily along, gathering dancers of all stripes, from street urchins and strumpets to fire eaters and a Chinese dragon, only to end with a Broadway flourish as sparklers and flags of all nations fill the sky. "Sperm" is easily the most polarizing song in the film, and a sure sign that the Pythons were not about to cater to Christian conservatives after *Life of Brian*.

Protestantism and Sex

As Palin's doomed children file sadly out onto the street, a dourly proud Protestant, Mr. Blackitt (Chapman), who considers himself morally and financially "superior" to his neighbors, eyes them imperiously through his window.

Blackitt rages on about the (potential) joys of being a Protestant, while his wife (Idle) grows more and more flustered about the possibilities of French ticklers, Black Mambos, crocodile ribs, and . . . having sex more than twice in a marriage. Character-wise, it's more than a bit like "Woody and Tinny" from the last season of *Flying Circus* all over again, but Chapman's self-righteous rant on modern sexual liberation and Martin Luther's Theses (back in 1517) lends a new dimension to the situation. Of course, given the Pythons' penchant for high-brow/low-brow juxtaposition, intellectual theological satire devolves quickly into sexy religious silliness via a deleted scene, aptly named . . .

The Adventures of Martin Luther

Cut from the original release (Idle believes American preview audiences didn't get the historical references and he's probably right), "The Adventures of Martin Luther" (filmed in Reform-o-Scope!) depicts the great reformer (Jones) as, essentially, Benny Hill with a spoon fetish. Compared to the polished "Sperm" dance number and quiet madness of Chapman in the previous sketches, this is all nudge-nudge/wink-wink slapstick and overacting. Still, had the "Martin Luther" sketch remained in place, there would have been a logical religious connection between "The Miracle of Birth" segment and the following "Growing and Learning" section.

Part 2: Growing and Learning

School Chapel / Oh, Lord, Please Don't Burn Us

As it is, the leap from Chapman's drawing-room tirade about prophylactics to a sermon in an English boarding school seems a tad abrupt. In a stained-glass chapel with uniformed youngsters lining the pews, the school's Chaplain (Palin) intones a quietly measured—if awfully silly—sermon on God's power and potential violence; meanwhile, the Headmaster (Cleese) shouts an endless litany of seemingly arbitrary school rules involving pegs (adding a casually brutal memo to young Jenkins: "apparently, your mother died this morning"). So far, we're back to the Pythons playing to type. But really, the school-chapel transition is just to lead into the gem of "Growing and Learning": "The Sex Lesson."

Sex Lesson / Rugby Match

Assisted by his "good lady wife" (Patricia Quinn of *Rocky Horror* fame), Cleese offers a very "practical" demonstration of heterosexual intercourse to a class of disaffected and distracted teen boys (among them, Jones, Chapman, Palin, and Idle). Well, Cleese offers a practical demonstration of everything between "vaginal juices" (covered last class) and "orgasm" at any rate. There's certainly practical nudity and a very convenient, but impractical, four-poster bed involved. Anyway, this being Python and all, the *coitus* is well and truly *interruptus* before we reach any sort of satisfactory finish; instead, after he is caught laughing at "something frightfully funny" in class, Jones is soon seen alongside other young boys on the rugby pitch being punished by the masters' students—a time-honored tradition at English schools, apparently. Sex and violence and sports: the Holy Trinity of Monty Python.

Part 3: Fighting Each Other

War

In what is easily the most artistically self-conscious transition in the film, we dissolve from a "boyish" Jones holding his head in his hands (as the violent horrors of rugby surround him) . . . to a "mannish" Jones holding his helmeted head in his hands (as the violent horrors of war explode around him); we have visually shifted in time and space from boarding school to the Great War! As Jones notes in his film commentary, there's even a pair of trees approximating the goal posts to aid in the visual transition. See, kids: that's directing! The violent parallels between rugby and war are likewise apparent, but are not the main point of the sketch.

Instead, we shift attention to a critique of British sensibilities and decorum (both here and in the "First Zulu War" sketch soon to come). In this sketch, the "loyal soldiers / retirement watch" trope is mocked, as Jones's faithful trench-mates present their captain with a series of elaborate timepieces (the expected wristwatch, a glass-encased ormolu clock, and a grandfather clock) as he prepares to storm the enemy gun post. While earnest expressions of loyalty are articulated, the men are shot down, one after another, to Jones's increasing dismay. Yet rather than let down his boys (especially the corpsing Idle), Jones relents and they begin to set up an incongruous final tea on the battlefield . . . dying all the way.

Marching Up and Down the Square (RSM)

Happily (?), we find that the previous sketch was all part of a training film (*The Meaning of Life* is a nesting doll of filmography) being shown by a modern-day British General (Chapman), who informs his audience that the meaning of life is a constant struggle between warring ideologies: hence the need for armies. At which point an animated Gilliam finger (*quelle Holy Grail!*) descends and vaporizes him. So . . . we'll stick a pin in the General's proposed "meaning of life" for now, shall we?

Pulling back from the Hand of God, we find ourselves on the tarmac of a military base where the Regimental Sergeant Major (Palin) verbally transitions from Chapman's scene by shouting, "Don't stand there gawping like you've never seen the Hand of God before!" He then utterly fails to cow his recruits into marching up and down the square with him. Part of the humor of the scene—beyond the critique of British military practices—is that "milquetoast" Palin seems to be finally playing an "angry" Cleese role . . . only he isn't. The best we can say about the RSM is that he's a loud, brash, blustery old softie. As we knew he would be.

The First Zulu War 1879 / Tiger Hunt

And then we are suddenly back in time again (thanks to a voice-over heralding the "calm leadership" of the British army), reinvestigating the "stiff upper lip" character of nineteenth-century British officers . . . even in the face of Zulu attack, curiously missing limbs, and costumed *felis horribilis*. Although "The First Zulu War" sketch was beset by production difficulties and illness (Cleese had eaten some bad prawns; the weather conspired against Jones; and—thanks to a local rebellion—most of the "local/colored" actors needed to be replaced by white actors in blackface), it remains one of the most maturely acted scenes from the boys . . . at least until Gilliam shows up as a zippered negro.

Really, this is where the film begins to go off the rails, narratively speaking. The understatement of the "Zulu War" (war as shaving inconvenience; dismemberment as mosquito bite; giant tigers as tiny viruses) is replaced by the campy appearance of Palin and Idle as two halves of a costumed tiger . . . and likely leg amputators. We'll never know, of course, because before "the mystery of the officer's missing leg" is resolved, we slow pan to a nearby nearly naked "native" who unzips his dark, dark skin (from chops to nave, as 'twere), revealing the very white Gilliam in a very white dinner jacket very whitely announcing: "Hallo, good evening, and welcome to the Middle of the Film."

The Middle of the Film

Waiting for us after the throw is a reasonably sane and attractive Lady TV Announcer (Palin) who introduces the mid-film diversion, "Find the Fish."

And now we're completely off the rails, folks. Set within "another film," we are treated to a Dada-esque visual barrage served up via a fish-eye lens: a tuxedoed Jones with elongated arms; a pachyderm-faced butler serving drinks; and a silver-wigged, corseted Chapman in high heeled-boots, faucet-nipples, and opera/boxing gloves searching for "the fish" among the Victorian corridors of the Battersea Power Station.

It all makes virtually no sense, but has a goofy self-reflexivity that (as Gilliam has noted of the previous tiger scene) certainly reminds one of "the old Python." It's almost as if—halfway through the film—the Pythons realized they hadn't been weird enough. Yet. *This* certainly corrects that oversight.

Fishy fishy fish.

Part 4: Middle Age

Eschewing any sort of logical transition at this point, the film simply cuts back to the tanked fish from the opening scene; they metatheatrically comment on the film's progress so far and—like much of the audience, we assume—their opinions are divided as to whether the Pythons will actually say anything worthwhile about the meaning of life or not before this whole shebang is over.

Long considered by most humans as the most boring stage of life, "Middle Age" is represented by two Americans (Idle and Palin, voicing barely passable middle-American accents) on vacation at the Super Inn Hotel. It is, as they say repeatedly in a brief bit of cut material, really "super." A more mundane contrast to the preceding surreal scene at Battersea can scarce be imagined.

Of course, the Super Inn Hotel isn't entirely normal; in fact, we'll find out later in the film that it's also Heaven (but more on that later). For now, a transvestite Gilliam (as M'Lady Joeline in full Bo Peep garb and exaggerated Minnesotan accent) greets the Hendys and takes them to "The Dungeon Room," where "real Hawaiian food [is] served in an authentic medieval English dungeon atmosphere." It's a wonderful satire on the inauthenticity of American, well, American *everything*, really.

In another scene sadly cut from the original release, the Hendys are seated by Diane the Waitress (Carol Cleveland, poured into "sexy Beefeater costume" . . . and yes, you read that right: they cut the scene!). Ahem. Anyway, Diane unceremoniously plops appetizers on the table—cawfee, ketchup, a TV, and a phone—then gruffly offers the two tourists square-shaped green things or squiggly shaped brown things for dinner. Again, the satire on American "taste" is rather thick here, so it's hardly a wonder that the scene was not embraced by American preview audiences; still, it's a pity more audiences didn't get to hear Cleveland say, "Have a nice fuck!" in an over-the-top New York accent while wearing a flounced Beefeater skirt and tiny top hat. No, no . . . go ahead: Google it. We'll wait. [Please avoid requesting that readers use rival media!—Eds.]

See? That'll stay with you for a while (and in your browser history forever). Cleveland aside, the cleverest bits of the scene are the dinner conversation options offered by the waiter (Cleese, chewing on an exaggerated Chicago accent): football or philosophy. To the delight of the fish eavesdropping from their death-tank, the Hendys choose philosophy: "a viable hypothesis to explain the meaning of life." Unfortunately for the fish, the Hendys are utterly dim (Oh, Americans!), and even with repeated prompts from Cleese, can't wrap their heads around philosophy; and so they are offered something "off the menu": Live Organ Transplants.

Part 5: Live Organ Transplants (!??)

Liver Donor

As noted earlier, the Pythons had been writing bits and pieces of "The Fish Film" since *Life of Brian* wrapped; this is clearly a sketch the troupe enjoyed and subsequently shoe-horned into the film regardless of thematic unity. Still: the sketch gives us Gilliam as a Jewish Rastafari with a Hitler mustache (!), and presents the best mash-up of high-brow/low-brow humor in the film . . . from the Grand Guignol splatstick of organ donation to the harmonic galactic geography of "Galaxy Song." The whole section is a treat, but it's out of place in the Seven Stages of Man thematic (and Cleese's menu-based transition from the previous scene is terribly fawst . . . erm . . . forced).

The basic conceit—before blood and guts start flying—is that Mr. Bloke (Gilliam) has elected to be a "live organ donor." And so, logically (or at least logically predicated upon the ambiguity of the phrase "live organ donor"), Cleese and Chapman arrive at Gilliam's door to forcibly take his liver from him, despite his vehement protest. As Cleese and Jones (as Gilliam's frumpy hausfrau) make small talk in the background (witness the world's most inappropriate meet-cute!), a wild-eyed Chapman viciously vivisects the flailing Gilliam, theatrically brandishing slimy organs before the camera as blood spurts in mass quantities from his victim. On the splatstick scale, it's somewhere between the "Black Knight" scene in *Holy Grail* and "Showdown at the House of Blue Leaves" in *Kill Bill: Vol. 1*. On the "they owe us six quid for the idea!" scale, the organ-repossession flicks *Repo: The Genetic Opera* (2008) and *Repo Men* (2010) are both a tenner.

Galaxy Song

In stark contrast the gross-out comedy of organ donation going on in the next room (which remains partially visible through a pass window), a salmon-suited lounge singer (Idle) calmly—if utterly unexpectedly—walks out of a small refrigerator, cane in hand, to lead Jones through a star-filled animated universe while singing the reassuringly melodic "Galaxy Song." Gilliam animates a universal "big bang" that recalls the "Miracle of Birth," music crests and swells, Jones seems full of wonder and hope: it's all very pleasant. Honestly, it's hard to imagine a more disparate pair of sketches joined under a single banner; truly, "Live Organ Transplants" is where comic vivisectionists go to die.

The Very Big Corporation of America / Interruption

One tenuous, hand-painted transition later . . . and the prequel featurette— *The Crimson Permanent Assurance*—bursts onto the scene, attacking the main film. Sadly, the doughty old pirate accountants are unceremoniously crushed by a falling American glass-and-steel monstrosity. Also sadly, one of the American businessmen (Idle), is distracted before fully examining the metaphysical development of the soul (so you're saying "souls don't develop because people become distracted . . ."); we were so close, people! So close!

Part 6: The Autumn Years

Penis Song

Screw the transitions! On with the film!

Another lounge singer—who is definitely "Not Noël Coward" (but is definitely Idle again)—entertains a polite crowd in an elegant restaurant with the "frightfully witty" little number, "The Penis Song." It's a great, late example of the thesaurus sketches the Pythons were so fond of back on *Flying Circus* (here Idle sings a series of euphemisms for "penis," including: dong, stiffy, dick, tadger, prick, Willy, John Thomas, one-eyed trouser snake, piece of pork, your wife's best friend, Percy, and cock). Oh . . . thank you very much.

Mr. Creosote

Ah, Mr. Creosote. The figurative buckets of blood in the "Liver Donor" sketch suddenly seem quaint following the literal buckets of vomit issuing forth in this scene from Mr. Creosote (Jones in an incredibly fat "fat suit"). Waddling into the expansive high-end restaurant, Creosote plays against conventional "sensibilities" and offers another example of escalation humor: Creosote is uncouth, gluttonous, and doomed; the waiter (Cleese) is polite, obsequious, and duplicitous. Cleveland—as a nearby patron—slips in some accidentally vulgar menstruation comedy in a failed attempt at being polite, but the bulk (hah!) of the humor in this sketch derives from the sheer volume of vomit streaming from hidden tubes and bile cannons. After the overstuffed Creosote finally explodes, the casual demeanor of Cleese—picking tidbits from the hollowed-out carcass of a still-living Creosote—is the icing on the vomitus cake (a wafer-thin wafer of comedy, if you will).

The Meaning of Life

Immediately following the cartoon humor of the "Mr. Creosote" bit, Cleese and a cleaning lady (Jones) briefly discuss the meaning of life amidst the now-empty restaurant-cum-vomitorium. Although Jones's sage reflection upon life is poetic and initially encouraging (in a Boethian "Consolation of Philosophy" kind of way), it ultimately devolves into vulgar anti-Semitism. Cleese dumps a bucket of vomit on his/her head, and the camera drifts to nearby French waiter Gaston (Idle), who urges the camera to follow him; clearly, we've broken the fourth wall yet again and reentered reality TV.

After a reasonably long buildup—as Gaston the Waiter and the camera shuffle across town—we arrive at an idyllic little cottage at the edge of a park, where he recalls the words his mother taught him: "You must try to make everyone happy, and bring peace and contentment everywhere you go." Which is nice, but sets up what a modern audience would recognize as a clear humblebrag: "And so . . . I became a waiter." Looking expectantly to the camera, Gaston becomes dismayed at the lack of acknowledgment, and totters away, telling the audience to "Fuck off!" That's philosophy, that is!

Part 7: Death

Falling Leaves

Anyone remember Gilliam's animated interstitials from *Holy Grail*? This is like that. We missed you, the Animator—glad the heart attack in 1974 wasn't fatal.

Terry Jones's Mr. Creosote, pre-detonation.   *Universal Pictures/Photofest*

God is a fine spell-checker!

Arthur Jarrett

Boobies!

According to legend, the "Arthur Jarrett" sketch was one of the many floated early on, perhaps when *The Trial of Monty Python* was the potential thematic for the film. In it, Jarrett (Chapman) "has been allowed to choose the manner of his own execution" after having been "convicted by twelve good persons and true, of the crime of first degree making of gratuitous sexist jokes in a moving picture." Jarrett's self-determined mode of death: pursuit by topless women. By allowing Jarrett to construct his own Dantean *contrapasso* (wherein the punishment both fits the crime and is the crime), the Pythons take a typically sexist booby joke (and they made plenty back on *Flying Circus*) and infuse it with metatheatrical humor and self-deconstructive irony (on multiple levels, really). Rather than follow the traditional pixilated-motion-and–"Yakety-Sax" route toward sexist comedy, the Pythons (especially Chapman) play it utterly straight; we witness—in partial slow motion—a deadly serious chase sequence that shows the troupe's only openly homosexual member being chased to death by a bevy of "lovely ladies" bouncing along in thongs and colorful roller-derby pads.

It's as if the Pythons spliced the gravitas of *The French Connection* with a surreal side of *The Prisoner* . . . and then wrapped it in the goofy sexism of *Benny Hill*. Chapman's animated swan dive off a cliff into his own open grave along the rocky English shore is probably symbolic of something as well, but . . . boobies!

The Grim Reaper / Salmon Mousse!

Cleese gets to wear a big black cloak and kill the rest of the Pythons. That in itself was probably enough to get him to sign on for the film. In short, the Grim Reaper (Cleese, wielding scythe and articulated skeletal hand) arrives at a secluded dinner party to hurl insults at both the English ("You're all so fucking pompous and none of you have got any balls!") and Americans ("Shut up! . . . you Americans, you talk and talk . . . Well you're dead now, so shut up!") before they all drop dead of salmon poisoning, get in their spectral cars, and drive through a very nice portal into the afterlife.

"The Grim Reaper" sketch offers another inspired performance from Palin, by the way, as a self-pleased American wife (to Gilliam's pompous American husband) who rather steals the scene and punctuates the absurdity of the moment with an apparently ad-libbed final line en route to Paradise: "Hey, I didn't even eat the mousse. . . ."

Christmas in Heaven

In the end, *The Meaning of Life* well and truly swallows its own tail: we're back at the Super Inn Hotel (aka Heaven). There, the recently departed salmon-eaters (plus one) enter a grand restaurant theater and we see pretty much every dead character from the film so far: Yorkshire urchins, British soldiers, Zulu warriors, live organ donors, Creosote casualties, and topless roller-derby executioners (because: boobies!). On a magnificent tiered stage with a grand neon staircase, a sequin-tuxed lounge singer (Chapman as "Tony Bennett") leads dozens of falsie-wearing female dancers (dressed as Santa/Angel hybrids) in a disco-esque final number, "Christmas in Heaven." The music is simultaneously catchy and bland: a perfect echo to the wry anticommercialism of the lyrics.

Further throwing this final scene into metatheatrical self-awareness, the camera pans from the stage to a nearby television, where we see Chapman (still singing) in front of another TV; diving into that TV, we see Joseph and Mary at the manger, then the Three Magi . . . all singing about the many "gifts for all the family" that matter. Unsurprisingly at this point, Chapman's grand performance is cut short and we find (via an abrupt pull-back) that the scene in Heaven is just a film being watched on a TV—unceremoniously clicked off—by the Lady Presenter from the Middle of the Film (Palin). Russian nesting dolls have nothing on Monty Python. Nothing, we say!

The End of the Film

Under a banner now reading "The End of the Film," the Lady Presenter (Palin) curtly announces "The Meaning of Life" as if reading the results of an Academy Award nomination: it's nothing very special. More important, to her at least, is ranting about the dismal state of cinema these days. I mean, really.

Finally, the theme song rises and we are treated to one last bit of Gilliam animation as the credits roll: a television set—playing the opening title sequence from *Flying Circus*—drifts off into space and we hear a reprise of Idle's "Galaxy Song."

Good night.

17

Post-Python: "Jolly, Jolly Good!"

John Cleese—The Most Prolific Python

Cleese was always the most prolific Python: writing, directing and acting in hundreds of projects. While Cleese is the key to Monty Python coming together, he is in many ways the most difficult of all the Pythons to deal with. He is a masterful comedian, but also (as he would admit) a bundle of contradictions.

A perfectionist who labors over projects, sometimes for years, Cleese would simultaneously have cameos in a dozen mediocre films and commercials. Cleese was instrumental in putting Python together. But he was also the first to question whether the original series could go any further than they already had after Seasons Three, the first to (for a while) leave Monty Python, and the one to most vigorously resist calls to get back together after the release of *The Meaning of Life* in 1982, but paradoxically, was also the keenest to try it again, as evidenced by the announcement that Python would reunite for a new tour in 1998. While this announcement was a bit premature and not all the Pythons were fully on board, it does show that Cleese can change his mind and revisit old works when in the mood. But even though various Pythons vacillated at various times about whether to "get the band back together," a reunion never materialized in the 1990s or early 2000s. It was only Cleese's desperate need for money after a devastating divorce settlement in 2008 as well as a loss in a lawsuit brought by Mark Forstater, one of the producers of *Monty Python and the Holy Grail*, over *Spamalot* profits, which affected the finances of all the Pythons, that led to their reunion in 2014 at the O2 Arena in London.

Now, we are not psychiatrists, but we play them on TV, so we could examine the psychological reasons for Cleese's ambivalence about continuing with Python (Cleese talks frankly about his years in therapy in *So, Actually . . .* and in many interviews). But a more charitable view of why Cleese always turned down Python reunions while continuing to work with individual members of Python, especially Palin, also could be that Cleese has always been just so darn busy!

Since the 1960s, Cleese has had well over 150 roles in movies; television shows as star, guest star, and the occasional "Wait, that's John Cleese over there!" cameo; radio program appearances; voice-overs for video games, commercials; and training films; not to mention writing, directing, and producing films. Cleese was busy before Python, during Python, and after Python. In this chapter, we'll look at some of the many, many, *many* projects that Cleese has been involved in as well as his involvements with Monty Python. (Not counting *Fawlty Towers*, but you've already read about that now, haven't you?) While all the Pythons were productive after the demise of the group following Chapman's death, none was quite so ubiquitous as Cleese.

The 1960s and '70s

Cleese put *most* of his writing and acting work aside during *Monty Python's Flying Circus*, except for *I'm Sorry, I'll Read That Again*, which Cleese contributed to whenever he had the time while working on Python. During the live radio broadcasts, if Cleese was not present, it would be explained that he was off somewhere else, "ranting." *Flying Circus* was in fact the first full-time job to which Cleese dedicated all his comedic strength, and his dedicated work on the series showed.

Cleese had a couple of small film roles in 1969, the year that *Flying Circus* got started, appearing in *The Best House in London* (and if you were thinking "Texas" and "Whorehouse," yes, that's the connection) and *The Bliss of Mrs. Blossom*. Among his more substantial engagements at the time were his and Chapman's screenplays for the 1969 comedy *The Magic Christian* and the adventurous but unsuccessful Peter Cook–starring 1970 political satire *The Rise and Rise of Michael Rimmer*, both of which films he also had small roles in, of course.

He and Chapman also worked on the execrable *Rentadick*. This was a film they'd originally written as *Rentasleuth* and had high hopes, but it was sold out from under them to producer Ned Sherrin (who should have known better, he had previously worked as the producer of *That Was the Week That Was*) and the cast and writers walked away. It was rewritten, released as *Rentadick* in 1972, and promptly tanked at the box office. Critic Alexander Walker later described the film as "another nail in the coffin of the British film industry."

Cleese was actively working on Monty Python projects through the 1970s and while that took up much of his time, he still squeezed in some writing for Ronnie Barker and *Doctor at Large* even while involved in the first three seasons of *Flying Circus*.

One view of Cleese says he is the Python most difficult to work with. But it could also simply be that Cleese gets bored more easily and craves new comedic challenges. We are inclined to agree with the latter. Either way, after three seasons of *Flying Circus*, and countless arguments while writing the third season, a dissatisfied-as-usual Cleese became convinced that Python had stretched the limits of television as far as they could.

Cleese largely absented himself from Season Four and began to look around for new projects. That, of course, raised the question of what does one do after being a pivotal part of the most influential comedic television series of all time.

One new part of his career was an unexpected step sideways. In 1972, Cleese cofounded a company called Video Arts, which produced short educational and work-training films, some of which are quite funny. This ultimately involved the crème de la crème of British comedic royalty, including appearances by Ricky Gervais, James Nesbitt, Hugh Laurie, and Dawn French. Cleese sold his share of the company in the 1990s, although he continued to appear in their videos.

Since Cleese was apparently still not busy enough, he also created and starred in *another* one of the most influential comedy programs of all time, *Fawlty Towers*. If *Monty Python's Flying Circus* completely deconstructed and tore apart the premise of almost every trope of television, *Fawlty Towers* proved that there was still a way to make the situation comedy work, but also by tearing apart the idea of the sitcom, over and over and over. (See the chapter on *Fawlty Towers* for more on that, but keep reading this one until you are done and then go back to that one, okay? We are also skipping *Holy Grail* for the moment as there is a sparklingly shiny chapter on that film, just a few pages over, so go and read that and then jump back to this paragraph. Please do.)

After *Monty Python and the Holy Grail* helped cement the Pythons' status with ground-breaking American comedians, more offers for work came in. This was especially true after the Python-inspired *Saturday Night Live* opened the doors for an edgier and more deconstructive American comedy. *SNL* producer Lorne Michaels suggested that Cleese and Palin become a comedic duo. Although watching them in *A Fish Called Wanda* and *Fierce Creatures* suggested how successful this could have been, the two also did not want to become a better-written version of the *Two Ronnies*. So, while they worked together when they could, this fascinating comedic duo never came to pass.

Cleese spent most of the 1970s on either Monty Python projects or *Fawlty Towers*, only taking a little time off to have a daughter (Cynthia, born in 1971) and get divorced from Connie Booth (August 1, 1978). However, as discussed in the chapter on *Fawlty Towers*, Booth and Cleese continued to work together after their divorce and remain friends to this day.

As the 1980s dawned, Cleese started to eye writing and directing his first film, something that would be uniquely his vision, *A Fish Called Wanda*. As is usual with a Python-related project, it was not to be as easy as he hoped.

The 1980s

While the expectations of a Cleese and Palin comedy duo never came to fruition, Cleese did spend some time in the 1980s working with several of the Python members in movies, including a memorable role in *Time Bandits* as an exceedingly polite Robin Hood ("thank you, very, very much!") alongside Palin in the Terry Gilliam–directed movie (three out of six Pythons, not bad at all), also appearing as Blind Pew in the Chapman vehicle *Yellowbeard* along with Idle, Spike Milligan, and Marty Feldman (we are also scoring this one as a three out of six Pythons), and as Haldan the Black in Jones's *Erik the Viking*. Of course, there was also some work with Python to do, such as the tour leading to the film release of *Live at the Hollywood Bowl* (1982) and, of course, *The Meaning of Life* (1983), the last Python feature film.

A Fish Called Wanda

In the 1980s, Cleese's dreams of becoming a writer, director, and leading man were closer than ever to being realized. While Cleese had worked extensively in commercials and industrial videos, he was also busily working on the project that eventually became *A Fish Called Wanda*, the first film that Cleese had full artistic control over.

An arduous process that started around 1984, *A Fish Called Wanda* went through many rewrites and a prolonged struggle for funding. While the plot is a bit convoluted—both Jamie Lee Curtis's character and Palin's pet fish are named Wanda—the film is a throwback to classic Ealing Studios–style heist comedies like *The Lavender Hill Mob*. It was just for that reason that Cleese brought on that film's legendary director, Christopher Crichton.

Although Cleese agreed to be codirector (the studio was nervous about Crichton's health), he only directed a few scenes toward the end.

The plot device is a jewelry heist planned and executed by a gang including doofus weapons expert Otto (Kevin Kline), clever glamour stooge Wanda (Jamie Lee Curtis), East End–style hard man George (Tom Georgeson), and perpetual stutterer Ken (Palin). After the successful robbery, the thieves start double-crossing one another, George ends up in prison, and only he and Ken know where the jewels are. In order to find them, Wanda seduces George's barrister, Archibald Leach (Cleese, using Cary Grant's real name, and nodding to the legal career he never had), stuck in a loveless marriage and busy raising an ungrateful daughter, Portia (played by Cynthia Cleese, his and Booth's real-life daughter). All the while Ken (Palin) is haplessly trying to kill the witness who identified George in a lineup, but ends up mistakenly killing her three dogs one by one; each little doggie funeral sadder than the other. Oh, the humanity!

Upon finally being released in 1988 to worldwide critical and box office acclaim, the film won Kline an Oscar for Best Supporting Actor and Cleese

Archie (John Cleese) gets worked over by Wanda (Jamie Lee Curtis) in Cleese's hit jewel-heist caper *A Fish Called Wanda*. *MGM/Photofest*

a Best Actor BAFTA. While there was immediate talk of a sequel, that never quite happened. Though Cleese did reunite the cast for the disappointing zoo-based comedy *Fierce Creatures* (1997). As with every other Python-related project, there has been talk of a musical version of *Wanda*, but no solid news on that front as of this writing.

Other than that, films that Cleese appeared in during the 1980s, whether in lead roles or bit parts, included memorable roles in *The Great Muppet Caper*, *Privates on Parade*, *Silverado* (a rare dramatic role for Cleese), *Clockwise*, *A Fish Called Wanda* (see above for more on *Wanda*), and *The Big Picture*, as well as the concert film *The Secret Policeman's Ball*. All of this is not including his industrials or numerous commercials in the decade. Cleese also made time along the way to marry Barbara Trentham in 1981 and have a second daughter, Camilla, in 1984.

Cleese was stunned by the death of Chapman to cancer in 1989 and delivered a memorable speech at his memorial, which included using much of the "Dead Parrot" sketch, to eulogize Chapman.

At the end of the 1980s, Cleese's career was on full throttle, though it seemed at the time that the death of Chapman meant Python would never perform again.

The 1990s

Cleese was just as ubiquitous in the 1990s as he was in the '80s, even going out on a limb and producing a wine-tasting video with his wife and several celebrity friends. Cleese also spent a good deal of the 1990s trying to get the "sequel" to *A Fish Called Wanda* made, although it had permutated so much over the last decade that calling it a sequel is a bit disingenuous as the actors were the same but the characters were completely different. He found it difficult to get financing despite the success of *Wanda*, and ended up taking on even more roles than usual. Cleese also divorced his second wife, Barbara Trentham, in 1990. Although the settlement was nowhere near as contentious as it would be for his next marriage, it was nevertheless traumatic. Cleese moved to Los Angeles to further work on his movie career, which was going better than ever.

Alongside the usual number of commercials (refreshing can of Schweppes, anyone?), Cleese's 1990s movie appearances included *Bullseye!*, *An American Tale: Fievel Goes West* (voice only), *Splitting Heirs*, *Mary Shelley's Frankenstein*, *The Jungle Book*, *The Swan Princess*, *The Wind in the Willows* (with fellow Pythons Idle, Jones, and Palin, and directed by Jones), *Fierce*

Creatures, George of the Jungle, The Out-of-Towners, and *The World Is Not Enough*, in which Cleese briefly joined the James Bond franchise, as "R," the eventual replacement for Desmond Llewellyn's "Q" character, who had been with the franchise almost from the start.

Cleese, who had endured virtual abuse as a child and two traumatic divorces at this point, wanted to share the insights that he had achieved in therapy. The result was two books he cowrote with therapist Robyn Skinner: *Families: How to Survive Them*, and *Life, How to Survive It*.

The 1990s also saw the failure of *Fierce Creatures*, which after multiple rewrites opened to tepid reviews and general negative reaction. A problem with the film was that after deciding to reshoot the ending, Cleese had to wait months until global traveler Palin had an opening in his schedule. In the meantime, noted screenwriter William Goldman was brought in for a "last-minute touch-up" and a second director, Fred Schepisi, came in to handle the reshoots that ended up taking an additional five weeks and cost an estimated $7 million. As a result, the film is uneven at best and does not have *Wanda*'s giddy dark humor. Cleese moved on but has not written a feature film since.

The 1990s also saw the surviving members of Monty Python, as well as an urn supposedly containing Chapman's ashes (which Gilliam "accidentally" kicks over), appear at the Aspen comedy festival in 1998 where they announced that they would be commencing with a reunion tour. However, Palin immediately had second thoughts and after Idle proposed booking them on a prolonged stay in Las Vegas, he walked away from the project, essentially scuttling it.

The announcement of a Python tour was one that fans had awaited for decades. The only trouble was that the announcement turned out to be premature by only sixteen years. Palin records in his diary an angry e-mail from Idle "which has a severe go at me for changing my mind on the stage show and suggests therapy." Cleese, after seeing Palin's reluctance, silly-walked away from the project as well.

The 2000s

In the new millennium, Cleese maintained a vigorous schedule of acting in various films and getting divorced yet again, but we'll get to that in a minute.

Now picking his roles with more care, Cleese appeared in two popular movie franchises, as King Harold in *Shrek 2* and two subsequent sequels, and as Nearly Headless Nick in two *Harry Potter* movies, roles that introduced Cleese to a new generation of comedy fans. Cleese also did several solo tours, which might have been necessitated by his third divorce.

His movie work blossomed, including *Isn't She Great, The Magic Pudding, Harry Potter and the Sorcerer's Stone, Harry Potter and the Chamber of Secrets,* Roberto Benigni's *Pinocchio, Die Another Day* (this time fully promoted to the role of "Q"), *The Adventures of Pluto Nash, Charlie's Angels: Full Throttle, Scorched, George of the Jungle 2, Shrek 2, Around the World in Eighty Days, Shrek the Third, Igor, The Day the Earth Stood Still, Charlotte's Web, The Pink Panther 2,* and *Planet 51,* among others. Not necessarily a list of comedy classics, but it's a living. He also had a recurring role in 2004 on the sitcom *Will & Grace,* where he could deliver some of his old ironic Python disdain: "You're behaving *like Italians!*"

Cleese also went through yet another divorce in 2008, this time to his wife of sixteen years, Alice Faye Eichelberger. The divorce was acrimonious and in the end Eichelberger won a whopping great settlement of £12 million, almost $19 million in American money. This left Cleese furious and he constantly railed about the injustice of his settlement for the next eight years at almost every public forum or interview. The bright side of Cleese's divorce (well, for his fans) was that it led him to tour again and was one of the major reasons for the Python reunion show in 2014. Cleese toured New Zealand and Dubai, Scandinavia, the United Kingdom, South Africa, Australia and the United States on the "Alimony" tour, telling stories and answering audience questions.

The 2010s and Beyond

After 2010, Cleese didn't slow down. Aside from the 2014 reunion, he also toured Canada on his own with the "Last Chance to See Me Before I Die" tour. More recently, he has been touring with Idle.

In 2015, Cleese published the first volume of his long-awaited memoir, *So, Anyway . . .* The book takes a long look at Cleese's family, particularly problems with his mother's mental illness and his own years in therapy. He did speaking engagements to promote the book across the United States and the United Kingdom, and is probably still on tour somewhere promoting something when you are reading this.

In terms of Cleese's 2010s film output, he appeared in or did voice-overs for *Shrek Forever After, The Big Year, Winnie the Pooh, God Loves Caviar, Spuds 2,* and *Absolutely Anything.* Much of his more recent work has in fact been voice-overs. They're less taxing, after all. Cleese was going to star in a live-action film, *Hunting Elephants*, but it proved to be too much for him and so he was replaced by the sprightly up-and-coming young actor Patrick Stewart.

Cleese's solo career outside of Python is certainly much more prolific than the other Pythons, and the quality of the work outside of a few clunkers (*Pluto Nash*, anyone? Anyone? *Anyone?*) is exemplary. And, as Cleese's memoir is both refreshingly candid ("You know, *candid* autobiographies?") and hilarious, it looks as though Cleese will remain in the public eye, at least until the last alimony and lawsuit checks are cashed.

Cleese also launched his own YouTube channel in 2016, which, due to unpopular demand, led to Anne Elk coming out of retirement to present her latest theory (Ahem! Ahem, ahem!), this time on "why some women have mustaches." Needless to say, it is her theory and it belongs to her (ahem!).

By the time you are reading this, Cleese will have already left for another continent to do one more show, one last tour, one more book, another radio series, several more sequels to *Shrek*, and get divorced again. Well, let's hope that's a no on the last one anyway.

To understand Cleese is to understand a force of nature, one that is constantly on the move and needs to leave situations after they become less humorous. Palin offered a wonderful travel metaphor for Cleese in 2012, writing that: "[T]he image I always have of him is of this 747 coming in to land. Teams of people, pipes underneath, doors open, people scurrying to service it. Then off it goes again, to the next destination" (Palin). The most indefatigable Python, indeed.

Cleese has also kept going as a screenwriter, even working on the story for the animated caveman family flick *The Croods*, and hopefully working on a second volume of *So, Anyway . . .* In his *The Greedy Bastard Diary*, Idle bemoans a friend

> whose love for the odd nickel leads to him being constantly yearning for a hammock, and island and a book, but who we all know will never make it. He has been saying this non-stop since 1968, but he works so hard, he'll never stop. In fact, he's in so many movies with a "two" on them, that we have labeled him "*The First Among Sequels*."

One More Thing: Those Commercials . . .

Cleese has been doing commercials for well over forty years now and for a bewildering array of products. Despite his own careful accounting, it is still unclear exactly how many he has filmed. Our accounting makes it clear that

One must read the book to find out what happened to the mustache.

he has appeared in at least forty-five different commercial campaigns, some ranging over a period of years, potentially totaling up to several hundred different commercials. Major clients have included Sony, Schweppes, TBS, Westinghouse, Canadian Club, Lexus, Sainsbury's, and even ads for the 2012 Czech Olympic team!

Cleese, while not as bad as Chapman when it came to frittering money away, nonetheless did get involved in various businesses and had several costly divorces. So his need for quick cash from the commercials (some aren't bad, look for the Schweppes ads on YouTube) is understandable. Cleese plays himself, more or less, in most of the commercials. Even when he is playing a "character" it is of the British "stiff-upper-lipped" but actually "quite-mad-below-the-surface" type well familiar to fans of Python and *Fawlty Towers*. Which is as it should be.

18

Post-Python: "I'm . . . Dead Yet!"

Graham Chapman—The Least Alive Python

C hapman would open his one-man shows in the 1980s by asking a "favor" of the audience: to heap abuse upon him for a full thirty seconds. And, oh, would they oblige: vile invectives, slurs, and profanity were flung at their idol with glee and volume—utterances that would make Chapman's professional abuse counselor from the "Argument Sketch" sit up and take notes. It takes a special kind of secure insecurity to make such a request before opening up to a roomful of strangers, even if, as Chapman often said immediately afterward, "That will save us some time later."

Abuse

In the spirit of Chapman's live tours, let's get the abuse over with first: Graham Arthur Chapman was an alcoholic. A drunkard. A sot, lush, wino, barfly alky boozer. A card-carrying dipsomaniac. Inebriated tosspot pisshead. Bereft of sobriety, he's pie-eyed, blotto, wellied, and well-hammered. Three sheets by noon, the man was plastered, legless, and barking at the moon. Pissed. Shit-faced and ploughed, sober as a judge and ready to hurl. Chapman was, in short, a three-pints-of-gin-a-day-aholic.

Although he hid it from his friends and peers for years, he made no bones about his addiction later in life. In the early days of *Flying Circus*, the other lads may not have realized the extent of his addiction, but—when he was consuming, by his own reckoning, over two quarts of gin *after* a few vodkas for brekkie—the secret eventually got out. By the end of *Flying Circus*, Chapman's drinking was jeopardizing his career. Writing partners began to note that he'd be "fizzing and popping"—really productive—until maybe half past ten in the morning, but by noon . . . it was off to the pub and that's the day. Costly on-site shoots would drag on interminably, as Chapman might require dozens of takes before recalling his lines.

The first days of shooting *Monty Python and the Holy Grail* in 1974 were particularly telling: Chapman, an avid mountaineer, had the DTs so bad

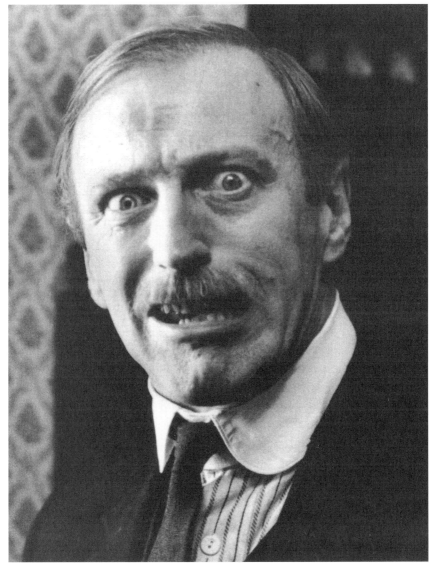

Graham Chapman in a moment of quiet self-reflection from *The Meaning of Life.*
Universal Pictures/Photofest

on set near the Gorge of Eternal Peril that he couldn't get himself to cross the perfectly safe Bridge of Death. This was a turning point for Chapman, who immediately vowed to stop drinking . . . eventually. He struggled with that decision for years, until ultimately going cold turkey around Christmas 1977. He underwent a miserable three-day withdrawal before ending up in the hospital to ring in the New Year. He never drank again, however, and was thereafter very public about his alcoholism and actively helped others with the disease. His story—as he recalls it—appears as part of *The Courage to Change: Hope and Help for Alcoholics and Their Families* (1984).

Ironically, of course, Chapman—a physician schooled in 1960s medicine—abandoned the booze but never put down the pipe. He died of throat and spinal cancer in 1989. He was forty-eight.

Are You a Pooftah?

Legend has it that the Pythons once received a complaint letter from a woman who had heard—*quelle horreur!*—that one of the men on *Flying Circus* was a homosexual. In addition to offering her prayers for his eternally damned soul, she included a Bible verse suggesting that the offending Python should be taken out and killed. Even though Chapman was publicly out at the time, the woman was unable to identify which of the Pythons was leading such a depraved lifestyle, so Idle—who was in charge of "fan mail" that day—sarcastically responded via post that they'd rounded up all the lads, figured out which was gay, and had him shot. As Cleese left the show soon after, Chapman later wondered what rumors were spread in the sticks after Ms. Biblefan received Idle's missive. Chapman related this story several different ways, including on his college tour in 1988. But keeping the facts straight was never one of his strong suits.

Although Chapman self-identified as homosexual (or the less politically correct "pouf," as he was wont to say) he occasionally had what he called "naughty sex" with female fans during his touring days across North America. His relationship with David Sherlock was an open one, and the other Pythons were keen in interviews to nudge-nudge wink-wink Chapman about his dalliances with Canadian Mounties, exuberant fans, and random acts of excess.

As an openly gay celebrity before it was fashionable to be an openly gay celebrity, Chapman was no role model. But he was available, visible, and unabashed about his sexuality at a time when homosexuality was still considered taboo by many. While Cleese was involved in Amnesty

International and Jones was illuminating environmental issues, in 1972 Chapman cofounded *Gay News*, a British newspaper he hoped would help homosexuals in the hinterlands of England realize that they were not alone. In the August 1972 issue, Chapman and Sherlock were interviewed over drinks at their home and Chapman offered some reasonable credos, including: heterosexuals need to stop telling boys to stop being so "butch"; the Gay Liberation Front needs to promote the idea of homosexuality as "normal" rather than "different"; and that "[we] mustn't try to persuade people that they should be totally homosexual at the expense of loving ladies, that are quite nice things really."

Chapman went on to appear as a charming raconteur on various talk shows in the United States and the United Kingdom, speaking openly about his homosexuality, equal rights, overpopulation, "what the neighbors will say," peer pressure, alcoholism, comedy, and why people should just generally get back to "loving each other." He really was a very nice fellow, when he wasn't falling-down drunk. Or trying to shock the crap out of people. Or both.

The Writer/Performer

Doctor, et al

As *Flying Circus* drew to a close, Chapman picked up script work on shows like *The Two Ronnies* (1973–1974), *The Prince of Denmark* (1974), and *Marty Back Together Again* (1974). But his lengthiest non-Python residency was with a medical-comedy television series. Like all the young Pythons, Cleese and Chapman often had multiple projects going at once, and when *Flying Circus* was starting the two also wrote the premier episode of a medical comedy series called *Doctor in the House* (1969–1970).

Chapman—whose practical medical experience gave him a wealth of ideas for the series—would return to the show sporadically . . . whenever he needed a few quid. All told, Chapman would coscript some thirty episodes over the various iterations of the series, including *Doctor at Large* (1971), *Doctor in Charge* (1972–1973), and *Doctor on the Go* (1977). While Cleese continued to write for the show on occasion, the two didn't formally write together after the first episode; instead, the *Doctor* series paired Chapman with other writing partners (Barry Cryer and Bernard McKenna) who would end up contributing to his future projects . . . including one that wouldn't see the light of day until 2000, some eleven years after his death.

Out of the Trees

Chapman and Adams, alongside Bernard, cowrote a pilot for a new BBC comedy sketch show, *Out of the Trees* (1976). It was, if possible, weirder than *Flying Circus* . . . at least in premise. Two linguists would start each sketch with a word or phrase. Their etymological investigations would—obviously!—lead to surreal comedy. The pilot aired—once!—opposite a football match and the BBC promptly erased the tape. The series (such as it is) was generally forgotten, although a copy was eventually found in Chapman's collection; it was subsequently shown at BFI Southwark (formerly the National Film Theatre) in 2006. Otherwise available to those with solid Internet connections and disconnected moral compasses.

The Odd Job

Chapman first hit the big screen on his own with *The Odd Job* (1978), a dark comedy he cowrote with McKenna. The film involves a depressed husband (Chapman) who believes his wife has left him; despondent, he repeatedly attempts suicide, until an odd fellow (David Jason of *DNAYS!*) suddenly appears, offering to do "odd jobs." The husband hires the man to kill him. When his wife unexpectedly returns, the husband is elated, but continues to be dogged by Jason, who remains intent on finishing the job. It sounds like a quirky enough premise (shadows fall upon *Throw Momma from the Train*, certainly), but the film failed to make any impact at the theaters or with critics. Fun (?) fact: Chapman's drinking chum, Keith Moon of the Who, was intended to play the odd fellow role, but he was going through detox at the time and had to withdraw. A mis-hit.

A Liar's Autobiography

In 1980, Chapman released *A Liar's Autobiography Vol. VI*, a semi-lucid, semi-factual, semi-autobiography he'd written with the help of his partner, David Sherlock, his friend Douglas Adams . . . and Alex Martin . . . and David Yallop. Full of stream-of-consciousness ramblings, fuzzy recollections, stylized memoirs, and outright balderdash, the book offers a distinct departure from the diaries of Palin or the memoirs of Cleese. *A Liar's Autobiography* highlights, in a scattershot way, the "major formative experiences" of young Chapman—from childhood to Python—but sifting through the text for a real history of the man is an exercise in some frustration. And perhaps that was his intention; the cover blurb offers the following disclaimer: "[T]his

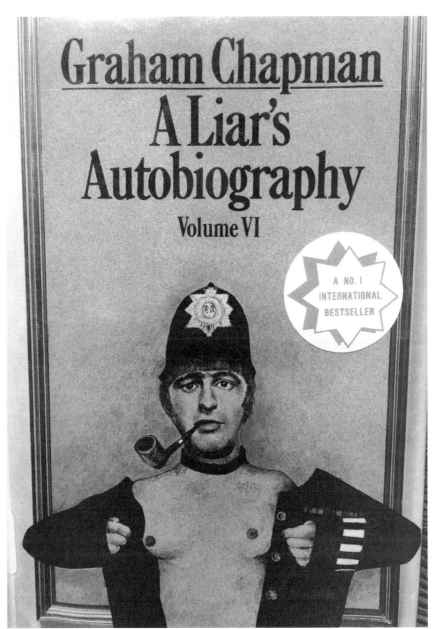

At least the title is true . . . ish.

book is not a history. It is a heady mixture of wild invention and outrageous honesty." So perhaps Chapman is offering the reader a challenge: to discern invention from honesty. Or perhaps, as Cleese has opined, Chapman "lived in a fantasy world" and *A Liar's Autobiography* simply reflects the fantastic world as he saw it. Or as five lying authors saw it.

The book was made into a 3-D animated feature-length film in 2012, with most of the Pythons lending their voices to various roles (less Idle, plus Cleveland, and including Chapman, who had recorded some bits before his death). Two producers of *A Liar's Autobiography*—Ben Timlett and Bill Jones (yes, Bill, son of Terry)—also codirected the far more lucid *Monty Python: Almost the Truth* (2009). But if you're into a trippy *Yellow Submarine* version of the Pythonverse, *A Liar's Autobiography* could be your bag.

Yellowbeard

The most heartbreaking of Chapman's "almost" projects is undoubtedly *Yellowbeard* (1983), a pirate comedy that could have, *should have*, been great. By the 1980s, Chapman was sober, he had seasoned scriptwriter McKenna and comic legend Peter Cook on board as cowriters, and a cast to die for. And yet . . . the nicest thing to say about *Yellowbeard* is that the 1980s were a tough time for the genre; just see Roman Polanski's 1986 debacle *Pirates*, with Walter Matthau(!) as the lead buccaneer for proof of that claim. Arrgh.

Like *The Odd Job*, Chapman had initially written the script for *Yellowbeard* with his chum Keith Moon in mind for the lead, but Moon had died (in 1978, battling alcoholism) well before the project became a reality. With Moon gone, Chapman stepped into the lead role to captain an all-star comedy cast including Peter Boyle, Cheech and Chong, Peter Cook, Marty Feldman, Idle, Madeline Kahn, James Mason, Cleese, Spike Milligan . . . and yes, that's David Bowie in there as well. Unfortunately, the film is not the "shipload of laughs" promised by the posters. Whether one blames the overlong time in "development hell" before shooting began, or the constant script rewrites (Idle recalls it was the worst script he'd ever read), or the repeated edits, or the pall that hung over the final production after Feldman died on set in 1982, in the end *Yellowbeard* was not to be Chapman's post-Python triumph. It's honestly hard to argue with Cleese's evaluation: *Yellowbeard* is "one of the worst six movies made in the history of the world." Contemporary critics were generally (but not always) a tad kinder, but *Yellowbeard* hardly made a splash at the box office. The failure hit Chapman hard and—although he served as executive producer of the rehab-thriller *Love Potion* (1987)—*Yellowbeard* would be his last feature-length film.

Given the density of comic talent on board, a documentary was made during the filming of *Yellowbeard*, and, as a historical artifact, the behind-the-scenes doc is definitely worth a look. In the days before multi-disc DVD releases, director's cuts, commentary tracks, or online "grassroots" leaks, *Group Madness: The Making of Yellowbeard* could have drummed up some excellent publicity for the film. However, rather than air widely in the weeks before the film's release (as the producers had planned), the behind-the-scenes teaser aired only once on U.S. television (preempting an episode of *Saturday Night Live*) in 1983. The documentary subsequently disappeared until its 1990s VHS release, then resurfaced again in 2007 on DVD.

Love Potion

Although he didn't have much hand in the creative end of things, Chapman was the executive producer ("grubbing around for money") on *Love Potion* (1987), a low-budget but trippy thriller set in an English rehab clinic; the film was also known as *Shock Treatment* and/or *Drugs Unlimited*. Not to be confused with Richard O'Brien's *Rocky Horror* sequel, *Shock Treatment* (1981) or Sandra Bullock's rom-com *Love Potion #9* (1992).

American TV

Chapman appeared now and again on American television, popping up on *Saturday Night Live* as "The Colonel" (1976 and 1982), and on *Hollywood Squares* (1979) or talk shows as himself. He hosted the short-lived *Dangerous Film Club* (1987), which featured weird home movies, newsreel footage, and music videos; Chapman also guest-starred on the made-for-TV movie *Still Crazy Like a Fox* (1987) as a detective inspector who matches wits with American sleuths during their London vacation.

In 1988, Chapman and Sherlock began work on a possible CBS television series, *Jake's Journey*, a takeoff on Mark Twain's perpetually reimagined *A Connecticut Yankee in King Arthur's Court*. The two wrote a number of episodes, and Chapman was cast to play a "cranky old knight" on the show, before CBS changed its mind and decided the comedy-fantasy would be "too British" for American audiences. The series never saw the light of day, but Chapman's pilot script for *Jake's Journey* was eventually published as part of *OJRIL: The Completely Incomplete Chapman* (1999). Unfortunately, *Jake's Journey* and *The Odd Job* reflect Chapman's post-Python career: a series of near-misses that could have been but never quite were.

Ditto

That's not to say Chapman ever gave up. He and Cleese had been tinkering with an old script titled *Ditto* they'd started in the years just before Chapman's death. Although Chapman often said it had been completed, Cleese has kept mum about the script since his passing. There's little likelihood it will ever see the light of day again.

The Live Performer

Apart from Python, Chapman toured extensively, lecturing at North American colleges and smaller venues. The shows were often semi-biographical, semi-promotional, semi-Pythonesque ramblings. He would discuss Python projects, non-Python projects, his alcoholism, his involvement with the Dangerous Sports Club, and sexuality (his, mostly). After the initial call for abuse, he would go on to intersperse his recollections with the occasional "Pythonic" or "Dangerous Sports" film clip, and end sessions with an open Q&A. The shows were surprisingly informative, sporadically funny, and very intimate; currently a few are available in various formats, including *A Six Pack of Lies* (1997) and *Looks Like a Brown Trouser Job* (2005); bootleg and amateur videos surface on the Internet from time to time as well. Hello, Syracuse!

Chapman found himself joining—more or less—the Dangerous Sports Club in 1985. This was a group of Oxford-based daredevils devoted to extreme sports back before there were extreme sports; although the club is credited with inventing bungee-jumping, many of the "dangerous sports" the group attempted now feel more like upper-class *Jackass* dares. In Chapman's first outing with the club, he joined others for a round of "surrealist skiing"—Chapman scoots down the slopes riding a five-foot wooden gondola; at the Sport Aid benefit in 1986, he is hurled some 130 feet into the air via bungee slingshot. But by his own account, Chapman was more mascot than member, attending events and showing clips of other daredevils doing dangerous things (hang-gliding over an active volcano, bungee-jumping, and so forth) during his college lectures. Rumor had it that Chapman was writing a film script for the club, full of outrageous stunts, in the months before he died.

Chapman was close with a number of rock musicians, as were many of the Pythons, who were—let's face it—rock stars of comedy. He even emcee'd a few shows by the Who back in 1975. Perennially popular with musicians and college students, he appeared as a guest VJ on MTV in 1987. It's worth

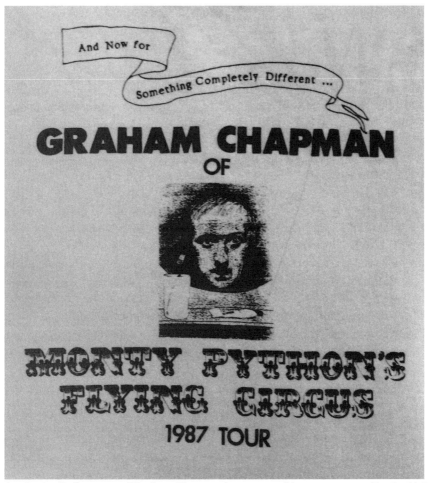

A prized relic from one of Graham Chapman's many speaking tours.   *Lisa Bocchini*

noting that within a year of Chapman's MTV stint, Cleese would be a guest DJ on a classical radio station.

Even given his connection to MTV, it's still something of a surprise to find Chapman starring in an Iron Maiden music video, for their hit single "Can I Play with Madness" (which charted at #3 in the United Kingdom). In the video, Chapman plays a spectacled schoolmaster / art teacher who looms over his students in the ruins of Tintern Abbey. After the usual "angry teacher" moment so central to the 1980s heavy-metal video mise en scène [Pretentious.—Eds.], Chapman falls into a pit (Chislehurst Caves) while contemptuously reading a confiscated *Iron Maiden* magazine. Naturally, he then explores the crypt and watches a Maiden concert video on a cobweb-covered underground television. Then, in a metatheatric nod to *The Meaning of Life*, he opens a refrigerator (labeled "LIFE") and sees Eddie the Head—the band's necrotic animated mascot—leering at him. The video ends with Chapman still lost underground, observed by a mystical beardo via crystal ball. It's an odd one. The video is available on the *Iron Maiden: From There to Eternity* compilation VHS (1992) and *Looks Like a Brown Trouser Job*.

Cancer

In the second season of *Flying Circus*, Gilliam animated a mock–fairy tale interstitial known as "The Spot" (Episode 19) about a handsome prince who ignores—to his peril—a black spot upon his face. The spot grows, and (as Cleveland narrates off-camera) "three years later he died of cancer." The bit wackily goes on to show "the spot" bouncing along, getting married, and spawning little specks that take over the neighborhood. Curiously, the BBC censored the word *cancer* in reruns, dubbing in a male voice saying "gangrene" to obscure the offensive word. Gilliam recalled being simply "dumbfounded" about the censorship. But Chapman, as a physician, took offense for more practical reasons, as included in Roger Wilmut's *From Fringe to Flying Circus*:

> "Why not use a word like 'cancer'? It's so silly to be afraid of it and hide the thing away—a lot of people do die of cancer, and if more people spoke about it more openly then more of them would be cured. It's silly to have this fear—and that's what censorship is, really—it's fear."

Chapman often feared he would die, but he thought it would be of alcohol. He'd smoked since he was fifteen, and there's rarely a shot of him on set without a pipe handy. Despite his medical training, despite not fearing the word, he simply didn't see the cancer coming.

In November 1988, Chapman noticed a pain in his throat after a dentist visit; an exploratory operation a month later revealed a tumor on his tonsils. He underwent radiotherapy treatment; after an operation to remove the growth, he seemed to be on the mend. Unfortunately, post-surgery backaches persisted for weeks, then he lost perception of his leg. After a self-diagnosis (aided by Sherlock), Chapman realized that the cancer had spread to his spinal cord. He was on the operating table the very next day, where they removed a rapidly growing tumor. As he noted afterward, the emergency surgery probably saved him from irrevocable paralysis. He remained in the hospital for nearly two months before being released in a wheelchair, unable to move his legs but certain he would overcome this setback. By September 1989, he had made progress through physical therapy and appeared publicly optimistic; although frail, he joined the other Pythons (and Steve Martin) to film two sketches for the upcoming anniversary special, *Parrot Sketch Not Included: Twenty Years of Monty Python*. They would be his last performances.

In an interview with the *Sun* soon after, on September 18, 1989, Chapman talked about his health, noting "I want to tell people loud and clear: DON'T be afraid of cancer; it CAN be beaten."

He was rushed to nearby Maidstone Hospital two weeks later, and died the next day, surrounded by friends and family (including Sherlock, Cleese, and Palin). Chapman's final words—to his nurse—were reportedly "Sorry for saying 'fuck.'" On October 4, 1989—almost twenty years to the day since *Monty Python's Flying Circus* first aired—Chapman, the cocreator of the "Parrot Sketch," was no more.

The Eulogy

Chapman was quietly laid to rest at Vinters Park Crematorium in Maidstone, near his home, on October 13, 1989. His fellow Pythons sent a Bronzino-style flower arrangement with the postscript: "Stop us if we're getting silly." In early December, the Pythons and other celebrities attended a memorial service for their fallen King/Colonel at St. Bartholomew's Hospital in London. The Fred Tomlinson Singers performed "Jerusalem" in his honor, and Idle led a chorus of "Always Look on the Bright Side of Life." Palin suggested that the recent twentieth anniversary of *Flying Circus* only mattered now that Chapman, who represented the proudest bits of Python—"awkward, outrageous, unconventional, unpredictable, impatient, and often very angry indeed"—was gone. But fittingly, it was his longtime writing partner, Cleese, who wrote the eulogy Chapman truly deserved.

After opening with a gentle riff on the "Parrot Sketch" in which he noted that Chapman has "kicked the bucket, hopped the twig, bit the dust [. . .] gone to meet the great Head of Light Entertainment in the sky," Cleese added: "Good riddance to him, the freeloading bastard! I hope he fries." And that's as Chapman would have wanted it, for Cleese to shock the audience on his behalf: "Anything for him but mindless good taste." So, while Cleese facetiously states that he lacks the courage—without Gray—to say "fuck" at a British funeral service (which he just did, of course), he encourages all sorts of inappropriate behavior of the other speakers to follow—"trousers dropping, blasphemers on pogo sticks, spectacular displays of high-speed farting, synchronized incest"—to perform "The Aristocrats" of funeral services, really. Because the ex-Chapman would have wanted them all to shock one another, as he had done over the years, to give "others a momentary joy of liberation" and the recognition "that the social rules that constrict our lives so terribly are not actually very important."

Fuck.

The Afterlife

Although gone, Chapman has scarcely been forgotten. In 1999, the august English Heritage society commemorated his early life with a Blue Plaque at King Edward VII School Melton, which Chapman attended in his youth. In 2012, Palin, Jones, and Cleveland unveiled another blue plaque—this one from the British Comedy Society—attached to the Angel Pub in London . . . a site Chapman attended frequently in his "second youth." A dubious honor, perhaps, but an honor nonetheless.

The "ghost of Chapman" continues to manifest itself, not only in familiar haunting grounds about England, but in exotic locales like the American South. For example, although Chapman never saw a play of his own produced in the West End during his lifetime, his long-lost *O Happy Day* finally opened in (of all places) Georgia in 2000.

Started by Chapman and Barry Cryer during the 1974 filming of *Holy Grail*, it was never finished or produced until Sherlock sent it for safekeeping to Jim Yoakum's Graham Chapman Archives in Atlanta. Yoakum thought the material deserved an airing, and gave it to an improv comedy group named Dad's Garage in Athens, Georgia; the group filled in the missing bits and ad-libbed with the "spirit of Chapman" in mind. As Cleese (he and Palin served as consultants) noted on the show's playbill: "Graham would have just been tickled to know that a bunch of American boys were doing his British farce. Then again, Graham had a very tenuous relationship with reality." An *Atlanta Journal-Constitution* theater report opined that *O Happy Day* is a "Pythonesque tale taking on family, drinking, weddings, birth, cross-dressing, drinking, overbearing mothers, mistaken identity, drinking, and all the other facets of being British." Dad's Garage went on to produce *Out of the Trees* in 2003 as well, a collection of short Chapman-esque sketches.

Of course, Chapman is always with the Pythons, *in spiritus* if not *in corpus*. At the *Monty Python Live at Aspen* semi-reunion in 1998, Chapman was infamously present, ensconced in a funeral urn ceremoniously set upon a steamer trunk, a placard with his pipe-clenched grinning face tacked unceremoniously upon the trunk. The urn is conspicuously ignored by the Pythons as they are interviewed by comedian Robert Klein for a full five minutes. Then, in a bit of tasteless slapstick that Chapman would have certainly enjoyed, Gilliam "accidentally" knocks over the urn, spraying ashes upon the stage rug. Silliness with brooms and a DustBuster ensues, before the interview continues, Chapman's grinning mug leering from the steamer trunk throughout the show.

The surviving Pythons kept Chapman involved in their "final" reunion as well, featuring him prominently in the 2014 *Monty Python Live (mostly): One Down, Five to Go* shows at the O2 Arena in London. In fact, Chapman appears "on stage" before the surviving five in every performance: after an introductory bit of dramatic *2001: A Space Odyssey* fanfare from the orchestra, his coifed face—as Mr. Neutron—appears like a demented Teletubby sun upon the central Megatron screen, only to be punted across the universe by a giant foot, bouncing about like a pinball. As with the Aspen urn, it's a fine and irreverent way to bring the dead to mind, then immediately hurl them to the void.

Archival footage of Chapman punctuated the O2 show; he appeared as the Colonel, for example, interrupting one bit and throwing to the next "good clean healthy outdoor sketch." In some of the live sketches that typically involved Chapman, the rest of the Pythons chipped in for their lost mate.

Cleese, for example, occupied Chapman's seat in the "Four Yorkshiremen" sketch (although he and Chapman helped originate the sketch on *At Last the 1948 Show*, the seats were typically filled by Chapman, Idle, Palin, and Jones during the Python's previous stage shows). Palin ranted as Chapman's proudly Protestant Mr. Blackitt; Idle played Chapman's interviewer on "Science Today" opposite Cleese's Anne Elk (Miss). Gilliam was atypically on stage as "Second Bruce" in the Philosopher's sketch and as the Pope's highly informative servant (both typically Chapman roles); while Jones played a Chapman-esque Pepperpot sitting alongside Cleese while "The Death of Mary, Queen of Scots" plays on the radio and a penguin sits on the telly. Happily, even Carol Cleveland got to honor the fallen Python, playing Chapman's Spam-hating Mrs. Bun in the Spam sketch opposite Idle and Jones. The newcomer to the show, Samuel Holmes, also tagged in from a recorded Chapman to complete "Christmas in Heaven" as Tony Bennett.

All in all, it was a lovely way to honor Chapman, really; possibly even more endearing than knocking his ashes all over Colorado.

19

Post-Python: "There's Nothing Quite as Wonderful as Money"

Eric Idle—The Showman

Not So Idle: Rutland to the Rutles

As any survivor of the 1970s can attest, television was then still a frequently crude and ill-put-together medium with lots of airtime to fill. The plethora of cheap-to-produce talk shows with tatty-looking sets made for an instantly mockable genre. The spoof-heavy *SCTV* (launched in 1976) and Martin Mull and Fred Willard's darker *Fernwood Tonight* (1977) relentlessly worked the contrast of grungy production values and over-the-top sunniness, while *Saturday Night Live* went back to the "weird local talk show" sketch format so often it became a cliché. Although the United Kingdom had fewer channels, the cheapie local show was still a recognizable genre, ripe for mockery.

In March 1974, months before the Pythons started recording the final season of *Flying Circus* (a good part of which was made up of sketches about odd invented talk shows), the BBC commissioned Idle to produce a six-episode comedy series with an even lower budget ("It was made on a shoestring," Idle told *Radio Times*, "and someone else was wearing the shoe") but almost as broad a remit. The idea behind *Rutland Weekend Television*—whose name supposedly came from a Cleese gag that Idle paid him a pound for—was that of a cheesy local-interest show broadcast from Rutland, the smallest county in England before it was merged into Leicestershire.

The premiere episode, "Rutland Weekend Gibberish," was first broadcast on May 12, 1975. Zipping from one eager-to-please and poorly suited host to the next, Idle shows off his ability to instantly morph character while maintaining a familiar tone; a feat that few if any of the other Pythons could have managed.

Idle, described by Chapman as "a word freak" and one of the only Pythons who could have pulled off the "Man Who Speaks in Anagrams" *Flying Circus* sketch, also used *Rutland* to highlight his lexicographical predilections. In one of the more infamous sketches, Idle plays an interviewer speaking in Burroughs-esque cut-up sentence fragments that loudly clang with the kind of giddy word-absurdity that Cleese and Chapman would have adored. Closing his introduction with "tip-toe rusting machinery [pause for effect] rustically inclined," Idle introduces the guest, who instead of being bewildered comes right back with more of the same: "Saddlebag, saddlebag, lechery billboard kettlebum . . ." and so on. Idle closes with the query "Machine wrapped with butter?" to which the interviewee replies in happy singsong confidence, "Machine wrapped with *butter*." Musical interludes and sketches follow in varying degrees of chaos, noted by the frantically grinning host as "a few slight teething problems."

Later episodes play out like bargain-basement *Flying Circus* sketches, minus the studio audience but plus anarchic cross-cutting. They mix Idle's wordplay with some snappy cultural subversion—the "Philosophy Corner" segment includes both "Kung Fucius: The Aggressive Philosophy!" and "Noam Chomsky's theory that Plato wore no panties"—and *Do Not Adjust Your Set*–style musical interludes from Neil Innes.

One standout bit in which Idle bargains with Satan, who wants more than his eternal soul since those just aren't worth that much, works like a classic Cleese-Palin shopkeeper sketch from *Flying Circus*. The first season's six episodes concluded on June 16, 1975, and a Christmas episode was broadcast on December 26.

Idle did his best to turn the Rutland universe into his own miniature franchise. In 1976, he published *The Rutland Dirty Weekend Book* (whose cover teased that it was "without an introduction by HRH Prince Charles"). A kind of highly libidinal *National Lampoon*–styled tabloid scrapbook, it mixed fake advertisements ("The 10 most asked questions about the Army: What's It Like in Northern Ireland?") with articles like "Who's Having Who in Television?," "The Vatican Sex Manual . . . Seventy-four positions in which to prevent lovemaking." Also in 1976, Idle and Innes released *The Rutland*

Weekend Songbook, a full-length album that was designed to sound like a full day's worth of the show.

Since neither caught on with the public, and *Rutland Weekend Television* was never given a proper DVD release, the world of Rutland lives on mostly in hazy memories, books like this one, and grainy YouTube clips. The one exception to that rule comes due to another rule: it's always good to be friends with a Beatle.

The legend that will last a lunchtime.   *Lisa Bocchini*

For the Christmas special, Idle's friend George Harrison popped in to sing his and Idle's "The Pirate Song." Besides being a buzzworthy cap to the show's first year, Harrison's appearance foreshadowed the following year's appearance of Idle's faux-Beatles mock-band the Rutles: Dirk McQuickly (Idle), Barry Womble (John Halsey), Stig O'Hara (Ricky Fataar), and Ron Nasty (Innes).

Ironically, the first appearance of the Rutles outside of advertisements in *The Rutland Dirty Weekend Book* wasn't even on the BBC. Idle hosted *Saturday Night Live* for the first time on October 2, 1976. Idle is castigated by Lorne Michaels for supposedly having suckered the show out of money meant for the Beatles to perform. As a substitute, Michaels premiered a clip from the Rutles episode of *Rutland Weekend Television*, which kicked off the second and final season on November 12, 1976. The reaction was so immediate that audience members were mailing in Beatles albums (edited to read "The Rutles") for signatures. Michaels offered to produce a feature-length Rutles film to air on NBC. The money wasn't astronomical but pretty good for those used to BBC starvation wages.

Idle wrote the film in February 1977, buying every Beatles book he could find and enlisting Harrison, who helped by screening *The Long and Winding Road*, a then-unseen Beatles documentary. In Keith Badman's *The Beatles: Off the Record 2*, Innes said, "The next thing I know is, I'm being asked to write sixteen songs by next Thursday lunchtime in the style of the Beatles." Innes had his own personal connection to the Beatles, as the Bonzo Dog Doo-Dah Band appeared in the band's *Magical Mystery Tour* and Paul McCartney (under the name Apollo C. Vermouth) produced their hit "I'm an Urban Spaceman."

All You Need Is Cash aired on NBC on March 22, 1978. As many sticklers would point out later, that was a good four years before *This Is Spinal Tap*. But while Rob Reiner's mockumentary was a deep embed inside the group psychology of its genre- and decade-spanning metal band, Idle's was more a stylistic goof happy to imitate the Rutles' transformation from mop-top teen idols playing at "Che Stadium" to guru-following hippies on their "Tragical History Tour" without ever getting into the Rutles' collective head. John Belushi, Bill Murray, Mick Jagger, and Paul Simon pop by for extended cameos in between the lengthy ersatz-Beatles re-creations that are so close to the originals that some sound more like covers.

The critics were impressed by the story of the band "whose legend will last a lunchtime." Audiences were less enthused: *All You Need Is Cash* came in dead last in the ratings for the week. That still meant far more viewers than Idle had ever enjoyed in Britain. He told *Entertainment Weekly*, "I came off BBC2, where there were 12 people and a donkey watching. So for me, being No. 76 on American television was exciting."

However, perhaps due to the anthropological attention to detail provided by Idle's writing and codirecting and Innes's spot-on musical mimicry, the film hit a chord with Beatles fans. One legend has it that an audio recording of Innes performing the John Lennon-ish "Cheese and Onions" on *SNL* the second time Idle hosted in April 1977 appeared later on bootlegs that claimed it was actually a Lennon demo.

The Rutles played to these fans by carrying on in the same kind of alternate universe as Spinal Tap and *A Mighty Wind*'s the Folksmen. The Rutles' 1978 self-titled release was essentially the soundtrack for *All You Need Is Cash*; its impersonation of the Beatles was actually so spot-on that Innes had to settle out of court with Beatles music publisher ATV. *Archaeology* (1996) was supposedly a greatest hits album with a design that parodied the Beatles' *Anthology*. Idle did not perform on either release. Everything came full circle in the new millennium with the reputed appearance of Ouch!, an actual Rutles tribute band.

Billed as a sequel, 2004's *The Rutles 2: Can't Buy Me Lunch* was basically a rehash, swapping in previously unused footage and some new celebrity interviews (Steve Martin, Tom Hanks, Carrie Fisher), which helped cash in on Idle's well-honed ability to befriend the rich, famous, and talented types that we imagine we would be hobbing and nobbing with, were we also rich, famous, and talented. (Call us, Steve Martin!)

There's an Idle on the Telly-Vision Set

After *All You Need Is Cash*, Idle was almost nearly finished with Rutland, except for a 2003 comedy album, *The Rutland Isles*, a mostly disregarded spoof on BBC documentaries with no real connection to the Rutland of yore.

Following Rutland, the most visible parts of Idle's career were the next three Python feature films: *Life of Brian, Monty Python Live at the Hollywood Bowl*, and *The Meaning of Life*. But even while he wrote books and plays and toured (with Pythons and without), Idle kept his hand in the acting game, soon becoming a dab hand at the guest comic spot.

Idle hosted *Saturday Night Live* three times between 1978 and 1980. It was a halcyon era when the show didn't always demand the host be a celebrity with a film to promote or a scandal to exorcise.

In 1981, Idle and ex-Herman's Hermits singer Peter Noone played touring rock stars on an episode of *Laverne & Shirley* that laid on the drug humor so thick it was pulled from reruns. The following year, Idle directed and narrated the premier episode of the anthology show *Faerie Tale Theatre* ("The Tale of the Frog Prince," with Idle's friend Robin Williams, plus Teri Garr and Shelley Duvall). Idle's up-and-down television career included everything from starring roles in the series *Nearly Departed* (he played a ghost; it was a comedy; it lasted one season) to Passepartout in a middling *Around the World in 80 Days* miniseries with Pierce Brosnan. He even cowrote and performed the theme song for the BBC sitcom *One Foot in the Grave* (1990–2000).

After Judd Nelson left the extremely 1990s sitcom *Suddenly Susan* (think sets thick with bric-a-brac and similarly overextended writing), Idle took over the role of blustery male foil to star Brooke Shields. In *The Greedy Bastard Diary*, Idle lamented that he was enticed onto the show by "the notion that, as [Shields's] boss, my character would do nothing but abuse her." A couple episodes in, one focus group treated by the network as holy writ got rid of that idea. "And so, sadly," Idle wrote, "my character spent the rest of the year being nice to her . . . I gnashed my teeth and took the quite enormous amounts of money they paid me not to be funny."

Following that, most of Idle's appearances on American television were audio only, and generally only appreciated by the schoolyard set who took whatever Nickelodeon and the Disney Channel threw at them. This wasn't unusual for a Python; several have lent their vocal cords to animated characters. Idle's voice acting began rather oddly in 1986, though, when he voiced the character/vehicle Wreck-Gar for *The Transformers: The Movie*. His character's first appearance is to the sounds of Weird Al Yankovic's "Dare to Be Stupid." But, as Idle noted later, at least he got to be in the same film as (the voice of) Orson Welles.

Later on, Idle has paid the bills voicing animated characters on everything from *Pinky and the Brain* to *Hercules*. His most memorable animated character, though, is probably the supremely cynical and condescending British documentary filmmaker Declan Desmond (part Nick Broomfield, part Michael Apted, all evil) on *The Simpsons*.

You, Too, Can Be a Great Actor!

Of all the Pythons, Idle has made the least fuss about acknowledging that he's out for filthy lucre. That's true even though he loves to repeat a gag where Cleese, he of the corporate training videos and many, many adverts, said he'd do literally anything for money, Idle offered him a pound to shut up, and Cleese took it. Idle's even made it part of his shtick. See: *The Greedy Bastard Tour, Eric Idle Exploits Monty Python*, "The Money Song" ("There is nothing quite as wonderful as money / There is nothing quite as beautiful as cash"). Influenced perhaps by his less-than-secure upbringing in that Wolverhampton boarding school, Idle took work that others in his place might have turned their nose up at, leaving some fans deeply discombobulated.

Like the other Pythons, Idle never graduated to that rarified level where once-groundbreaking comics like Steve Martin, Robin Williams, and Louis C.K. suddenly become hot properties rolling in their millions. Palin and Gilliam carved out specific roles for themselves (genial travel chronicler, cinema fantasist). But Idle was more of an odd-jobber in the Jones mold, albeit without the medievalist sideline. Thus, his mix of sitcom and voice-over work, not to mention appearances in a string of films that often left Python fans underwhelmed, to put it mildly.

Following his Rutland/Rutles period and *Life of Brian*, Idle started off relatively slow in films. He showed up for Chapman and Peter Cook's 1983 pirate spoof, *Yellowbeard*, one of the relatively few films he did with fellow Pythons. More memorably, two years later he jumped out as the unfortunate bicyclist who is continually being run over by the Griswolds in *National Lampoon's European Vacation*. Here, Idle not only showed his ability to convey a particularly English stoicism but also his willingness to pillage old bits from the Python past for a laugh; "It's just a flesh wound, honestly," he scoffs as blood spurts out in front of the horrified American tourists.

Not long afterward, Idle entered the months-long tribulation that was Terry Gilliam's *The Adventures of Baron Munchausen*. In the film's *Wizard of Oz* doubling of fantasy upon fantasy, Idle played both a cockney actor trying to survive in a besieged city and one of the baron's henchmen, able to run at Mercury-like speeds. While Idle's turn is note-perfect in both roles, he groused later to the *Guardian* in 2012 (possibly tongue in cheek, he loves to get reporters' goat) that it was one of the only things he regretted in his career: "[It] was shitty and horrible and filming went on forever."

Once *Munchausen* finally limped its way out of theaters, Idle's acting career took a definite swerve. Through the 1990s and onward, one was most likely to see Idle on the movie screen mugging in broader than broad comedies. For *Nuns on the Run* (1990) a wannabe *Some Like It Hot* sans Marilyn Monroe and Billy Wilder, Idle and fellow *European Vacation* costar and English comedy legend Robbie Coltrane hid out from gangsters while dressed as nuns. *Casper* (1995) capitalized mostly on Idle's rubbery-faced aspect, as did *Honey, I Shrunk the Audience* (1994), a short film made for a ride at Epcot, which one hopes at least paid well.

Idle received unusually high marks for his performance as Rat in Jones's 1996 studio-crippled adaptation of *The Wind in the Willows* (coming full circle from Idle's childhood, when his first stage role was as Second Fieldmouse in a school play of the same book), idiotically renamed *Mr. Toad's Wild Ride*.

The following year, Idle did his level best in *An Alan Smithee Film: Burn Hollywood Burn*, a hardworking, of-the-moment, cameo-riddled trainwreck of a satire that wanted ever so much to be *The Player*. Idle plays a hapless director stuck in the crossfire of studio interference and star egos. It's a Hollywood footnote now for the irony of having its in-joke title—Alan Smithee is the traditional pseudonym assigned by the Director's Guild when a director either walks off or is taken off a film—come true in real life. Writer and then–Hollywood powerhouse Joe Eszterhas removed director Arthur Hiller and recut the film, leading Hiller to fulfill the title's prophecy by removing his name from the credits.

In recent years, like with his television work, Idle's film résumé has been of the voice-only kind, though very occasionally in adult fare like *South Park: Bigger Longer & Uncut*.

Ultimately, little of Idle's post-Python acting on the big and little screen has measured up to either his work with the Pythons or the frantic creativity he brought to the Rutland/Rutles mini-universe. But he has managed to keep his hand in an industry that is initially welcoming and ultimately vicious to comedians of his vintage; just witness the attempts of Marty Feldman and other 1960s British comedy veterans who tried to make a go of it in Hollywood.

It's possible, as well, that Idle has turned his attention to pursuits more worthy than Hollywood. As part of a Python fete at the 2015 Tribeca Film Festival, Idle pointed out how *Flying Circus* worked in part because there were no executives telling them what to do. "That's why it's so shit over here at times doing work for the studios," he said. "You've got people who came out of the William Morris mailroom giving notes on comedy. The only possible response is 'Fuck off!'"

Novel- and Screenwriting, Live!(!!!)! from Pasadena

Like other Pythons, Idle is thought of primarily as a performer. But excepting Gilliam, each came up as a writer as well. During the Python years, it was Idle, the odd Python out in the troupe who didn't have a writing partner, who did the yeoman's work of assembling the troupe's various bestselling books. Idle kept writing through the post-Python period, and not just sketches.

Idle is an inveterate bookworm, a survival technique for those years in Wolverhampton. As he put it in *The Pythons*: "I was more well read than most teenagers because at boarding school there was nothing else to do in the evenings." Today, the reading list that he posts on his website is smashing in its depth and variety, and shared with friends by the likes of Dave Eggers.

Idle's first stand-alone book came out in 1975. About as difficult to find now as the *Rutland Dirty Weekend Book*, *Hello Sailor* is similarly randy but more politically inclined. Caught somewhere between William S. Burroughs and *Dr. Strangelove*, the novel throws together a batch of farcical plotlets ranging from a gay prime minister to a man trying to make history by bedding the daughters of each member of the cabinet to a comically disorganized Middle East escapade by the British military. Frantically dense and stream-of-consciousness, it's emblematic of the kind of work Idle was still doing in the mid-1970s and would turn away from not long after.

During the early 1980s, Idle briefly turned screenwriter. He describes this period on his blog as "being paid a fortune to re-write films that were never made." According to a 1987 interview from *Q Magazine*, the never-produced screenplays included Rutland-related projects (one of which, *And Now This*, came to light as the 2003 CD *The Rutland Isles*), and the promisingly titled *Hamlet Prince of Dallas*. Idle's screenplay for *Splitting Heirs* (1993), a reversed-at-birth farce starring himself, Rick Moranis, and a young Catherine Zeta-Jones, was about the only full-fledged film to result from this period.

In the early 1990s, Idle and his frequent musical collaborator (following his Rutland/Rutles work with Innes) John Du Prez started kicking around the idea of an animated musical for children based on Edward Lear's nonsense poem "The Owl and the Pussycat." Steven Spielberg passed. Never one to let a good bit of material lie fallow, Idle transitioned the musical into the charming 1996 children's book *The Quite Remarkable Adventures of the Owl and the Pussycat*, with a Grammy-nominated audio version on which Idle narrates and performs the sneakily subversive songs.

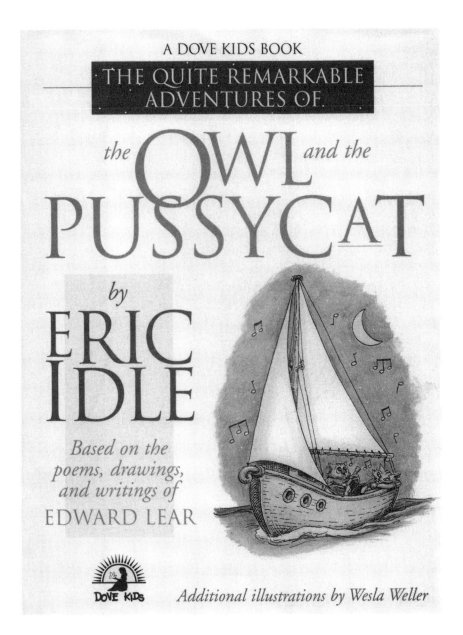

A DOVE KIDS BOOK

THE QUITE REMARKABLE
ADVENTURES OF

the OWL *and the*
PUSSYCAT

by
ERIC
IDLE

*Based on the
poems, drawings,
and writings of*
EDWARD LEAR

DOVE KIDS   *Additional illustrations by Wesla Weller*

In 1982, Idle worked on a futuristic comedy called *Science Friction* (yay, puns!) that was to have starred Robin Williams and Dan Aykroyd as comics traveling the solar system circuit with their android who looks like David Bowie (to be played, of course, by the Thin White Duke himself). Nothing ever came of the film.

Idle reworked the story and published it in 1999 as a Douglas Adams-esque science-fiction picaresque under the (far better) title *The Road to Mars: A Post-Modem Novel*. It remains the most successful of his books to date, and for good reason. The pun-spattered plot about planet-hopping comics meanders, to be sure. But the sidelong narration by Carlton, in which the 4.5 Bowie android works out an academic theory of comedy, benefits from both Idle's encyclopedic grasp of the medium and his less-used (since the Python days, at least) ability to write in a drier idiom.

The Greedy Bastard Diary: A Comic Tour of America (2005) is just that: Idle's recollections from the 2003 Greedy Bastard tour. Both dashed-off and highly focused, it's bawdy and sentimental, equal parts thoughtful insight and stooping-low vaudevillian humor, padded out with Python song lyrics and interruptions by a grumpy editor, the latter a repeat gag from *Hello Sailor*, and not exactly good enough to repeat, as who wants to hear from editors? [Harrumph.—Eds.] Dipping away from the road show to his family life and a harrowing if brief glimpse at his childhood, it's a glimpse of what Idle could produce if he ever got around to a full-fledged memoir.

Idle's third novel, *The Writer's Cut*, came out in 2015. A Hollywood satire, it follows an author who becomes the center of a media firestorm by saying he's going to write a book about all the stars he's slept with, and name names. The TMZ mania balloons at the same rate as the writer's ego and greed, even while he never quite manages to get around to *writing* the damn thing everybody's talking about. It's like an anxiety-fueled fever-dream that mines Idle's Hollywood experiences for all they're worth.

The Song and Dance Man

Despite, or perhaps because of, all the smarmy announcers and showbiz types that he played on *Monty Python's Flying Circus* (somehow coming off as a little less smarmy than the more naturally sincere and uncynical Palin), Idle has a striving quality that wouldn't have seemed out of place in the world of prewar show business. At the same time, Idle eagerly embraces the panto, or English pantomime, style, with all its silliness, mugging, and cross-dressing. Those strands of ambition and playing to the back row come together in Idle's stage work.

In the interregnum between the Footlights and *Flying Circus*, Idle started off treading the boards. He performed in a revue called *My Girl Herbert* in 1965 and the satire *Oh, What a Lovely War!* the following year before moving into the David Frost comedy factory. But even though Idle early on swore off a career as an actor in favor of being a creative multi-hyphenate, the theater bug continued to bite.

Idle's first stage play, *Pass the Butler,* premiered in Coventry in 1981. An Ealing-ish drawing room comedy with some of the satirical mania of *Hello Sailor,* it's about a minister of defense who's surrounded both by a cluster of life-support machines and his cuttingly cold-blooded aristocratic family waiting ghoulishly for the switching-off ceremony. The plot doesn't move so much as spin as the one-liners fly thick, including one that would be recycled soon after for *The Meaning of Life*'s "Galaxy Song": "I do hope there's intelligent life in the Universe, because there's bugger all down here on Earth." It opened in London's West End in 1982 and ran for five months.

Fittingly for a performer who would reinvent himself as a song-and-dance man decades later, Idle's first big stage appearance was in one of the great musicals of the English tradition. In 1986, Idle was in high form as Ko-Ko the Lord High Executioner in Jonathan Miller's innovative reinterpretation of Gilbert and Sullivan's 1885 light operetta *The Mikado.* Stripping out some of the original's Japanese Orientalism, Miller made it a sort of 1930s Marx Brothers musical comedy, heavy on the greasepaint and waggling eyebrows, beloved by some and despised by others. Idle reprised his role at the Houston Grand Opera in 1989. By being allowed to rewrite the song "Little List," which lists people who "won't be missed," with modernized targets for execution, Idle changed the direction of how the play would be mounted. While controversial among purists at first, the updated and topical "Little List" is now a *Mikado* tradition.

What's All This, Then?
Bugger All Down Here

"Galaxy Song" is one of Idle and Du Prez's more chipper compositions, but with a darker edge. Originally used in *The Meaning of Life,* it later appeared on the *Monty Python Sings* album and was resuscitated yet again for the 2014 reunion concert at the O2. After Idle became acquainted with Brian Cox, the physicist informed him that in the years since "Galaxy Song" had been written, its scientific details had become less accurate because of new research. So, with Cox's help, Idle rewrote the song to better reflect new science. For the concert, a video was recorded in which Cox points out the song's inaccuracies, only to be run over by the motorized wheelchair of Stephen Hawking, who tells off Cox for being "pedantic."

Idle's first musical was actually not *Spamalot*, but *Behind the Crease*, a radio play that he wrote for the stage (as *Sticky Wicket* or *The Back Page*). The musical, with songs by Idle and Du Prez, about a cricketer and the tabloid reporter (Idle) tagging along with him through the West Indies, was broadcast on BBC in 1990.

In 1998, Idle was signed on to write the book for a musical based on the works of Dr. Seuss. He told the *New York Times* that he envisioned an anarchic show filled with mayhem centered on the Cat in the Hat (whom he played at an early reading), "like the M.C. in *Cabaret*." Idle left the show after the original producers declared bankruptcy. A far more conventional *Seussical* opened on Broadway in 2000 and swiftly closed.

Idle returned to live performance in 2000, when he launched the *Eric Idle Exploits Monty Python* tour with a small cast that ran through as many Python chestnuts as possible. The previously referenced *Greedy Bastard Tour* in 2003 was essentially a broader, longer version of the same.

After that, Idle left the rock and roll touring lifestyle behind for a bit, in order to crank up a little thing called *Spamalot* and a littler thing called *Not the Messiah* (see Chapter 25 for the full story on that wee adventure).

Eric Idle with his instrument, 2012.   *PythonProfessor/Wikimedia Commons*

A prized relic from Eric Idle's 2000 tour.   *Lisa Bocchini*

Say No More!

Although *Spamalot* and *Not the Messiah* took up several years of Idle's career, he kept the ball rolling on several creative fronts.

In April 2012, Idle premiered a new stage production, *What About Dick?* A revamping of an old idea he'd been kicking around since the 1980s—when it was a Merchant-Ivory parody called *Remains of the Piano* (rim shot!)—the show was a faux 1940s radio play whose gags and improvisation revolved around the idea of (as Idle put it) "the decline and fall of the British Empire as seen through the eyes of a piano." A star-heavy cast, mainly of Idle's mates, from Billy Connolly to Tim Curry and Eddie Izzard and Jane Leeves, performed it live for four nights. The result was edited together into a film for digital download.

As Idle was always the keenest on keeping the Python flame alive, having endlessly pillaged their back catalog on his live tours and starting PythOnline back in 1997, it was no surprise that he was the one tapped to direct the O2 reunion show. He spent roughly a year writing and directing *Monty Python Live (mostly)* before its ten performances in July 2014.

In 2015, Idle did a stint in the three-night stand of *Spamalot* at the Hollywood Bowl. That year he also started a tour with Cleese: *Together Again at Last . . . For the Very First Time.* Interestingly, back in 1971, Palin had observed in his diary that "John and Eric see Monty Python as a means to an end—money to buy freedom from work."

Desired or not, it's a freedom that Idle doesn't appear to have very much interest in.

20

Post-Python: "It's Only a Model"

Terry Gilliam—The Director-y Python

Cultural guerrillas like Magritte and William S. Burroughs, with their anonymous suits and anodyne countenances, mask the slashing subversion of their art like prisoners keeping a razor blades in their mouths. Terry Gilliam, the would-be missionary from Minnesota, was also one of those hiding-in-plain-sight subversives. His status as the non-Oxbridge outsider in Monty Python and willingness to do the goofiest, most physical mugging made him the least likely to be recognized on the street. This was just fine for a guy who would, in the post-Python years, be defined mostly by what he did behind the camera rather than in front of it.

Un Film de Gilliam

Jabberwocky (1977)

Coming two years after *Monty Python and the Holy Grail*'s instant success, *Jabberwocky* was a great step forward for the burgeoning filmmaker, who had been codirector on *Holy Grail* with Jones. (Gilliam did camera angles and smoke, while Jones interfaced with the humans.) For his big-league debut, he chose as his source material Lewis Carroll's short nonsense poem about a monster with "the jaws that bite, the claws that catch!" who gets its head snicker-snacked off by a boy who "left it dead and with its head / He went galumphing back."

Cowritten by Gilliam and Charles Alverson, the Kurtzman assistant at *Help!* whose job Gilliam snapped up back in New York, *Jabberwocky* was billed incorrectly as a Monty Python film for its American premiere. After all, it had one Python behind the camera, another (Palin) in a starring role, and a third (Jones) making an appearance in the pre-credits sequence.

The cover of *Gilliamesque* provides an idea of what the inside of Terry's head might look like.

Lisa Bocchini

Admittedly, some might be forgiven for thinking that this excrement-smeared and purposefully antiheroic extended gag of a medieval monster flick was going to be the further adventures of the old Arthurian gang from *Holy Grail*. The *New York Times*'s critic Vincent Canby (who called it "a comedy with more blood and gore than Sam Peckinpah would dare use") even approvingly termed *Jabberwocky* "a sort of stepson" to *Holy Grail*.

In the mock epic, Palin plays Dennis the Apprentice, a gormless lad who gets convinced by a princess to go off on a quest to slay the ravening Jabberwock beast that's been ravaging the countryside. The linked string of bits and skits skewers all the expected targets, from royalty and authority (King Bruno the Questionable) to religion (a cynical bishop and a cult leader preying on fear caused by the Jabberwocky) and the general grimy misery of daily life in the fantastic Middle Ages (there's never a moment of grandeur or pomp and circumstance that isn't almost immediately undercut).

Jabberwocky's ramshackle air is born part of intention, part of necessity, and part of Gilliam's original pitch, which he described in his memoir as "Here's the eight-line poem, we've got a monster, let's go!" [Actually, the poem is twenty lines long.—Eds.] The typically tongue-in-cheek trailer promised that *Jabberwocky* would be "so terrifying" that nobody would be admitted to the theater until the last ten minutes of the film. Although the end results are certainly nothing close to a horror film (and in fact Gilliam

What's All This, Then?
The Anglophile Python

Gilliam easily adapted to life in England and became a dual citizen in 1968, only renouncing his American citizenship in 2006, in part to protest the Iraq War and in part for tax reasons. (It was a process he described later as rather comical, given all the very nice people at the U.S. Embassy who tried to talk him out of it.) Gilliam started working with the other Pythons as an outsider, listed separately from the other Pythons in the first season of *Flying Circus*, but his design sense proved an integral part of early Python and, American or not, he shared the same rebellious sense of absurdity that marked the English Pythons. He fit in so well that he married Monty Python's makeup and wardrobe specialist, Maggie Weston, who worked with Gilliam on several of his films and gave birth to his three children, Amy, Holly, and Harry. Along with Palin, Gilliam is the only other Python to stay married to his first wife, an unusually stable move in such a chaotic group.

tried unsuccessfully to cut the film as more of a comedy to please worried producers who wanted *Holy Grail* shenanigans), he continually bears down on the blood and carnage. It's a half-Python kind of thing.

Time Bandits (1981)

Gilliam next returned to the director's chair for an idea he came up with in 1979. At the time, he was annoyed by the sanitized versions of fairy tales being fed to young people and wanted to return children's fantasy to its darker, more meaningful roots. A band of six dwarves steal a map of the universe showing where all the time-traveling wormholes go and start looting everything they can from throughout history. Along the way, they bust into the twentieth-century bedroom of an eleven-year-old boy, who follows along on their adventures.

The oddness of the story was a tough sell in a time when fantasy film meant *Star Wars* and *Superman*. But Gilliam's enthusiasm (he physically acted out the entire scenario for the producers) carried the day. Palin agreed to help write the script, the producers signed on for an (at the time) incredibly low budget of $5 million, and that was it. A car crash of influences from C. S. Lewis to classic adventure tales, *Time Bandits* also toyed with ancient mythology and religion. Incredibly for a children's film, a highly officious and non-loving God, aka the Supreme Being, aka "SB," appears as an imperious Ralph Richardson (who would occasionally cross out lines of dialogue, explaining "God wouldn't say that").

The film's production was a close-run thing, given some serious time and budget constraints. HandMade Films mortgaged their office to fund everything. Gilliam and the producers scrapped numerous times, presaging much of his cinematic future. Robert Sellers's *Very Naughty Boys* quotes Idle on Gilliam's relationship with the business side of the film business: "You try to discuss a budget with Terry Gilliam, it's kind of ridiculous. Terry is completely mono, he's taken several businesses out of existence. Several companies have fallen victim to the Gilliam piracy."

Released with low expectations in November 1981, *Time Bandits* was a commercial and popular success, earning back its production budget on opening weekend. One of the few hands-down hits in Gilliam's repertoire, it played on constant rotation during the early years of cable television in America.

As with most beloved blockbusters, rumors have floated for years about ways to continue the franchise. In late 2015, it was reported that Gilliam was working on a TV series adaptation of *Time Bandits*. Immature adults of a certain age eagerly await the day when their bedroom walls will once again reveal to them the wonders of the universe. Ahem.

Brazil (1985)

Around 1978, Gilliam conceived a film about a totalitarian future where a functionary of the Ministry of Torture tries to escape his dull, horrific life by way of fantasy. Gilliam later described *Brazil* to the *New York Times* as "a post-Orwellian view of a pre-Orwellian world" or "Walter Mitty meets Franz Kafka." The latter succinctly describes the nervy and uneasy blend of tragedy and comedy that would become his masterpiece, *Brazil*.

Gilliam had initially pitched it and *Time Bandits* to producer Denis O'Brien, who preferred the kids' movie. After finishing *The Meaning of Life*, Gilliam went back to *Brazil*. He brought in playwright Tom Stoppard (whose 1975 television play *Three Men in a Boat* starred Palin) to tighten up the story and bring a dash of verbal élan. Some more screenplay cutting and tucking later with Charles McKeown (an occasional script doctor who also had a few small roles in *Life of Brian*), and Gilliam was ready to shoot.

The quasi-British world of *Brazil* looks as though everything froze technologically and aesthetically sometime right before or after World War II and spiraled down from there. The visuals are a rattletrap mix of German Expressionism and shabby Art Deco, *Metropolis* in decline, overlaid with a kudzu-like growth of slapped-together ducts and bureaucracy that's as slow and inefficient as it is murderous. Propaganda posters exhort people to "Don't suspect a friend / Report him."

The film's Rube Goldberg plot rumbles into action once a fly drops into a teletype machine, causing an arrest warrant for terrorist / rogue duct repairman Harry Tuttle (Robert De Niro) to misprint, sending the police after the innocent Archibald Buttle, who is summarily tortured and executed. Bureaucrat Sam

What's All This, Then?
McVeigh-Tuttle

When Oklahoma City bomber Timothy McVeigh was looking for an alias, he pulled from *Brazil*. Reportedly, when the movie-loving terrorist was making the rounds of the gun-show anti-government militia subculture, McVeigh used the name Tuttle, in homage to Robert De Niro's anarcho-repair man. "It's like Manson being inspired by 'Helter Skelter,'" Gilliam told the *Chicago Tribune*. "My Tuttle fixed things! He didn't blow them up."

Oooh, Criterion edition. Fancy.

Lowry (Jonathan Pryce) believes his brightly smiling, secretly sadistic friend Jack (Palin) might be involved. He dreams of fighting the system and falls in love with spiky-haired trucker Jill (Kim Greist), the symbol of all that is good and pure in this corrupted world.

There's a lot that's too, too much in *Brazil*, as though Gilliam just couldn't stop hanging new ornaments from the spiny tree Stoppard had written for him. But amid all the clutter and noise, *Brazil* is brutally effective in savaging a public oblivious to the horrors occurring around them and the horrors they are complicit in. A black comic opera set to a backbeat of random institutional and revolutionary violence, it denounces the decade's stifling consumerist conservatism. Spoiler alert: it doesn't *really* end well.

Universal Pictures was shocked, *shocked!*, when Terry Gilliam gave them a Terry Gilliam film. Even though he delivered *Brazil* on time and under budget, all they saw was a loopy and grim satire where love does not triumph. In the documentary *The Battle of Brazil*, Gilliam says that just by looking at the clenched body language of the executives after his first screening, "I knew we were in trouble." Just as a nervous Warner Bros. dealt with *Blade Runner*, another dyspeptic and narratively obscure science-fiction story, by slapping on a this-is-what-everything-means voice-over and a happy ending, Universal decided *Brazil* couldn't be released without changes. Top on their list: How about a happy ending?

Gilliam refused, taking out a full-page ad in *Variety* that read simply, "When are you going to release my film, 'BRAZIL'?" He also held surreptitious screenings, one to a packed house of students at CalArts (who went wild for it) and another for critics and friends. One was writer Harlan Ellison, who went (in his words) "absolutely bugfuck" for the film and wrote a column railing against the injustice of studio suits cutting a masterpiece to bits like they had Orson Welles's *The Magnificent Ambersons* decades earlier.

Universal was submarined at the last minute when the Los Angeles Film Critics Association named the (as yet unreleased) *Brazil* best picture of the year and also awarded it best direction and best screenplay. Forced into a corner, Universal opened *Brazil* in just a couple theaters right before the end of the year to qualify for the Academy Awards. It was nominated for two Academy Awards, original screenplay and art direction. But in the end, audiences were more on the side of Universal. Even though *Brazil* is now considered one of the great science-fiction films of all time, then it was just another critical darling and box office failure.

The Adventures of Baron Munchausen (1988)

The third film in what critic Jack Mathews termed Gilliam's "Dreams" trilogy (after *Time Bandits* and *Brazil*) would also turn out to be something of a Waterloo for the filmmaker. He's had a lot of those.

On paper, the project looked like just the thing. Based on the frequently filmed nineteenth century adult-ish fairy tale *Baron Munchhausen's Narrative of His Marvellous Travels and Campaigns in Russia*, the titular hero's exuberant blurring of reality and Don Quixote–like faith in his abilities have obvious Gilliam parallels. After all the well-publicized production disasters, the film that finally resulted remains a glorious, knockabout thing, a stumbling white elephant of a latter-day Powell and Pressburger event picture, the likes of which we are unlikely to ever see again.

Munchausen cranks up in full meta-mood. In a European city besieged by a massive Turkish army, a ragtag touring company has their sad-sack Baron Munchausen production interrupted by an imperious fellow (John Neville) being chased by Death itself. The old guy insists he's the *real* Baron and that everybody must listen to his stories. Over the course of the overstuffed hullabaloo of a film that follows, Gilliam sends the Baron and an entourage that includes Idle and a nine-year-old Sarah Polley on an exploding-firecracker-string of adventures.

The Baron's knockabout exploits, lavishly detailed by a team that included the great production designer Dante Ferretti, are unusually luxe for Gilliam's guerilla taste. But it's all cheery fun, running from the favorite cannonball-riding bit to a centerpiece Méliès-like sequence on a moon ruled by a motormouthed king (Robin Williams) and a hard-to-forget shot showing a horse-borne Baron lopping the heads off a line of Turkish troops. Gilliam strings the whole unwieldly assemblage together on a thin thread of a theme about the Baron's overgrown child's insistence on believing in magic. "Your 'reality,' sir, is lies and balderdash," the Baron declaims at one point, with all the conviction of Don Quixote. "And I'm delighted to say that I have no grasp of it whatsoever." For all its allegiance to whimsy and the empire of dreams, though, *Munchausen* is also vinegared with an adult's crook-eyed awareness of bloody, bloody history.

That mixture of moods made *The Adventures of Baron Munchausen* a bear of a thing to market. The fiascos piled up: expensive on-location shoots in Spain and Italy, lengthy and poorly handled pre-production that ate up millions before a single frame was shot, a multilingual crew that could barely communicate, and a rogue's gallery of producers, financiers, and insurers who fretted and poked and prodded Gilliam as budget overruns cascaded.

By the time *The Adventures of Baron Munchausen* opened in March 1989, it already had a stink on it, generated by an entertainment press that have been feasting over the carcasses of so-called "troubled" productions since the days of *Cleopatra*. Like many other thoughtful children's films (the initially ignored *Iron Giant* comes to mind), it was seen as too complicated for the kids and too lighthearted for the adults. Its acquisition of what Gilliam called "bad financial ju-ju" had the studio limiting its release and thus their exposure. All of this meant that financially *Munchausen* was a disaster, pulling in just $8 million gross on a budget that by some accounts soared well over $50 million. Although critical favor and cult attention later swung more in the film's favor, its status as full-fledged debacle (Gilliam's first) made the next stage of his career even more unlikely.

The Fisher King (1991)

Incredibly, Gilliam's career wasn't submarined by *Munchausen*. His relatively short dry spell ended with a dream screenplay essentially falling out of the heavens and launching him on the second distinct phase of his filmmaking career.

Up until this point, Gilliam had been something of an admitted control freak. Part of that control was his always having at least part of a hand in the screenwriting. He also generally had at least one of his old Python friends on hand to deliver some crackling British dryness. Both of those habits were laid to the side for *The Fisher King*.

Producer Lynda Obst had been working for years to make Richard LaGravenese's fanciful buddy script when an agent suggested Gilliam. According to a laser disc edition commentary track, Gilliam noted that he actually smashed all three of his major rules on that film: never make anybody's script but his own; never work for a major studio; never work in America. In any case, it beat directing another project being pushed on him: *The Addams Family*.

LaGravenese's script is stippled with Arthuriana and clashes of dreams and reality; right up Gilliam's alley. It's also a character piece that leans heavily on gouts of emotions: quite unlike anything in Gilliam's repertoire. The protagonist is Jack (Jeff Bridges), a lavishly paid troll of a shock jock who has a meltdown after unwittingly inspiring a man to commit mass murder. He befriends Parry (Robin Williams), a fellow fallen soul who was once a college professor but fell to pieces after his wife was murdered. The redemption story shows Jack regaining his humanity by helping Parry get past his traumatic visions of a Red Knight and obsessions with a trinket he believes is the Holy Grail.

The first film that Gilliam directed with nary a Python to be seen is also in some ways his least recognizable. The expressionistic canted angles and distrust of corporate America are straight Gilliam, not to mention the Red Knight's thrift-shop nightmare costumery. But the male leads' broken-heart bonding and Parry's sweet and courtly (if manic) wooing of the quiet Lydia (Amanda Plummer) stands out as something new for the director. Although the film is filled with all the mugging that one would expect, it's also a more quietly acted thing than anything Gilliam had done until that point. Even his great bravura moment, that dream of a waltz sequence in Grand Central, which came from Gilliam and not the script, has nary an ounce of Python snark to be found. It's pure love.

With its squishy paeans to the imagination and vaguely New Age anti-yuppie sentiments, not to mention a neatly optimistic therapeutic break-through, *The Fisher King* became something of a touchstone for sensitive dreamers. It was nominated for five Oscars, winning one for Mercedes Ruehl, who played Jack's girlfriend. Although not a runaway hit, the film was enough of a success to put Gilliam back in Hollywood's graces. Fortunately, that didn't result in Gilliam making *The Addams Family II*.

Twelve Monkeys (1995)

For *Twelve Monkeys*, the second film where Gilliam was brought on as a hired gun, he was given certain constraints in exchange for having final cut: he needed to keep to a $29 million budget, an R rating, and a running time no longer than 135 minutes.

The script by David Webb Peoples (*Unforgiven*), inspired by Chris Marker's twenty-seven-minute experimental film *La Jetée*—a circuitous loop of black-and-white stills about a time-traveling experimental subject from a postapocalyptic future who keeps remembering his own future-past death—is a clockwork piece of ingenuity, threading cause and effect through Marker's impressionistic dreamscape. Order is brought to chaos.

Instead of Marker's nuclear apocalypse, in this version humanity has been devastated by a virus. The few survivors have moved underground, where in the year 2035 a cabal of scientists researching time travel as a way of stopping the virus from starting send convict James Cole (Bruce Willis) back in time. Cole ends up in 1990, where he's tossed into an insane asylum.

Cole tries to solve the mystery of the Army of the Twelve Monkeys who supposedly released the deadly virus, while trying to convince his psychiatrist (Madeleine Stowe) that not only is he from the future but in fact the future of humanity *does* depend on him. Further clues are provided by a madman (Brad Pitt) who might actually not be entirely insane (look for the guys in the straightjackets in Gilliam films: they always hold the answers). The story ties together as Marker's does with a killing at an airport, only with an extra aura of doom layered over it.

Twelve Monkeys represents the peak of Gilliam's Hollywood period; it was also one of the last times that he was handed the keys to the kingdom: prestige script, name-above-the-title movie stars, and an actual budget. Interestingly, it's also one of his finest films. A genre piece, to be sure, but a superbly crafted one where all the pieces fit together with precision and intelligence. Even the usual Gilliam madhouse playacting (Pitt's bug-eyed performance is the closest thing the decade saw to a live-action Looney Tunes cartoon) and scatological mucking about in the gutter, which could be so distracting when inserted into a more romantic piece like *The Fisher King*, locks into an end-of-days, we're-all-inmates-in-a-great-asylum vibe. The film was popular enough to spark an entire subgenre of viral-centered apocalypse thrillers that continues today, as well as a TV series that started in 2015.

Fear and Loathing in Las Vegas (1998)

In Hunter S. Thompson's most famous work, he delivers a semi-factual recounting of a drug-stoked road trip to Las Vegas where he was ostensibly supposed to report on . . . something. Hunter's panicky doom-whispering and kamikaze humor made for a wicked mix, bringing a tweaked gravitas to its dark seam of post-1960s gloom and paranoia. In other words: obvious box-office gold.

It's fair to say that both Hunter and Gilliam had similar feelings about America, even though they came at it from different perspectives. Thompson was a well-bred Southern boy who never tired of peeling back the façade of American hypocrisy and jabbing at it with his cigarette holder in virulent disgust, like Gore Vidal's disreputable intellectual cousin. But Thompson also never quite lost that inherent love of his great and vulgar homeland. Gilliam, the clowning cartoonist from the Valley, just got the hell out of America as soon as he could, and seemed to resent ever having been associated with the place.

All that makes *Fear and Loathing* a fitting farewell to Hollywood. Gilliam's strength was never in finely crafted satire. In fact, for all his vocal anti-Americanism, his most viciously cutting material tended to lacerate his adoptive country: the blasé attitude of most of the characters in *Brazil*, no matter what savagery their government throws in their faces, makes for a damning critique of British "Keep Calm and Carry On" stiff-upper-lip attitudes.

Fear and Loathing tips all that on its head. The story isn't much, just Hunter trying to keep his head above water while ingesting all manner of drugs, splashing out expense-account money, freaking out over whatever animalistic hallucinations are ripping through his brain ("The sky was full of what looked like huge bats"), and tripping through the late–Roman Empire decadence of Las Vegas while ruminating on where the country has gone wrong. Any film of *Fear and Loathing* is bound to get lost in the weeds trying to keep up with Hunter's jabbering (expertly supplied by Johnny Depp, the kind of rubber-faced circus performer who slots neatly into the Gilliam carnival) and the unhinged lunacy of his traveling companion Dr. Gonzo (Benicio Del Toro).

The problem with *Fear and Loathing in Las Vegas*, as with any literary adaptation (even one with hallucinated reptiles, a carload of drugs, and Johnny Depp), is that late-1990s Hollywood was not equipped to sell something like this. The film opened against *Godzilla* and was crushed at the box office like a cardboard Tokyo.

Thus ended Gilliam's middle period of filmmaking, his brief sojourn in the belly of the filmmaking beast. After this point, he would continue working with marquee performers but the shoots would mostly be in Europe with stitched-together financing and (more common than not) production headaches. They also evinced a grimmer and narrower creative perspective in which the grand satire of *Brazil* or the wonderment of *The Adventures of Baron Munchausen* was nowhere to be found. These late-period Gilliam films are among his most chaotic and boundary-pushing. But perversely they are also increasingly repetitive, and among his least memorable works.

The Brothers Grimm (2005)

The new millennium started off roughly for Gilliam's cinematic career. His on-again, off-again *Don Quixote*–inspired project ran aground in Spain during 2000, the victim of everything from freakish storms to NATO fighter planes to injuries and the usual run of bad Gilliam luck. The period also involved a few other tantalizing films that never happened (*Good Omens, Harry Potter and the Sorcerer's Stone*). In 2001, Gilliam served on the jury at the Cannes Film Festival, where he was photographed happily displaying a T-shirt that read: "Can Be Bribed."

Finally, in 2003, Gilliam started shooting *The Brothers Grimm*, a lavish action-fantasy extravaganza with some very uncharacteristic elements—a matched pair of heartthrobs, Matt Damon and Heath Ledger; fight scenes; a script from Ehren Kruger of *Transformers* infamy; and buckets of money, more than Gilliam had ever seen before. Gilliam also unfortunately had as executive producers the Weinstein brothers, who didn't mind slapping their fingerprints all over Gilliam's work.

The conceit is that the Brothers Grimm, who wrote all those malevolent fairy tales centuries before, are really a pair of German con men. Will (Damon) and Jacob (Ledger) roam the countryside circa 1812 looking for gullible peasants to whom they can charge exorbitant amounts to supposedly exorcise evil spirits. They get in over their heads once they come across *actual* supernatural occurrences (fearsome creatures in the Black Forest kidnapping children for their dark queen) that they have no idea how to fight.

Early skirmishes were waged between Gilliam and his producers Bob and Harvey Weinstein, who didn't like anything they saw, from Gilliam's cinematographer to his desire to cast Samantha Morton in a key role to the bump that Gilliam wanted to use on Damon's nose. The Weinsteins won on all accounts. "I'm used to riding roughshod over studio executives," Gilliam told *Time*, "but the Weinsteins rode roughshod over me."

As filming ground on, the producers found themselves disturbed once they realized the full implications of hiring *Terry Gilliam* and giving him $80 million. So the tinkering and second- and third-guessing began. The nonsensical nature of it all—it's like the movie-business version of the old story about the scorpion and frog crossing the river: the Weinsteins *knew* he was Terry Gilliam, did they think they'd hired Michael Bay?—would be enough to drive filmmakers less determined than Gilliam out of the business altogether.

By the time that *The Brothers Grimm* wrapped in the fall of 2003, the relationship between Gilliam and the Weinsteins was so parlous that the director essentially took a break and shot another film. *The Brothers Grimm* didn't open until late summer 2005; that seven-year gap since *Fear and Loathing* was the longest time in Gilliam's career without a single picture in release.

The film is lush and colorful, richly brocaded with Black Forest detail, and as painterly as anything Gilliam had managed since *Munchausen*. It fights the good Gilliam fight against reason, with Will serving up a line that could stand as a solid summation of Gilliam's method: "Life's little subterfuges make it all worthwhile."

However, there's no escaping that it feels like an orphaned work. There are flickers of Gilliam's visual bric-a-brac and slapstick humor. But the whole endeavor is jammed so uneasily into action-blockbuster mode (climaxes upon climaxes) that neither mainstream nor Gilliam fans would be pleased.

Tideland (2006)

The Brothers Grimm took forever to edit, not least because the director and producers were barely on speaking terms. Gilliam ended up having so much time off, in fact, that he shot a whole other film during that time. It's his most creatively uncompromising film, as well as his absolute worst.

Based on a novel by Mitch Cullin, *Tideland* is about young Jeliza-Rose (Jodelle Ferland), whose parents are hopeless drug addicts. After her mother (Jennifer Tilly) overdoses, Jeliza-Rose and her father, Noah (Jeff Bridges), retreat to his old family farmhouse. There, things in the real world turn from horrible to much, much worse, with putrefying corpses and suggestions of incest. Meanwhile, Jeliza-Rose's imagination roars into overdrive as compensation. These flights of fancy mark her as a similar figure to Robin Williams's Parry from *The Fisher King*, escaping trauma by fleeing into a fantasy world where things make sense.

Described by Gilliam as *"Alice in Wonderland* meets *Psycho,"* *Tideland* has in fact none of the former's mind-twisting flights of fancy and precious little of the latter's skillfully honed horror. Instead, the film is a grueling and well-nigh unwatchable disaster with the most unfunny humor and least-impressive visuals of any Gilliam film before or since.

While *The Brothers Grimm* showed what happens when an artist like Gilliam was subjected to too much studio interference, the guerrilla indie *Tideland* illustrates what can happen when an artist like Gilliam is left completely to his own devices.

The Imaginarium of Doctor Parnassus (2009)

An *echt*-Gilliam work crawling with darkly dreamy enchantments and fallen humanity, *The Imaginarium of Doctor Parnassus* was conceived as the

Terry Gilliam at New York's IFC Center on his 2006 publicity tour for
Tideland.   *The Wrong Man/Wikimedia Commons*

rollicking tale of a roaming band of performers trawling through mod-
ern-day London in a medieval horse-drawn wagon. Their titular leader
(Christopher Plummer) has a secret involving the devil himself, Mr. Nick
(Tom Waits in the satanic carnival-barker role he was always meant for).
Parnassus fights to save his daughter from the consequences of a pact
with the devil that will either save or doom her, resulting in them zipping
through a magic mirror and traveling to fantastical dreamworlds. Heath
Ledger, fresh off playing the Joker in *The Dark Knight*, is Tony, a mysterious

stranger whom the troupe finds hanging from a bridge and who later plays a key role in their otherworldly adventures.

Filming started in December 2007 in London. During a break in filming the following month before the production moved to Prague, Ledger was found dead in New York, having suffered an accidental overdose of sleeping pills and anti-anxiety medications. The death was devastating for Gilliam, who had become fast friends with the actor. "Terry was to Heath what Tim Burton is to Johnny [Depp]," Ledger's assistant told film journalist Peter Biskind. Ledger had told one interviewer that he would do anything for Gilliam on a film, including working catering.

Initially, Gilliam considered shutting everything down, a decision that wouldn't have been difficult for the backers to countenance given that the film had just lost its star. But after Gilliam's cinematographer Nicola Pecorini and his daughter Amy (a producer on this and later films of her father's) talked him around, Gilliam turned to persuading other actors to finish Ledger's work. In quick order, Johnny Depp, Colin Farrell, and Jude Law agreed to step in and play Tony during different trips through the magic mirror. When it premiered at the Cannes Film Festival, *The Imaginarium of Doctor Parnassus*, an interesting curiosity, was given a ten-minute standing ovation.

The Zero Theorem (2013)

Not surprisingly for an artist who celebrates breaking away from reality, Gilliam has frequently used the past as a storehouse for imaginative raw material. Interestingly, his two future-set films, *Brazil* and *Twelve Monkeys*, were also among his most successful. *The Zero Theorem* was not on par with those major-studio releases, being another scavenged-together indie production that relied (as Gilliam told *Wired*) on "people working for scale, working their asses off, being very clever, and filming in Bucharest."

The dystopia envisioned in *The Zero Theorem* is far different from the Orwellian nightmare of *Brazil* or the virus-ravaged apocalypse of *Twelve Monkeys*. It's something far closer to the modern-day world, in which corporations, not governments, have assumed control over people's lives. It's against all these seductive screens and advertisements that the protagonist Qohen (Christoph Waltz), a computer savant with a buzzing brain but dead eyes, is waging his existentialist fight. One doesn't have to look too far from Qohen to see another of Gilliam's half-cracked, half-chivalrous warriors, declaiming to the modern world that it'll never take them alive.

Shorts and Miscellany

The Crimson Permanent Assurance (1983)

The original idea for this short film was as an animated introduction to *The Meaning of Life*. But eventually Gilliam convinced the others to let him film it as a live-action piece. It still serves as the start to that feature, but it's a wonderful stand-alone film. (See Chapter 16)

The Secret Tournament (2002)

During his post–*Fear and Loathing in Las Vegas* years of wandering in the filmic deserts, Gilliam directed a pair of ads for the shoe company Nike as part of their $100 million 2002 World Cup campaign. The ads were dramatic and noirish science fiction mini-films (set to a remix of Elvis's "A Little Less Conversation") imagining twenty-four of the world's best soccer players gathering on a cargo ship to play a cage match–like "first goal wins" secret tournament. Although some saw this kind of work as out of step for Gilliam, they forget that he worked in the ad business back in the 1960s, and on 1972 animated commercials for gas cookers, called "The Great Gas Gala." That doesn't mean he necessarily craves the work. Gilliam told one interviewer that he does a commercial about every five years, when he gets really depressed.

The Wholly Family (2012)

Curiously, when the Garofolo Pasta company, based near Naples, paid Gilliam to make a twenty-minute film, he said, Sure! The story follows a bickering couple on vacation in Naples, getting lost in all the tangled alleyways and frustrated by their son and his fascination with the stalls selling figurines of the Holy Family and Pulcinella (the Italian version of Punch), who goes to bed without supper and has troubling dreams involving pasta and dolls. If nothing else, the non-advertisement is not immediately recognizable as Gilliam.

The Damnation of Faust (2011) / *Benvenuto Cellini* (2014)

In 2011 Gilliam was hired to direct a production of Berlioz's *The Damnation of Faust* for the English National Opera. It was a risky choice, given that Gilliam was admittedly no lover of opera. He compensated by opting for visual overkill, using the opera as a lens for viewing Germany before and during the Nazi era (as one opera critic noted, this ignores the fact that Berlioz was French and Christopher Marlowe English). By the time Gilliam got around to crucifying Faust on a swastika-shaped cross, more than a few critics thought he'd crossed a line. The director described it as a cross between Goethe and *Cabaret*, only with a Kristallnacht dance sequence. Three years later, he directed another Berlioz opera, the more rarely performed *Benvenuto Cellini* (the sculptor being a favorite of Gilliam's), in a carnivalesque staging replete with stilt walkers and a full-on Mardi Gras celebration.

The Ones That Got Away

Over the years, Gilliam has been involved with or in some ways attached to more than his fair share of projects that never came to fruition. Here are a few of the ones that we would love to see someday:

- *1884*—A mysterious project that's been talked about since at least 2010, when *Variety* announced Gilliam's involvement with an animated steampunk fantasy about an alt-history 1884 (in which dirigibles crowd the skies over London and the British Empire has conquered the moon).
- *The Defective Detective*—One of Gilliam's longest gestating projects is this story that he wrote after *The Fisher King* with that film's writer, Richard LaGravenese. It's about a cynical New York cop who has a breakdown that sends him into a fantasy world where the old rules of crime-fighting no longer apply.
- *Good Omens*—Terry Pratchett and Neil Gaiman's comic apocalypse fantasy novel stars a pretty nice demon and a bibliophilic angel, and also features the Antichrist and the fact that the world is probably going to end Saturday . . . after tea. At one point, Johnny Depp was going to play the demon and Robin Williams the angel.
- *Harry Potter and the Sorcerer's Stone*—According to some accounts, Gilliam was author J. K. Rowling's first choice to helm the first installment of the *Harry Potter* film series. Gilliam later pronounced himself relieved: "I would have gone crazy," he told *Total Film* magazine. "It's a fucking factory, working on *Harry Potter*."
- *The Man Who Killed Don Quixote*—Multiple attempts to make this time-travel fantasy-comedy came to naught over the years, the most infamous

collapse being during filming in 2000 (captured in the tragicomic 2002 documentary *Lost in La Mancha*), when a mix of financing issues, weather catastrophes, general chaos, and finally star Jean Rochefort's injury killed the production. A more recent version was scuppered when star John Hurt was diagnosed with pancreatic cancer. As of 2017, the film was back in the production yet again, with Palin as the deluded Don Quixote.

- *Sandman*—Gilliam has been connected to the hard-to-imagine film version of Gaiman's genre-redefining fantasy epic graphic novel cycle for years, though perhaps more as wish fulfillment for Gaiman, who has said that he thought Gilliam would have the right temperament for the project.

- *Son of Strangelove*—If a 2013 interview with the film site Twitch is to be believed, Stanley Kubrick had been working on a *Dr. Strangelove* sequel with the original's writer, Terry Southern, with the idea that Gilliam would direct. Kubrick had many years earlier asked Gilliam to contribute animation to *A Clockwork Orange*, but on such a tight deadline that Gilliam had to turn him down. The mind boggles.

- *A Tale of Two Cities*—In the 1990s, Gilliam was set to direct Mel Gibson in an adaptation of Dickens's novel of the French Revolution. But money became an issue, Gibson took off to direct *Braveheart*, and an attempt by Gilliam to save the project with a smaller budget and Liam Neeson in the starring role went nowhere.

- *Watchmen*—Years before Zack Snyder's 2009 adaptation of Alan Moore's landmark 1986–1987 graphic novel about troubled superheroes and the American Dream, action impresario Joel Silver considered Gilliam for the project. Everyone from Darren Aronofsky to Paul Greengrass was also attached before Snyder mucked it up with his faithful-to-the-book but uninspiring take.

In some ways, the list of Gilliam's never-completed projects says almost as much about his restless and always-hunting creative temperament as the many astounding works he's completed in the post-Python years. Like his fellow Pythons in the post–*Flying Circus* years, Gilliam reinvented himself as a unique artist whose body of work outside the troupe is as, or in some cases, more impressive than the work he helped create within it. Whatever else the coming years see from Gilliam, it will almost certainly be cantankerous, busy, and overreaching.

As Gilliam wrote in his autobiography: "At my most self-pitying moments in the midst of one wide-screen disaster or another, I have been known to visualise myself as a kind of Pinocchio messiah who takes on the sins of the world, and then gets nailed to himself."

Come to think of it, *Pinocchio Messiah* would be an utterly brilliant film for him to make. . . .

21

Post-Python: "I'm Bounder of Adventure"

Michael Palin—The Nicest Python

And then there's the affable, reliable, and altogether "nice" Palin. Compared to those of his peers, Palin's post-Python career (which included memorable turns in partial-Python projects such as *Time Bandits*, *A Fish Called Wanda*, and *Brazil*) took a rather unexpected turn when he largely abandoned movies after the failure of *American Friends* (a film he was personally invested in) to start spotting trains professionally in 1980; following the success of his stint on *Great Railway Journeys of the World*, Palin went on to become a highly regarded and astoundingly popular travel show host.

To date, he has traveled *Around the World in 80 Days* (1989); traversed *Pole to Pole* (1992); been spotted on the *Irish Railway Journey: Derry to Kerry* (1994); gone *Full Circle with Michael Palin* (1997); retraced the legendary author's steps in *Michael Palin's Hemingway Adventure* (1999); trekked the *Sahara with Michael Palin* (2002); wandered about *Himalaya with Michael Palin* (2004); toured *Michael Palin's New Europe* (2007); and experienced *Brazil with Michael Palin* (2012). Such success abroad—"off the main stage" as it were—is both surprising and revelatory, a career path largely unheralded by his previous work on *Flying Circus*, *Do Not Adjust Your Set*, and *The Complete and Utter History of Britain*. A surreal comedy, a children's show, and a historical mockumentary in retrospect seem tangential to his success as a travel host.

Palin in Film and Television

When Python was winding down after the difficult production of *The Meaning of Life*, it looked as though the group was not going to make another movie. This was further cemented by Chapman's death in 1989, which all but assured that Python would not work together again. All the Pythons began focusing on their solo careers, and Palin was no exception. Numerous offers came in and Palin appeared as a frequent guest on talk shows where his natural charm came through easily. But Palin was leery of Lorne Michaels's idea to turn him and Cleese into a comedic duo, fearing they would just become a latter-day Abbott and Costello or Laurel and Hardy. (Although thinking about it today, an Abbott and Costello vehicle starring Cleese and Palin seems like a wonderfully silly idea.)

Palin had started writing outside of Python with longtime partner Jones. When the BBC offered the chance to make a series of their own, they came up with a fantastic concept: *Ripping Yarns*, which parodied things familiar to British people of a certain age—schoolboy adventures, Indian regiments, crime stories, and the like, only reimagined with a Pythonesque sensibility.

After shooting the January 1976 pilot, "Tomkinson's Schooldays," that starred Palin and Jones, the BBC asked that Palin alone appear in the show as he had a more traditional "leading-man" type look. Jones, although

Michael Palin and Roy Kinnear in the "Escape from Stalag Luft 112B" episode of *Ripping Yarns*.
BBC/Photofest

disappointed, took it in stride and cowrote all two seasons with Palin. The first season of six episodes ran in September and October 1977, with a second season of three episodes following in October 1979.

Ripping Yarns is decidedly British, most especially "The Testing of Eric Olthwaite," which parodies a boring British childhood. Unlike Cleese's *Fawlty Towers*, which translated well in America, *Ripping Yarns* is a relatively unknown part of Palin's work to this day. However, the best of the episodes, "Escape from Stalag Luft 112B," "Roger of the Raj," and "Tomkinson's Schooldays," still hold up and have enough universal appeal that they could have been shown more frequently in the States. Sadly, *Ripping Yarns* was more or less the end of the Palin-Jones team, as each moved on afterward to his own projects.

Palin wanted to see if he could work on his own as a scriptwriter and movie star. As strange as it seems now, considering the varying career paths that he and Cleese took, Palin was for a time seen as the most bankable ex-Python. He found himself getting green-lit for movies that might not have found financing without his presence.

Palin's first major project as a writer and performer was *The Missionary* (1982), a very Pythonesque look at a repressed missionary who becomes rather bawdy against his better judgment. Think the "Dirty Vicar" sketch, only with more restraint. A minor hit, *The Missionary* was strangely enough Palin's only real comedy out of the three features he wrote. His next writing and acting gig was *A Private Function* (1984), which starred him as a black-market pig thief in postwar England. While the film went over well in England, winning BAFTA awards for his costars Maggie Smith and Denholm Elliot, it did not cross over well in America, most likely because of the, well, "Britishness" of the bloody thing.

While Palin did appear in several other films (more about that soon), his last film as a screenwriter was not released until 1991. *American Friends* was a more personal project, based on a true incident involving Palin's great-grandfather Edwards, who met a mother and daughter while traveling and then found him in a quandary when they stay with him in the ultra-masculine environment of Oxford. More drama than comedy, *American Friends* was poorly received, essentially sinking Palin's career as a writer and creative force who could create his own feature projects.

Palin's acting credits remain small compared to most of the other Pythons. Unlike Cleese, who had been writing and appearing in films before Python, Palin didn't appear in his first film until the somewhat stilted *And Now for Something Completely Different*; his only non-Python-related film

Michael Palin in *American Dreams* (1991).   *Photofest*

for a few years was *Three Men in a Boat* (1975), Tom Stoppard's adaptation of Jerome K. Jerome's 1899 British comic travel memoir.

He appeared in several Terry Gilliam films, starting with *Jabberwocky* (1977). His next role was his memorable cameo in Idle's Beatles parody *All You Need Is Cash* (1978). Palin also worked with Gilliam in *Time Bandits* (1981) and more notably playing against type in *Brazil* (1984), where essentially he is the quintessential amiable and utterly harmless company man right up until he tortures his friend (Jonathan Pryce). Even though most of the publicity around *Brazil* was how the studio had butchered the ending, it was striking to see Palin play such a complex and villainous character.

Cleese's *A Fish Called Wanda* (1988) featured one of Palin's most memorable roles as the stuttering criminal Ken, a performance partially based on his father's stuttering issues. Both pathetic and heroic, a shy animal lover who could also rob and kill without compunction, Ken is one of Palin's quintessential non-Python characters and remains a fan favorite. While there was talk of a sequel to *Wanda* for years, the eventual sequel that reunited the original cast was the poorly received *Fierce Creatures* (1997), which was one of Palin's last major film roles for several decades (he did not appear in any films between 1997–2010), and from then on he concentrated on his travel projects.

Although Palin never became a leading man, he did briefly attempt to work within the Hollywood system once. One of his most high-profile film projects was a memorable cameo left on the cutting room floor in the Tom Hanks–Meg Ryan rom-com *You've Got Mail*. In it, Palin played it pretty straight as a major author (based apparently on Thomas Pynchon) who flirts with Meg Ryan's character before she inevitably ends up in Hanks's arms. Apparently, it didn't work plot-wise, although those who have seen the DVD extra do confirm it was a memorable turn.

Even though most Americans have never seen it, Palin's most powerful dramatic role was a 1991 British miniseries, *GBH* (a police charge which stands for Grievous Bodily Harm). Here, Palin played it straight as a headmaster intimidated by an out-of-control councilman who ferments unrest and sends thugs to Palin's school for disturbed children. The miniseries is a good example of Palin in a completely dramatic role and is one of his best performances.

More recently, Palin's multi-role work in the 2014 Monty Python reunion concerts showed that his deft touch for live performance hasn't faded one bit.

Excepting a role as Molotov in Armando Iannucci's *The Death of Stalin* (2017), Palin was largely absent from film and television in recent years. But he had a good excuse . . . he was traveling around the world.

Palin and Travel

When Palin was approached to host travel programs, first about classic British railway trips and then a much more ambitious project attempting to retrace Phineas Fogg's fabled trip in *Around the World in 80 Days*, even he had a difficult time seeing himself as a natural raconteur. As Palin noted in his diary while working on the far more ambitious *Pole to Pole* journey in 1991, "Should I be doing this programme? [. . .] Have I not taken a journey round the world as a convenient way of avoiding other career decisions?" While this entry was written after the relative failure of his dream film project, *American Friends*, it also shows his inherent insecurity, even after years of being in the public eye. Perhaps Palin was not meant for the life of a major celebrity. Upon his return, Palin wrote in his diary: "I think the journey has, in a way, calmed and settled me. It's been much nearer to sanity than the phone-ringing, celebrity-conscious world I left at home."

While the life of a celebrity can indeed be harsh (just look back at the "Working-Class Playwright" sketch for further details: writer's cramp!), the trips that Palin took around the globe were not exactly a walk in Hyde Park. The pace on many of the series was extremely hectic; as Palin recounted about *Around the World*, "Thirty days have gone. We've been through twelve countries, spent two nights on trains, 13 nights on boats, including seven on an open dhow and I've slept in 13 different beds since we left London." Palin even wondered if the rigors of the trips he took were taking a toll on his once-boyish features. Palin wrote:

> Home to look at the "Great Railway Journey" to compare my efforts with what I've seen today. There seems to be little difference except that I've aged a lot. I look preternaturally school boyish and unblemished in 1980. Can I have turned into W. H. Auden so quickly?

Despite concerns about aging and how travel was taking its toll, Palin was clearly identifying himself as a Python apart, one who could still carry the spirit of Python within him, even as he forged his own career path outside the main stage.

In 1994, while in Belfast preparing for the BBC series *Great Railway Journeys of the World: Derry to Kerry*, Palin remarked in his ubiquitous diary on the extraordinary security measures typical to Northern Ireland at the time:

These quasi-military presences must be as much a provocation as a necessity. They represent institutionalized force, embattled and dug in against the outside world. No wonder the men of both sides who attack them have a chance of becoming heroes.

Palin was an astute critic and did not want to whitewash the countries he visited on his journeys.

Palin's attitude was most likely atypical for most of his generation, who even while fighting for progressive issues most likely saw (or rather didn't see) the Irish struggle through anything other than highly censored British news reports. While Palin had not come out on the side of the IRA itself, he did demonstrate a tendency to question the official British accounts of what was, up until then, a literally occupied country. Palin, while wealthy himself, could still see the British occupation of Northern Ireland through the lens of British class issues.

As another book by two out of the three coauthors of this very work, *Everything I Ever Needed to Know About ___* I Learned from Monty Python* (available now!), has observed, Python used their natural antiauthoritarian principles to highlight the inherent silliness in the British class system. Years after Python, Palin was still investigating and observing that "silliness," just now with more resignation than before. Palin's trips, it must be noted, were not just vacations; he was putting himself through arduous, sometimes dangerous conditions to show his audience locations and peoples that they might not get a chance to see. But unlike the Whickers of the world, Palin examined the parts of the world he saw both with a critical eye and exuberant glee.

Most people forget how truly revolutionary Python's comedy was both at the time and today, and how so much of Python was designed to attack the dominant British class system. To Palin, Python's comedy was all about resisting the urge to tell people how to behave and how not to behave. They expounded the freedom of the individual, a very 1960s thing. Palin applied that worldview in his travels around the world, noting the very real issues of poverty, class, and colonialism still present in former (and present) British colonies.

While in Belfast in 1994, Palin was watching on TV as the Good Friday Agreement went into effect, stopping most military activities and leading to the first prolonged stretch of peace that Northern Ireland had seen for almost four decades. Palin watched in wonder, thinking that the peace agreement was as momentous as the end of apartheid or the collapse of communism. He marveled on his journeys that he was not just seeing places most people would never visit, but that he was also seeing history unfold before his eyes.

The more that Palin traveled, the more the stark contrast between the first and third worlds became apparent. Sometimes the reality of travel did not live up to Palin's romanticized expectations, as he noted about visiting Riyadh for *Around the World in 80 Days*. Having been raised on *Arabian Nights*–style fantasies, he did not discover the mysterious "Kasbah" of his imagination, but an overbuilt, neon-lit urban metropolis, bereft of romance and myth. Palin found it depressingly "commercial," excepting the regional Islamic culture, which the West didn't know or care about. This was not his childhood fantasy come to life, but the reality of how cultures adapt to modern times. Palin was not trying to be overtly political, but his longstanding contempt for the notion of British exceptionalism clearly irked him from the start. By the time he had a chance to travel the world for a living, he was a host who showed you not just the beauty of the rest of the world, but also the ugly scars left from the past.

Although Palin's "nice guy" persona has often been viewed—particularly by the cynical—as a weakness, a sham, or an irritant, it has served him remarkably well as a traveler. Almost without exception, he has been affably unobtrusive, the type of foreigner whom people seem almost magically willing to accommodate and even embrace. His presence in other countries, even if he was taking part in local ceremonies and rituals, was not meant to be disruptive, but accommodating, understanding, and (against his initial wishes) educational as well.

Palin pulled off a modest everyman character better than most professional travel presenters. Indeed, Palin seems to be without ego or self in his travels, something like the Taoist "Uncarved Block" or a human Winnie-the-Pooh. His relative selflessness enables him to experience the journey as it presents itself, rather than (as so many of us do) turning the journey into the thing we already expected it to be: "I am going to Paris to find love," we say, or "I am traveling to Israel to rediscover my heritage," or "I am going to Disneyland to get in touch with my inner child." Palin just boards the train to see what happens; he is willing to experience the experience, not control the experience.

In *Traveling to Work*, Palin saw his role as travel correspondent very particularly: "My contribution, I think, will not be precision, analysis, and revelation, but honesty, directness, openness, and enthusiasm." This enables Palin to succeed as a traveler in ways that the other Pythons could not. Can we imagine Cleese floating down the rivers in Saudi Arabia or traveling the Antarctic without looking for a desk where he could "register a complaint"?

Yet in the beginning, Palin could not know that he would be a "natural" as a travel reporter, and his self-doubt suggests that, had any other Python so chosen, they too could have traveled as he had, experienced the world as he did. This is poppycock. While one might argue that, had Palin chosen to devote himself to acting or writing rather than travel, he might have rivaled the Hollywood success of Cleese, or the academic success of Jones, it is preposterous to suggest that Cleese or Jones (or Idle, or Gilliam, or Chapman) could have succeeded as Palin did as a world traveler.

To new generations born long after Python was in their prime, Palin is the consummate travel host, a genial everyman who takes them around the world and back again. But while Palin was not working as much as an actor while doing his travel documentaries, he was spending more and more time at his writer's desk. When he not adding entries to his ubiquitous diaries, Palin was busy working on book projects both connected to travel and as far afield as children's books, novels, and plays.

Palin as a Writer

Palin isn't the most prolific Python in terms of appearances on television and movies. At his best, he's nowhere near as active as Cleese or Idle, who are probably filming five cameos and a voice-over as you read this. However, Palin has been extraordinarily busy as a writer. In the post-Python years, Palin has written three filmed screenplays and well over a dozen books, and has even kept a consistent diary, which has now been published in three volumes: *Diaries 1969–1979: The Python Years* (2006), *Diaries 1980–1988: Halfway to Hollywood* (2009), and *Diaries 1988–1998: Traveling to Work* (2014).

The diaries are fascinating for the amount of minutiae and acute observations that Palin made along the way. Although not intended for publication originally (one entry describes him arguing with his agent about this), the diaries do provide a view into the inner life of both Palin and Python. The diaries reveal arguments about script and plot from Python, musings about real estate and the state of the British film industry, and brutally painful personal details. Even an event that would have shaken most people to their core, like the suicide of his long-depressed sister Angela in 1987, is included here in all its tragic reality.

While Palin details the turmoil that surrounded his work (Python work meetings could descend into chaos seemingly at any moment) and the setbacks in his personal life, he was mostly concentrating on the things that brought happiness to himself and his family. He does not mince words, even expressing disappointment in some of his children's choices, but in reading Palin's diaries, one is struck by his strong sense of honesty and dedication to his wife, Helen, and their children, who occupy far more space than all his professional work combined.

"Michael Palin is not just one of Britain's foremost comedy character actors, he also talks a lot. Yap, yap, yap he goes, all day long and through the night . . . then, some nights, when everyone else has gone to bed, he goes home and writes up a diary."

—JOHN CLEESE

MICHAEL PALIN
DIARIES 1969-1979

Palin published travel books to accompany each of his journeys, including: *Around the World in 80 Days*, *Pole to Pole*, *Full Circle*, *Hemingway Adventure*, *Sahara*, *Himalaya*, *New Europe*, *80 Days Revisited*, and *Brazil* (no connection to the movie, it's also an actual country, you know).

Palin, who clearly had the best investment advice of any of the Pythons (read his diaries for proof of this), also allows visitors to his website to read his travel books for free. These are breezy and amusing accounts that sometimes omit the behind-the-scenes struggles described in more detail in the diaries. Nonetheless, Palin's sometimes coffee table–sized accounts are full of witty and illuminating stories about his adventures.

Palin has also worked on numerous literary projects beyond his diaries and travels. Some from his period of collaborating with Jones are wonderfully silly, such as the must-have *Bert Fegg's Nasty Book for Boys and Girls* (1974), which was later expanded and reissued as *Dr. Fegg's Encyclopedia of All World Knowledge* (1984).

Among Palin's numerous children's books are *Small Harry and the Toothache Pills* (1982), *Limericks or the Limerick Book* (1985), *Cyril and the House of Commons* (1986) and *Cyril and the Dinner Party* (1986), and *The Mirrorstone* with Alan Lee and Richard Seymour. In addition to his literary works, Palin is also the author of one play: *The Weekend* (1994), which received middling reviews and did not last that long. All in all, the *Fegg* books are the best of the Palin solo or collaborative works in that they are consistently silly and could easily be seen as a continuation of his lighter side, as opposed to the "serious" books that are both comedic but hint at an inner sadness not explored by Palin in public.

Palin also wrote two novels, *Hemingway's Chair* (1995) and *The Truth* (2012), which both received good reviews, but in all honesty are not major canon in terms of Python solo projects.

Palin, These Days

Ultimately, Palin *is* the nicest of the Pythons, but that doesn't mean that his post-Python work was among the most minor works of post-Python solo material. Sadly, that award goes to the late Chapman, who never did well when trying to work on his own.

Palin has much to be proud of in terms of post-Python. His travel host career aside, he wrote one film that can be considered a comedy classic (*The Missionary*), worked successfully with Jones on a very hilarious two-season run on *Ripping Yarns*, and made many memorable appearances in films, most particularly in *A Fish Called Wanda*. While Palin did not become a movie star, none of the Pythons did. Star or not, his work after Python has an enormous depth and range that Cleese and Idle, for all their ubiquity, cannot match. Palin may be the "nicest" Python, but perhaps he is also the most revealing of all the members of Python, with years of success and dreams deferred detailed for all the world to see.

22

Post-Python: "He's a Very Naughty Boy!"

Terry Jones: The Medieval-est Python

Terence Graham Parry "Terry" Jones—the perennial Pepperpot and mother hen who always seemed most keen on keeping the Pythons together—has had a surprisingly diverse career after Python. Since codirecting *Monty Python and the Holy Grail*, Jones has directed a variety of Python and non-Python films, but he's also written children's books and academic treatises, political columns and historical documentaries; he cofounded a microbrewery; directed (and researched!) a film about an infamous London madam; starred as Toad in the live-action *The Wind in the Willows*; cowrote *Lady Cottington's Pressed Fairy Book* and *Dr. Fegg's Nasty Book of Knowledge*; penned a libretto or two; and hosted a host of historical documentaries on topics from sex in the ancient world to Renaissance falsehoods to modern weather. He even wrote an outline (abandoned) for Joe Dante's *Gremlins 2* and an actual script (much abandoned) for Jim Henson's *Labyrinth*.

In short, Jones has gone on to make quite a name for himself in a variety of fields. Although the moniker would surely pain a man who has spent a portion of his life debunking misconceptions about the "Dark Ages," he is quite the Renaissance man. But as much of a *bricoleur* as Jones has become, he is generally acknowledged as the most academic of the Pythons, and it is probably with his intellectual pursuits—spurred in part by his role as codirector on *Holy Grail*—that got him started on the path that led to his wildly diverse output. So we'll begin there, shall we?

The Scholar

Before *Flying Circus* took off, Jones had fostered an interest in and talent for writing, English literature, and—in particular—medieval studies; as

Palin recalls in *Monty Python Speaks*: "Terry and I were both interested in history—Terry because he read medieval English and was very interested in Chaucer and all that and me because I'd done three years of a history degree at Oxford. I was brim full of all this useless information."

Useless information? Hardly! Jones's readings in medieval English were instrumental in crafting the verisimilitude of *Holy Grail*: the film may have been parodic and low budget, but it certainly seemed "real" to the audience . . . right up to the point that it became temporally surreal. In fact, Jones had been noodling some ideas regarding Chaucer during the shooting of *Holy Grail*. Gilliam recalled a particular "aha!" moment for his codirector when they were investigating castles and the two were shown the "defensible partition" between the lord and his retinue and the "hired mercenaries" (who, by necessity, also lived in the castle). Effectively, the lord could protect himself *from his own knights*, as it were.

Jones would go on to write his seminal—and at the time, academically controversial—cultural-historical reevaluation of one of the "most worthy" characters in fourteenth-century fiction: Geoffrey Chaucer's unnamed Knight from *The Canterbury Tales*. You know the story, right? With all the pilgrimage and talking chickens and bed-swapping and hot pokers up the ass, right? Anyway, in *Chaucer's Knight: Portrait of a Medieval Mercenary* (1980), Jones uses close readings and cultural parallelism to identify repeated moments of ironic representation in the depiction of the Knight throughout the *Canterbury Tales*: moments that the naïve narrator misses, but that the author (and the reader) should pick up on. As a result, Jones suggests that the Knight en route to Canterbury alongside the other pilgrims is not a bastion of nobility and chivalry (as had been taught in schools since time immemorial), but a sword-for-hire couched in ironic pseudo-chivalric garb. After all, Chaucer—like the Pythons six hundred years later—was a master satirist: Why would he un-ironically uphold the dominant paradigm with an overly adulatory depiction of the Knight?

Now, academics are a cowardly lot . . . no, wait, sorry: that's criminals. Academics are an insular lot, and—certainly in the 1970s—they tended to look down upon "amateurs" without PhDs who dared to opine about such august authors as Geoffrey Chaucer (*the* Father of the English language). But Jones's cultural historicism was compelling—convincing, even—and spurred an entire generation of medievalists to reevaluate previously established readings. If Chaucer's worthy (worthy, I say!) Knight were in fact a potential thug (as Jones argues), who knows what else we might have gotten "wrong" about the Middle Ages?

Jones has maintained a voice in medieval academia over the years, writing for the *Cambridge Review* (1981) and *Studies in the Age of Chaucer* (2000), as well as presenting at various conferences (he's something of a celebrity among medievalists). He also recorded audiobooks for another famously popular "medieval" Oxfordian, J. R. R. Tolkien, whose translations of *Sir Gawain and the Green Knight*, *Sir Orfeo*, and *The Pearl* are well worth giving a listen to (try NOT to imagine *Holy Grail*'s Black Knight while listening to Jones describe the head-lopping in *Sir Gawain*!).

More recently, Jones came out with another controversial historical conjecture: *Who Murdered Chaucer?: A Medieval Mystery* (2003). Working alongside bona fide professional medievalists to "stage a coroner's inquest on Chaucer's death," Jones speculates that Chaucer—a "politically inconvenient" author who suddenly disappeared from public record in 1400—could have been intentionally eliminated from history by a suppressive authority (Henry IV and Archbishop Arundel). As Jones admits, it's "less of a Whodunnit? than a Wasitdunnatall?" but the book offers an engaging investigation into history and historicity.

It also shows that modern academics now take Jones seriously: in 2003, Jones was honored to unveil the historical Blue Plaque at the site of the Tabard Inn, "from which Chaucer's pilgrims set off in April 1386." In 2012, he was recognized with a premortem Festschrift titled *The Medieval Python: The Purposive and Provocative Work of Terry Jones* . . . and nothing says "one of us" among professional medievalists like a good old-fashioned Festschrift (a collection of essays that are published to honor a scholar, don't you know). Perhaps someday he'll find a home for his planned production of François Rabelais's enormous medieval satire *Gargantua*; that the play (intended for the West End in 1992) has never seen public performance is a travesty.

The Docent

Happily, Jones's insights into history have not been confined to the ivory towers of academe. He has championed historical reevaluation on the telly as well. After a brief foray into what might be deemed the smallest field of meteorology—historical weather analysis (*And God Blew* in 1992), Jones set forth to write and host a very successful string of popular historical documentaries: *The Crusades* (1995), *Ancient Inventions* (1998), *The Surprising [Hidden] History of Egypt* (2002), *The Surprising [Hidden] History of Rome* (2002), *The Surprising [Hidden] History of Sex and Love* (2002), *Terry Jones'*

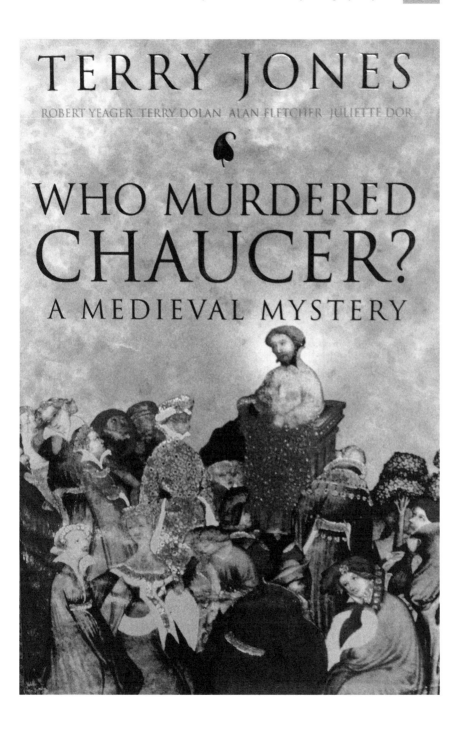

TERRY JONES

ROBERT YEAGER · TERRY DOLAN · ALAN FLETCHER · JULIETTE DOR

WHO MURDERED CHAUCER?

A MEDIEVAL MYSTERY

Medieval Lives (2004), *The Story of 1* (2005), *Terry Jones' Barbarians* (2006), and *Terry Jones' Great Map Mystery* (2008).

Jones has also taken to the radio: *The Routes of English* (1999) discussed Chaucerian Middle English; *The Medieval Ball* (2000) reexamined how medieval thinkers saw the world around them; *The Anti-Renaissance Show* (2002) debunked the presumption that the Renaissance was more enlightened than the medieval era; *Heroes and Villains* (2003) questioned the too-simple hero/villain dichotomies historically assigned to Alexander the Great and Attila the Hun; and *Let's Hear It for the King of Judea* (2004) reassessed the reputation of King Herod.

In all these engaging documentaries, Jones plays the role of self-assured docent, doling out factoids and debunking misinformation from an authorial pulpit with a wry smile and cocked eyebrow. He enjoys, it seems, informing folks of their erroneous beliefs . . . even the misinformation he helped promulgate in *Holy Grail* (the medieval had decent teeth, as he admits, and not everyone was "covered in shit").

Between his comic and academic output, Jones's literary erudition was recognized early on, and the BBC tapped him to host their weekly *Paperbacks* discussion program (1981). Jones's run on the literary review included a week dedicated to independent authors, another to the nuclear threat, and one to children's books (among others). He's continued to promote literature of all stripes over the years, supporting the Hay-on-Wye Festival of Literature on more than one occasion.

The Politico

Jones has also shared his political (and social, and ecological) opinions with the masses via the medium of newspapers (for the under-forties: newspapers are dead-tree versions of the right-scroll on Facebook; for the under-twenties: Facebook is what your dad is looking at on the computer when he's not watching porn). While Chapman was championing gay rights and Cleese was organizing Amnesty International concerts, Jones was financially backing *Vole*, an environmental magazine (1977–1980), and voicing his social concerns in print.

Jones began writing op-ed pieces for the *Young Guardian* in 1987; these were collected in *Attacks of Opinion* in 1988, and reveal his breadth of knowledge (and generally liberal opinions) on topics from ecology to taxation to the media. After the events of 9/11, Jones wrote a series of columns for the *Observer*, the *Guardian*, and the *Independent*, criticizing the reactions to terrorism by the Anglophone powers that be. These "little outbursts of indignation" (as Jones calls them) were collected in *Terry Jones's War on the War on Terror: Observations and Denunciations by a Founding Member of Monty Python* (2005). (Which leads us to ask the following heated political question: If Jones is a "founding member" of Monty Python, who the hell are the second-generation members?) Jones also co-wrote and co-directed *Boom Bust Boom* (2008), a documentary about mankind's tragicomic ability to repeat preventable economic mistakes in one generation after another. Jones brightened up the dreary science with songs and puppets, as more professors should.

The Fabulist

Speaking of the next generation, Jones has not relegated himself to the role of revisionist-historian and neo-politico: he has remained as capable of entertaining children as he was in his *DNAYS!* days. Jones and Palin kept their Oxford partnership alive immediately after *Flying Circus* wrapped by coauthoring *Bert Fegg's Nasty Book for Boys and Girls* (1974) (aka *Dr. Fegg's Nasty Book of Knowledge* [1976] and *Dr. Fegg's Encyclopaedia of All World Knowledge* [1984]); the book presents an *almost* child-friendly series of comic tales, something like *DNAYS!* meets Shel Silverstein's *Uncle Shelby's ABZ Book*.

Jones and Palin also cowrote and costarred in the somewhat sporadic *Ripping Yarns* series (nine episodes airing 1976–1979); the series is fondly remembered as an often-surreal lampoon of Edwardian "literature for young boys" so popular in prewar England. Bears, Nazis, and frogs are involved. And yes: it's often as weirdly fun as *Flying Circus*.

When not in front of or behind the camera, Jones is a father ("I have a home life, you know!"), and began writing fairy tale-esque stories for his children in the late 1970s, some of which later became available to the public (the stories, not the children). These include:

Fairy Tales (1981); *The Saga of Erik the Viking* (1983); *Nicobobinus* (1985); *Goblins of the Labyrinth* (1986); *Curse of the Vampire's Socks and Other Doggerel* (1988); *Fantastic Stories* (1992); *A Fish of the World* (1993); *The Beast with a Thousand Teeth* (1993); *The Fly-By-Night* (1993); *The Sea Tiger* (1993); the delightfully dark *Lady Cottington's Pressed Fairy Book* (1994) and the follow-up, *Strange Stains and Mysterious Smells: Quentin Cottington's Journal of Fairy Research* (1996); *The Goblin Companion* (1996); *The Knight and the Squire* (1997) and its sequel, *The Lady and the Squire* (2000); and *Animal Tales* (2011). Many of these tales are creative "reimaginings" of traditional legend, informed by Jones's

---

What's All This, Then?
Like Cannibalism for Chocolates

Palin and Jones also cowrote the decidedly unpopular *Secrets* (1973), a decidedly un-child-friendly hour-long BBC dark comedy dealing with cannibalism at a chocolate factory. One assumes the elevator pitch went something like this: "See, it's *Sweeney Todd* meets *Soylent Green* at the Whizzo Chocolate Company . . ." Sold! Despite being utterly wiped by the BBC, a VHS recording of *Secrets* survived and the film is now available as an extra on the *Ripping Yarns* DVD (parental discretion is advised). Oddly enough, Vanessa Redgrave and Jonathan Pryce (along with *Fawlty Towers* alumna Prunella Scales) starred in a remake of *Secrets* called *Consuming Passions* (1988). Neither film, alas, is as funny as a crunchy frog covered in lark's vomit.

---

deep knowledge of narrative structure and variant mythologies. Often the result of a partnership with the award-winning (and highly prolific) children's illustrator Michael Foreman, Jones's kid-lit has been generally well received, oft-nominated for awards, and sometimes adapted for stage. To call Jones the Pythonic equivalent of Shel Silverstein might be a bit of a stretch, but there's no doubt that the two seemed comfortable writing on topics timeless and political, ridiculous and sublime, darkly satiric and warmly genial.

Jones also cocreated the very popular but short-lived *Blazing Dragons* animated series for ITV (1996–1998); set in "Camelhot," the series flips the script of most Arthuriana by presenting a civilization of noble dragons who are attacked by evil humans. Fun fact: when released in the United States on the Toon Disney network, the shows were—shocker!—bowdlerized within an inch of their life. A pity some idiomatic Lancelot couldn't get there in time to save the rather flamboyant Sir Blaze. . . .

The Director

Madam Cyn

Jones—who once famously argued "What's wrong with masturbation?" with a group of BBC censors—remained interested in more than child's fare after *Flying Circus*. The most "adult" film Jones ever completed is *Professional Services* (1987), the lightly veiled tale of London's most (in) famous madam. Cynthia Payne, whose "House of Cyn" had been famously raided in 1978—compromising an MP, a "peer of the realm," and several vicars—served as Jones's model for his film's heroine, Christine Painter (played by Julie Walters). The story gives Jones room to simultaneously criticize authoritarian morality and be as bawdy as he liked (David Leland's script features plenty of bluntly clever language). And yet somehow, despite the juicy narrative upon which the film is based, the production ultimately proved more interesting than the film itself. One wonders if Jones ever took Gilliam aside and said, "So, about *Don Quixote* . . . "

Jones gained some extra-Python notoriety by attending a sex party at Payne's house in 1985 as "research" for his *Professional* project. Then, in an impossible-to-script moment of life-imitating-art-imitating-life, tabloids reported that Payne's house was raided for the second time in 1986, on the very night Jones was filming his version of the 1978 raid for his film (admittedly, later court documents report that the raid occurred during the "wrap" party for the film, but that's another pun for another day).

After their second "House of Cyn" raid, police reopened their case against Payne; although she was acquitted this time, Jones delayed release of his completed film lest his portrayal of Painter paint a distorted pretrial picture of Payne. Many of the Pythons (and Payne) attended the film's delayed premiere (1987) in a show of solidarity; this was, after all, the first film Jones had directed outside of Python. Despite the free publicity

What's All This, Then?
The Venerable Jonesy

Jones married Alison Telfer, a biochemist, in 1969; they have two children, Sally (b. 1974) and Bill (b. 1976). The two also secretly enjoyed an open marriage until the mid-1990s, when Jones let slip their arrangement during an interview. Telfer was reportedly less than pleased that Jones had made their private life so public; unlike the socially open attitude of entertainment in which Jones traveled, Telfer's career as a biochemist at London University may have been a tad less open to open marriages at the time. Still, the two remained married until 2004, when Jones began seeing Anna Söderström, an Oxford student he met at a book signing. To the delight of the *Daily Mail* and other British tabloids, and to the apparent displeasure of Telfer, Söderström was twenty-one at the time . . . nearly ten years younger than Jones's and Telfer's children. After his divorce to Telfer, Jones and Söderström had a child, Siri (b. 2009) and were secretly married (2012). Madam Cyn would certainly have approved.

afforded by the second Payne scandal, and despite favorable critical reviews (Roger Ebert gave it 3.5/4 stars), the film was not widely popular. But as Jones rather proudly noted in a promotional interview with Terry Wogan, three of the four films ever banned in Ireland (*Crimes of Passion*, *Professional Services*, *Life of Brian*, and *The Meaning of Life*) were directed by him, so he must be doing something right.

Erik the Viking

After *Professional Services*, Jones directed and scripted *Erik the Viking* (1989), a comedy-fantasy very (!) loosely based on a story he had originally written for his son, Bill, some years earlier. The revised script deals with an oddly guilt-ridden and morally modern Viking (Tim Robbins) who seeks the gods' aid in ending Ragnarök (the Norse end of days). Cleese plays one of the baddies, Eartha Kitt plays a witch, Mickey Rooney is alive in it, and Jones himself plays a "terribly nice" (if hapless) king. The film has a few good moments (over the edge of the world!), and a cool concept, but it's all rather dour and uneven . . . Robbins in particular seems confused by everything going on around him. However, in a fine bit of "Jörmungandr biting its own tail,"

Terry Jones and Tim Robbins in Jones's *Erik the Viking*.   *Orion Pictures/Photofest*

the DVD re-release (2006) features a pared-down "Director's Son's Cut" (by Bill, who knew the original material intimately) that is worth another look.

Young Indiana Jones

Moving from ancient Norse mythology on the big screen to modern American legend on the small screen, Jones next directed an episode of *The Young Indiana Jones Chronicles* (1992). Jones cameos in the episode (titled "Espionage Escapades") as well, which revolves around bungling spies, Russian ballet, German baddies, and Pablo Picasso. The lighthearted and kid-friendly romp—a fan favorite that season—may have encouraged Jones to return to directing less obviously "adult" films, which is fortunate, as his next directorial endeavor likely ranks as his best post-Python work behind the camera.

The Wind in the Willows

Adapting Kenneth Grahame's beloved children's novel *The Wind in the Willows* (1908) for the big screen, Jones put together an utterly charming live-action film: with himself in the starring role as the paunchy Toad of Toad Hall. *The Wind in the Willows* (1996) also brought together four-fifths of the remaining Pythons, with Idle as Rat, Cleese as (naturally enough) Toad's lawyer, and Palin as the Sun (Gilliam was allegedly game, but scheduling conflicts prohibited his contribution).

But beyond strong casting (the film also stars Steve Coogan as Mole and Stephen Fry as the Judge), Jones takes a rather adult tack toward the material, lacing Grahame's original tale with—as a contemporary *New York Times* review noted—"an Orwellian parable that upholds the virtues of civility and decency while baring the evils of naked yuppie greed." Given the pap that usually passed as children's filmmaking at the time, Jones's contribution was welcome indeed. *The Wind in the Willows* went on to win awards at both the Chicago and Wisconsin International Children's Film Festivals.

Unfortunately, the film grossed less than it deserved, having been screened in the United Kingdom almost exclusively in the afternoon (targeted solely at kids), and—thanks to legal wrangling between Columbia and Disney over distribution—only received limited release in the United States. in 1997. Disney eventually (in 1998) released the film on VHS (and again on DVD in 2004) under the title *Mr. Toad's Wild Ride* . . . to tie in with their

What's All This, Then?
Jones & Adams

Jones's connection to Douglas Adams runs deeper than Adams's fourth-season appearances on *Flying Circus* and one bad movie review. The two stayed chummy over the years, and when Adams grew increasingly involved with production of his *Starship Titanic* video game, Jones stepped in to write the 1997 novelization. Reviewers gave a collective "meh." Apparently, Adams didn't write entirely convincing Python, and Jones didn't write entirely convincing Adams.

by-now defunct amusement ride (which sadly closed its creep-tastic neon doors in 1998). Still: Jones is spot-on as Toad, and the film well worth every parent's time.

Animated Aliens

After a somewhat protracted directing hiatus, Jones wrote and directed another semi-animated affair which fully saw (or at least heard) all five surviving Pythons reunited on the big screen for the first time since *The Meaning of Life*; unfortunately, *Absolutely Anything* (2015)—about a group of aliens who "test" humanity by giving one human (Pegg) the ability to do "absolutely anything"—is a dismal failure, despite a great cast (Simon Pegg and Kate Beckinsale are the leads, while Eddie Izzard, Robin Williams, and Joanna Lumley all lend their talents). As a critic for the *Guardian* noted, *Absolutely Anything* is anything but funny: "[T]his low-budget Brit film is just depressing, a sub–Douglas Adams sci-fi comedy." Happily, the Pythons' live (mostly) reunion shows in 2014 rather obscured this less-than-stellar CGI reunion.

The Zymurgist

Jones—a Welshman by birth and by choice—liked to opine about beer as well as politics (and art and the environment and censorship and . . . well, you get the point). In 1977, he cofounded Penrhos Brewery at a sixteenth-century farm on the Welsh-England border. The brewery—a microbrewery under the guidance of brewmaster Peter Austin, back when microbreweries were a novelty—helped revive a national interest in porter; Jones helped promote the microbrewery by pouring six pints of Penrhos over his own head at the Great British Beer Festival in London later that year. Although Penrhos Brewery closed in 1983, Jones kept his taste for beer and even wrote an article on "real ale" for the *Good Beer Guide 2003*.

Beer, beer, beer, beer, wonderful beer!   *Lisa Bocchini*

Fittingly, Jones is the only Python to appear on the post-Python cult comedy *The Young Ones*. He played a drunken vicar in a 1984 episode aptly titled "Nasty."

Although Penrhos is no more (alas, to having never tasted a walloping pint of Jones' First Ale), there is still Python beer, thanks in part to Jones's enthusiasm. Black Sheep Brewery in Yorkshire crafted (and licensed) a thirtieth-anniversary beer in honor of the troupe, called "Monty Python's Holy (Gr)ail Ale" (1999). According to the label, the beer is "tempered over burning witches"; according to the Black Sheep brewmaster, it has "more hops than a killer rabbit"; according to your authors, it's a reasonable English pale ale (4.7%, for those planning to play a round of "Sir Bedevere's

Visor" later today). Apparently, there's a "Holy Grail Dark" now available, so if you'll excuse us, it's time to nip off to the pub for a pint.

Sadly, in late 2016—just as Jones was to accept a Special Award for Outstanding Contribution to Film and Television from BAFTA Cymru—it was announced that he had been diagnosed with primary progressive aphasia, a type of dementia that hinders verbal communication. Jones, with the help of his fellow Pythons (and a teleprompter), had generally hidden his growing aphasia throughout the O2 reunion. But by September 2016, the neurological syndrome had progressed to the point that he needed to cancel speaking engagements. With the help of his son, Jones silently accepted his BAFTA before a decidedly emotional crowd of fans in early October, roughly a week after the announcement of his condition.

As Palin noted on his Facebook page, aphasia is "the cruellest thing that could befall someone to whom words, ideas, arguments, jokes and stories were once the stuff of life." Still, Jones—whose verbal humor was so strongly evident in Python—remained in good spirits throughout 2016 with his family and friends, who continue to enjoy his companionship and occasional moments of "the old Terry" while watching musicals at home or socializing at the local pub. It is hoped that the revelation of his disease will spark an increase in dementia awareness throughout Britain, and that other sufferers of the disease will be treated with more sympathy than before. Say no more, eh?

23

Seven for Seventh

The Semi-Pythons

Monty Python was an insular operation, written (almost) entirely by the original Python Six—men who also played nearly every key role—from twit to Gumby to Pepperpot and all points in between. There was, it seems, little room for outsiders. However, the Pythons did have several long-term collaborators who all, in their own ways, contributed to the success of Monty Python. Their august numbers include stalwart "glamour stooge" Carol Cleveland, *Fawlty Towers* cocreator Connie Booth, Bonzo minstrel Neil Innes, *Hitchhiker's Guide to the Galaxy* author Douglas Adams, and superfan/Beatle George Harrison. At various points in time and space, these—and others—have been cited as "The Seventh Python." And yet, to paraphrase the ever-erudite Kurgan: "There can be only one [seventh]!" So read on, squire, as we present, for the final time . . . *The Case of/for the Seventh Python!* (In 3-D wherever available; in 5-D wherever not.)

I: Mark Forstater: The Profit-Sharer

We're going to start off this list of candidates for "The Seventh Python" with a man who has, somewhat crudely, put forth his own name to be considered. We think he's a bit naff, but let's hear him out before we rule against him, shall we?

According to the *Hollywood Reporter,* Mark Forstater—one of the *Holy Grail* producers whom Palin noted in 1973 was seething with "jealousy and rivalry" over shares of the film—sued the Pythons in 2012 for a share of the profits from *Spamalot,* the Broadway musical that was "lovingly ripped off" from *Monty Python and the Holy Grail.* In short, since *Spamalot* is a "spin-off" of the film he helped produce some forty years earlier, Forstater argued that he was entitled to additional monies—some $400,000—from the Python Six.

In the end, Forstater's lawyer successfully argued that—"for purposes of profit-sharing"—Forstater must be considered the "Seventh Python" on *Holy Grail*... with subsequent spin-offs and merchandise rolled into his "Top Half" share (whatever the hell that means). Quite honestly, it's all rather lawyerly and—if it weren't all so expensive—silly. But the Pythons in 1974 weren't the most business-savvy young comics in the world, so most likely they'd signed something that, like a vicious bunny with razor-sharp teeth, came back to bite them in the end. Ultimately, the judge ruled in favor of the plaintiff, and the Pythons reportedly paid Forstater some £800,000 in royalties and legal fees. On the "plus" side, Forstater's lawsuit has been cited as the primary reason the Pythons got back together for the *Monty Python Live (Mostly)* shows in 2014, so fans—if not actual Pythons—owe him some small thanks for compelling the band to get back together.

However, regardless of a lawyer's argument or a judge's decision, Mark Forstater is no more the Seventh Python than the Legendary Black Beast of Arrghhh. Less so.

2: George Harrison: The Superfan

While nine out of ten zoologists agree that a Beatle is not, by nature, a Python, we might make an exception for George Harrison. A dedicated fan, bit player, sugar daddy, and devoted friend, Harrison played a role in the Pythons' success that is often underestimated. Even if he'd never been directly involved with the Pythons (and he certainly was!), the troupe owe Harrison—and the rest of the Beatles—a debt of thanks for starting the British Invasion... without which *Flying Circus* would never have crossed the Big Pond, nor *Holy Grail* become so Anglo-cultish.

Harrison was a vocal Python fan from their BBC days; while the Beatles' less-than-amicable divorce was going on, Harrison was quoted in Robert Ross's *Monty Python Encyclopedia* as saying, "the only thing worth getting out of bed for is *Monty Python's Flying Circus*." As if to punctuate his fandom, Harrison's touring pseudonym at hotels in the 1970s was "Jack Lumber." Idle—who was Harrison's closest friend among the Pythons—recalls that Harrison "was always a raving certified Python Fanatic." Indeed, the two had a connection even before there was a Monty Python; Harrison had appeared in the Ronnie Corbett situation comedy *No, That's Me Over Here* (1967), which Idle had written. The two met at a screening of *Holy Grail* in Los Angeles. Idle told a *New Yorker* writer that Harrison said, "Let's go and have a reefer in the control booth," and the pair ended up talking for

George Harrison's cameo in *Life of Brian*; well, it was the least they could do . . . .
Mary Evans/Ronald Grant/Everett Collection

two days. Later, Idle would often jam with Harrison, along with part-time Python and sometime-devoured minstrel Neil Innes; the Beatle and the Bonzo subsequently appeared on Idle's *The Rutland Christmas Special* in 1975.

Later still, Harrison appeared with the Pythons on stage at City Center in New York dressed as a choral Mountie for the "Lumberjack Song" (according to legend, no one in the audience noticed this cameo by the most famous person on stage). Harrison also appeared in Idle's hilarious mockumentary *All You Need Is Cash*, playing an interviewer who eventually loses his microphone to a worker as he disassembles the offices of the now-bankrupt mega-band. Oh, the irony!

Harrison's most famous connection to Python, however, was as a financial angel on their most controversial film, *Life of Brian*. In 1978, hearing that Python was having financial difficulties after their deal with EMI had collapsed, Harrison (along with Denis O'Brien) formed HandMade Films and saved the day by backing the Pythons to the tune of $4 million.

In return, the Pythons cast him in a small role as Mr. Papadopoulos, one among a "sea of fans" crowding about Brian (Chapman). It's all of fifteen seconds' worth of silent screen time: as Idle has noted, Harrison essentially bought the world's most expensive theater ticket. HandMade Films went on to produce *Monty Python Live at the Hollywood Bowl* (1982) and continued to work with various members of *Flying Circus*, producing Gilliam's *Time Bandits* (1981), Palin's *The Missionary* (1982) and *A Private Function* (1984), and Idle's *Nuns on the Run* (1990).

Harrison and Idle remained particularly close friends throughout their lives; Idle noted fondly years later in his *The Greedy Bastard Diary* that "I never knew a man like him. It was as if we fell in love. His attention, his concern, his loving friendship was so strong and powerful that it encompassed your entire life." Idle was bedside at Harrison's demise, helping to scatter rose petals on his body in the Hindu ritual that Harrison had requested before his death. As a sign of their deep respect for Harrison, the Pythons reunited (minus Cleese and Chapman; plus Innes, Cleveland, and Tom Hanks) at the *Concert for George* in 2002. They all sang the "Lumberjack Song" in his honor.

Harrison almost singlehandedly ensured that *Life of Brian* became a brilliant lightning rod of controversy and kept the Pythons in the public eye when no one else would take a chance on their potentially blasphemous material. But at the end of the day, Harrison wasn't so much the "Seventh Python" as he was their "Number One Fan." And really: Do we really need to bestow yet another honor upon the "Third Beatle" at this point?

3: Ian MacNaughton: The Producer

Edward Ian MacNaughton—while never quite a teen heartthrob like Harrison—was an invaluable behind-the-scenes advocate who helped facilitate their early success on the "small screen"; the Glaswegian MacNaughton directed nearly all four seasons of *Monty Python's Flying Circus*, *And Now for Something Completely Different* (1971), and both *Monty Python's Fliegender Zirkus* shows (1972). Prior to working with Python, though, he been an in-demand actor, producer, and director.

A former Royal Marine, MacNaughton took up acting as part of the Globe Players (the Marine version of the Footlights). He played many roles on British television in the 1950s and '60s, including the comedy *Tell It to the Marines* (1959–1960); he even garnered smaller parts in films ranging from *Lawrence of Arabia* (1962) to the 1956 science fiction cheapie *X the Unknown* (actually playing a character named Haggis, which seems like a human rights violation for a Scotsman). Later, he saw an ad for a directors' training program at the BBC. Afterward, he worked as a producer and director on several BBC television shows through the 1960s, and eventually found himself paired with the Pythons.

What set MacNaughton apart from the rest of the BBC—and what also connected him to the Pythons—was his experience working with Python idol Spike Milligan on his series *Q . . .* (1969). The Pythons' respect for both Milligan and *Q . . .* transferred to their respect for MacNaughton.

MacNaughton was asked to join *Flying Circus* after the fourth episode—he'd been on vacation when the show began—at which point the BBC told him that he had to "save" the show, as it was not (per the BBC) "funny." Fortunately, his directorial (and comic) sensibilities were closer to the Pythons' than to the stodgy BBC's. After some initial friction between MacNaughton and Jones (who already had his own ambitions to become a director), MacNaughton was accepted as part of the team and subsequently spent much of his time explaining the show to his bosses at the BBC. Jones, who wrote an obituary for MacNaughton in the *Guardian* in 2002, noted "he made it his business to protect us against the antipathy of the BBC hierarchy—not an enviable task. He found himself having to defend a program that the BBC seemed to regret having commissioned in the first place."

As a director with acting chops, MacNaughton often appeared as an extra or bit character in *Flying Circus*. However, after producing *And Now for Something Completely Different* (1971)—which the Python Six generally considered a low-budget and unimaginative repackaging of their vintage material—MacNaughton parted ways with the Pythons, and the "two Terrys" (Gilliam and Jones) began directing. Still, there wasn't really any "bad blood" between the Pythons and MacNaughton: in fact, he directed the pilot for Chapman's failed comedy show, *Out of the Trees* (1976).

But with the Pythons generally off to greener pastures and larger screens, MacNaughton returned to work with Milligan in the 1970s, going on to direct the many sequels to *Q*, including *Q6* (1975), *Q7* (1977), *Q8* (1978), and finally *Q9* (1980). MacNaughton also directed art films and plays into the 1990s, working until a car crash seriously injured him in 2001, ultimately leading to his death in 2002.

Although Monty Python proved they could succeed without MacNaughton's direction, he provided them the freedom to initially develop their warped and groundbreaking comic vision. Indeed, without the judicial directorial interference of Ian "Mixed Grill" MacNaughton, the Pythons might not have survived their first season with the BBC; while that may not be worth a seventh share, it's certainly worth seven shillings sixpence . . . and our thanks.

4: Douglas Adams: The Hitchhiker

Douglas Noël Adams (1952–2001) is best known for his hilarious and justly praised *The Hitchhiker's Guide to the Galaxy* science fiction–comedy series (which has been adapted for radio, television, movie, comics, and gaming), but many forget that he got his start as a comedy writer working on Season Four of *Monty Python's Flying Circus*. Although a decade younger (but certainly no shorter) than most of the Pythons, Adams followed their path. Raised in London (then Brentwood in Essex), he showed an aptitude for creative writing early on; he then studied English literature at Cambridge and (of course!) joined the Footlights Club, where the Pythons were already legends.

After Adams graduated, his work for the *Footlights Review* (1974) was "discovered" by Chapman. Adams was subsequently recruited to write with Chapman after Cleese departed *Flying Circus*. Chapman, who was not accustomed to writing on his own (or writing much at all, if some of Cleese's observations are accurate) cowrote the "Patient Abuse" sketch with Adams for the final episode of the entire series. Fun fact: Adams and Neil Innes are the only two non-Python members to receive a writing credit on a Python album or television series. Adams also appeared as a bit actor in two episodes of *Monty Python*: one as a masked doctor in the metatheatrical "Film Trailer" sketch (Episode 42) and another as a metal-salvaging Pepperpot in the opening of "Mr. Neutron" (Episode 44). Both are mute roles, so the less said about them the better.

After Python left the BBC, Adams and Chapman continued to collaborate, working with Bernard McKenna on *Out of the Trees* (1976), a failed "linguistically based" comedy show in the surrealist vein of *Python*; *Trees* only aired once and was subsequently wiped by the ever-cost-conscious bean counters at the BBC. Fortuitously, a rough copy was eventually found in Chapman's videotape collection; it was subsequently "cleaned up" and shown at BFI Southwark in 2006. Several small parts of Chapman's *A Liar's Autobiography* contain material cowritten with Adams, including a revised sketch about Genghis Khan. Honestly: Did any of the Pythons *not* write a sketch about Khan?

After *Trees* died, Adams hit a bit of a dry patch; although he pitched ideas about to television and radio, no one was sassing the hoopy frood at the time, and he ended up taking a series of odd jobs to get by. Although he paired with Chapman once again in 1977 to write an episode of *Doctor in the House* (then called *Doctor on the Go*), the two never struck gold as Chapman and Cleese had.

But then Adams hit (the heart of) gold elsewhere: he (and producer Simon Brett, with some eventual material from John Lloyd) pitched the pilot for *The Hitchhiker's Guide to the Galaxy* to BBC Radio 4 . . . and the rest is long and convoluted history that led to a successful weekly radio series in both the United Kingdom and the United States (on NPR, the radio equivalent of PBS). The radio series gave birth to Adams's subsequent series of novels (which, honestly, also fed back into the radio series: it's all rather quantum); the increasingly inaccurately named "Hitchhiker's Trilogy"—*The Hitchhiker's Guide to the Galaxy*; *The Restaurant at the End of the Universe*; *Life, The Universe, and Everything*; *So Long and Thanks for All the Fish*; and *Mostly Harmless* (1979; 1980; 1982; 1984; and 1992)—were huge hits, and not inaccurately described as Pythonesque science fiction. Then came the comic book adaptations, television series, films, and video games. After *Monty Python*, Adams made a name for himself as a prolific—if legendarily tardy—writer.

He had his hand in many projects over the years, including editing and writing for *Doctor Who*; in the "it's about time" category, Cleese appeared in one of Adams's scripted episodes, "City of Death" (1979). Adams was a vocal advocate for technology, atheism, the environment, and video games; in the "it's a small universe" category, Adams's *Starship Titanic* CD-ROM adventure game (1998) was novelized by Jones (1999) after Adams had blown multiple deadlines. His once-speculative science fiction is now reflected in the practical technology of the online translator Babelfish and the instant messaging software Trillian.

Unfortunately for the worlds of science fiction and comedy, Adams suffered a fatal heart attack in 2001. As his concrete and ethereal tombstone declared after his death: "So long and thanks for all the fish."

As a pinch hitter and comic author in his own right, Douglas Adams is formidable. But his contributions to the televised Pythonverse come late, and—through no fault of his own, really—during their nadir (Season Four . . . oh, Season Four!). As the Pythons went on to larger screens and venues, Adams went his own, ultimately science fiction, way. Like George Harrison, Adams shone far brighter apart from the Pythons than when he was a part of them. Is he the Seventh? No. But Forty-Two isn't too shabby.

5: Connie Booth: The Other Cleese

For Python fans, Constance "Connie" Booth is best known for her frequent roles in *Flying Circus* and her appearance as the "witch" in *Monty Python and the Holy Grail*; but Booth contributed far more to the legacy of the Pythons than playing bit roles, cocreating and cowriting *Fawlty Towers* with husband (and later ex-husband), Cleese.

Born in Indianapolis in 1944, Booth moved to New York City to study acting at the American Theater Wing. Soon after, she began a promising acting career, appearing at New York's Shakespeare Festival and at the Bard in San Francisco. Cleese and Booth first met in 1964 when he was performing in the Cambridge Circus while she was working as a waitress at a Third Avenue café. A smitten Cleese kept returning to the café until he worked up the nerve to ask her to see him perform. As the show started, Cleese was doing two of the things he was least adept at: singing and dancing; Booth's initial reaction was one of horror. But once she saw him performing comedy, she quickly warmed and they started dating. After enduring several years of long-distance romance (Cleese was primarily working in England and seeing her on holiday breaks), Booth moved to England and the two finally married in 1968; they had a daughter, Cynthia, in 1971.

Booth first performed (and wrote) alongside Cleese—and future Pythons Chapman and Palin—in *How to Irritate People* (1968), the lesser-known pre-Python David Frost project we discussed earlier. Despite some nascent proto-Python in the acting and themes, the cast was largely disappointed with the way the show turned out. Cleese remarked in *So, Anyway . . .* that he "felt bad that Connie had such a terrible television baptism."

Booth appeared in a half-dozen episodes of *Flying Circus*, as well as *Monty Python's Fliegender Zirkus* and *And Now for Something Completely Different*. Some of her more memorable roles include the particularly perplexed and disappointed "best girl" to Palin's cross-dressing lumberjack, a rather racy Ophelia, and the knocked-out target of a gleeful boxer (Cleese). While she never had the screen time of Cleveland, Booth certainly played the part of glamour stooge with aplomb and confidence. Booth later showed a genuine flair for situation comedy and a penchant for pantomime—while mostly nekkid alongside Cleese—in the Chekhov-inspired short film *Romance with a Double Bass* (1974). Her rather put-upon witch in *Holy Grail* (1974) who locks eyes with the camera and deadpans, "It's a fair cop," voices the shoulder-shrugging inevitability of many caught up in the Pythons' surreal world.

After leaving *Flying Circus*, Cleese and Booth created a writing and acting partnership that produced arguably the best traditional British sitcom of all time. The first season of *Fawlty Towers* (1975) saw Booth cowriting and costarring as Polly Sherman, the set-upon maid at Fawlty Towers, who deplores—yet usually goes along with—the schemes of the hapless and vile proprietor Basil Fawlty (Cleese). Although Booth and Cleese separated in 1976 (ultimately divorcing in 1978), they still worked in relative harmony, producing a second season of *Fawlty Towers* (1979) as hilarious as the first. In *So, Anyway . . .*, Cleese describes his relationship with Booth as tumultuous, but somehow still right.

After *Fawlty Towers*, Booth had notable roles in *84 Charing Cross Road* (1987) and *High Spirits* (1988), and appeared alongside Palin on *American Friends* (1991). She continued to work in television until 2000 when she married *New Yorker* critic John Lahr and largely retired from acting; she currently works as a psychotherapist.

Had she also written for *Flying Circus*, Booth might be considered a solid Seventh Python; as history stands, however, her work on *Fawlty Towers* merely places her among the elite pantheon of brilliant television writers. Merely.

6: Neil Innes: The Bonzo Rutle

Neil James Innes—musician/composer, extra/tasty minstrel, and longtime Python collaborator—has often been referred to as the "Seventh Python," sometimes even by some of the Pythons themselves. Born in 1940, Innes showed an early interest in music, one that was furthered when he met future collaborator Viv Stanshall in high school; both were heavily interested in music from the 1920s and '30s. Later, at Goldsmiths, University of London, he and Stanshall joined forces with Rodney "Rhino" Desborough Slater, Roger Ruskin Spear, and "Legs" Larry Smith; together they formed the revivalist Bonzo Dog Doo-Dah Band.

Words are hard to describe this band: on stage, they seemed to enact live-action versions of Terry Gilliam's surreal animation. Dada, jazz, lounge, blues, psych-pop, and calypso were all part of their makeup. They hit the charts with "I'm the Urban Spaceman" in 1968, and their unorthodox songs caught the attention of more traditional musicians: the Bonzos even appeared (as themselves) in the Beatles' *Magical Mystery Tour* (1967), playing "Death Cab for Cutie" (and yes: the alt-rock band was named after them). The Bonzos released four proper records during the 1960s, as well as an early '70s reunion record (a bit of a contractual obligation, that); the surviving members put out a last record in 2007, *Pour L'Amour des Chiens*.

Innes first worked with two-thirds of the soon-to-be-Pythons (Palin, Jones, Gilliam, and Idle) as one of the Bonzos, who were the house band (and occasional extras) on the proto-Python series *Do Not Adjust Your Set* (1967–1969). On *DNAYS!*, the anarchistic band would usually perform a song along with props, costumes, and general chaos (think a psychedelic—if typically G-rated—version of Gwar).

Soon after, when Jones sought out period-specific music for *Monty Python and the Holy Grail* (1974), Innes wrote and recorded a soundtrack for the film; ultimately, the music didn't "work" comically, and so it was dropped, but Innes remained on the film as a self-punishing monk (thump!), a doomed page (bovine death from above!), and an overly forthright minstrel (cannibalized by peckish knights). With the exception of Gilliam, no one is more abused in the film; a dubious honor, to be sure.

In addition to his pleasant musical collaboration on *Holy Grail*, Innes worked with the Pythons proper (save Cleese) as a writer during the abbreviated fourth season of *Flying Circus*; significantly, Innes cowrote the grossly popular "Most Awful Family in Britain" sketch and played an intentionally awkward guitar version of "The Liberty Bell (March)" to close out the series. Fun fact: other than the original Python Six, only Innes and Douglas Adams have been credited with writing material for the series.

Innes frequently toured with the Pythons afterward, singing and acting (or acting as a singing interstitial). In *Live at City Center* (1976), for example, he performed his Bob Dylan parody "Protest Song." In *Monty Python Live at the Hollywood Bowl* (1982), he performed the oddly affecting "How Sweet to Be an Idiot Song," as well as the Bonzo classic "I'm the Urban Spaceman" (he also milled around in the background for some sketches). Innes also rejoined most of the Pythons at the *Concert for George* (2002) in honor of the late George Harrison. In short, Innes was often with the Pythons throughout the years, if not entirely integrated with the Pythons, as it were.

Of the Pythons, Innes had his closest relationship with the similarly musical Idle, whose parodic sketch show *Rutland Weekend Television Show* (1975–1976) featured Innes in various roles, including that of chief musician. The show mocked low-budget local television while being in fact low-budget television. Although the show was comically spotty and only lasted thirteen episodes, *Rutland* premiered the genius "fab faux" Beatles satire, the Rutles.

Cocreated by Innes and Idle, the Rutles produced "real" albums, appeared on "real" television (*Saturday Night Live*, for example), and were the subject of "real" mockumentaries. The first, *All You Need Is Cash* (1978), paved the way for future mockumentaries like *This Is Spinal Tap* (1984). A parody of Beatlemania, *Cash* is so uncannily canny about the Beatles and the music business that George Harrison, Mick Jagger, and Ron Wood had cameos. Yet while songs from the Pre-Fab Four (Nasty, Stig, Dirk, and Barry . . . all written, composed, and produced by Innes) were intended to be taken as Beatles parodies ("Get Up and Go" is dangerously spot-on), not everyone got the joke; ATV Music—which then held the Beatles' music catalogue—sued, leading to most of the songs by the Rutles now being referred to as "written by Innes/Lennon/McCartney." But for the legal bills, that's a high compliment, if you ask us.

Soon after, in 1979—a few years before the advent of MTV—Innes starred in the BBC series *The Innes Book of Records*, which featured numerous comedic music videos. Ever the pioneer, Innes has continued to tour, work in children's television, form various bands, play Rutles songs, and produce his solo compositions to the present day.

Sadly, Innes and Idle eventually had a falling out over (you guessed it) money. According to a 2005 article in the *Chicago Tribune*, the two first sparred over the second Rutles film (Idle called Innes "determined to be a failure," while the more politic Innes said that "if people want to be possessive and don't want to share their toys in the sandpit, I couldn't care less") and then over *Spamalot*, which uses the music that Innes wrote for two songs. Innes was never paid for the rights and was subsequently left out of the Monty Python reunion tour in 2014.

Is Innes a Python? Honestly, the man had a documentary called *The Seventh Python* (2008) devoted to his career and everything. However— according to legend—Innes and

What's All This, Then?
Honorary Pre-Python

Humphrey Barclay started as a performer in Footlights at around the same time as Cleese. He later became a key ingredient in the Python creative recipe, directing 1963's Cambridge Circus revue (with Chapman and Cleese), producing *I'm Sorry, I'll Read That Again* and *The Complete and Utter History of Britain*, crafting the creative team for *Do Not Adjust Your Set*, and bringing in a goofy-looking American animator named Gilliam (introduced to Barclay by Idle) for *We Have Ways of Making You Laugh*. Barclay also produced the various *Doctor . . .* series and thought that the episode written by Cleese could be a series itself; Barclay appeared prescient when in 1975 Cleese did just that with *Fawlty Towers*. Incredibly, after all that, Barclay somehow *wasn't* involved with *Monty Python's Flying Circus*.

Cleveland were once asked during a radio interview which had the better claim to be the Seventh Python; when Cleveland suggested that the honor should fall to her, Innes rather gallantly stepped aside . . . or at least remained nobly silent. So, while Innes was often a close, if sometimes sporadic, Python collaborator, he will probably be best remembered as a quarter of the Rutles . . . truly a "legend that would last a lunchtime."

7: Carol Cleveland: *The* Glamour Stooge

In the years before *Flying Circus*, every sketch comedy on the BBC—shows dominated by white male Oxbridge performers—seemed required to have a "token" actress, a regular female for the boys to react to/with. The pre-Python / post-Frost shows were no exception: *I'm Sorry, I'll Read That Again* had Jo Kendall; *At Last the 1948 Show* had the lovely Aimi MacDonald; *DNAYS!* had Denise Coffey. Make no mistake: some of these women were comediennes in their own right, as accomplished on stage as the blokes beside them. But they were, at the time, generally seen as comic appendages: what the Brits then called "crumpets." Into this conventional role—a requisite of the BBC for *Flying Circus*—came Carol Cleveland. But like the Pythons themselves, Cleveland turned convention on its ear and ultimately made the role her own: she even coined the term "glamour stooge" to describe herself. She's been comically enchanting Python fans ever since.

Born in London in 1942, Carol Gillian Frances Spreckley (later Cleveland: "she whose tracts of land exhibit great cleavage") moved to San Antonio, Texas, in her youth as an Air Force brat and attended high school in Pasadena, California. Modeling alongside her mother as a baby, Cleveland won various "Miss" pageant titles in her teens. She returned to London in 1960, studied at the Royal Academy of Dramatic Art (RADA) on a grant, tried life as a Playboy Bunny ("Didi"), and then hit the stage and screen. Before joining *Flying Circus*, Cleveland landed "serious" (albeit typically singular) roles on various cultish British television shows, including *The Saint* (1963–1965), *The Avengers* (1966), and *Randall & Hopkirk (Deceased)* (1969). She also cut her comic teeth with Spike Milligan, Roy Hudd, and the Two Ronnies. With her established comic résumé—and obvious assets—in mind, she was cast for the first four episodes of *Flying Circus* by the show's original producer (John Howard Davies).

In her first on-air role (one of the first recorded for the series), Cleveland plays the silent but ravishing Deirdre Pewtey—wife of Palin's milquetoast Arthur Pewtey (suspected and subsequently confirmed cuckold) in the

"Marriage Guidance Counsellor" sketch. And she certainly is glamorous: "a beautiful buxom wench in the full bloom of her young womanhood" as the script notes heralding her first appearance state ("37-25-37," as her own website notes). Idle—as the counselor utterly enchanted by Cleveland—describes her in rapt detail during the sketch, voicing what many a young lad in the audience was thinking at the time. Ahem.

Her pantomime reactions and general "stage presence" are in full effect early on, especially when there weren't many actual lines for her to voice. She stars—alongside Palin—in the silent-film sketch "Seduced Milkmen" (Episode 3): Palin's the milkman; she's the seductress whose "come hither" body language serves as a perfect counterpoint to his nebbishy shyness. Cleveland also gets to play against expectation in the "Erotic Film" sketch (Episode 5) opposite the cinemaphiliac Jones, who ignores the terribly attractive woman pouting on his bed: "Oh Bevis, are you going to *do* anything or are you just going to show me films all evening?" As Jones's bride in "Buying a Mattress" (Episode 8), Cleveland gets her first go at the (already running) "It's my only line!" gag.

By this point, she's clearly a favorite among the Pythons, who—as Palin has admitted—weren't terribly adept at writing roles for "real" women; still, after the first few episodes they started writing roles with her in mind. Jones considered her a seventh Python, while Cleese and Palin were both impressed by her professionalism and eagerness to give just about anything a go.

Although Ian MacNaughton often brought in new girls for *Flying Circus*, the Python Six had a vocal preference for Cleveland, upon whom they knew they could rely. Simply put, "Carol Cleavage" was far more than a crumpet: she was naturally Pythonesque.

Cleveland garnered the lioness's share of glamour stooge roles on the series, appearing in two-thirds of the episodes over four seasons; along the way, she has played: an unfaithful wife, a seductress with a penchant for milkmen, a milkmaid, nurses, stewardesses, a French au pair, a newlywed in search of a mattress, a selection of royal ladies, various receptionists and secretaries, a hippie, maids of all sorts, a "very-silly looney," a masculine-voiced strip-tease politician, mothers, daughters, pretty girls, waitresses, a pantomime-horse lover, Antoinette (soon-to-be) Montgolfier, a BBC announcer, a showgirl, a customer with a flamethrower, and a woman dancing on a table (this last to ring out the very last sketch of the series . . . forever). It's a reasonable range, really, rather wider than the cross-dressing lads with their narrow repertoire of Pepperpots and grannies.

On stage, the Pythons capitalized upon Cleveland's inherent sexuality—and the welcome absence of BBC censors—by offering her unrestrained retorts that twisted, in some ways, the expectations of audiences who had memorized every line of *Flying Circus*. She appeared with the Python Six in *Monty Python's First Farewell Tour* (1973) and she's been touring with them ever since. In *Live at the Hollywood Bowl* (1980), for example, her deadpan (and ad-libbed) secretarial query, "Or are you here for a blow job?" in the "Bounder of Adventure" sketch caught audiences—and the inquisitive Tourist (Idle)—by surprise, lending a saucy freshness to her staged appearances.

Having played a reasonably wide variety of roles on *Flying Circus* and on stage, Cleveland was approached with a particularly "tricky" role for *Holy Grail*, a part that the boys—according to Cleveland—thought she "might have to work at a bit": a nineteen-year-old virgin. As she mischievously notes in the on-set documentary *The Making of Monty Python and the Holy Grail*: "Maybe I pulled off half of it—don't ask me which half." Clearly, the lads found their match in Cleveland. Her turn as the alluring and metatheatrically inclined twin caretakers of Castle Anthrax—Zoot and Dingo—is remarkably controlled and understated, enabling her final, exasperated "Shit!" to really pull a laugh.

In addition to the twins Zoot and Dingo in *Holy Grail*, Cleveland has appeared on the big screen as Mrs. Gregory ("What's so special about the cheesemakers?") in *Life of Brian*; and as a Beefeater Waitress ("Have a nice fuck!"), a Rich Restaurant-goer ("We have a train to catch . . . and I don't want to start bleeding over the seats") and a Heavenly Hotel Receptionist ("Happy Christmas!") in *The Meaning of Life*.

Even after the Pythons (essentially) called it quits, Cleveland could be counted on to keep the name alive: she's been interviewed repeatedly about her role as the "female Python," hosted the thirtieth anniversary "Long Live the Dead Parrot" BBC radio special (1999), and performed—along with Cleese, Jones, Palin, and Gilliam—as part of the four-hour "Python Night" on BBC TV (1999); she pouted as the "best girl" to Palin's Lumberjack in the *Concert for George* (2002) and appeared in *Not the Messiah (He's a Very Naughty Boy)* (2009). Cleveland—like the surviving members of the Python Six—voiced several characters in the Chapman biopic, *A Liar's Autobiography* (2012), and was honored with one of Chapman's former roles—Mrs. Bun in the "Spam" sketch—during the *Monty Python Live (Mostly)* reunion shows (2014).

Outside of the Pythonverse, Cleveland has appeared in film, stage, and radio; she's also starred in her own one-woman show, *Carol Cleveland Reveals All* (1994), and presented dramatic readings of her parents' WWII diary—titled *War Baby*—on stage and radio (2007 and 2013). But as her memoir—*Pom Poms Up!: From Puberty to Python and Beyond* (2014)—points out, Monty Python has been, at times, "a bit of a ball and chain" in the sense that casting directors forget she can play anything but a glamour stooge.

In short, Carol Cleveland has been with the Pythons since their *Flying Circus* days, has joined them on stage and screen throughout the lands, has unflaggingly promoted Python during the lean years, and has, more than anyone else on this list, evidenced a natural affinity for the boys' particular brand of lunacy. She deserves—in the eyes of this august tribunal—to be upgraded from "glamour stooge" to official "Seventh Python." Congratulations, Carol.

PS: The fact that she helped put two-thirds of the current tribunal through puberty has NOTHING to do with our decision to include her here. Ahem.

24

After Python

The Influencers and Referencers

Not surprisingly for a creative garbage type like him—see "The Architects' Sketch," *Flying Circus* Episode 17, or don't, not really our business (bloody masonic handshakes)—Cleese is often asked how to get started as a comedy writer. In *So, Anyway . . .* , he presents a real cracker of an idea: outright theft: "Steal an idea that you know is good, and try to reproduce it in a setting that you know and understand." Genius!

Fortunately for anybody who came along after the Pythons and wanted to riff on their material, Cleese laid that idea right out there for them. What's fascinating, though, is how few comedians *have* stolen from the Pythons over the years. That fact becomes even more amazing when one considers just how many comedians and other artists cite exposure to the Pythons' work as a formative experience somewhat akin to Saul getting knocked off his horse on the road to Damascus.

The Python effect runs so deep now, getting on to a half century after John Sousa first blared over Gilliam's animation, that it's as threaded into the DNA of modern comedy as the Marx Brothers, Eddie Murphy's *Delirious*, *Seinfeld*, Del Close, Lucille Ball, or "Who's on First?" David Sims wrote in *The Atlantic* that:

> Showing *Holy Grail* to a young comedy fan now can almost be like showing *Casablanca* to someone who watches a lot of Hollywood dramas—it's like seeing the template for success; one that's been repeated, tweaked, challenged and paid homage to over and over again.

Python was of course a hit in its native land, and its sketches and songs remain very much a part of the British lingua franca. Feed the first line or two of "Always Look on the Bright Side of Life" to the average crowd on pub quiz night and you will likely get the rest of the song belted back at you with enough gusto that the whistling chorus will feel like a stiff breeze. *Flying Circus* and the albums and live shows that followed were new and developed cult followings with ease. But they also built on established traditions like *The Goon Show* and *Beyond the Fringe* and so were seen as part of a continuum.

Over in the States, Python was always a more acquired taste, even at their height. But it was likely that sense of surprise that made their impact on American comics so explosive. The wickedly funny combination of tight and economical writing (honed by so many years in the David Frost factory) and an expansively surrealist willingness to chop sketches off in the middle or just before the punch line or leaving off the punch line entirely, set against the troupe's nose-thumbing intellectualism, resulted in something that the American comedy establishment hadn't quite seen before. Python was funny as hell, of course, but it was their *daring* that almost made the bigger impact.

When *Flying Circus* and *Holy Grail* started making the rounds in the mid-1970s (see Chapter 12 for the full-ish story there) alternative American humor was primarily defined by institutions like *National Lampoon* and comics and writers like Lenny Bruce and Harvey Kurtzman. They all broke with the style of earlier generations; the shorthand way to think of this transition is to contrast the cliché of some Borscht Belt ba-dump-dump joke-slinger in a dinner jacket with a mumbly and insecure confessional "comic" storyteller bumming people out in some Greenwich Village basement club. But the new comics didn't play with the form as much as one would think. Even when breaking taboos on language or nudity, or taking on controversial political content, alternative American comedy still worked in much the same idiom as before. Now they just took on the establishment vociferously and directly.

Monty Python, on the other hand, took a more circuitous route to its satire. In fact, its members usually denied they were even being satirical at all, just "silly." Python's obvious political content might have been relegated to the occasional Enoch Powell reference. But their subversion in terms of structure and content was far deeper and more destabilizing than anything coming out of the *Lampoon* / *Saturday Night Live* combine, whose satire was all too easily absorbed right back into the mainstream it supposedly stood apart from.

In part for being so new and boundary-shattering, when Python hit America, the response from certain quarters was near electric. Even before *Flying Circus* hit the PBS circuit, Python's albums had acquired a certain cultish status among the traveling circus of comics and rock stars who would populate the early years of *Saturday Night Live*.

When that show, produced by Python fan Lorne Michaels, first hit the airwaves in October, just months after the premiere of *Holy Grail* (Chevy Chase was hired after Michaels watched him crack wise while they were in line for a midnight screening), the Pythons' influence could be seen in its mix of skits with filmed inserts before a live audience and a certain willingness to let chaos reign. Several cast members were great fans, though many were probably disappointed when Idle (who first hosted in 1976) told them

April 24, 1976: Lorne Michaels offers the Beatles a cool $3,000 if they'll reunite on *Saturday Night Live*. He got the Rutles.   *NBC/Photofest*

that in fact the Pythons' writing sessions had a clock-punching discipline: morning shift, lunch, afternoon shift, be done at six.

Oddly, as Zack Handlen points out in *If You Like Monty Python . . .* , one of the few true heirs to the Python legacy during the 1970s could actually be 1977's *The Kentucky Fried Movie*. This idea seems a stretch at first, as John Landis's influences pulled less from Oxbridge and more from the exploitation / B-movie side of things. But the chaotic (and even punk rock, as Nicholas Rombes argued in *A Cultural Dictionary of Punk: 1974–1982*) attitude of this rackety assemblage of sketches and spoofs cares as little for overt logic or bothering with punch lines than the average *Flying Circus* sketch.

KFM writers David Zucker and Jim Abraham later turned their sensibility to more lucrative fourth-wall-breaking spoofs like *Airplane!* and *The Naked Gun*. It might be difficult to imagine those films existing without Python, but their high yuk-yuk factor keeps them from existing in quite the same comedic universe.

Today's comedy occasionally skews more surrealist. But even though the out-there likes of *Broad City*, *Flight of the Conchords*, or various Adam McKay films (*Anchorman*, in particular) push the boundaries of reality or cause-and-effect narrative, they never quite do away with them entirely.

The irony is that for all the comedians who express a deep love for Python, precious few have followed in their footsteps. In *The Pythons*, Cleese called out the irony of this "immediate reverse effect" in which the Pythons loomed so large that comics would intentionally steer away from anything that seemed too derivative. "This is a paradox," Cleese said, "and I don't understand it."

Another reason for the lack of direct heirs to the Python throne is logistics: There just aren't that many bands of talented and complementary writer-performers out there who could bring the necessary battery of skills to bear. Most groups working in the comedy mines these days tend to be loose improv troupes like the Groundlings or Upright Citizens Brigade who are more tied to a founding sensibility than the Pythons' rock band–like unit. The closest analogy to the Pythons would likely be the Kids in the Hall. Kevin McDonald admitted to *Entertainment Weekly* that they, at least subconsciously, had stolen from Python: "We tried not to, but what can you do? It's like how every rock group sounds like the Beatles."

No matter how hard the Pythons tried, from the guerrilla culture-jamming of *Flying Circus* to the mordant Buñuel-esque bleakness of *The Meaning of Life*, they were never able to kill the punch line.

The Other, Reference-y Bits

In which we look at the ways that Python fans have signaled their admiration over the years.

Freaks and Geeks

Judd Apatow's one-season 1999–2000 series *Freaks and Geeks* is a Rosetta stone for understanding modern American comedy, in part because so many of its alumni went on to basically redefine the form; stars like Seth Rogen, Jason Segal, Martin Starr, and James Franco to writers and directors Paul Feig, Jake Kasdan, Miguel Arteta, and Mike White. But the Apatow outsider comic sensibility that later spread through Hollywood also showed its hand here in terms of critical influences.

Set in a Michigan suburb in 1980, the show centered on an outcast bunch of kids who did what they could to find succor and community in

Freaks and Geeks (left to right) Martin Starr, John Francis Daley, and Samm Levine; an important part of *Monty Python and the Holy Grail*'s core audience.   *NBC/Photofest*

those who shared similar tastes, or at least a dislike of what mainstream culture was pitching at them.

In the show's final episode, "Discos and Dungeons," the trio of nerdy stars have a plan for the night of their school's homecoming dance: a local theater is showing *Monty Python and the Holy Grail*. They're going to see it. *Twice.* When the understanding but concerned mother of Sam, the runtiest of the three, asks if he wouldn't rather go to the dance, he is just confused: "No. Why would I do that?"

Later in the episode, when Sam complains about all the years that he's going to go through life as an outcast geek before things will get better for him, the teacher in charge of the school's A/V club hands him a film canister with a 16mm print of *Holy Grail*. You might be a nerd now and life is going to be rough, the teacher is saying, but *this* will help you get through the tough years.

Game of Thrones

Although the HBO adaptation of George R. R. Martin's epic *Game of Thrones* novels is set in a fantasy world where dragons occasionally darken the sky and dead people sometimes get a yearning to stay less dead, it does take pride in staying true to a certain kind of pseudo-medieval verisimilitude. Yes, there's gleaming armor and castles and lords and grand battles, but none of it comes without blood, mud, pestilence, and cynical power-grabbing. In that sense, it's not terribly surprising that at some point they would get around to referencing Monty Python.

In "Breaker of Chains," Episode 3 of Season Four, the Champion of Meereen (it's a long story) barks a long string of insults at blond dragon-mastering Daenerys Targaryen that nobody without a doctorate in Low Valyrian would be able to decipher. It turned out later that the champ was giving her the business in the manner of the French taunter from *Monty Python and the Holy Grail*. He started with "Your mother was a hamster" and proceeded from there.

Only a few dedicated fans noticed at first, but later the show's creator eventually acknowledged that the reference was slipped in there by David Peterson, the linguist in charge of crafting the show's entirely made-up languages that nevertheless correspond to an entirely authentic grammatical structure in the same manner as Tolkien's various Elvish dialects.

Ready Player One

Ernest Cline's 2011 novel is a dystopian action-adventure epic about Wade, a young gamer fighting to win a contest to control OASIS, the virtual gaming universe that almost everybody in the crumbling world of the future spends most of their time in. To succeed, he must navigate a web of clues left by the game's late programmer, who was an obsessive fan of the pop and geek culture he mainlined during a prototypical 1970s and '80s suburban childhood. In between understanding all the references to Rush, *The Last Starfighter*, and obscure anime series, Wade must also prove his knowledge by literally performing his way through geek classics like *WarGames*. Spoiler Alert: At one point near the climax, he can only proceed by acting out every gesture and line of dialogue as performed by Chapman's Arthur King in *Monty Python and the Holy Grail*, a movie Wade fortunately happens to have seen well over a hundred times. As any self-respecting geek most certainly has. (Ni!)

Nixon or Python?

To celebrate the fortieth anniversary of Richard Nixon's resignation, on December 31, 2014, the *Washington Post* published a quiz: "Did Richard Nixon Actually Say That?" Question #2 was "Who said this, Richard Nixon or a character on *Monty Python's Flying Circus*?":

> You ever see what happened, you know what happened to the Greeks. Homosexuality destroyed them. Sure, Aristotle was a homo, we all know that, so was Socrates.

The answer, as you could probably guess, was Tricky Dick himself, just chatting in the Oval Office with a couple of his Watergate coconspirators (Haldeman and Ehrlichman) about Greek philosophers and the supposed civilization-destroying threat that was homosexuality. One does wonder what the Pythons could have done with that scenario.

Monty's Boffins

It's no secret that nerds love Monty Python. Maybe it has something to do with their predilection for singsongy, punning, and reference-laden humor that once upon a time skewed toward the likes of They Might Be Giants, the Dead Milkmen, Weird Al Yankovic, and Dr. Demento. In any case, the fondness of the tech community (i.e., grown-up nerds) for Python is revealed in a couple quirks of nomenclature. Guido van Rossum named his programming language Python for the group—talks at Python conferences are sometimes called "The Spanish Inquisition."

A slightly more obscure tech-world Pythonism is the likelihood that referring to junk e-mail as "spam" is a tip of the hat to the "Spam Sketch." That reportedly happened after users of early Internet formats like chat rooms and bullet boards started referring to irritating postings and repeatedly unwanted messages as "spam" after the Python sketch's usage of the word in rapid-fire repetition.

25

Spamalot!

The Pythons Go to Broadway . . . and a Long Line for the Restroom Ensues!

he year: 2005.

The place: The men's loo in the Shubert Theater, NYC.

The quote: "Look: there's a penguin on the urinal!"

(Or so one of your authors recalls. It was a weird night.)

So how did we get here? To a time when pissing ruffians can misquote Python at the will-calls and bathroom stalls of a Broadway theater?

How? Well . . . I'll tell you . . .

In the Beginning

It all started when a young man had a dream: to make money. Lots and lots of money. This is not an unusual story, but it is one that—statistically speaking—oft ends as it begins: with a lad dreaming of money. But this particular lad was Idle, and if there's one thing Eric "The Greedy Bastard" Idle knows, it's how to pursue mon . . . his dreams.

Teaming up with his longtime friend and musical collaborator, John Du Prez, Idle saw an opportunity to take his love of money, British panto, and Python to the American stage . . . by taking Arthur and his Knights of the Round Table to a place they had turned their backs on back in 1974: Camelot! (It's only a model. . . .) In the elevator-pitch patter of Hollywood, *Spamalot* is "the musical *Camelot* meets *Monty Python and the Holy Grail*": cha-ching!

It'll be a collector's item someday! *Courtesy of Playbill*

The sketch-y plot of *Spamalot*—if not the WTF? ending—remains in step with *Holy Grail*: Arthur and his coconut-clattering sidekick, Patsy, roam the lengths and breadths of the land seeking knights to join in their quasi-medieval quest. Along the away, they encounter God, French taunters, self-abusive monks, not-yet-dead serfs, overly accurate minstrelsy, knights who say "Ni!," a soon-limbless Black Knight, constitutional peasants, and a killer rabbit. But other bits of non-*Grail* Python lore sneak onto stage as well: a Finland travel ad (from their *Contractual Obligation Album*); the fish-slapping dance (from *Flying Circus*); and two utterly un-ironic choruses of "Always Look on the Bright Side of Life" (from *Life of Brian*).

On top of all this Pythonic *mishegoss*, Arthur and company meet the Lady of the Lake (and her aptly named Laker Girls), sing about theater production and the uneven allocation of stage time vis-à-vis star power, seek out the support of theater-savvy Jews, stage a Broadway show, come out of the closet, happily embrace a Vegas-style Camelot (complete with musical numbers, oversize gambling props, and showgirls), and eventually get married: the official "grail" of every comedy since Aristotle was a lad.

In keeping with the general Python brand, *Spamalot* is predictably meta-theatrical: it's a Broadway musical that recognizes it is a Broadway musical. But it's also a lighthearted romp through a decidedly optimistic Middle Ages, that—rather than avoid the silly idealism of Camelot and *Camelot* as *Monty Python and the Holy Grail* did—embraces it. In other words: not much room for Jones-style medieval verisimilitude. What's truly surprising is that Idle builds an entire musical around a crappy musical number that once proved Monty Python hates musicals. Well, that Monty Python circa 1974 hated musicals. Okay, fine: *Monty Python and the Holy Grail* hated musicals. Don't believe us? Witness:

- Arthur—Dourly dismisses the silly Camelot-inspired choral knights at Camelot: "On second thought, let's not go to Camelot: 'tis a silly place."
- Musician Neil Innes (off-screen)—Wrote a whole score for *Holy Grail* that never got used!
- Musician Neil Innes (onscreen)—Rabbit-bashed and cow-crushed!
- Prince Herbert of Swamp Castle—Whose father cuts him off every time the music swells.
- King Brian of the Wild—Delights in the killing of "close harmony groups"; granted, the scene was never shot, but check out *Monty Python and the Holy Grail (Book)* for all the gory details. Look at the *bones*, man!
- Minstrel Cannibalism!!!—"In the frozen land of Nador, they were forced to eat Robin's minstrels . . . and there was much rejoicing. Yay."

Tastes like killer rabbit. *Lisa Bocchini*

That's hate speech, that is. Yet there they are, thirty years later, "a bunch of British knights / prancing 'round in woolly tights," singing up a storm, dancing with chorus girls, still chasing after that damned grail.

Given such a dramatic tonal shift from the immediate source material, it's a wonder the other Pythons ever permitted this cheery domesticated version of their earlier angry avant-garde film effort to appear on Broadway. As Idle admitted in a 2005 *New York* magazine profile, "The history of post-Python projects has been like middle-aged courtship, fraught with frustration, Byzantine negotiations, hot flashes, disappointing flurries of enthusiasm usually ending in stalemate, and droopy disappointment."

Yet (per Idle), the surviving Pythons reacted to his proposed project with an almost universal enthusiasm ("loved it," "overjoyed," "a jolly good project," "pretty spiffing"); and "not only did they like it, they wanted to help!" Idle cites Gilliam as being particularly "tempted to get involved with the design" of the sets ("I think the sets should be based on the medieval illustrated manuscript artwork I used for the animations [in *Holy Grail*]") before he admitted the danger of getting too involved in Eric's project while working on his own film projects.

Of course, other sources suggest that not all the Pythons were exactly thrilled with Idle's staged resurrection of their earlier cinematic endeavor.

Cleese seemed the most on board, even early on, and prerecorded the voice of God for the show. Palin—ever the mediator—took the middle road: "It's not 'Python' as we would have written it. But then, none of us would get together and write a 'Python' stage show." Gilliam—contrary to Idle's recollection—considered the *Spamalot* project nothing more than "Python-lite" but acknowledged that it was futile to try to stop something "with a life of its own." The "blessed and venerable Jonesy" (as Idle calls him) was the most vocally dismissive, yet after seeing the show, he changed his mind, admitting on a local New York radio show that *Spamalot* "was terrific good fun," even while pointing out "it isn't really Python. It is very much Eric . . . the best parts of the musical are the new things." Chapman, ever the recluse, refused to comment.

In retrospect, Jones is right: while nostalgia for Python may have drawn audiences to the theater initially, the new musical numbers—which effectively poke fun at the artifice of Broadway itself—are what made *Spamalot* a lasting success. The "Diva's Lament (Whatever Happened to My Part?)" pulls back the curtain on stage performance and actor anxiety; "The Song That Goes Like This" goes exactly like, uhm, "this," riffing on predictable

What's All This, Then?
John "Trevor Jones" Du Prez

While perhaps not the "Seventh Python," John Du Prez certainly deserves the title of the "Eighth-Measure Python" or at least the "Second Idle." Du Prez—an award-winning musician, composer, and conductor—began his musical career as a member of the Top 40 British pop band Modern Romance, joined the Music Department at London University, and composed a score of film scores that include three *Teenage Mutant Ninja Turtles* films (that's three more than Elmer Bernstein, the overrated hack) and the Weird Al masterpiece *UHF*. He has been working with Idle for years, arranging the music for (most of) *Spamalot* and the original "Galaxy Song."

On the Python side of things, Du Prez composed or arranged music for *Life of Brian* (1979), Gilliam's *Time Bandits* (1981), *The Meaning of Life* (1983), Palin's *A Private Function* (1984), Cleese's *A Fish Called Wanda* (1988), and Idle's *Not the Messiah (He's a Very Naughty Boy)* (2010). He was also the conductor for *Live at the Hollywood Bowl* (1982), *Not the Messiah* (2010), and *Monty Python Live (Mostly)* (2014).

Not bad for a man living his life under an alias.

Andrew Lloyd Webber stage duets (doing so twice, really, by returning as "Twice in Every Show" in Act II); "I'm All Alone" draws attention to otherwise "invisible" stock characters on stage; and "You Won't Succeed on Broadway" just opens up all sorts of metatheatrical self-reflection as the show that puts on a show realizes it has always been, in fact, a show.

A Formal Function

In short, Idle and Du Prez are terribly clever, folks: they're just not as angry as the Pythons were back when they filmed *Holy Grail*. And it would have been foolish to try to replicate 1970s Python on 2000s Broadway anyway. Monty Python flourished within a 1960s counterculture that saw a world controlled by a hierarchical class-based system, a world normalized by a medium (television) that promulgated simple assumptions and biases while trivializing serious thought and discussion.

Marcia Landy posits that as a product of Oxbridge wise guys, *Flying Circus* was "acutely conscious of television as perpetrator of misinformation." Although the individual Pythons held diverse theoretical approaches to comedy, they all had one thing in common: a complete and utter disrespect for the conventions of genre television. Cleese, for example, had vocally grown "tired of formats" on television, while Gilliam always thought that a driving impulse behind Python's comedy was to get rid of punch lines. *Flying Circus*—a television show, mind you—recognized the inherent silliness of television shows and exposed their conventions as absurd.

Given the Pythons' deft subversion of television and film genres, it is no wonder that the stage musical *Spamalot* would play with theater conventions. Idle and Du Prez knew that some televisual or filmic conventions could be translated to the stage (the "Finland" travelogue that begins the show, for example). But they also realized that Broadway had its own conventions and visual codes. To create a truly Pythonesque Broadway production, they would need to violate and remix those conventions as readily as Python had done to television or film earlier.

In addition to the many self-reflexive song lyrics, Arthur and the Lady of the Lake draw audiences back to "reality," breaking the fourth wall or encouraging characters on stage to reevaluate their existence as characters on stage: "Have a drink and a pee, we'll be back for Act Three . . . ," "What a dark and extremely expensive forest!," and so on.

So rather than rail angrily against the establishment as Monty Python was wont to do in their heyday, *Spamalot* is content to—very effectively—nudge-nudge-wink-wink its way to pointing out Broadway's foibles and conventions. It is, on the whole, a far less dour affair than *Monty Python and the Holy Grail*: no one plays it "straight," no one wallows in filth, and no one has to suffer through Scottish weather in sopping wet armor.

Performance

Of course, this time around the Pythons aren't there to wear the woolen chainmail. "Real" actors—some who could even sing!—were brought on board: Tim "Dr. Frank-N-Furter" Curry as Arthur; Sara "Dr. Callie Torres" Ramirez as the Lady of the Lake; David Hyde "Dr. Niles Crane" Pierce as Sir Robin; Hank "Dr. Nick Riviera" ("Hi, everybody!") Azaria as Lancelot . . . a lotta doctors, really. And a lotta "real theater" actors as well, including Michael McGrath as Patsy, Christopher Sieber as Galahad, Steve Rosen as Bedevere, and Christian Borle as Not Dead Fred / the Historian. As you may have noticed, there's a real live woman in the cast! And she steals the show. Naturally.

Under the able direction of Mike Nichols—who was acing improv comedy back when the Pythons were still taking their A-levels, or O-levels, or whatever the hell test the Brits take at university—*Spamalot* is performed as silly, camp, and more parodic than satiric. There is no straitlaced Chapman leading the way through the madness: Curry's King Arthur is every bit as prone to double takes and over-the-top vamping as the rest of the cast. There are puns. Topical humor. And—horrors!—the cast sometimes stops to explain a joke to the audience. It is not, as Palin notes, something the Pythons would have written.

And yet, it works. It really works. And it sold. Oh, how it sold.

Spamalot premiered at Chicago's Shubert Theatre in December 2004, and opened at New York's Shubert Theatre (former home to *A Chorus Line* and *Chicago*) in February 2005. The five surviving Pythons attended the Broadway premiere and came on stage to end the show with a chorus of "Always Look on the Bright Side of Life." *Spamalot* ran through January 2009, pulling up stakes after over 1,500 performances, having taken in an estimated $175 million at the box office. The Broadway show was a critical favorite as well, gathering rave reviews and accolades; *Spamalot* was nominated for fourteen Tony Awards, winning three: Best Performance by a Featured Actress in a Musical (Sara Ramirez), Best Direction of a Musical (Nichols), and Best Musical. Idle won two Drama Desk Awards for the show that year: Outstanding New Musical and Outstanding Lyrics, while

What's All This, Then?
A Brief History of Coconuts

While the origins of *Holy Grail*'s conflation of coconuts and horses origi-
nated in penury and BBC Radio, the sheer numbers of coconut "events"
brought on by the Pythons is impressive. Herewith a short history:

- April 1975—At the hotly anticipated New York premiere of *Monty Python and the Holy Grail*, the Pythons distributed a thousand coconuts to fans stretching around the block.
- June 1975—Jones and Chapman gave out a mere five hundred coconuts at the opening of the *Holy Grail* in Chicago.
- March 2006—In honor of *Spamalot*'s first anniversary on Broadway, 1,789 fans—led by the New York cast—set the Guinness World Record for "Largest Coconut Orchestra," knocking out their version of "Always Look on the Bright Side of Life" in the Shubert Alley outside the theater.
- April 2007—A year later, Jones and Gilliam (alongside the London cast of *Spamalot*) lead 4,382 fans in Trafalgar Square, London; their rendition of "Always Look on the Bright Side of Life" utterly crushes the previous record.

Du Prez and Idle won a Grammy for Best Broadway recording of the cast album in 2005. The original West End cast was also nominated for seven Laurence Olivier Awards, although sadly, their particular Grail-quest came up empty. Still, by most measures of musical theater, *Spamalot* has been a roaring success.

Spamalot has enjoyed multiple U.S. tours, a repeat run on London's West End (2006–2008 and 2012–2014), and worldwide productions from 'stralia to 'Zealand (with alphabetic stops at Belgium, Canada, the Czech Republic, France, Germany, Hungary, Ireland, Italy, Japan, the Netherlands, Poland, South Korea, Spain, Sweden, and the United Kingdom). It even had a *highly* metatheatrical run at the Grail Theater in Las Vegas (2007–2008, with over five hundred shortened ninety-minute performances in fifteen months). From July 31 to August 2, 2015, Idle returned to the Hollywood Bowl—thirty-three years after he and his fellow Pythons first conquered America—with an all-new all-star cast (including Craig Robinson as Arthur, Merle Dandridge as the Lady of the Lake, Warwick Davis as Patsy, and Christian Slater as Lancelot). As history has proven, whether served in a can or on stage, *Spamalot* lasts forever.

Michael McGrath and Tim Curry make Broadway into a very, *very* silly place.

Joan Marcus

Every iteration of *Spamalot* adds its own spin to the proceedings, with updated topical humor, stunt casting, and altered staging. The original Broadway shows, for example, "starred" Cleese as the voice of God (prerecorded); in the London productions (2013–2014), a string of famous English celebrities appeared in the role via "visual recording" . . . including Palin and Idle. Due to time constraints, the Vegas shows cut entire numbers ("All for One") and shortened others ("Run Away"). In Europe, jokes about Jews and the New York theater scene simply didn't translate, so "You Won't Succeed on Broadway" is often changed to "You Won't Succeed in Showbiz" and the lyrics altered significantly. The Hollywood Bowl shows added a scattering of showbiz-attuned jokes ("Oh yeah? Well I'm Lady Gaga!") during their brief summer fling. Even the original Broadway show updated itself after Ramirez won her Tony. A previous line in "The Diva's Lament" went: "I've no Grammy, no rewards / I've no Tony awards"; this was soon changed to "My Tony awards / won't keep me out of Betty Ford's." When Ramirez left the show, the new Lady of the Lake (Lauren Kennedy) sang, "My predecessor won awards / and now she's in Betty Ford's." And so it goes.

These many staged alterations speak to the continued adaptability of *Spamalot*, of *Holy Grail*, and of Arthurian legend in general. The "Once and Future King" rises and falls, rearranges and runs away, only to reappear in time of greatest need. Or when Cleese gets his next divorce. In three . . . two . . .

The Messiah Ariseth! Again!!

Like any would-be theatrical magnate looking for another big score—a parallel could be drawn here with Mel Brooks, who had a massive hit with the stage adaptation of *The Producers* and had substantially less success with his follow-up musical of *Young Frankenstein*—after *Spamalot*, Idle zeroed in next on the next-most-popular film in the Python canon after *Holy Grail*: *Life of Brian*.

(That's true at least in the United States; *Life of Brian* has a much stronger fan base in the United Kingdom. This could be due to differing attitudes on religion. As Idle said about the *Life of Brian* controversy in the documentary *Almost the Truth*, he discovered that the United States exhibited a level of "fanaticism" about religion that was quite surprising to him.)

Idle's concept for the *Life of Brian* musical went through several drafts over the course of nine months. But in 2005, any work was summarily cut off

It's only a model . . . *Lisa Bocchini*

after what Idle called an "unexpected and unanticipated" veto by one of the other Pythons.

Commissioned by Toronto's Luminato Festival and the Toronto Symphony Orchestra, *Not the Messiah (He's a Very Naughty Boy)* premiered in June 2007. Featuring a libretto by Idle and music by Du Prez, it was conducted by Toronto Symphony Orchestra music director and Idle's cousin Peter Oundjian. The show was later performed at several festivals, as well as Carnegie Hall in New York, the Sydney Opera House, and the Hollywood Bowl.

The five-part oratorio takes the guts of the film and reshapes them musically as a parody of Handel's *Messiah*. Idle and Du Prez didn't limit themselves, of course. The story of the somewhat witless Brian's accidental and unwilling transformation into a religious leader is there. But, not surprisingly, the satirical critique of organized monotheistic religion and revolutionary zealotry gets a little lost in the shuffle; admittedly, it might have proved difficult to work the Judean People's Front's mass suicide into a musical number.

Each part had its own cheeky name: "Apocalypso Now," "Boy Next Door," "The Temptation of Brian," "Baroque and Roll," and "Miserie Loves Company." The music is packed with nods to everything from Shostakovich and Mozart to (somewhat cringingly) spirituals, and even doo-wop; the sublimely catchy "Woe Woe Woe!" sounds like a fantastic bonus track from the *Grease* cast recording. The last song from part four, "Individuals," is a superb piece of ersatz Dylan gibberish, complete with high-then-low wheezy mumbling and the occasional blat from a harmonica.

The overture was Sousa's "The Liberty Bell (March)" and it concluded with "Always Look on the Bright Side of Life." Originally about an hour long, it was eventually expanded to roughly an hour and a half.

The Royal Albert Hall performance on October 23, 2009, was something of a reunion and Python jamboree, tacking the UK premiere onto a fortieth-anniversary bash, or Ruby Jubilee, for the troupe. Idle was there, in proper tails and all, as a soloist. Although not precisely a classically trained singer, like some of the Pythons he can hold his own as a self-described "baritonish" performer. He started things off with an appropriately self-aware gag about celebrating "four hundred years of some of these jokes."

Palin appeared in a very non-Pepperpot outfit as Mrs. Betty Parkinson to act as narrator and provide a nod toward topicality (obligatory Sarah Palin reference). Both Terrys made appearances as well, one musically (Jones) and the other not (Gilliam). Their cameos and an eagerly anticipatory audience (there was an entire row of Gumbys up front) made the Ruby Jubilee celebration appear to be the most important aspect of the evening, with the performance of a "new" piece of musical theater almost beside the point. All that seemed to be missing was a giant video screen showing the "Philosophers' Football Match."

What made the Royal Albert Hall *Not the Messiah* show stand apart from so many other live Python events was in part the setting, quite grander than many of their venues. There was also the rather formidable sight and sound of the BBC Symphony Orchestra and Chorus, a veritable battalion of musicians and singers who gave Idle and Du Prez's material everything they had, and certainly helped elevate some of the rather sketchier numbers to a grander height.

Of course, Idle was not about to leave anything to chance, whether or not it had anything to do with *Life of Brian*. Witness the bagpipers who make a couple key appearances and the light wands distributed to the audience. That's also why, after the audience sings along to "Always Look on the Bright Side of Life" (already pillaged for the company bow at the end of *Spamalot* and just about every one of Idle's live performances anywhere), Palin returns to the stage to give the "Lumberjack Song" one more go.

All in all, a respectable night's entertainment, but certainly needing a lot more shaping and fine-tuning before it could be booked into a theater for eight shows a week.

26

We're Not Dead Yet!

The Recurring Resurrections, Reunion Tours, and Ex-Chapmans

Man, for a bunch of guys who bickered about reunions for years, they sure did get together a lot. Below is a list of the major live performances, reunions, and gatherings of "not-yet-dead" Pythons. Over the years, they've gathered in bits and bobs, in twos and fives (threes, m'lord), for shows like the Amnesty International "Policeman Balls" and a host of random interviews (many of which asked: "Will you ever have a reunion?"). Chapman and Idle toured "solo" for years, performing old Python material alone, or with "reasonable facsimiles" of their absent brethren. As Idle notes in the invaluable *Monty Python Live!* guide, the Pythons began doing live shows before they were Pythons, really. As (mostly) products of "smokers" and campus stage shows—meeting one another at the Edinburgh Festival Fringe and so forth—the lads were all comfortable going live before doing so with Python. And while it wasn't exactly a tour, their first album—*Monty Python's Flying Circus* (1970)—was recorded before a live audience at the Camden Theatre in London. Perhaps surprisingly, the Pythons continue to muck about together a bit nowadays, even after the O2 shows in 2014 that purportedly paid all their outstanding debts; Cleese and Idle have been making the rounds in the United States of late.

1971: Coventry Arts Theater: Three Nights Only!

According to Idle, this string of three midnight shows at the Belgrade Theatre was a smash, in part because the audience—college students from Warwick University—were themselves smashed. These first live shows were arranged against all odds. The *Coventry Telegraph* reported at the time that the Warwick student union organizer had simply hoped to book "one or two" Pythons for the second year of their campus festival, only to find Idle looking for a venue where the whole troupe could perform "away from London in case it didn't work." The £1 tickets disappeared almost immediately. Students dressed as Gumbys lined the front rows, and stalked the Pythons after the show. It was only once the Pythons got some perspective by stepping outside of London that they truly comprehended their growing cult. A fine start.

1973: Monty Python's First Farewell Tour: Thirty Shows, Thirteen Cities, Three Weeks Across the United Kingdom

Although a "chaotic" affair, prone to dope-related technical glitches, missed cues (Chapman's alcoholism was reaching ludicrous levels), "lipstick competitions" (as various Pepperpots engaged in makeup one-up-womanship), and "corpse wars" (Palin lost to Cleese), the tour was another success, building at the height of the troupe's television popularity in England. Such was their UK success that the lads (and Cleveland and Innes) decided to continue the tour overseas . . . on to balmy Canada!

1973: Monty Python's First Farewell Tour: Canada, Eh?

In his *The Greedy Bastard Diary*, Idle recalls that as the Pythons were staged through Canadian customs, there was a "tremendous screaming and we looked behind us to see which rock and roll stars were arriving, only to be amazed by the realization that the yelling crowd was there to greet us: our first experience of the hype that occasionally surrounded Python": they were fookin' rock stars in Canada! It was Beatles-esque . . . or at least Rutles-esque. Most of the Pythons embraced the wackiness of comedy rock-stardom (they behaved like naughty schoolboys, as Cleveland recalls). But Cleese—experiencing problems in his marriage to Connie Booth at the time—was a bit of a bear, preferring to eat dinner by himself. It was on this tour that Cleese announced to the others that he'd not be returning to *Flying Circus* for a fourth season. But the antics of the others—both onstage and in the intermittent interviews—cemented the Pythons as absurd and wacky comic gods. The tour crisscrossed the Great White North and eventually they all (sans Cleese) wound up in San Francisco, then LA, and then the *Tonight Show*, where they bombed. So they went back to England.

1974: Monty Python Live at Drury Lane: Four Weeks in London

Aka "Monty Python's First Farewell Tour (Repeat)," the two-week booking was in such demand that they almost immediately extended to four weeks. Performed in the comfort of their hometown, as it were, the show had an atmosphere that was radically different from the previous tours. Yet they were still comedy rock stars . . . who drew real rock stars to their shows (their loyal supporters among the Beatles, Stones, and Floyd, in particular). Happily, a taste of what their early live shows were like is available to laity as well: the March 23 show was recorded and released a few months later as *Monty Python Live at Drury Lane* (on Charisma). One of their best. (Pop Quiz!: Who played the role of Palin's Lumberjack's "best gal"? Since Cleveland was touring elsewhere in 1974, her replacement was Idle's first wife, Lyn Ashley, billed on *Flying Circus* appearances as "Mrs. Idle.")

1976: Live at City Center: Three Weeks in NYC

As Jones notes, Python were "the toast of the town" in New York, hobbing with the nobs and all that. All the Pythons had some sort of "star experience" during their stay, running into such luminaries as Katharine Hepburn, Martin Scorsese, Jim Henson, Leonard Bernstein, Paul Simon, the original *SNL* cast, and so forth. George Harrison (among others) joined the troupe on stage, incognito, for their closing "Lumberjack Song" sketch at the April 20 show. To the Pythons' wry dismay, by this point the audiences had memorized their routines, which made the shows less comic performance than religious ceremony. But considering their last experience in the United States (crickets), this was a definite uptick.

In addition to the usual star sightings that the city had on offer, the Pythons enjoyed the full New York "tourist" package: Innes's apartment was burgled twice, Cleese was rolled by two hookers, Chapman was bashed at a gay club, and Cleveland was nicked. Good times. (One imagines that if the lads had been able to perform instead at the Palladium that year with Python freak Julie Andrews, as she had asked them to, things might have been a *touch* more civilized.) A U.S.-only album of "best bits" followed quickly in May.

This is like the American version of *Live at Drury Lane*. Michael Palin's *Esqurie* essay "Monty Python's American Diary" is reprinted on the back.   *Lisa Bocchini*

1980: Hollywood Bowl: Four Nights Under the Stars

By most recollections, the Hollywood Bowl show was Peak Python. But the acoustics of an outdoor stadium were a challenge, as were the eight thousand fans . . . eight thousand stoned fans . . . eight thousand stoned fans who knew the material *dead on*. So the troupe goofed around a bit, ad-libbing to get the others to corpse, and changing lines to keep the audience on their toes. Cleveland, for example, stunned the crowd by shifting "Have you come about a holiday, or would you like to come upstairs" to "Have you come about a holiday, or would you like a blow job?" A stunner, that one.

Overall, the Hollywood Bowl show is a bit more raw, over the top, and vulgar than their typical fare, but then again: they were playing to the

Eric Idle as one of many philosophical Bruces in *Monty Python Live at the Hollywood Bowl.*
Columbia Pictures/Photofest

American festival crowd, fans who treated them like the second coming of the Beatles. California had the weather, the celebrities, the parties, and the adulation. And no one got burgled, rolled, bashed, or nicked. Gooder times. Columbia Pictures released a feature film of the concert soon after (1982); the book, *Monty Python Live!* (2009), includes a repro of the "Official Programme" for the show, as well as typical transcripts of the sketches.

1989: Parrot Sketch Not Included: One Sad Afternoon in September

In a bittersweet final mini-reunion after nearly a decade apart, the Python Six gathered together with super-fan Steve Martin to record some new material in honor of the troupe's impending twentieth anniversary . . . and their impending twentieth-anniversary televised clip-show. The Pythons recorded two new sketches on September 3: a bit where they play schoolchildren, and another with them all crammed into a cupboard. They disliked the schoolchildren bit so much that it didn't make it to air. Chapman passed away a month later, leaving a six-second "crammed in a cupboard" cameo as the last Python Six appearance on record. The show aired in England two months later, on November 18, 1989.

1998: Comedy Arts Festival Tribute to Monty Python: One Hour in Aspen

The surviving Pythons—plus the ashes of Chapman in an urn—were interviewed by comic Robert Klein on March 7, 1998. The troupe discussed their comic legacy, BBC censorship, and . . . oh, dammit, Gilliam knocked over Chapman's ashes again! The rogue. The interview aired on HBO on March 21.

2002: The Concert for George: One Night at the Royal Albert Hall

In honor of their fallen super-fan, George Harrison, four of the five surviving Pythons—Idle, Palin, Gilliam, and Jones—joined together with Innes and Cleveland (and Tom Hanks) and performed "Sit on My Face" and the "Lumberjack Song" (Harrison's favorite) in the Royal Albert Hall, London. Not quite a full "survivors' reunion" without Cleese, but adding in two top contenders for the "Seventh Python" (−1 +2 x ½) made this one difficult to dismiss. Or add up.

2014: Monty Python Live (Mostly): One Down Five to Go: Ten Shows Over Two Weeks in London

The Final Sell-Out

After losing that *Spamalot* royalties lawsuit, the Pythons decided to put on a show. Yep: just like the *Little Rascals*, or your average Mickey Rooney and Judy Garland musical, only with far more torture-happy Jesuits. Originally intended as a one-night-only event, after those tickets sold out in 43.5 seconds the Pythons added nine more nights. Apparently, the old bastards still had fans. Fans with credit cards and high-speed Internet connections.

The show was a mix of classic sketches (of course), new dance numbers, and old clips. Chapman got some face time via the Megatron, and a few sketches were dusted off and updated (professors Brian Cox and Stephen Hawking add to "Galaxy Song," for example). Carol Cleveland joined the boys, as did various guest stars on the odd night: Eddie Izzard, Stephen Fry, Warwick Davis, Mike Myers, Simon Pegg, and Noel Fielding, among others. Newcomer Samuel Holmes danced and filled in for Chapman (as do the rest of the Pythons, including Cleveland) throughout the night. It was a gala event that went beyond the usual late-career victory lap. The sold-out final show was simulcast to select theaters in the United States and the United Kingdom, and available on DVD soon after.

One of our writers actually got on one of those mechanical birds and flew over to England to see the last Monty Python reunion show at the O2 Center in London. These are the things we do for the reading public. Here's his thrilling report.

The Cogan Diaries

When the second wave of shows went online, I was up at 3:00 a.m. After several minutes of frantic waiting, the tickets were secured! The bank account was emptied! (Retirement, that's for suckers!) We were off to England.

Lumberjacks and Gumbys and Mounties. Oh, my! While I expected some cosplay at the reunion show, I wasn't aware of how popular the lumberjack trope would be. The Gumby look was easy to assemble (the souvenir stands were selling Gumby bandanas for those who came unprepared), and the lumberjack look could be taken from your old grunge outfit from 1991, presuming it still fit, but . . . Mounties? That took some effort, so my I tipped my hat to the fans who had somehow gotten their hands on Canadian uniforms, who did stand out even among tens of thousands who clearly were there for the Python show.

The line to the O2 was reasonable . . . it only took about an hour to get to our seats. While I noticed many people my age or older, I was pleasantly surprised by the number of people who had not been born when *The Meaning of Life* was in the theaters, meaning a new generation of rabid Python fans were out there. Us old folks could die in peace, just put me on the ice floe and push me off to oblivion now! Well, er, after the show. And maybe a pint. Or three.

I've been to many a concert where people were listening to the band's music in the parking lot. But I had never been to a show where almost all the fans, without exception, were trading favorite Python lines and reenacting entire sketches. It was almost as though people could not believe that the surviving Pythons had gotten together and that unless they repeated words from the sacred tomes (movies, TV shows, and records) the Pythons would not materialize. We would have to will them back into existence. Maybe it was the fact that the final show would be broadcast live and would later be released as a DVD, but the crowd was almost more Python than Python. There were no casual fans the last night of the reunion.

The lights dimmed, and after a brief video cameo by Chapman, the living Pythons came out on stage. All around me I realized that grown men were weeping and that I was one of them. I had never expected to see this day (I've seen all the others live expect for Jones, and yes, that does mean Chapman before he was an "ex-Chapman"). Then the show commenced with dancing and singing (mostly not by the Pythons, although they all did sing at one point or another), followed by the "greatest hits" the fans were expecting, plus appearances by Eddie Izzard, Mike Myers, Brian Cox, and a memorable cameo from Stephen Hawking, who was in the audience. Although there were some flubs (Jones was clearly reading from notes during one sketch, which led to Cleese taking them away and reading them himself), it was brilliant.

Obviously, you can buy the DVD, or if you are reading this book, probably already have a copy, plus a backup in case you lose that copy, so you know what sketches they did. But to me, it wasn't just seeing them live that made me feel so alive, it was the fans. Almost all of them were laughing before the best bits and not in an annoying way, but out of love. The Pythons may have done these shows for the money, but for the fans, it was bliss.

As the entire stadium sang along to "Always Look on the Bright Side of Life" at the end (naturally followed by "piss off!"), it didn't feel like a "Greedy Bastard Tour" or a nostalgia trip, it felt like being part of a lovable, slightly bonkers community and part of something bigger than ourselves. We left feeling like we had come from a kind of church service, having done our part to make the world a better, sillier place.

Selected Bibliography

Articles

Adams, Sam. "John Cleese." *AV Club*, October 22, 2009.

Adams, Stephen. "Dead Parrot Sketch Is 1,600 Years Old." *Telegraph*, November 13, 2008.

Barnett, Laura. "Eric Idle, Portrait of an Artist." *Guardian*, November 20, 2012.

Bay, Samara. "Answers to Your Top Ten Questions About Monty Python's *Spamalot* at the Hollywood Bowl." *Playbill*, August 1, 2015.

Bennetts, Leslie. "How Terry Gilliam Found a Happy Ending for 'Brazil.'" *New York Times*, January 19, 1986.

Biskind, Peter. "The Last of Heath." *Vanity Fair*, August 2009.

Bradshaw, Peter. "Monty Python's Flying Circus Is Deeply Uninfluential." *Guardian*, August 13, 2007.

———. "*Absolutely Anything* Review: Cheap and Cheerless Sci-Fi Comedy." *Guardian*, August 13, 2015.

Caro, Mark. "Feuding Founders of the Rutles: You Can't Buy Them Love." *Chicago Tribune*, June 2, 2005.

Clemons, Pete. "Look and Watch: Monty Python Reunion Plan Sparks Memories of First Live Appearance—In Coventry." *Coventry Telegraph* 14:29, January 15, 2014.

Corliss, Richard and James Inverne. "Terry's Flying Circus." *Time*, August 1, 2005.

Dutka, Elaine. "Handmade Man: An Interview with George Harrison." *Film Comment*, May/June 1988.

Ebert, Roger. "Review: *Personal Services*." *Chicago Sun-Times*, May 29, 1987.

Finke, Laurie A. and Linda Aronstein. "Got Grail? Monty Python and the Broadway Stage." *Theatre Survey* 48:2, November 2007.

Gallagher, Paul. "Eric Idle's Brilliant, Nearly Forgotten Comedy Classic 'Rutland Weekend Television.'" Dangerousminds.net, January 19, 2015.

Gardener, Eric. "Monty Python Members Lose 'Spamalot' Musical Profits Dispute." *Hollywood Reporter*, July 5, 2013.

Grow, Kory. "'Game of Thrones' Episode Revealed to Contain Monty Python References," *Rolling Stone*, May 12, 2014.

Harrod, Horatia. "Terry Gilliam Interview: If I Had Stayed in America, I'd Be Throwing Bombs." *Daily Telegraph*, March 14, 2014.

Hertzberg, Hendrik. "Aspects of Show Biz." *New Yorker*, May 12, 1975.

Hill, Logan. "Influences: Terry Gilliam." *New York*, December 5, 2012.

Housego, Mike, and Jean Richie. "I Knew It Was Cancer." *Sun*, September 18, 1989.

———. "I Nearly Died on Three Bottles of Gin a Day." *Sun*. September 20, 1989.

Hughes, Laura. "What's Europe Ever Done for Us?" *Telegraph*, March 1, 2016.

Johnson, Kim and Albert Williams. "Eric Idle Talksalot." *Chicago Reader*, December 16, 2004.

Jones, Terry. "Ian MacNaughton." *Guardian*, December 26, 2002.

———. "With this elephant, we gave birth to the Pythons." *Guardian*, February 9, 2005.

Journal. "New Chapter for Black Sheep." January 31, 2004.

Lemon, Denis. "Graham Chapman Interview." *Gay News Collective*, August 1, 1972.

Make, Andrew. "Monty Python: The Vinyl Years." *Mojo*, November 21, 2013.

Massey, Jeff, and Brian Cogan. "*Spamalot*: Lovingly Ripping Off / Ripping On the Establishment." *Medieval Afterlives in Contemporary Culture*. Ed. Gail Ashton. London: Bloomsbury, 2015.

McGrath, Charles. "Terry Gilliam's Feel-Good Endings." *New York Times*, August 14, 2005.

Moore, Bo. "Terry Gilliam on His Epic New Dystopian Film *The Zero Theorem*." *Wired*, September 18, 2014.

O'Sullivan, Kevin. "TV Python Comic at Sex Orgies." *Sun*, January 24, 1987.

Pogrebin, Robin. "How 'Seussical: The Musical' Was Puffed into a Big Flop." *New York Times*, July 18, 2001.

Press Association. "Monty Python's Terry Jones Leads Tributes at Funeral of Cynthia Payne." *Daily Mail*. December 9, 2015.

Q Magazine. "Monty Python Interview," August 1987. http://www.skeptictank. org/treasure/COWTEXT/HUMOR/MONTPYTH.HUM

Rea, Steven. "Graham Chapman Off on Solo Tour of US." *Chicago Tribune*. April 16, 1987.

Rechler, Glenn. "It's . . .: Graham Chapman reminisces . . ." *Spin*, July 1987.

Schulman, Michael. "Jester." *New Yorker*, December 22 / 29, 2014.

Sellers, Robert. "It's a Miracle That Terry Gilliam's *Time Bandits* Even Got Made." *i09*, September 17, 2013.

Sims, David. "How *Monty Python and the Holy Grail* Influenced Film by Satirizing It." *Atlantic*, April 9, 2015.

Spitz, Marc. "Rutlemania is Back, and It's Unreal." *New York Times*, December 19, 2013.

Teodorczuk, Tom. "John Oliver Hears Monty Python's Many Secrets." *Daily Beast*, April 25, 2015.

Van Gelder, Lawrence. "Film Review: An Orwellian Tale about Animal Behavior." *New York Times*, October 31, 1997.

Wilmington, Michael. "Worlds in Collision." *Chicago Tribune*, January 14, 1996.

Zehme, Bill. "King Mike and the Quest for the Broadway Grail." *New York*, March 14, 2005.

Books

Badman, Keith. *The Beatles: Off the Record 2*. London: Omnibus, 2009.

Berg, William, trans. *Philogelos: The Laugh Addict*. London: Yudu, 2008.

Birkenstein, Jeff, and Anna Froula and Karen Randell. *The Cinema of Terry Gilliam: It's a Mad World*. New York: Columbia University Press, 2013.

Boak, Jessica, and Ray Bailey. *Brew Britannia: The Strange Rebirth of British Beer*. London: Aurum Press, 2014.

Chapman, Graham, and David Sherlock, Alex Martin, David Yallop, and Douglas Adams. *A Liar's Autobiography Volume VII*. New York: Methuen, 1980.

Chapman, Graham, et. al. *The Complete Monty Python's Flying Circus: All the Words, Volume One*. New York: Pantheon, 1989.

———. *The Complete Monty Python's Flying Circus: All the Words, Volume Two*. New York: Pantheon, 1989.

———. *Monty Python and the Holy Grail (Book)*. London: Methuen, 1992.

———. *Monty Python Live!* New York: Hyperion, 2009.

———. *Monty Python's The Meaning of Life*. London: Methuen, 1999.

———. *The Pythons: Autobiography by the Pythons*. New York: St. Martin's Press, 2003.

Cleese, John. *So Anyway . . .* New York: Crown Archetype, 2014.

Cleveland, Carol. *PomPoms Up!: From Puberty to Python and Beyond*. London: Dynasty, 2014.

Cogan, Brian and Jeff Massey. *Everything I Ever Needed to Know about ___** *I Learned from Monty Python*. New York: Macmillan, 2014.

Dempsey, Luke. *Monty Python's Flying Circus: Complete and Annotated . . . All the Bits*. New York: Black Dog & Leventhal, 2012.

Fischer, Dennis. *Science Fiction Film Directors, 1895–1998*. Jefferson, NC: McFarland & Company, 2000.

Gilliam, Terry. *Gilliamesque: A Pre-posthumous Memoir*. New York: Harper Design, 2015.

Handlen, Zack. *If You Like Monty Python . . .* Milwaukee, WI: Limelight, 2012.

Johnson, Kim "Howard." *Monty Python's Tunisian Holiday*. New York: Thomas Dunne, 2008.

Jones, Terry. *Chaucer's Knight: The Portrait of a Medieval Mercenary*. New York: Methuen, 1980.

———. *Terry Jones's War on the War on Terror*. New York: Nation, 2005.

Jones, Terry, and Robert Yeager, Terry Dolan, Alan Fletcher, and Juliette Dor. *Who Murdered Chaucer?: A Medieval Mystery*. New York: Thomas Dunne, 2003.

Idle, Eric. *The Greedy Bastard Diary: A Comic Tour of America*. New York: HarperEntertainment, 2005.

Landy, Marcia. *Monty Python's Flying Circus*. Detroit: Wayne State University Press, 2005.

Larsen, Darl. *A Book About the Film* Monty Python and the Holy Grail. Lanham, MD: Rowman & Littlefield, 2015.

———. *Monty Python's Flying Circus: An Utterly Complete, Thoroughly Unillustrated, Absolutely Unauthorized Guide to Possibly All the References from Arthur "Two Sheds" Jackson to Zambesi*. Lanham, MD: Scarecrow Press, 2008.

Matthews, Jack. *The Battle for Brazil: Terry Gilliam v. Universal Pictures in the Fight to the Final Cut*. New York: Applause, 1987.

McCall, Douglas. *Monty Python: A Chronology, 1969–2012*. Jefferson, NC: McFarland & Company, 2014.

Morgan, David. *Monty Python Speaks!* New York: Dey Street, 2005.

Palin, Michael. *Michael Palin Diaries 1969–1979: The Python Years*. New York: St. Martin's Press, 2006.

———. *Diaries 1980–1988: Halfway to Hollywood—The Film Years*. London: Weidenfeld & Nicolson, 2009.

Perry, George. *Life of Python*. London: Pavilion Books, Ltd., 1994.

Ross, Robert. *Monty Python Encyclopedia*. London: Batsford, 2001.

Sterritt, David and Lucille Rhodes. *Terry Gilliam: Interviews*. Jackson, MS: University of Mississippi Press, 2004.

Stott, Andrew. *Comedy (The New Critical Idiom)*. New York: Routledge, 2014.
Topping, Richard. *Monty Python: From the* Flying Circus *to* Spamalot. New York: Virgin Books, 2008.
Wilmut, Roger. *From Fringe to Flying Circus*. London: Eyre Methuen, 1980.
Yeager, R. F. and Toshiyuki Takamiya, eds. *The Medieval Python: The Purposive and Provocative Work of Terry Jones*. New York: Palgrave Macmillan, 2012.

Media

The Aristocrats. (Dir. Paul Provenza) Documentary, 2005.
Marty Feldman: Six Degrees of Separation. (Dir. Jeff Simpson) BBC Wales, 2008.
"Monty Python's Fliegender Zirkus!," BBC Radio 4, May 7, 2011.
Monty Python: Almost the Truth (The Lawyer's Cut). (Dirs. Bill Jones, Alan G. Parker, Ben Timlett) IFC miniseries, 2009.
"Monty Python 1989 Memorial to Graham Chapman." BBC TV. https://www.youtube.com/watch?v=nb7YVkoSyXQ
"Monty Python's Graham Chapman's Curious, Courageous, Poignant Video Op-Ed, 1984." Dangerous Minds. November 11, 2013.
"Terry Jones and Wogan Talk about *Personal Services*." https://www.youtube.com/watch?v=I8ru4l0BGJE

Websites

Allmusic.com
Boxofficemojo.com
Dailyllama.com
Discogs.org
Drdemento.com
Ericidle.com
H2g2.com
Imdb.com
Montypython.com
Montypython.net
Rutlemania.org
Screenonline.org.uk
Tcm.com
Terrygilliamweb.com

That's it.
Seriously, there's no more.
(Well, that's not totally true, there's still the index. Plus, the back cover,
if you haven't read that already. It's very nice!)

*   *   *

You don't gotta go home,
but you can't stay here.

*   *   *

Now piss off, you.

Index

Numbers in italics refer to photographs

A Private Function, 285, 312, 336
Absolutely Anything, 230, 306
Adams, Douglas, 140, 238, 258, 306, 309, 314–315, 318
Adventures of Baron Munchausen, The, 254, 270–271, 274, 276,
Airplane!, 327
All in the Family, 151
All You Need Is Cash, 251–252, 287, 311, 318
American Friends, 283, 285, 288, 317
And Now for Something Completely Different, 36, 97, 98, 102–110, 146, 156, 159, 207, 285, 312, 313, 316
Apatow, Judd, 194, 328
Aristocrats, The, 143, 246
Around the World in 80 Days, 253, 283, 288, 290, 293
At Last the 1948 Show, 3, 19, 26, 27–39, 40, 41, 45, 49, 64, 66, 79, 247, 320
Azaria, Hank, 338

BAFTA, 34, 181, 209, 210, 228, 285, 308
Barbados, 1
Barclay, Humphrey, 7, 10, 31, 40, 43, 319
Barker, Ronnie, 3, 5, 23–24, 48, 54, 225
BBC, xi–xiii, 4, 5, 7, 10, 11, 13, 15, 17, 19, 20, 23, 25, 27, 28, 31, 32, 33, 41, 45, 46–58, 64, 67, 73, 84, 85, 88–90, 95, 101, 106, 111, 114, 118, 121, 127, 130, 131, 133, 135, 137, 142, 143, 147, 151, 154, 161, 181, 203, 204, 238, 244, 248, 251, 252, 253, 260, 284, 288, 300, 302,
310, 313, 314, 315, 319, 320, 321, 322, 339, 343, 350
BBC Television Centre, *49*, 56, 111
Beatles, the, 47, 50, 97, 146, 251–252, 287, 310, 317–319, 327, 346, 347, 349
Benny Hill Show, The, 64, 65, 74, 78, 81, 221
Bentine, Michael, 14–16, 19, 20
Bert Fegg's Nasty Book for Boys and Girls, 301
Beyond the Fringe, 11, 12, 13, 50, 325
Biggles, 74, 83–84, 122
Biôlek, Alfred, 111
Black Beast of Arrrghhh, 174–175, 310
Bonzo Dog Doo-Dah Band, 43, 45, 251, 309, 311, 317–318
Booth, Connie, 5, 25, 38, 71, 91, 130, 165, 179, 181, 186, 187, 189, 192, 226, 227, 309, 316–317, 346
Brazil, 211, 267–269, 270, 274, 278, 283, 287, 293
Brexit, 76, 200
Broadway, 5, 156, 186, 211, 260, 309, 332–341
Bronzino, 8, 43, 79, 245
Brooke-Taylor, Tim, 5, 10, 24, 26, 27, 28, 29, 31–32, 33, 34, 36–39, 79
Brooks, Mel, 27, 34, 35, 84, 209, 341
Brothers Grimm, The, 274–276
Buddah Records, 147
Burma, 1
Burns, George, 4

Cambridge Circus, 3, 5, 7, 11, 27, 29, 31, 37, 316, 319

Cambridge University, 3, 4, 5, 7, 10,
    11, 21, 23, 27, 29, 31, 32, 33, 37,
    38, 40, 314
Camelot, 158, 165, 166, 167, 171, 332,
    334
Camelot, 156, 167, 209, 332, 334
Canada, 141, 148–151, 230, 339, 346
Canterbury Tales, The, 296
Carroll, Lewis, 263
Castle Arrrghhh, 176
CBC, 149
Chapman, Graham, xi, *xii*, 2–4, 5, 10,
    11, 12, 21, 23, 24, 25, 26, 27,
    31, 32, 33, 34, *34*, 35, 37, 38,
    41, 45, 48, 49, 54, 56, 60, 62,
    63, 64, 65, 68, *68*, 69, 70, 71,
    72, 76, 77, 79, *82*, 83, 86, 87,
    88, 89, 90, 91, 92, 99, 100, 101,
    106, 116, 119, 120, 121, 122,
    123, 127, 128, 129, 131, 133,
    134, 135, 137, 140, 142, 143,
    144, 149, 154, 155, 159, 161,
    167, 169, 171, 176, 177, 196,
    199, 205, 211, 212, 213, 214,
    215, 216, 221, 222, 224, 226,
    228, 229, 233, 234–247, 249,
    254, 284, 291, 293, 300, 312,
    313, 314, 315, 316, 319, 322,
    330, 336, 338, 339, 345, 346,
    347, 350, 351, 352
Chaucer, Geoffrey, 77, 157, 296, 298,
    300
*Chaucer's Knight: Portrait of a Medieval
    Mercenary*, 296
Christmas Card, 54
Cleese, John, xi, *xii*, 2, 3, 4–6, 7, 8,
    10, 11, 12, 15, 19, 21, 22, 23,
    24, 25, 26, 27, 28, 29, 31, 32,
    33, 34, *34*, 36, 37, 38, 40, 41,
    43, 45, 48, 49, 50, *51*, 52, 53,
    54, 55, 56, 58, 59, 60, 62, 64,
    65, 67, *68*, 69. 70, 71, 72, 73,
    74, 75, 76, 78, 79, *82*, 83, 85,
    87, 88, 89, 90, 91, 92, 93, 94,
    95, 96, 97, 99, 100, 101, 104,
    105, 106, 109, 111, 112, 113,
    115, 116, 117, 119, 120, 121,
    122, 123, 125, 127, 128, 130,

    131, 133, 134, 135, 149, 156,
    157, 162, 164, 165, 167, 171,
    172, 176, 179–193, *180*, 198,
    199, 203, 204, 205, 209, 211,
    212, 213, 214, 216, 218, 221,
    223–233, *227*, 236, 237, 238,
    240, 242, 243, 245, 246, 247,
    248, 249, 254, 262, 284, 285,
    287, 291, 294, 300, 304, 305,
    312, 314, 315, 316–317, 318,
    319, 321, 322, 324, 327, 336,
    337, 341, 345, 346, 347, 350,
    352
Cleveland, Carol, xiv, 35, 62, 64, 65,
    66, 70, 72, 75, 78, 79, 86, 90,
    91, 93, 96, 104, 118, 120, 129,
    131, 134, 136, 141, 144, 169,
    209, 215, 216, 218, 240, 244,
    246, 247, 309, 312, 316, 320–
    323, 346, 347, 348, 350, 351
Clifton College, 4
Clump of Plinths, A, 5, 10, 32
Coffey, Denise, 40, 41, *42*, 43, 45, 320
Colbert Report, The, 21
*Complete and Utter History of Britain,
    The*, 12, 13, 45, 47–49, 60, 62,
    157, 283, 319
Cook, Peter, 13, 24, 26, 31, 104, 224,
    240, 254
Corbett, Ronnie, 3
Crichton, Charles, 226, 227
Crimson Permanent Assurance, The, 210,
    217, 279
Curry, Tim, 192, 262, 338, *340*
Curtis, Jamie Lee, 226, 227, *227*

Dad's Army, 47, 128, 137
Daily Show, The, 21
Dangerous Sports Club, The, 242
Davis, Warwick, 339, 351
Devillier, Ron, 151, 153, 154
Diaries (by Michael Palin), 15, 24, 238,
    291, 292, 293
Dibley, Mr., 92
Do Not Adjust Your Set, 7, 10, 12, 13, 19,
    28, 31, 40–45, *45*, 48, 49, 52,
    54, 91, 128, 238, 249, 283, 301,
    318, 319, 320

Doctor in the House, 3, 237, 315
Don Quixote, 270, 274, 280–281, 303
Doune Castle, 158, 167
Dr. Demento, 147, 330
Dr. Fegg's Encyclopaedia of All World
     Knowledge, 301
Dr. Fegg's Nasty Book of Knowledge, 293,
     295, 301
Du Prez, John, 210, 256, 259, 260, 332,
     336, 337, 339, 342, 343, 344,
Dürer, Albrecht, 112

Edinburgh Festival Fringe, 5, 10, 13,
     345
Eliot, T. S., 115
Emmanuel College, 2
Erik the Viking, 226, 301, 304–305, *304*
Everything I Ever Needed to Know About
     ____* I Learned from Monty
     Python, 289

Falklands War, 205
Fawlty Towers, 55, 130, 179–193, 224,
     225, 226, 233, 285, 302, 309,
     316, 317, 319
Fawlty, Basil, 179–193
Fear and Loathing in Las Vegas, 273–274
Feldman, Marty, 23, 26, 27, 28, 29, 31,
     33–35, *34*, 37, 38, 48, 49, 226,
     240, 255,
Fierce Creatures, 225, 228, 229, 287
Firesign Theater, 147
Fish Called Wanda, A, 225, 226–228,
     229, 283, 287, 294, 336
Fisher King, The, 271–272, 273, 276,
     280
Fliegender Zirkus, 38, 61, 110–112
Footlights Club, 2, 5, 10, 11, 21, 24, 31,
     33, 258, 312, 314, 319
Forstater, Mark, 223, 309–310
Freaks and Geeks, 328–329, *328*
Fred Tomlinson Singers, The, 71, 72,
     99, 100, 120, 121, 205, 245
From Fringe to Flying Circus, 3, 58, 244
Frost Report, The, 3, 5, 6, 10, 11, 13,
     21–25, *22*, 27, 28, 29, 31, 33,
     41, 49, 54

Frost, David, xii, 2, 3, 5, 6, 10, 11, 13,
     21–26, *22*, 27–29, 31, 32, 33,
     35, 40, 41, 47, 49, 50, *51*, 54,
     92, 128, 258, 316, 325

Game of Thrones, 329
Gay Boys in Bondage, 115, 126
Gilliam, Terry, xi, *xii*, 2, 6–8, 10,
     15, 21, 29, 36, 38, 40, 43, 45,
     48, 52, 54, 55, 56, 59, 62, 65,
     66, 67, 70, 75, 76, 79, 83, 87,
     89, 90, 91, 92, 98, 99, 100,
     101, 102, 106, 108, 114, 115,
     122, 125, 126, 128, 130, 131,
     134, 137, 140, 141, 142, 143,
     144, 153, 154, 158, 159, 161,
     162, 164, 165, 169, 170, 172,
     173, 175, 176, 178, 179, 195,
     196, 200, 207, 209, 210, 214,
     215, 216, 217, 218, 221, 222,
     226, 229, 244, 247, 254, 256,
     263–282, 287, 291, 296, 303,
     305, 312, 313, 317, 318, 319,
     322, 324, 335, 336, 337, 339,
     343, 350
Gleneagles Hotel, 179
Golden Rose of Montreux Prize, 25
Goodies, the, 20, 27, 31, 32
Goons, the, xii, 13, 14–20
Goon Show, The, 2, 4, 6, 13, 14–20, 43,
     50, 110, 146, 325
Great Railway Journeys of the World, 283,
     288
Greedy Bastard Diary, The, 231, 253,
     258, 312, 346
Greedy Bastard Tour, 254, 258, 260
Greek, 112, 185, 192, 330
Greer, Germaine, 10
Guevara, Che, 98, 127
Gumby, 67, 72, 78, 88, 97, 121, 149,
     150, 155, 194, 309, 343, 346,
     351

HandMade Films, 50, 195, 196, 266,
     311, 312
Harold the Sheep, 54, 62

Harrison, George, 50, 147, 195, 196, 251, 309, 310–312, *311*, 315, 318, 347, 350
Harrods, 133, 134, 158
Hawking, Stephen, 259, 351, 352
Hello Sailor, 256, 258, 259
Help!, 6, 7
Hill, Benny, 146, 212
Hitchhiker's Guide to the Galaxy, The, 309, 314–315
Holy (Gr)ail Ale, 161, 165, 307
How to Irritate People, 4, 25–26, 31, 71, 86, 316

I'm Sorry I'll Read That Again, 10, 31, 40, 224, 319, 320
Idle, Eric, xi, *xii*, 4, 7, 8–10, *9*, 11, 12, 24, 25, 26, 33, 40, 41, *42*, 43, 45, 46, 47, 48, 54, 55, 57, 58, 60, 64, 65, 66, 67, 69, 71, 72, 73, 74, 75, 76, 78, 79, *82*, 86, 87, 88, 89, 90, 91, 92, 94, 95, 96, 97, 98, 99, 108, 112, 114, 117, 120, 122, 123, 125, 127, 128, 131, 133, 134, 136, 137, 141, 142, 143, 144, 145, 149, 153, 162, 165, 167, 168, 170, 171, 173, 174, 176, 179, 194, 195, 201, 205, 210, 212, 213, 214, 215, 217, 218, 222, 226, 228, 229, 230, 231, 236, 240, 245, 247, 248–262, 266, 270, 287, 291, 294, 305, 310, 311, 312, 318, 319, 321, 322, 326, 332, 334, 335, 336, 337, 338, 339, 341, 342, 343, 344, 345, 346, 347, *349*, 350
Imaginarium of Doctor Parnassus, The, 276–278
India, 1
Innes, Neil, 40, 45, 137, 144, 164, 168, 169, 249, 251, 252, 256, 311, 325, 312, 314
Iron Maiden, 243, 244
It's Man, 59, 61, 65, 74, 78, 79, 80, 85, 88, 90, 97, 113, 116, 121, 123
ITV, 32, 33, 40, 41, 45, 47, 127, 302
Izzard, Eddie, 20, 262, 306, 351, 252

Jabberwocky, 263–266, 287
Jackson, Arthur "Two Sheds," 60
Jamaica, 1, 207
Jones, Terry, xi, *xii*, 5, 7, 10–12, 13, 15, 24, 33, 34, 35, 40, 41, *42*, 45, 47, 48, 49, 53, 54, 56, 57, 58, 60, 62, 63, 65, 66, *68*, 70, 72, 73, 74, 76, 78, 81, 82, *82*, 83, 85, 86, 87, 88, 89, 90, 91, 92, 93, 94, 95, 97, 98, 99, 106, 108, 112, 113, 117, 121, 122, 125, 127, 128, 129, 131, 133, 135, 136, 137, 140, 141, 142, 144, 145, 153, 154, 155, 157, 158, 159, 162, 164, 167, 169, 171, 172, 195, 197, 198, 204, 209, 211, 212, 213, 214, 215, 216, 217, 218, *219*, 226, 228, 237, 240, 246, 247, 254, 255, 256, 263, 284, 285, 291, 293, 295–308, 313, 315, 318, 321, 322, 334, 336, 339, 343, 347, 350, 352

Kentucky Fried Movie, The, 327
Kenya, 1
Khan, Genghis, xi, 60, 314
Kids in the Hall, the, xiii, 20, 62, 109, 135, 327
King Arthur, 133, 156–158, 161–168, 170–174, 176–177, 241, 265, 330, 332, 334, 337, 338, 339
Kline, Kevin, 227
Knights of the Round Table, 156, 158, 162, 165, 166, 167, 168, 172, 173, 174, 175, 176, 296, 318, 332, 334
Kray brothers, 82–83
Kurtzman, Harvey, 6, 7, 263, 325

Lady Cottington's Pressed Fairy Book, 295, 301
Larsen, Darl, 109
Latin, 5, 164, 198, 199, 205
Led Zeppelin, 65, 146, 147, 155
Leicester, 2, 93, 99
Lenin, 98

Lewis, Nancy, 110, 147, 149, 151
Liar's Autobiography, A, 3, 238–240, *239*, 314, 322
Life of Brian, 5, 15, 35, 70, 95, 128, 194–206, 207, 209, 211, 216, 252, 254, 267, 304, 311, *311*, 312, 322, 334, 336, 341, 344
Lownes, Victor, 104, 109
Luftwaffe, 1

MacDonald, Aimi, 27, 28, 29, 35–37, 320
MacNaughton, Ian, 55, 57, 106, 108, 312–314, 321
Mad, 6, 149
Marx Brothers, 4, 57, 259, 324
Marx, Karl, 98, 127
Matching Tie with Handkerchief, 147, 154
McTeagle, Ewan, 85–86
Meaning of Life, The, 24, 29, 144, 207–222, 223, 226, *235*, 244, 252, 259, 267, 279, 283, 304, 306, 322, 327, 336, 352
Michaels, Lorne, 21, 225, 251, 284, 326, *326*
Mikado, The, 137, 259
Milligan, Spike, 14–20, *18*, 50, 52, 53, 104, 226, 240, 313, 320
Mills, Michael, 52
Minnesota, 6, 215, 263
Missionary, The, 285, 293, 312
Monty Python and the Holy Grail, 92, 100, 102, 109, 125, 130, 133, 144, 154, 155, 156–178, 181, 194, 195, 196, 197, 203, 209, 214, 217, 218, 223, 225, 235, 246, 263, 265, 266, 295, 296, 298, 300, 309, 310, 316, 318, 322, 324, 325, 326, 329, 330, 332–341
Monty Python Live (mostly): One Down, Five to Go, 38, 247, 262, 310, 322, 336, 351–353
Monty Python Live at City Center, 311, 318, 347–348, *348*
Monty Python Live at the Hollywood Bowl, 11, 38, 78, 108, 120, 196, 226, 252, 312, 318, 322, 336, 348–350
Monty Python Live at Theatre Drury Lane, 92, 154, 347
Monty Python: Almost the Truth (The Lawyer's Cut), 50, 52, 240, 341
Monty Python's Big Red Book, 102
Monty Python's First Farewell Tour, 149, 156, 322, 346, 347
Monty Python's Flying Circus, xii, xiii, xiv, 3, 6, 8, 15, 19, 21, 22, 24, 25, 26, 28, 29, 33, 34, 35, 36, 37, 39, 40, 41, 42, 43, 45, 46–101, 102, 104, 105, 106, 108, 109, 110, 111, 112, 113–145, 147, 148, 149, 151–155, 156, 158, 159, 161, 177, 179, 180, 190, 200, 203, 204, 207, 209, 210, 212, 217, 221, 222, 224, 225, 234, 236, 237, 238, 244, 245, 248, 249, 255, 258, 265, 281, 283, 295, 301, 302, 306, 310, 312, 313, 314, 316, 317, 318, 319, 320, 321, 322, 323, 324, 325, 327, 330, 334, 337, 345, 346, 347
Moon, Keith, 238, 240
Moore, Dennis, 127
Moore, Dudley, 13, 104
Morgan, David, 108, 153
Mozart, Wolfgang Amadeus, xi, 60, 343
MTV, 242–243, 319
Muggeridge, Malcolm, 203–204
Muppet Show, the, 15, 36, 63, 228
Murder in the Cathedral, 115

Naked Gun, The, 327
National Lampoon, 147, 249, 254, 325
New Zealand, 3, 5, 23, 230, 339
Nichols, Mike, 338
Nixon, Richard, 21, 26, 46, 112, 153, 330
Norwegian Blue, ix, 25, 70, 71
Not the Messiah (He's a Very Naughty Boy), 206, 260, 261, 322, 336, 341–344
Nuns on the Run, 255, 312

O Happy Day, 246
O2 Arena, xiv, 67, 71, 123, 223, 247,
    259, 262, 308, 345, 351, 352
Occidental College, 7, 43
Odd Job, The, 238, 240, 241
Oddie, Bill, 5, 31, 32
Office, The, 192
Oxford University, 10, 11, 12, 13, 24,
    285, 296, 301, 303

Palin, Michael, xi, *xii*, 5, 7, 10, 11,
    12–13, 15, 24, 25, 32, 33, 34,
    38, 40, 41, *42*, 45, 47, 48, 49,
    52, 53, 54, 56, 59, 60, 61, 62,
    63, 64, 65, 67, 69, 70, 71, 72,
    73, 74, 75, 76, 77, 78, 79, 80,
    82, 83, 84, 85, 86, 87, 88, 89,
    90, 91, 92, 94, 95, 96, 97, 98,
    104, 105, 106, 110, 111, 114,
    115, 116, 117, 120, 121, 122,
    123, 124, 126, 127, 128, 129,
    132, 133, 134, 135, 136, 137,
    140, 141, 142, 143, 144, 145,
    147, 151, 153, 154, 155, 157,
    161, 162, 163, 165, 167, 169,
    170, 171, 172, 173, 176, 197,
    199, 200, 203, 209, 211, 212,
    213, 214, 215, 221, 222, 224,
    225, 226, 227, 228, 229, 231,
    238, 245, 246, 247, 249, 254,
    258, 262, 263, 265, 266, 267,
    269, 281, 283–294, 296, 301,
    302, 305, 308, 309, 312, 316,
    317, 318, 320, 321, 322, 336,
    338, 341, 343, 344, 346, 347,
    348, 350
Pass the Butler, 259
PBS, xii, 151–155
Peckinpah, Sam, 96, 123, 124
Pepperpot, 29, 60, 62, 64, 65, 70, 73,
    75, 76, 78, 87, 88, 89, 96, 102,
    117, 121, 129, 137, 140, 144,
    197, 247, 295, 309, 314, 321,
    343, 346
Pierce, David Hyde, 338
Playboy Club, 104
Powell, Enoch, 46, 270, 325

Presley, Elvis, 147, 279
Prince Herbert, 144, 171, 334
Producers, The, 341
Professional Services, 302, 304
Proust, Marcel, 73, 75, 97, 118, 119,
    119, 120, 121
Pryce, Jonathan, 269, 287, 302
Python (programming language), 331
Pythons: Autobiography, The, 2, 9, 15,
    47, 256

Q5, 52, 55, 313
Queen Victoria, 62, 127, 135
*Quite Remarkable Adventures of the Owl
    and the Pussycat, The*, 256

Ramirez, Sara, 338, 341
Ready Player One, 330
Rentadick, 224
Richards, Keith, 1
Rise and Rise of Michael Rimmer, The,
    26, 224
Road to Mars, The, 258
Rolling Stones, the, 1, 146
Round the Horn, 33, 50
Rowling, J. K., 69, 280
Rutland Dirty Weekend Book, The, 249,
    251, 256
Rutland Isles, The, 252, 256
Rutland Weekend Television, 248–250,
    251, 318
Rutles, the, 97, 251, 252, 254, 255,
    256, 318, 319, 320, 326, 346
Rutles 2, The: Can't Buy Me Lunch, 252

Sachs, Andrew, 181, 184, 186, 192
Saturday Night Live, xiii, 21, 26, 118,
    133, 140, 147, 149, 225, 241,
    248, 251, 252, 318, 325, 326,
    347
Scales, Prunella, 181, 193, 302
SCTV, 98, 149, 248
Secombe, Harry, 14, 16, 18, 19, 20
Sellers, Peter, 14, 15, 16, 18, *18*, 19, 20,
    104, 146
Shakespeare, William, 112, 115, 126
Sherlock, David, 3, 120, 236, 237, 238,
    241, 244, 245, 246

Simpsons, The, 253
So, Anyway . . . , 4, 22, 230, 231, 316, 317, 324
Sousa, John Philip, xi, 8, 56, 324, 343
South Park, xiii, 255
spam, 331
Spam, 74, 98–100, 167, 247, 322, 331
Spamalot, 100, 144, 167, 206, 223, 260, 261, 262, 309, 319, 332–341, 344, 351
Spanish Inquisition, the, xiv, 64, 81, 83–85, 89, 204, 331
St. Bartholomew's Hospital, 3, 245
St. Peter's Preparatory School, 4
Starship Titanic, 306, 315
Stoppard, Tom, 267, 269, 287

Terry Jones's War on the War on Terror, 301
That Was the Week That Was, 14, 21–23, 22, 31, 224
Thatcher, Margaret, 71
This Is Spinal Tap, 251, 319
Three Men in a Boat, 267, 287
Tideland, 276
Tim the Enchanter, 172
Time Bandits, 196, 226, 266–267, 270, 283, 287, 312, 336
Toad the Wet Sprocket, 53
Together Again at Last . . . For the Very First Time, 262
Tony Award, 338, 341
Took, Barry, 33, 49
Toulouse-Lautrec, 128

Trotsky, Leon, 125
Tse-Tung, Mao, 98
Tunisia, 195, 196
Tuttle, Harry, 267
Twelve Monkeys, 272–273, 278

Uganda, 1
Uphill, 4
Upright Citizens Brigade, 109, 327

Viking, 65, 99, 100, 114, 176, 304

Wales, 10
We Have Ways of Making You Laugh, 43, 319
West End, 27, 186, 246, 259, 298, 339
Weston-super-Mare, 4
What About Dick?, 261–262
Whitehouse, Mary, 121, 204
Who Murdered Chaucer?: A Medieval Mystery, 298
Who, the, 146, 238, 242
Wilmut, Roger, 3, 244
Wind in the Willows, The, 228, 255, 295, 305–306
Wolverhampton, 8, 46, 99, 254, 256
World War II, 14, 61, 90, 111, 187, 192, 267
Writer's Cut, The, 258

Yellowbeard, 35, 226, 240–241, 254
Young Indiana Jones, 305

Zero Theorem, The, 278

Index of Bits, Episodes, Sketches, and Songs

"Albatross," 78

"Always Look on the Bright Side of Life," 201, 205, 209, 245, 324, 334, 338, 339, 343, 344, 353

"Ant, an Introduction, The," 70–72

"Appeal on Behalf of Extremely Rich People," 144

"Archaeology Today," 94–95

"Army Protection Racket," 70

"Art Critic," 65

"Art Gallery," 65

"Attila the Hun," 79, 93–94

"Bank Robber (Lingerie Shop)," 72–73

"Batsmen of the Kalahari, The," 144

"Battle of Pearl Harbor, The," 74, 75, 107, 109

"Bishop, The," 88–89

"Black Knight, The," 163–164, 209, 217, 298, 334

"Blackmail," 81, 90, 107, 119

"Blood, Devastation, Death, War and Horror," 117–118

"Book at Bedtime, A," 127–128

"Bookshop," 29, 33, 37–38, 70

"Bounder of Adventure," 322

"Bridge of Death, The," 175–176, 236

"Bruces," 81, 95, 96

"Buying a Bed," 70, 71, 77

"Buzz Aldrin Show (or: An Apology), The," 87–89

"Captain Fantastic," 41

"Cheese Shop," 37, 70, 122, 123, 184

"Class Sketch, The," 23, 24, 33

"Come Back to My Place," 79

"Confuse-a-Cat," 66

"Constitutional Peasants," 133, 162–163, 167, 169, 334

"Court Scene," 64

"Creosote, Mr.," 218, *219*, 222

"Cycling Tour, The," 60, 124–125, 127

"Dead Bishop on the Landing," 117

"Dead Parrot Sketch," xiii, 3, 11, 37, 65, 70, 71, 73, 93, 107, 151, 228, 245, 322, 350

"Déjà Vu," 85–87, 88

"Detective Sketch, The," 75

"Dirty Fork, The," 107

"Dirty Hungarian Phrasebook," 81, 98, 99, 107, 109

"Dirty Vicar, The," 129, 285

"Dull Life of a City Stockbroker," 58, 67

"E. Henry Thripshaw's Disease," 126

"Eighteenth-Century Social Legislation," 75

"Election Night Special," 92–93, 121

"Every Sperm is Sacred," 209, 211

"Explorer Sketch," 117

"Face the Press (Or Dinsdale)," 81–83

"First Man to Jump the Channel, The," 73

"Fish-Slapping Dance," 41, 76, 115, 334

"Four Yorkshiremen," 29, 37, 38–39, 247

"Full Frontal Nudity," 70

"The Funniest Joke in the World," xi, 61, 108, 137

"Galaxy Song," 209, 216, 217, 222, 259, 336, 351

"Germany vs. Greece Philosophers' Football Sketch," 61, 112

"Golden Age of Ballooning, The," 131–133

"Gorilla Librarian," 74

"Grandstand (or: The British Showbiz Awards)," 128–129

"Gumby Flower Arranging," 150

"Hamlet," 137–140

"Hell's Grannies," 62, 70, 107

"History of Slapstick," 5, 11

"Hitler, Mr.," 76

"Housing Project Built by Characters from Nineteenth-Century Novels," 125

"How Far Can a Minister Fall?," 77

"How Not to Be Seen," 97–98, 106

"How to Recognise Different Parts of the Body," 95–96

"How to Recognise Different Types of Trees from Quite a Long Way Away," 64–65

"Intermission," 57, 77–80

"It's a Living (or: School Prizes)," 91–93

"It's the Arts," 58, 60, 67–68

"Italian Lesson," 60

"Ken Shabby," 77, 97

"Knights Who Say Ni!, The," 170, 171–172, 334

"Larch, The," 64

"Liberty Bell (March), The," xi, xiii, 56, 59, 134, 144, 318, 343

"Light Entertainment War," 135–137, 154

"Literary Football Discussion," 61, 74

"Live from the Grill-O-Mat," 89–91

"Live Organ Transplants," 207, 209, 216–217

"Lumberjack Song," 71, 72, 107, 112, 153, 311, 312, 316, 344, 347, 350

"Man Who Finishes Other People's Sentences, The," 144

"Man Who Speaks in Anagrams," 117, 249

"Man's Crisis of Identity in the Latter Half of the 20th Century," 66–67

"Michael Ellis," 126, 133–135

"Ministry of Silly Walks," 81, 82, 83

"Miracle of Birth, The," 209, 210–212, 217

"Money Programme," 116–117

"Money Song," 117, 254

"Most Awful Family in Britain, The," 142, 143, 145, 318

"Mouse Organ," 63

"Mouse Problem, The," 26, 63, 64

"Mr. and Mrs. Brian Norris' Ford Popular," 115–116

"Mr. Neutron," 94, 140–142, 247, 314

"Naked Ant, The," 76–77

"Nude Organist (or: the Nude Man), The," 121, 125

"Nudge, Nudge," 54, 64, 65, 108, 150

"Operating Theatre (Squatters)," 79

"Oscar Wilde Sketch, The," 128–129

"Owl-Stretching Time," 65–66

"Party Political Broadcast," 121, 142–145

"Penis Song, The," 217

"People Falling Out of Buildings," 108

"Pet Conversions," 73

"Philosopher's Football Match, The," 61, 112, 343

"Picasso/Cycling Race," 60

"Police Station (Silly Voices)," 77

"Probe-Around on Crime," 79

"Putting Down Budgies," 151

"Queen Will Be Watching, The," 100–101

"Restaurant Sketch," 64

"Royal Philharmonic Orchestra Goes to the Bathroom, The," 74–76

"Salad Days," 96, 122–124
"Salvation Fuzz," 79
"Science Fiction Sketch," 69
"Scott of the Antarctic," 96–97
"Seduced Milkman," 64
"Sex and Violence," 53, 56, 57, 61–64
"Sit on My Face," 350
"Society for Putting Things on Top of
    Other Things, The," 81, 90,
    91, 117
"Spam," 81, 98–100, 247, 322, 331
"Spanish Inquisition, The," 83–85
"Strangers in the Night," 74

"Tale of Happy Valley, The," 112
"Tale of Sir Galahad, The," 169–170
"Tale of Sir Lancelot, The," 159,
    170–171
"Tale of Sir Robin, The," 168–169
"Tale of the Piranha Brothers, The,"
    82
"Travel Agent," 76, 120, 189
"Trim-Jeans Theatre," 115

"Trojan Rabbit, The," 168
"Tudor Job Agency," 126
"Twentieth Century Vole," 68

"Upper Class Twit of the Year," 24, 77,
    107, 109

"Vocational Guidance Counsellor," 73

"Wacky Queen, The," 55
"War Against Pornography, The,"
    121–122
"What Have the Romans Ever Done
    for Us?," 199, 200, 205
"What the Stars Foretell," 70
"Whicker's World (or: Njorl's Saga),"
    113–114
"Whither Canada?," 53, 57, 60–61
"Whizzo Chocolates," 68, 302
"Working-Class Playwright," 63, 288
"World Forum," 98

"You're No Fun Anymore," 69

THE FAQ SERIES

AC/DC FAQ
by Susan Masino
Backbeat Books
9781480394506................$24.99

Armageddon Films FAQ
by Dale Sherman
Applause Books
9781617131196.......................$24.99

The Band FAQ
by Peter Aaron
Backbeat Books
9781617136139.........................$19.99

Baseball FAQ
by Tom DeMichael
Backbeat Books
9781617136061.........................$24.99

The Beach Boys FAQ
by Jon Stebbins
Backbeat Books
9780879309879.................$22.99

The Beat Generation FAQ
by Rich Weidman
Backbeat Books
9781617136016.........................$19.99

Beer FAQ
by Jeff Cioletti
Backbeat Books
9781617136115.......................$24.99

Black Sabbath FAQ
by Martin Popoff
Backbeat Books
9780879309572.................$19.99

Bob Dylan FAQ
by Bruce Pollock
Backbeat Books
9781617136078.......................$19.99

Britcoms FAQ
by Dave Thompson
Applause Books
9781495018992.....................$19.99

Bruce Springsteen FAQ
by John D. Luerssen
Backbeat Books
9781617130939.......................$22.99

A Chorus Line FAQ
by Tom Rowan
Applause Books
9781480367548......................$19.99

The Clash FAQ
by Gary J. Jucha
Backbeat Books
9781480364509.................$19.99

Doctor Who FAQ
by Dave Thompson
Applause Books
9781557838544.....................$22.99

The Doors FAQ
by Rich Weidman
Backbeat Books
9781617130175.......................$24.99

Dracula FAQ
by Bruce Scivally
Backbeat Books
9781617136009.....................$19.99

The Eagles FAQ
by Andrew Vaughan
Backbeat Books
9781480385412.....................$24.99

Elvis Films FAQ
by Paul Simpson
Applause Books
9781557838582.....................$24.99

Elvis Music FAQ
by Mike Eder
Backbeat Books
9781617130496.....................$24.99

Eric Clapton FAQ
by David Bowling
Backbeat Books
9781617134548.....................$22.99

Fab Four FAQ
by Stuart Shea and
Robert Rodriguez
Hal Leonard Books
9781423421382.......................$19.99

Fab Four FAQ 2.0
by Robert Rodriguez
Backbeat Books
9780879309688.................$19.99

Film Noir FAQ
by David J. Hogan
Applause Books
9781557838551.....................$22.99

Football FAQ
by Dave Thompson
Backbeat Books
9781495007484.....................$24.99

Frank Zappa FAQ
by John Corcelli
Backbeat Books
9781617136030.......................$19.99

Godzilla FAQ
by Brian Solomon
Applause Books
9781495045684.................$19.99

The Grateful Dead FAQ
by Tony Sclafani
Backbeat Books
9781617130861.......................$24.99

Guns N' Roses FAQ
by Rich Weidman
Backbeat Books
9781495025884.................$19.99

Haunted America FAQ
by Dave Thompson
Backbeat Books
9781480392625.....................$19.99

Horror Films FAQ
by John Kenneth Muir
Applause Books
9781557839503.....................$22.99

James Bond FAQ
by Tom DeMichael
Applause Books
9781557838568.....................$22.99

Jimi Hendrix FAQ
by Gary J. Jucha
Backbeat Books
9781617130953.....................$22.99

Prices, contents, and availability
subject to change without notice.

Johnny Cash FAQ
by C. Eric Banister
Backbeat Books
9781480385405................ $24.99

KISS FAQ
by Dale Sherman
Backbeat Books
9781617130915.................... $24.99

Led Zeppelin FAQ
by George Case
Backbeat Books
9781617130250 ....$22.99

Lucille Ball FAQ
by James Sheridan
and Barry Monush
Applause Books
9781617740824.....................$19.99

M.A.S.H. FAQ
by Dale Sherman
Applause Books
9781480355897.....................$19.99

Michael Jackson FAQ
by Kit O'Toole
Backbeat Books
9781480371064 ....$19.99

Modern Sci-Fi Films FAQ
by Tom DeMichael
Applause Books
9781480350618 .... $24.99

Monty Python FAQ
by Chris Barsanti, Brian Cogan,
and Jeff Massey
Applause Books
9781495049439 ....$19.99

Morrissey FAQ
by D. McKinney
Backbeat Books
9781480394483.................. $24.99

Neil Young FAQ
by Glen Boyd
Backbeat Books
9781617130373.....................$19.99

Nirvana FAQ
by John D. Luerssen
Backbeat Books
9781617134500.................... $24.99

Pearl Jam FAQ
by Bernard M. Corbett and
Thomas Edward Harkins
Backbeat Books
9781617136122 ....$19.99

Pink Floyd FAQ
by Stuart Shea
Backbeat Books
9780879309503....................$19.99

Pro Wrestling FAQ
by Brian Solomon
Backbeat Books
9781617135996......................$29.99

Prog Rock FAQ
by Will Romano
Backbeat Books
9781617135873................ $24.99

Quentin Tarantino FAQ
by Dale Sherman
Applause Books
9781480355880 .... $24.99

Robin Hood FAQ
by Dave Thompson
Applause Books
9781495048227 ....$19.99

**The Rocky Horror
Picture Show FAQ**
by Dave Thompson
Applause Books
9781495007477 ....$19.99

Rush FAQ
by Max Mobley
Backbeat Books
9781617134517 ....$19.99

Saturday Night Live FAQ
by Stephen Tropiano
Applause Books
9781557839510.................... $24.99

Seinfeld FAQ
by Nicholas Nigro
Applause Books
9781557838575.................... $24.99

Sherlock Holmes FAQ
by Dave Thompson
Applause Books
9781480331495.................... $24.99

The Smiths FAQ
by John D. Luerssen
Backbeat Books
9781480394490...............$24.99

Soccer FAQ
by Dave Thompson
Backbeat Books
9781617135989.....................$24.99

The Sound of Music FAQ
by Barry Monush
Applause Books
9781480360433.................$27.99

South Park FAQ
by Dave Thompson
Applause Books
9781480350649.................... $24.99

Star Trek FAQ
(Unofficial and Unauthorized)
by Mark Clark
Applause Books
9781557837929....................$19.99

Star Trek FAQ 2.0
(Unofficial and Unauthorized)
by Mark Clark
Applause Books
9781557837936.....................$22.99

Star Wars FAQ
by Mark Clark
Applause Books
9781480360181..................... $24.99

Steely Dan FAQ
by Anthony Robustelli
Backbeat Books
9781495025129 ....$19.99

Stephen King Films FAQ
by Scott Von Doviak
Applause Books
9781480355514.................... $24.99

Three Stooges FAQ
by David J. Hogan
Applause Books
9781557837882.....................$22.99

TV Finales FAQ
by Stephen Tropiano and
Holly Van Buren
Applause Books
9781480391444.....................$19.99

The Twilight Zone FAQ
by Dave Thompson
Applause Books
9781480396180 ....$19.99

Twin Peaks FAQ
by David Bushman and
Arthur Smith
Applause Books
9781495015861......................$19.99

UFO FAQ
by David J. Hogan
Backbeat Books
9781480393851 ....$19.99

Video Games FAQ
by Mark J.P. Wolf
Backbeat Books
9781617136306 ....$19.99

The Who FAQ
by Mike Segretto
Backbeat Books
9781480361034 .... $24.99

The Wizard of Oz FAQ
by David J. Hogan
Applause Books
9781480350625 .... $24.99

The X-Files FAQ
by John Kenneth Muir
Applause Books
9781480369740.................. $24.99

HAL•LEONARD®
PERFORMING ARTS
PUBLISHING GROUP

FAQ.halleonardbooks.com